DRINK AND THE CITY

Alcohol and Alcohol Problems in Urban UK
since the 1950s

JE McGregor

First published by Nottingham University Press

This reissued original edition published 2023 by 5m Books Ltd www.5mbooks.com

Copyright © Nottingham University Press 2023

All rights reserved. No part of this publication
may be reproduced in any material form
(including photocopying or storing in any
medium by electronic means and whether or not
transiently or incidentally to some other use of
this publication) without the written permission
of the copyright holder except in accordance with
the provisions of the Copyright, Designs and
Patents Act 1988. Applications for the copyright
holder's written permission to reproduce any part
of this publication should be addressed to the publishers.

British Library Cataloguing in Publication Data
Drink and the City: Alcohol and Alcohol Problems in Urban UK since the 1950s

ISBN 9781789182774

Disclaimer

Every reasonable effort has been made to ensure that the material in this book is true, correct, complete and appropriate at the time of writing. Nevertheless the publishers and the author do not accept responsibility for any omission or error, or for any injury, damage, loss or financial consequences arising from the use of the book. Views expressed in the articles are those of the author and not of the Editor or Publisher.

Typeset by Nottingham University Press, Nottingham

EU GPSR Authorised Representative
LOGOS EUROPE, 9 rue Nicolas Poussin, 17000, LA ROCHELLE, France
E-mail: Contact@logoseurope.eu

Men drinking: http://www.flickr.com/photos/national_library_of_australia_commons/6173555293/Trip to Jerusalem: http://www.flickr.com/photos/prisca_eyedea/5377989865/
Café culture: http://www.flickr.com/photos/duncanh1/4678071159/
The Bell: http://www.flickr.com/photos/stevecadman/61681770/

CONTENTS

Acknowledgements		vii
1.	**'Drink and the City'**	1
	What the book is about	2
	English society and alcohol: a brief history	3
	The politics of alcohol	5
	Targets of concern	7
	The role of medicine	8
	Book outline	10
	Notes	15
2.	**Medicine as Part of Social Concern, 1950s & 1960s**	19
	National developments	19
	Drink and drink problems in 1950s Nottingham	22
	Drink as a problem of ethnic minorities	23
	Women as targets	26
	Growing concern about youth	28
	The rise and role of Alcoholics Anonymous	29
	AA and the emerging medical response	30
	The regional alcohol treatment unit	33
	The prominence of poverty	36
	Medicine as part of social concern	37
	Conclusions	40
	Notes	41
3.	**Medical Responses to the Vagrant Alcoholic, 1970s**	47
	National policy developments	48
	Nottingham: a medical-penal alliance over vagrancy	50
	Co-ordinating the response: the Nottinghamshire Council on Alcoholism	59
	Conclusions	62
	Notes	63

4.	**Youth in Public View, 1970s**	67
	National developments	67
	Nottingham: Changing realities and perceptions of the local problem	69
	Women and drink	70
	Pubs, publicans and anxiety about youth	71
	CAMRA and the campaign over pub hours	73
	The 'problem' of the hooligan	75
	Conclusions	77
	Notes	78
5.	**Combining Drink and Drugs: Alcohol Treatment in the 1980s**	83
	National policy developments	83
	Nottingham and the impacts of national policy change	85
	Improved co-ordination and developments in the community	88
	The changing nature of homelessness and break-up of the medical-penal alliance	90
	The rise of the hostel sector and development of the 'wet' project	91
	Development of the Hostels Liaison Group (HLG)	92
	Handel Street Day Centre: the 'wet' project	93
	Conclusion	96
	Notes	97
6.	**'Drunken Yobs and Aggressive Beggars': the 1980s**	101
	National developments	101
	Nottingham: alcohol as a problem of young outsiders	104
	Football and riots: intensified responses to youth	106
	Riots and other hostilities	107
	Courting youth: a U-turn on approach	108
	Local and national moves on licensing	111
	The big city makeover	113
	Conclusions	115
	Notes	116
7.	**Politicisation and Fragmentation: Alcohol Treatment in the 1990s**	121
	National policy development	121
	Nottingham: new developments versus established norms	124
	Birth of 'The Nottingham Clinic'	126
	Impacts on the local treatment arena	130
	Modes of treatment and their effectiveness	131

Conclusions 135
Notes 136

8. 'Liberty's' and Licensing: Responses by the Police in the 1990s — 141

National developments 141
Nottingham's changing drinking scene 144
   The end of the pub and local brewing and the arrival of chameleon bars 146
Marketing alcopops: impacts on youth behaviour and the drink scene 147
Drugs and the intensification of police concern over drink disorder 150
The case of Liberty's nightclub and the relevance of the
   principle of need 152
Intensification of police responses to alcohol 155
Conclusions 157
Notes 157

9. 'Cldt Give a 4xxxx for Lst Ordrs': The National/Local Problem of Binge Drinking — 165

Developments in Nottingham (2000-2004) 167
   Towards tackling the problem of city centre disorder 169
National and local convergence over 'binge drinking' 174
Conclusions 176
Notes 177

10. UK Alcohol Policy: National-Local Interaction — 183

Binge drinking: a national problem? 184
   Changing face of the problem 188
Local-national interaction and the policy process 190
   Explanations of the frequent separation and occasional unity
     between local-national policy 190
   Social psychiatry's role in shaping the local response 192
   The rise and role of the criminal justice sector 194
   Changing realities 196
Conclusion 198
Notes 200

Reference Sources 203

Nottinghamshire Archives 203
   City Council records 203
   Mapperley Hospital records 203

v

Media Archives 204
   Films/broadcasts 204
Other Libraries and Sources 204
Official Reports 205
Other Reports 207

To Tim and Fin

ACKNOWLEDGEMENTS

The idea of researching the most recent history of drink originated from a discussion I had with students at Nottingham University, where I worked, and still do, as a lecturer in substance misuse. The students asked why Nottingham had been in the media spotlight over binge drinking. A lively debate ensued, which got going my interest in the issue. Subsequently, I was fortunate enough to secure a Wellcome Trust doctoral studentship (Grant No. 074237 'Enhancing history in public health') after submitting a proposal to research the interplay between local and national policy over drink, and with the help and guidance of my supervisor Professor Virginia Berridge of the Centre for History in Public Health at the London School of Hygiene and Tropical Medicine, I commenced doctoral studies in 2007, successfully completing my thesis in 2010. I am indebted to Wellcome for affording me such a great opportunity in the first instance, and to Virginia for being a first rate supervisor and mentor.

In turning the abovementioned PhD research into a book the aim was to document the changes in attitudes and responses to alcohol in the UK urban environment. Nottingham seemed a good choice because of its recent reputation as the 'Binge capital of Britain', however I make no claim that Nottingham is representative of urban UK. Even so, the city's history provides rich pickings for the alcohol historian and its convergences and deviations from the national view tell us something important, not only about the process of policy making but the recent history of alcohol in the UK. Some of the material in the book has been presented at conferences and seminars. I presented one paper, *'Youth, drink and the city: 1950s to the 2000s'* at a conference on Student Alcohol Use/Misuse held on March 30th 2010 at University of Northampton. I also presented a paper *'From Dependence to Binge: Alcohol in Nottingham 1950 to early twenty-first century'* at the Intoxicants and Intoxication in Cultural and Historical Perspectives Conference in July 22nd 2010 at Christ College, Cambridge, and presented another paper *'Mutual aid and community participation - alcohol and the local approach, 1950s-early twenty first century'* on January 31st 2011 at a seminar in Nottingham, held by Nottinghamshire Health Care NHS Trust. Some of the material used in this book was published in a paper 'Local and National Policy Making for Alcohol: Nottingham, UK, 1950-2007' in the journal *Social History of Alcohol and Drugs,* 25: 1-2 (2011) 148-164. Thanks to audiences of these conferences and seminars for their comments and contributions, especially Angela McShane, Phil Witherington and members of the ESRC network on Intoxicants in Historical and Cultural Perspective who helped me develop this work.

In undertaking the research for this book I accumulated a good many debts. Besides Virginia Berridge, there are many other people to thank for advice and support; Betsy Thom, John Greenaway, James Nicholls, Alex Mold, Rachel Herring, Susanne Macgregor, David Best, to name a few. I also need to thank the many people who helped me in other ways, finding archives and other primary sources for instance. Thanks therefore go to Dorothy Ritchie and colleagues at the Local Studies Library at Nottingham Central Library, the librarians at Duncan Macmillan House, the archivists at Nottinghamshire Archives and staff at the Wellcome Library, London. Thanks to the editorial staff at Nottingham University Press, in particular Sarah Keeling, who ironed out some awkward glitches. What errors remain are down to me. I also thank those who gave freely of their time to be interviewed, and those who granted me access to personal and institutions' records. On the subject of interviews, I had the great privilege of interviewing the author Alan Sillitoe at his home in Notting Hill in the summer of 2007. Sadly, Alan died in the spring of 2010. He was a wonderful character, full of warmth and humour. He vividly and touchingly brought 1950's Nottingham back to life, and in consequence quite a few of his recollections pepper the early chapters.

Finally, I thank my husband Tim, whose support and encouragement has been immeasurable and my son Fin, who joined me in the quest for material for this book. As a consequence his knowledge of alcohol and alcohol matters is exceptional for someone in their teenage years!

1

'DRINK AND THE CITY'

In August 2011, a ban on street drinking came into force in areas of Basford and Sneinton in Nottingham. Drinking bans were already in place covering the city centre, Hyson Green and The Forest recreation ground, while a ban was being considered for the inner city area of St Ann's. The move, named a Designated Public Place Order, was supported by the Nottingham City Council who aimed to clamp down on the antisocial behaviour of *"drunken yobs or aggressive beggars"*.[1] Street drinking, in different guises, has endured as a persistent policy concern in Nottingham. 'Binge drinking', the latest construction of the problem, emerged in the early 2000s and saw the city become a national flashpoint over the issue.[2] That Nottingham, or any geographical location, could represent 'Binge Britain' in this way provided the starting point for the research on which this book is based, for it suggested something important about problems in society and how they emerge onto the policy agenda.

Nottingham is situated at the heart of England. It has a relatively small population of 300,800, whilst the population for Greater Nottingham is currently 667,100.[3] The city has a liberal tradition and in keeping with this, it was chosen a few years ago as the site of a new 'Speakers Corner', which is situated in its central square (Old Market Square).[4]

Old Market Square, Nottingham

The Square is the largest town square still surviving and the second largest public space in Britain after Trafalgar Square, covering an area of about 11,500m².[5] Redesigned in 2007, it is an area of arena-like proportions, which adds to a sense of theatre and spectacle.

Since the eighteenth century onwards the Square has featured as a rallying point for the campaign of working people's rights and political enfranchisement. It has played an important role in amplifying concerns about alcohol over time; spotlighting vagrancy drinking and other forms of street drinking, including binge drinking. The city has a long-established association with drink. It was well situated for the supply of barley from the Vale of Belvoir and the local water was particularly good for brewing. These factors had an effect on its early trading history. 'Nottingham Nut Brown Ale' was produced in considerable quantities and exported to other parts of the country, though trade declined after it was out-performed by beer from Messrs. Bass's brewery at Burton around 1770.[6] Nottingham's inns and public houses flourished because workers migrated from the rural areas to work in the town over the course of the eighteenth and nineteenth century. Pubs became social centres for the lower orders but their activities often were regarded as problematic. Trade and political groups were prohibited from licensed premises by Parliament in 1799 because of fears generated by the French Revolution. After relaxation of the laws however, trade unions activities resumed in pubs. Branches often associated themselves with particular houses in the city. Shoemakers met at the Butchers' Arms, lace makers and printers met at the Durham Ox and framework knitters at the Dove and Rainbow, Seven Stars and King George on Horseback.[7] Pub going continued as an essential working class activity to recent times. This was captured in Alan Sillitoe's Nottingham based novel *'Saturday Night and Sunday Morning,'* first published in 1958. Arthur Seaton, the novel's anti hero, embodied the city's drinking culture, which was characterised as hardworking and offset by weekend drink binges. Sillitoe, born and bred in the city, described Saturday night as *"the best and bingiest glad-time of the week,"* a place where *"piled-up passions were exploded on Saturday night, and the effect of a week's monotonous graft in the factory was swilled out of your system in a burst of goodwill."*[8]

What the book is about

Alcohol use is rooted in British culture and the vast majority of adults in the UK regularly consume it. The circumstances and manner in which alcohol is consumed can tell us something about society and relations between the genders, different age groups and social classes. Drink acts as a social indicator, an instrument for the observation and analysis of social change. This book is a study in local history and, as such, joins a broad historiographical tradition.[9] But it aims to go further than simply local history *per se*, to examine the dimensions of the interaction between the local and the national, using the case study of alcohol policy making. Utilising a well populated urban area such as Nottingham, with its long associations with drink, provides plenty of opportunities to make connections between shifts in attitudes and responses to drinking and wider social change in society.

ENGLISH SOCIETY AND ALCOHOL: A BRIEF HISTORY

Even though heavy drinking among the English stretches back many centuries, evidence suggests that consumption levels have fluctuated over time. For example, if we look at consumption levels since the late eighteenth century, we see at first they declined, then rose in the nineteenth century, fell sharply in the early twentieth, and rose again from the 1960s to the present day.[10] Clearly trends in consumption are influenced by something, and it's likely that political, economic and cultural shifts play a significant role in transforming ideas about drink, and responses to it, over time; themes emphasised in historian James Nicholls book 'The Politics of Alcohol.'[11] He suggests there have been certain constants that have concerned society about drink. These include heavy drinking and rituals that encourage it, heightened concern about women's drinking, disputes over the role of licensing authorities, conflicts over the rights of moderate drinkers, and the role and responsibility of the state in preventing excess. Nicholls also suggests that often underlying these issues has been a failure to reconcile tensions between free trade ideologies and the need to maintain social order.[12] A much used case in point is the 'gin epidemic' of the eighteenth century. This was a period in the first half of the 18th century when the consumption of gin became popular with the working classes in Britain, especially in London. Historian Jessica Warner, an authority on the gin epidemic, called it 'the first modern drug'. The average annual consumption of spirits among adults increased from about one-third of a gallon in 1700 to 2.2 gallons in 1743.[13] There ensued an outbreak of extreme drunkenness that provoked moral outrage and a legislative backlash. 'Polite society' panicked and the authorities reacted by placing restrictions on the consumption of gin. Consequently five major Acts were passed between 1729 and 1751 designed to control the consumption of gin (in 1729, 1736, 1743, 1747 and 1751). The crisis was captured by William Hogarth in his print 'Gin Lane', which has been reused many times in discussion of class relations and alcohol. Hogarth also produced 'Beer Street', in the same year (1751), both prints in support of a campaign directed against gin drinking among London's poor.

Beer Street

Gin Lane

(William Hogarth, 1751)

Until recently historians tended to blame the increase in gin consumption for much of the social unrest that escalated during the period, and cited the Tippling Act of 1751 in defence of this argument. The Tippling Act eliminated small gin shops and left the distribution of gin to larger distillers and retailers. Within a few years consumption was down to 2 million gallons per year and the quality of gin improved. However, historians now argue that the social unrest prior to, and after, the Tippling Act was exacerbated by excessive gin drinking, rather than it having been its cause. A combination of displacement, poverty, unemployment, and the vast chasm between the 'superior' and 'inferior' classes, created an unstable social environment. Thus the 'gin epidemic' can be viewed largely as a social problem that centred on a particular location - London and its environs.[14] Warner argued that concern developed at a time; *'when nothing else seemed to be happening – and when the government was flush.'* [15] Furthermore, a number of commentators have noted recently parallels between the gin craze and the twenty-first century crisis over 'binge drinking'. The parallels include a range of issues; public health, crime and disorder, costs to the economy, the corruption of women, the threat to family life, and the English identity.[16] The gin craze is not the only period to have drawn comparison with the present. Some, including public health historian Virginia Berridge, have suggested parallels with the early years of the nineteenth century as this was a time when the issues of excessive alcohol consumption began to be defined as a social problem and crime and disorder was a concern of society, just as now. Berridge cited The 1830 Beer Act as an influential factor at that time because it liberalised licensing at the same time as drunkenness mounted.[17] Likewise drink also featured as a concern about social change in the Victorian era as historian Brian Harrison illustrates in his commanding book 'Drink and the Victorians'. In this, Harrison connected alcohol to concern about living standards and working class culture as well as to the nature of liberalism.[18] Thus the circumstance, frequency with which it is consumed, and who consumes it, appear to tell us a good deal about shared values or otherwise in society. The strongest narrative has been a story of the poor, as well as the working class man. Higher class disapproval of alcohol consumption by the lower social classes was an underlying issue in the Victorian era. Exacerbated by industrialisation, some middle class observers of working class life concluded the working man was his own 'worst enemy' due to his indulgence in drink.[19] Working class expenditure on 'intoxicating liquors' thus tended to be viewed as an obstacle for their improvement.[20]

THE POLITICS OF ALCOHOL

Even before the sixteenth century governmental responses in Britain reflected tensions between the desire to exploit drinking practices fiscally and a concern to regulate what were perceived to be their moral and social implications. However, the history of state action has been clouded by competing influences as historians Phil Witherington and Angela McShane suggest. They argue that state action has been hindered often by the difficulty of shaping drinking cultures 'on the ground'.[21] Policies of the past often focused on the timing of consumption and retail; the quantities sold or drunk; the venues at which retail could take place; and the strength of drinks through control of ingredients. The Victorians, however, proposed a number of solutions to this quandary. One involved the concept of 'moral suasion' where individuals were to be persuaded of their responsibilities or obligations to their fellow citizens. The idea was based on a belief that the state was unlikely to be effective in tackling intemperance and was taken up in the mid nineteenth century by liberals who saw the way forward through progressive education. One view of intemperance at this time was as a product of 'faulty social order'. The proposed solution was temperance, but whilst some saw this as a liberating move, others saw it as an instrument of the governing classes to undermine workers and their radicalism. The Victorians also used the conventional system of regulation to control alcohol consumption. In place since 1522 it had become established practice for local justices of the peace to issue licences for the 'on' sales of liquor. The purpose of licensing was to regulate trade in the interests of the 'public good', prevent disorder and raise taxes. Meant to protect the public from the excesses of drinking, regulation was not designed to influence drinking habits directly. Besides, from the early part of the nineteenth century, licensing restrictions increasingly came under attack with some arguing for freer sales rather than more restriction. Having parallels with the present, free traders argued that a free market would promote temperance since the worst drunkenness was caused by adulteration of liquor. But this view flew in the face of a new prohibitionist standpoint that swept Britain following developments in the US when a law prohibiting the sale of intoxicants was passed in Maine, New England in 1846. Subsequently, the United Kingdom Alliance (UKA) was founded in Manchester in 1853 to work for prohibition of alcohol in the UK. Prohibitionists believed the consumption of drink was dangerous and various mechanisms to restrict licensing were proposed, including heavier taxes against the strongest liquors. Because the measures were regarded as likely to be unpopular, not least with the government for no less than 30-40 per cent of the nation's revenue came from excise and licence duties, an alternative path was suggested, which was to reduce the hours of sale. The move was controversial and in 1854-55 attempts to introduce severe restrictions on Sunday trading led to rioting in Hyde Park.[22]

The early twentieth century saw renewed debates over the role of local magistrates in reducing the numbers of licences in their areas. Policies encouraging the closure of surplus pubs were adopted by the Liberal and Tory parties, but arguments ensued over the issue of compensation from the state for the withdrawal of licences. Then in 1914, with the outbreak of war, further restrictions were enforced, with a Central Control Board established in 1915 to manage the alcohol trade across most of the UK. Existing restrictions on opening hours and Sunday trading were tightened and excise duties on beer and spirits were increased significantly. The Second World War saw restrictions remain in place. Consumption of alcohol remained comparatively low, a situation that continued into the immediate post war period. The industry responded with the introduction of new drinks, particularly lager, targeted at the youth market and women drinkers. Over the following decade, the resurgence of the drink trade was aided by the expansion of the youth market and increased levels of affluence. In addition, the Licensing Acts of 1961 and 1964 were explicitly geared towards liberalisation of licensing.[23] In the late 1960s and early 1970s, alcohol abuse became more important in terms of government priorities. The reason for this was that the 'problem' had become more visible. Not because there was growth in the UK alcohol problem but because the issue received greater attention from the media, pressure groups and Parliament.[24]

The early twenty-first century saw the emergence of a new drink crisis, the so called 'binge crisis' with which Britain became linked ('Binge Britain'). 'Binge drinking', a purposeful style of drinking, and the modern epithet for consuming copious amounts of alcohol with the explicit purpose of becoming intoxicated over a short period of time, reportedly first developed as a drinking pattern among young people in a number of countries including Britain during the late 1990s/early 2000s. Due to the long-term effects of alcohol misuse, it soon was regarded as a major public health issue and community safety issue.[25] It quickly became associated with profound social harm, economic costs and an increased disease burden. A style of drinking noted to develop during adolescence and young adulthood, young people soon became targets of concern though this did not stop New Labour Government, re-elected in 2001, promising further liberalisation in licensing. On the contrary, Government from this time on frequently discussed ideas about the UK adopting European drinking styles with the Prime Minister, Tony Blair, claiming binge drinking '*a new British disease*' that only licensing reform could prevent.[26]

TARGETS OF CONCERN

Women's drinking has emerged, diminished and re-emerged as a focus of concern at different historical moments. In almost every society more men drink alcohol than women. From the London gin epidemic to the turn of the twenty first century, concern about women and drink in Britain has had much to do with fears over women's role in society. During the temperance era (the late nineteenth and early twentieth century) often women, though leaders of anti-drink sentiment and temperance activity, were blamed for many of the problems resulting from drinking. This was because at this time many people believed in the 'inheritance of acquired characteristics'.[27] This view was reinforced when during the years 1899-1907 a new critique of alcohol evolved which pointed to increasing female insobriety as a factor in infant mortality. This saw anti-drink doctors orchestrate concern over drink's deleterious impact on pregnant women and babies. By condemning alcohol as an important source of infant deaths and national inefficiency, these doctors encouraged the medical profession to adopt a more critical view of drink and compelled the government to permit hygiene and temperance instruction in elementary schools. This helped not only reinforce a particular view of women who drank, but translated proposals to prohibit children under the age of fourteen from licensed premises into legislation.[28] The theme emerged again in the immediate post war era of the 1950s, with the female 'alcoholic' presented as a stereotypical figure resorting to drinking in secret to cope with a life restricted to the home. In the 1970s

Foetal Alcohol Syndrome was identified as a significant concern after studies noted differences between the children of mothers who used alcohol during pregnancy or breast-feeding and those who did not. Later still, concerns were made about 'ladettes' in the binge-drinking culture of the 1990s/ early 2000s, though this account placed less emphasis on reproduction and motherhood than earlier episodes.[29] Hostile reaction to women's drinking persists in many cultures, with religious and social pressures, as well as gender roles and stereotypes, acting as mechanisms to restrain women's use of drink.[30] Sometimes women's drinking has been linked to major concerns of the era, as in the nineteenth century for example, where high infant mortality and an unhealthy working class weakened the national 'stock' and supremacy of the English abroad.[31] Furthermore there has been heightened concern at times of rapid change in women's roles.[32]

Young people too have been an important group of concern. In the past youth were portrayed as "the future" whereas in the near past and present they often tend to be viewed as a source of worry. This anxiety has contributed to a fear of adolescents, especially those from ethnic minority groups. There is a long history of them becoming scapegoats for concern about drink, as emphasised by Geoffrey Pearson in his work on hooliganism.[33] He argued that the most recent youth crime debate in the UK has been invariably accompanied by some notion of generational decline in terms of family, community, authority, tradition and morality, and is nothing new; there was a similar current of feeling in the 1920s and 30s, when, just as now, these sentiments were linked directly to problems of crime and criminal justice. He cited The King George's Jubilee Trust report (1939), 'The Needs of Youth', which summed up a catalogue of complaint that is uncannily familiar: *"Relaxation of parental control, decay of religious influence, and the transplantation of masses of young persons to housing estates where there is little scope for recreation and plenty for mischief ... The problem is a serious challenge, the difficulty of which is intensified by the extension of freedom which, for better or worse, has been given to youth in the last generation."* [34]

Dealing with problems of alcohol

THE ROLE OF MEDICINE

Although it was customary to deal with drink with penal measures, this was not the only approach at the disposal of authorities. Medical interventions especially in the twentieth century curried favour, with doctors taking a prominent role in managing alcohol problems during the period covered in this book, for example. This state of affairs materialised as the role of medical science became increasingly important, and excessive drinking became connected with theories of disease and treatment during the twentieth century. World War I helped further understanding that the effects of alcohol depended on how *much*, not what *kind* was consumed, as men came under the scrutiny of doctors as they entered the military. Furthermore, scientific discoveries altered the way doctors understood health and illness, and new philosophies and techniques helped the development of new medical specialties.[35] As the specialty of psychiatry took ownership of the problem of alcohol, the concept of alcoholism as a disease amenable to treatment was revisited. Habitual drunkenness or inebriety as a 'disease' though was not new, for Thomas Trotter (1804), 'the first scientific investigator of drunkenness' had earlier called alcoholism 'a disease of the mind'.[36] This was reworked after World War II, as psychiatrists became closely linked to the treatment of alcohol problems and had influence at the international level within policy making circles. Although alcohol had a low policy profile in the UK at the time, the World Health Organisation (WHO) saw alcoholism as a major policy issue. The changing perspective thus was influenced not only by the increasingly internationalised nature of medical research but by mounting international pressure from WHO, which published a report in 1951, which stressed the importance of alcoholism. The new medical version of the concept arose from ideas put forth by Elvin Morton Jellinek, a consultant engaged by WHO in 1952. Alcoholism was characterised as compulsive use of alcohol, loss of control over the amount and frequency of drink consumed and continued use despite negative consequences. A chronic condition, it was regarded as having the potential for relapse. Abstinence was put forward as the only way to stall the illness into remission.

These events occurred at around the time the National Health Service (NHS) became established in the UK. There existed close interaction between medical scientists and political actors between the 1950s and early 1970s, which meant psychiatry continued to dominate alcohol treatment at least until the 1970s although certain prominent individuals, including the psychiatrist Griffith Edwards, who established the UK Addiction Research Unit (later the National Addiction Centre) in London, held influence for considerably longer. Sociologist Betsy Thom, in her book 'Dealing with Drink', called this period the 'pioneering' phase, where many treatment responses emerged as a result of 'bottom up' initiatives.[37] In the 1970s the alcohol field entered a new phase in which treatment no longer featured on the policy agenda. This was due largely to a paradigm shift towards seeing the problem as one of too high per capita consumption, where the aim was to reduce the harms of alcohol in society.[38] By the 1990s policy increasingly concerned managing risks and reducing harms as opposed to treating 'alcoholism'. Furthermore, a management model, combined with an 'evidence based policy' approach, where research was set to become a central determinant of public policy, became the order of the day.

Book outline

As indicated at the outset, this book explores events associated with drink in Nottingham from the 1950s to the early twenty-first century, a time when Nottingham was an influence on national policy over drink. Much of the material used is primary source material (oral histories and new and previously archived material) tracked down in the course of my investigations. This is supplemented by secondary sources which are referenced as endnotes. The sources of primary material are listed at the end of the book.

Events at the national and local levels of policy making are dealt with chronologically. First, national trends are given attention before events in Nottingham are considered. This strategy is employed in order to draw attention to local integration and/or deviation from national developments. For the most part each decade is covered by two chapters; one looking at community responses and the other exploring the ways in which medicine responded to alcohol problems over each decade. The exceptions to this rule include chapter two, which focuses on the 1950s/1960s and merges the medical and community responses to drink because medicine's initial response emerged from local social concerns of the period, and chapter nine, covering the early 2000s, when medicine's role in managing drink became diminished. Elsewhere though, the approach helped draw attention to the important role of medicine in managing the local 'drink problem'.

Before the reader delves further into the book there are a few terms that probably warrant some explanation. 'Medicine', for instance, is used as a 'catch all' term to mean 'specialist medical alcohol services', an arena dominated by psychiatry from the 1960s. This seemed preferable to 'psychiatry' because it captured the broader, ancillary medical activity of general practitioners, hospital physicians, liver specialists, public health physicians and so on. The category also captured voluntary and mutual aid groups such as Alcoholics Anonymous (AA), not because the voluntary response was unimportant, quite the contrary, but because these were among the first to respond to alcoholism (from the mid 1950s) and formed part of specialist medical response. Emphasising 'community' responses in every second chapter provided a way of scrutinising emerging responses by groups and networks in the community that were, for the most part, outside medical influence. These included responses from the media, the general public, police and local council. It is recognised, however, that at times overlaps developed. The approach primarily was intended to aid analysis of the interplay/balance of power and to capture shifts in perceptions as well as behavioural and material changes over time. And finally on the subject of terminology, the words 'drink', 'alcohol' and 'alcohol consumption' are used interchangeably throughout the book. Terms were chosen to reflect changing definitions and used to emphasise that drinking and drink problems in society are not historically or culturally stable concepts. Any definitions, ascribed behaviours or styles of drinking (alcoholism, alcohol dependence, problem drinking, chronic or binge drinking) outlined in the book therefore should be regarded as historically and conceptually important rather than scientifically proven or disproved.

The chapter subsequent to this introduces Nottingham in the post war 1950s and analyses responses by the local community to drink through this and the ensuing decade, the 1960s. At that time particular groups; women, ethnic minorities and youth, periodically became targets of community concern over drink. This was the era when the concept of 'alcoholism' took hold internationally and nationally and began to filter down to the local level. The fellowship Alcoholics Anonymous (AA) with its ideas of mutual support and self help arrived in 1955 and was the first response to alcoholism in the city. However, psychiatrists at the local psychiatric hospital (Mapperley Hospital) were soon to join forces with AA soon after guidance was issued concerning treatment for the alcoholic from the Ministry of Health in 1962. Though developments were in line with wider policy developments over treatment for alcoholics, responses soon developed around the specific concerns of the local community. It was public reaction to concerns about poverty in Nottingham that helped galvanise support for the treatment of alcoholics and led to alcoholism becoming viewed as the extreme case of the homeless/vagrant alcoholic. Champions from medicine influenced developments in a significant way and took responsibility for co-ordinating local effort and the growing band of social workers, probation officers and ex-drinkers who sought to improve the lot of the alcoholic at the local level. The convergence between community, criminal justice and medicine offered a lasting legacy and a framework for responding to alcoholism which endured over successive decades.

The idea of the homeless alcoholic continued to inform local policy at a time when national discussion in the 1970s was moving towards a public health and population approach to the problem. Chapter three argues that responses became better co-ordinated with the establishment of the Nottinghamshire Council on Alcoholism in 1975, and more connected to the centre via institutions like the National Council on Alcoholism and the Royal Colleges (Psychiatry and Physicians). Responses developed a medical-penal nature whilst continuing to spotlight the vagrant alcoholic. This was largely owing to the particular orientation of the specialist psychiatrists at Mapperley Hospital and meant the local response stood apart. For though the Home Office in its report *'Habitual Drunken Offender'* of 1971 called for medicine and the penal sector to establish detoxification facilities for the habitual drunken offender, neither the vagrant nor the habitual drunken offender were of much interest to psychiatrists outside of London at that time.

Internationally as well as nationally, there was revived public health thinking on alcohol during the 1970s, with emphasis on the importance of total consumption in populations. This perspective saw other groups in the community, including women and ethnic minorities, become targets of concern. Nevertheless it was concern about youth that developed in the most sustained way. Chapter four analyses the shifts in public perception over the 1970s, highlighting some changing realities, such as young people taking up drinking as a leisure activity after new clubs and bars opened up in the city centre, aimed at a younger clientele. This shift contributed to the problematising of youth drinking, with much of the concern borne out of anxiety over the declining morality of youth. This concern was first articulated in the mid 1970s when publicans voiced concerns about a new problem of hooliganism in the city centre pubs. In an episode involving the consumer group Campaign for Real Ale (CAMRA), which called for longer pub hours, publicans alleged a new, young hooligan element was running amok in Nottingham's city centre. In consequence, CAMRA's application for an extension of licensing was turned down by local justices though the problem was overstated, for there was little evidence of a growing problem. In fact, drunken disorder rates were declining.

Although concern about alcohol in the community shifted to young people, medicine continued to place importance on the homeless alcoholic, owing to the particular orientation of psychiatrists working at Mapperley Hospital. Chapter five analyses the responses of the local specialist treatment arena in the 1980s at a time when the government faced a new drugs epidemic and an emerging problem of HIV/AIDS. These issues shifted the national policy focus away from alcohol and led to changed fortunes for the UK alcohol sector. In many parts of the country alcohol treatment developments came to a standstill but in

Nottingham, the issue remained important. Monies meant for drugs misuse were also spent on alcohol, specifically on tackling the problems of the homeless street drinker. The voluntary sector and medicine worked closely on some new initiatives. One was The Handel Street Wet Centre, the first of its kind in England, and a place where street drinkers could go and drink in relative safety and crucially, off the streets. This was a period when inter-agency co-operation was stepped up, and new formal co-ordination arrangements put in place. The period marked an important shift for it was the beginning of the end of the medical-penal alliance. It saw police moved on to tackle concerns about youth disorder, an issue which medicine did not engage with or become involved in.

Chapter six focuses on the problem as viewed by the police in the 1980s, whose concern switched fully to youth. In this chapter it is argued that behind the new framing lay a growing consensus that exposure of young people to the destructive dangers of the streets turned them into hooligans. A day of mass arrests of skinheads, punks and habitual drunks in the Old Market Square in the summer of 1980 characterised the new approach and signified the tension between the 'Establishment' and youth. Social unrest and changes in young people's behaviour; significant youth mobility and homelessness, drugs misuse, and a trend in 'circuit drinking,' all added to the visibility of, and concern surrounding, youth. Despite this, alcohol consumption among young people remained low and comparatively stable throughout the decade, which suggests concern was largely a matter of changed perceptions, arising in all probability because of liberalisation of drinking with the introduction of the Licensing Act 1988. This brought anxiety about the prospect of 'all day' drinking, but when no upturn in disorder was apparent when the Act was introduced, the Council forged ahead with radical plans to turn Nottingham into a '24 hour' city.

Whilst alcohol was shaping up as a policing and youth issue in the community, things were changing also in the alcoholism treatment sector. There were more networks and formal procedures, which formed part of a new 'top down' approach. Changes also took place in the wider sphere of health and social care policy, which impacted on the sector in a significant way. Illustrating the significant change that occurred in the 1990s, chapter seven focuses on the arrival and impact of a new private clinic, 'The Nottingham Clinic', a test case for a new type of NHS public/private finance initiative. Employing the 'Minnesota Method,' a model of abstinence-based treatment that utilised the ideas of AA and was derived from the United States, the clinic's arrival showed not only how politicised the sector was becoming, but that psychiatry was outmoded and out of step. Provoking debate about new and old approaches to treatment, the clinic's main impact was on local relations, for by the end of the decade, the once unified sector had become fragmented.

Medicine was out of step with the community by the 1990s, where the antics of young people were causing mounting concern. At first disorder in the night economy was linked to the growing problem of drugs as Nottingham faced a major drug crime crisis, as did other UK cities at the time. Nottingham ranked top of the crime polls and was under intense scrutiny of Government as it 'got tough' on crime. The focus on drug crime left police in the city with difficulties dealing with drunken disorder in the city centre at night-time. To prevent the problems from escalating, police began to routinely object to new late night licenses to counter the Council's permissive approach to licensing. But the police approach was upended when magistrates overturned objections to the granting of a licence for Nottingham nightclub, 'Liberty's' in 1996. A landmark case, it provided momentum for development of the wider UK night economy and the catalyst for intensified criminal justice responses to youth drinking in the city.

After the Liberty's case, and at the turn of the century, Nottingham's night-time economy grew rapidly, as did many other UK cities. Chapter nine looks at the issues from the perspective of the police, where the problems of night-time disorder persisted. The situation drove Nottinghamshire Chief Constable Steven Green to speak publically about the problem of drink disorder in Nottingham's night-time economy, and co-operate in the making of a television documentary on 'binge drinking'. The episode represented a key policy moment but Nottingham gained the unfortunate media tag, "Binge Capital of Britain.' It highlighted the important roles of individuals and campaigns in the policy process and the interplay between national and local levels in the policy making process. It showed that the local level can influence national policy; and the other way round. Occurring at the same time as '24 hour' licensing was debated in Parliament in 2004/5, Green's actions helped establish drink as a important criminal justice issue, whilst Government used the crisis to push through its proposals, suggesting licensing reform would end 'bingeing to catch last orders'.

The concluding chapter analyses the interaction between centre and local over drink for the whole study period. It provides explanations for the shifts in balance of power at the local level between medicine and other groups in the community over the problem of alcohol, and suggests local definitions are important to policy and influence the policy making process.

Notes

1 'New power could mean blanket bans on drinking in public,' *The Telegraph*, October 1st 2009.

2 'On the streets of binge Britain', *The Observer*, September 5th 2004; 'The revellers' paradise which is hell for police', *The Telegraph*, November 20th 2004.

3 Nottingham City Council data. Available from http://www.nottinghamcity.gov.uk/index.aspx?articleid=2399 [Cited March 10th, 2011]

4 The Speakers' Corner Trust (SCT) first UK project was launched in Nottingham in February 2008.

5 'The History of Old Market Square,' BBC Nottingham. Available from http://www.bbc.co.uk/nottingham/content/articles/2008/03/06/local_history_old_market_square_feature.shtml [Cited March 10th, 2011].

6 J. Holland Walker, 'An itinerary of Nottingham', *Transactions of the Thoroton Society*, 31 (1927).

7 P. Jennings, *The Local: a History of the English Pub* (Stroud: Tempus Publishing, 2007) p.132; J.J. Rowley, 'Drink and the Public House in Nottingham 1830-60,' *Transactions of the Thoroton Society*, 79 (1975), pp.132.

8 A. Sillitoe, *Saturday Night and Sunday Morning*. (London: Flamingo, 1994), p. 9.

9 Examples of historiographical work on Nottingham include: M. Ashfield, *Don't be late on Monday: Life in a Nottingham Lace Factory* (Derby: Derby Books Publishing Company Ltd, 2011); G. Oldfield, *The Illustrated History of Nottingham Suburbs Revised* (Derby: Breedon Publishing, 2009); A. Nightingale, *Murder and Crime in Nottingham* (Stroud: The History Press Ltd, 2007); J. Beckett and K. Brand. *Nottingham* (Manchester: Manchester University Press, 1997); J. Beckett, *A Centenary History of Nottingham*. Manchester: Manchester University Press, 1997.

10 J. Nicholls, 'Drinking cultures and consumption in England: historical trends and policy implications', in Alcohol Health Committee,: First Report of Session 2009-10 Vol. II, HC151-II, Ev 239-53; P. Withington and A. McShane, 'Fluctuations in English drinking habits: an historical overview', Report for the Parliamentary Select Committee on Health, April 2009 Vol. II, HC151-II Ev 231; J. Kneale, 'British Drinking from the Nineteenth Century to the Present,' in Alcohol Health Committee,: First Report of Session 2009-10 Vol. II, HC151-II, Ev 239-253.

11 J. Nicholls, *The Politics of Alcohol; a History of the Drink Question in England* (Manchester: Manchester University Press, 2009).

12 Ibid, p.2

13 J. Warner, *Craze: Gin and Debauchery in an Age of Reason,* (New York: Random House, 2002), pp.2-16.

14 The Tippling Act prohibited distillers from selling gin at retail, and levied severe penalties for non-compliance, such as imprisonment, whipping and even deportation for repeat offenders. As a result, gin prices rose, gin consumption steadily declined back to 2 million gallons whereas beer consumption, steadily increased to about 4 million gallons a year. See

also E. L. Abel, "The Gin Epidemic: Much Ado about What?" *Alcohol and Alcoholism* 36 (2001), pp. 401-405.

15   J. Warner, *Craze*, p.5.

16   P. Borsay, "Binge Drinking and Moral Panics: Historical Parallels?" *History and Policy*, 62 (2007).

17   V. Berridge, *Temperance: Its History and Impact on Current and Future Alcohol Policy*, (York: Joseph Rowntree Foundation, 2005).

18   B. Harrison, *Drink and the Victorians: The Temperance Question in England, 1815-1872* (London: Faber and Faber, 1971),

19   B. Harrison, *Drink and the Victorians*. Also J. Warner, *Craze: Gin and Debauchery in an Age of Reason*.

20   A.E. Dingle, "Drink and Working Class Standards in Britain; 1870-1914," *Economic History Review* 25 (1972), pp. 608-622

21   P. Withington and A. McShane, 'Fluctuations in English Drinking Habits: An Historical Overview'.

22   J. Greenaway, *Drink and British Politics since 1830* (Hamps: Palgrave Macmillan, 2003), pp. 11-18

23   J. Nicholls, 'Drinking Cultures and Consumption in England: Historical Trends and Policy Implications,'

24   R. Baggott, *Alcohol, Politics and Social Policy* (Aldershot: Avebury, 1990), pp.16-17

25   M. Plant and M. Plant. *Binge Britain* (Oxford: Oxford University Press, 2006), pp.131-153.

26   'Alcohol, 'the 'new British Disease', BBC News online, May 20th, 2004. Available from http://news.bbc.co.uk/go/pr/fr/-/1/hi/uk_politics/3731025.stm (Cited April 4th 2011)

27   Works on women in the temperance era; B. Harrison, *Drink and the Victorians* pp. 25, 32, 46-47; M. Barrow, 'Temperate Feminists: The British Women's Temperance Association,' Manchester: PhD thesis, 1999.

28   D.W. Gutzke, 'The Cry of Children: The Edwardian Medical Campaign against Maternal Drinking,' *British Journal of Addiction* 79 (1984), pp. 71-84.

29   V. Berridge, *Temperance: Its History and Impact on Current and Future Alcohol Policy*, (York: Joseph Rowntree Foundation, 2005).

30   For further discussion see M. Plant, *Women and Alcohol* (London: Free Association Books, 1997).

31   The promotion of temperance by women from the higher classes in society at that time placed working class women under the moral jurisdiction of health professionals, charitable organisations and ladies' organisations. For further discussion: B. Thom, 'Women and Alcohol: The Emergence of a Risk Group,' in *Gender, Drink, and Drugs*, ed. M. McDonald (Oxford: Berg, 1994), pp. 33-54.

32   J. Waterson, 'Gender Divisions and Drinking Problems,' in *Alcohol Problems in the Community* ed. L. Harrison (London: Routledge, 1996), pp. 170-99; J.Waterson, *Women and Alcohol in Social Context* (Hamps: Palgrave, 2000).

33   G. Pearson, *Hooligan: A History of Respectable Fears*. (Basingstoke: Macmillan, 1993); See also Stanley Cohen, *Folk Devils and Moral Panics: The Creation of the Mods and Rockers.*, 2nd ed. (New York: St. Martin's Press, 1980), for discussion of scapegoats and moral panics.

34   'The Generation Game', *The Guardian*, November 8th 2006.

35   W. F. Bynum, R. Porter and M. Shepherd, *The anatomy of madness: essays in the history of psychiatry, Volume 3.* (London: Routledge, 2004).

36   T. Trotter. *An essay, medical, philosophical, and chemical on drunkenness and its effects on the human body.* ed. R. Porter (London: Routledge, 1988). Quotation is from B. Harrison, *Drink and the Victorians*, p. 92.

37   B. Thom, *Dealing with Drink: Alcohol and Social Policy* (London: Free Association Books, 1999), p.5.

38   R. Klein, *The New Politics of the NHS: From Creation to Re-Invention* (Oxon: Radcliffe Publishing, 2006); C. Ham, *Health Policy in Britain* (New York: Palgrave Macmillan, 2004).

2

MEDICINE AS PART OF SOCIAL CONCERN, 1950S & 1960s

This chapter introduces Nottingham in the era of the 1950s and 1960s, and analyses responses to drink by the local community. This was a time when the concept of 'alcoholism' took hold at the international and national levels in both medical and policy circles, ideas that began to filter to the local level. The fellowship Alcoholics Anonymous (AA), with its ideas of mutual aid and self help was the first response in the city, arriving in 1955. This was followed by a response from psychiatrists at the local psychiatric hospital, Mapperley Hospital, where doctors were to join forces with AA to offer treatment for alcoholism following guidance from the Ministry of Health (1962). Within the NHS at that time, power over implementation of health policy was concentrated at regional and local authority level, and largely in the hands of individual consultants. This meant that although Nottingham was in line with wider policy developments over treatment for alcoholics, responses at Mapperley were able to develop around the perceived needs of the local community. Public reaction to research about poverty in Nottingham first helped galvanise local support and treatment for alcoholics. Though initially other groups - including women, ethnic minorities and youth - were targets of community concern over drink, the focus of concern on poverty saw alcoholism become defined with time as the extreme case of the vagrant alcoholic. Champions from medicine as well as the community influenced developments with a small, but influential network of doctors, social workers, probation officers and local activists taking responsibility for co-ordinating local effort, the convergence between these groups offering a lasting legacy and a framework for responding to alcoholism that endured over successive decades.

National developments

The Second World War had a profound effect on the way British people saw themselves in terms of their role in society, and in their expectations about the quality of everyday life. Nevertheless, a general mood of tolerance persisted towards drunkenness, with a blind eye often turned to individuals and families seeking help. Nevertheless, in the late 1950s concern began to mount over drink as part of a movement of renewed concern about health. Views on a number of health issues, including alcohol, began a process of redefinition and formed part of a broader move within public health involving emphasis on individual responsibility for healthy 'lifestyles' and behaviours.[1] A likely contributing factor to concern was the increase in the use of mood-altering substances, especially among soldiers, which in some cases continued after the Second World War ended as men attempted to re-join civilian life. Likewise, the slow but steady rise in alcohol consumption after the war was a trigger for concern following the removal of certain licensing restrictions, the growth in the number of off-licenses and increased uptake of home drinking. In many areas of life however, the values of pre-war society remained unchanged, with many general household items, including foodstuffs and alcohol, continuing to be rationed until 1948, with some remaining controlled until 1954. Drinking remained a fairly ritualised affair, with alcohol consumed most frequently within the confines of the public house or 'pub'. Within the context of the pub, locally brewed beers were popular and outshone nationally available products. The "permitted hours" of opening hours, determined by the 1921 Licensing Act, were five hours on a Sunday, otherwise eight hours (nine hours a day in London) from 11.00 am to 10.00 pm, with a two-hour break after noon. Local licensing authorities determined the actual times. In cities, pubs usually were open from 11.00 am to 3.00 pm, and from 5.00 or 5.30 pm to 11.00 pm, though country areas could be half-an-hour earlier. The 1923 Intoxication Liquor (Sales to Persons under Eighteen) Act made the legal age for the purchase or consumption of alcoholic drinks 18, but allowed the sale of beer, porter, cider or Perry (or pear cider) with a meal to those over 16. With the Licensing (Permitted Hours) Act of 1934, licensing magistrates could extend closing time until 10.30 pm for part of the year if it was in the public interest to so do.[2] The pub itself had suffered in terms of standard of comfort following the 1930s' economic depression and World War Two. But in the late 1950s and 1960s brewers began to improve their houses: serving meals, providing gardens, encouraging families and selling soft drinks as well as alcohol to make them more respectable and welcoming places. A number of legislative changes assisted the move, and offered the first revision of legislation for over forty years. The changes included restaurants and hotels being allowed licenses in 1961; the 1964 Act promoting growth in the number of off-licenses and facilitating their appearance in food shops with more liberal opening hours. Nevertheless, these developments were offset in 1964 by the abolition of Resale Price Maintenance, which encouraged more home drinking and had significant impact. In 1951 for instance, there were 26,200 off-licenses but by the late 1970s, the figure had risen to around 41,100.[3]

Around the time of these developments in the social realm, the concept of 'alcoholism' gained acceptance in medical circles. This defined the problem of persistent drunkenness in terms of disease and was taken up with enthusiasm by psychiatrists. World War Two had profound effects on the speciality of psychiatry, with notable advancement in new areas such as social psychiatry in the immediate post-war period. A new "holistic" view of the patient gained prominence; borne out of the lessons of war and its traumas.[4] That the new 'disease' was taken up so keenly by psychiatry is attributable to a branching of interests into new speciality fields at that time, which facilitated expansion into new areas including alcohol and drug addiction.[5] The concept, which emerged in the international medical research community in the Fifties, originated from ideas put forward by Elvin Morton Jellinek, a consultant engaged by the World Health Organisation (WHO) in 1952. Alcoholism was characterised as compulsive use of alcohol, loss of control over the amount and frequency of drink consumed and continued use despite negative consequences. A chronic condition, with the potential for relapse, abstinence was put forward as the only way to stall it into remission. Increasing concern about alcoholism was evident from 1958 when the Magistrates' Association, which had set up a committee to consider matters of 'common interest relative to the medical aspects of legal offences', turned its attentions to the rehabilitation of vagrants. This had the effect of shifting the policy focus towards alcoholism.[6] This was followed in the 1960s by pressure to respond to the problem from a number of sources. First, there was concern arising from the steady increase in the number of offences of drunkenness in the UK. Second, there was an increase in the number of prosecutions for drink-driving. And third, there was an increase in the admission rate to psychiatric hospitals of patients diagnosed as suffering from alcoholism.[7] Widespread acceptance of alcoholism, concern from general practitioners, the clergy and others, about the lack of suitable treatment provision for those suffering from the condition and evidence of a growing problem, inevitably increased pressure on government to treat it. In 1962 the Ministry issued an official statement concerning alcoholism treatment. The first statement, a Memorandum on Hospital Treatment for Alcoholism (1962) recommended the setting up of specialist NHS inpatient units; Regional Alcohol Treatment Units (ATUs), for the treatment of alcoholism and alcoholic psychosis.[8] This was followed by a second memorandum in 1968, but by then the emphasis was already shifting away from hospital/institution based care towards community care as was the general trend within the NHS.[9] Running in tandem with these developments in medicine was the rise of alcoholism as a moral/spiritual phenomenon in society. This perspective was promulgated by the self help fellowship Alcoholics Anonymous (AA). The fellowship had its beginnings in Ohio, United States in 1935 and was influenced by the Oxford

Group, a fellowship that emphasised universal spiritual values in daily living.[10] In 1939 AA published its central text, *Alcoholics Anonymous*, which explained the Fellowship's philosophy and methods, the core of which were the Twelve Steps of recovery.[11] With a focus on abstinence from alcohol, the perspective was moral-spiritual in outlook. Recovery was viewed as revival from a social/spiritual form of illness and as such, differed from the new disease perspective proposed by medicine. By the 1950s the Fellowship extended to other countries. In Scotland in 1949 meetings began in Perth, Edinburgh and Glasgow, and in England meetings were also established that same year in London.[12]

Drink and drink problems in 1950s Nottingham

As described in the introductory chapter, it was part of the culture of the city to work hard in the week and seek compensation by drinking hard at the weekends. Alan Sillitoe described it as *"a matter of letting your hair down after work in the factories."*[13] Drinking provided unity and fostered integration at a time when social cohesion was under threat. The pub acted as a meeting point or hub for voluntary groups, and played an important role in the subsequent campaign for social improvements during the 1960s. The writer, politician and activist Ken Coates, who was a researcher at Nottingham University, and engaged in research into poverty in the St Ann's area of the city during the 1960s, recalled no particular problem with drink in the community. He suggested its use was largely contained because most families could not afford to spend money on it. *"Nobody had much money and that alone diminished the scope for drunkenness"*.[14]

Red Cow Inn, Lenton, demolished in the 1960s
© Lenton Local History Society.

But Ray Gosling, the writer/broadcaster, who lived in St Ann's - a slum area of the city - and was an active member of its local residents' association, saw things differently; *"In those days [pre-demolition] St Ann's was one of the most fantastic drinking places in the world and it was a fantastic place for shebeens. There were pubs with pianos and music and sing-songs ...and when the pubs shut, the West Indians and Caribbeans had shebeens.*[15] Nevertheless, drinking occurred mostly in the confines of the pub where consumption was fairly well controlled by a mix of social regulation and restriction on licensing. Arrests for drunkenness were no worse than pre-war figures but up on war time figures when restrictions and rationing meant consumption levels were abnormally low.[16] But Nottingham was a *'hearty and feisty'* place, as Gosling put it. Fighting in the streets was commonplace; especially in the working class areas where drink formed *'part of the squabbles'*.[17]

Drink as a problem of ethnic minorities

The problem of drunkenness, perhaps inevitably, began to be viewed differently as the social landscape altered during the course of the 1950s and 1960s. Employment troughed in the late 1950s and there were other effects on family life. Major slum clearance programmes during the period saw families removed from their neighbourhoods and there was breakdown of long established communities. At the time the area of St Ann's, with its closely packed terrace houses, was home to around 30,000 people.

Edwin Street, St Ann's, Nottingham, 1969
© North East Midland Photographic Record

Like many in other slum clearance areas, including the Meadows, they resented being sent packing elsewhere. This was an era of massive change, change deemed necessary because of the poor state of the properties, but too abrupt for people living in these areas. Redevelopment affected perceptions of 'community spirit'; and as historian John Beckett argues, people moving to the new council estates viewed them as paradise for burglars' and muggers and believed that 'neighbourliness' ceased to exist.[18]

There was also a significant rise in population, which increased due to immigration that peaked in 1963 at 315,050.[19] In the inter-war years, Nottingham's foreign-born population numbered only 4,290 of whom the Irish formed the largest group, but the ethnic mix altered considerably by the 1950s with more than 5,000 European-born residents in the city and further immigrants arriving from Poland, Lithuania and other Eastern European states. The Poles had their own cultural associations and many, like the Irish who came before them during the industrial era, were Roman Catholics. There were an estimated six hundred Lithuanians, Latvians and Estonians living in Nottingham, many of whom believed themselves to be under Soviet threat of death.[20] The influx of immigrants tended to move into working class inner city residential areas such as the Meadows, New Lenton, Radford, the Forest and St. Ann's.[21] Different factions of the community held different beliefs and practices over a wide range of issues. Sometimes these differences were seen as threatening to the traditional way of life. Over the course of the decade the behaviour of certain ethnic minority groups with regards to drink, as well as other groups viewed as testing the social boundaries, including youth and women, became objects of suspicion and scrutiny. Nottingham's social problems were most often attributed to groups that were economically and socially marginal including prostitutes, vagrants, drugs users and petty criminals. With the disintegration of communities, alcohol problems were a visible sign of social distress and as other writers have noted elsewhere over other historical periods, drunkenness came to be viewed as a problem and as a perceived threat of the 'dangerous classes'.[22] Also in the 1950s, Italians, Asians and West Indians, Scots and Irish, Geordies and Liverpudlians, were drawn to the Midlands in pursuit of work. Many experienced downward occupational mobility, were employed as manual workers or worked in poorly paid occupations.[23] This movement of migrant workers into the inner city areas coincided with transfer of the more 'well to do' out of the city to rural and suburban areas.

Alcohol was linked to ethnic hostility that reared its head in Nottingham during the race riot of 1958. Minor assaults peaked between the years 1950-54 and a new pattern of assaults on police officers was emerging.[24] Though not directly linked to changing patterns of drunkenness, alcohol was frequently viewed as the cause of trouble when it started. More than 1,000 people went on the rampage on the streets of St Ann's on the evening of 30th August 1958. The *Nottingham Evening Post* reported: *"The whole place was like a slaughterhouse."* In many of the reports of what caused the riot, relationships between black men and white women featured. Some people later referred to the disturbances in Nottingham as the "teddy boy riots", a reference to the young men involved in the white, working class youth culture of the period.[25] After the riots, an enterprising bus company apparently offered tours of the riot-torn streets. Such was the interest that in early September, 1958, the Lord Mayor of Nottingham appealed to people not to go to St Ann's "for sightseeing purposes". Though the cause of the rioting and disturbances during 1958 most likely resulted from a growing problem of prostitution, housing shortages, unemployment and a growing concern about violence and crime; spatial polarisation and differences in cultural life undoubtedly led to tensions.[26] The riots in Nottingham and subsequent rioting in London's Notting Hill were reported and debated around the world; as this section of an article from US Time magazine emphasised;

> *"In Nottingham, a textile city of 312,000, where Negroes [sic] constitute less than 1% of the population; they make up 20% of the unemployed. Fist fights ....have become a common Saturday night feature in Nottingham's slum district around St. Ann's Well Road, an area noted for petty crime, poverty and prostitution. Last month a gang of white Teddy boys jumped a West Indian labourer and beat him with fists and clubs.....The pubs on St. Ann's Well Road ...were filled with edgy whites and Negroes. At Chase Tavern a young Negro drew angry mutters when he entered with a white girl. At closing time a band of Negroes ...neared the pub, knives flashing, left two white men writhing on the ground. Within minutes, as nearby pubs emptied, fighting became general...smashed bottle......... sticks and bricks and anything else handy."*[27]

In the aftermath, the community turned its attentions to its social problems with the hope of restoring its reputation. Nevertheless, the riots exposed discord in local relations and concern about the behaviours of 'outsiders' remained, as this comment from a police officer of the period exposed; *"The problem is the unlicensed shebeens where people drink after hours and drink all night. But that is mainly, and I say mainly, amongst the coloured [sic] fraternity where they illegally sell drink at these shebeens and the party goes on all night."*[28]

For many of the West Indian community however, the parties were a way of life. Interviewed by Ruth John for her book 'St Ann's Nottingham; Inner City Voices', Ray Gosling recalled the parties he attended. He described attending one in a big cellar, approached from Manning Street but in fact it was the cellar of the house opposite. Young black men were there, and white youths. Gosling recalled taking a girlfriend, *"You would stand there and bop, bop, bop and eat this chicken and rice out of a saucer... buy cans at enormous prices."*[29] Parties in the Hyson Green area often lasted several nights. Most were organised on a commercial basis, the organisers charging admission and taking on short term lets on flats from which to operate these events.

WOMEN AS TARGETS

Other social changes to occur at this time included changes in the role of women, not just within the home but in the workplace. Consequently women increasingly became targets of hostility, and women from ethnic minority groups were hit doubly hard. The following case study, which featured in the Annual Report of the Children's Committee 1969 -1970, illustrates the kind of concern roused;

FAMILY C – 'A HOPELESS CASE'

"The woman is Irish and lived for 12 years with a West Indian in derelict areas due for demolition. She spent her formative years in an Irish Convent. According to the man's culture, the woman is fully responsible for looking after the home and he feels justified in doing little. She has little idea of home-craft and is an alcoholic, drinking beer and cheap wine as a form of escapism. After much effort she is persuaded to take treatment and the four children are put into care. ...she has co-operated reasonably well and has been moved to a good area now...She is not a good timekeeper or worker and is often dismissed but the children are now at school...with alcohol problems there is always the possibility of further failure." [30]

Though for young men drinking was construed as a rite of passage, for women it was still largely discouraged by means of social convention. Even if it was acceptable for women to accompany men into the pub, they were still far less likely to drink alcohol there, for the pub remained the province of men. Unusually however, women occupied an important place in the workforce in

Nottingham, making up almost two fifths of the employed locally compared to slightly over one third nationally, which meant many women had more independence and income at their disposal than was usual for the times. Traditionally women were employed in the lace trade but as this industry faded out many were absorbed into the hosiery industry. Women also benefitted when Nottingham became a centre of light engineering and service industry. A quarter of Ericsson's telephones employees were women and within the pharmaceutical industry (Boots pharmaceutical company) they made up a significant number of the workforce, as they did at Players (tobacco industry).[31] As sought after employees, this added up to far greater opportunities for women to work, but also to afford to socialise and engage in activities like drinking. As Ray Gosling recalled; *"Women were not frightened to drink, they had the money. Not pints or anything but they used to go to Yates* [Wine Lodge]*"*.[32]

Young men and women at a popular Notts dance venue.
Reproduced by permission of Alan Fletcher/Chainline/The Notts. Mods

The guiding gender norms and expectations about women in relation to drink were not markedly different to anywhere else despite the new found freedoms. A local man recalled; *"We would drink beer, that's what the boys did ...our girlfriends stayed sober. There was a convention that young men drank beer (couldn't afford to drink spirits usually) and that girlfriends didn't drink or were certainly not expected to get drunk. It was rather shocking if a girl got drunk, so in the company of women and girlfriends it greatly reduced the amount of trouble because they were largely sober and could exercise some control. If they drank anything it was a dreadful drink called Babycham [a light, sparkling perry or pear cider] which was almost devoid of alcohol or anything else."* The distinctions between the genders were especially marked in the post war era with emphasis on re-constructing family life and fears about marital breakdown with greater access to fault-based divorce.[33] Poverty and unemployment were additional factors that distorted perceptions of women's roles because poverty tended to marginalise people, and particularly distorted the role of men in families, the hallmarks apparent in the findings of a local study, Patterns of Infant Care in an Urban Community, carried out in Nottingham in 1963. The study found Nottingham's rate of illegitimate births, at nine per cent, was twice the national average. The newly built council houses were often allotted to families with small children, so some communities were entirely made up of young families, affording women the opportunity to experience peer support but providing little support from the wider community.[34]

GROWING CONCERN ABOUT YOUTH

As already indicated, mostly it was men who engaged in the act of public drinking in the Fifties and early Sixties. As young men, they gained the *savoir faire* to engage in public drinking. This usually entailed individuals progressing from naïve to sophisticated drinker by learning how to hold their drink. Alan Sillitoe described his initiation into the world of drinking as a young man in Nottingham; *"At 14 or 15 I had started to drink, going to the pubs but I was going to work. Before the Christmas holiday.... we would chuck a penny or two into a common kitty and then, just as the factory broke up we would all go to the pub. They had to carry me back .... a pint or so just knocked me out. I soon took to it of course. You weren't supposed to go into a pub until you were 16. Nobody bothered – you just went in and had a pint of shandy or whatever you fancied. If a young man wanted a drink, well, it was in their family, in their blood. It was tradition as well."*[35]

Historically the norms governing youth access to alcohol have been at their most restrictive when adult and juvenile labour have been in low demand or when the status of adulthood has been postponed.[36] In the period immediately after the Second World, work was plentiful and the conception of the teenager emerged, largely in response to advertisers who realised that young people had money to spend which meant youths were rewarded with a postponement of adulthood not afforded their parents.[37] It meant drinking was able to transform into an essentially recreational activity, conducted outside the home and among groups, a shift that contributed substantially to the acceptability of youth drinking.

Mods outside the Council Building, 1965   Notts. Mods out on a bank holiday at Skegness
Reproduced by permission of Alan Fletcher/Chainline/The Notts. Mods

The rise and role of Alcoholics Anonymous

Much of the concern about alcoholism in the late 1950s and 1960s grew out of concern for the physical and social environment. The state of affairs gave rise to concern, mostly amongst older members of the community, about the erosion of traditional ways of life. Voluntary impulses were mobilised to combat not only degeneration of the physical environment, but to safeguard against declining moral standards. Hence alcoholics were not the only group to come into view at this time. Others including young single mothers, the mentally ill and homeless were also singled out for concern. Alcoholics Anonymous meetings were established in Nottingham in the mid-Fifties and later other enlightened self-interest groups became central to responses to social conditions and problems in the city. The 'self help' ethos of AA and similar groups set up at this time, left an indelible mark on the community. Developing initiatives of the 'community development' kind, meant Nottingham was in advance of developments nationally where the trend only properly took off during the 1970s and 1980s. [38] The self help ethos enabled the community to act to further the interests of particular marginalised groups yet still serve to benefit the community as a whole. [39]

AA was the first tangible response to alcoholism in Nottingham. [40] Before that, if someone in the local community had a problem with drink there was little in the way of direct help though doctors sometimes, if reluctantly, stepped in. Those with drink problems sometimes were admitted voluntarily to the City Hospital (general hospital) or one of the psychiatric hospitals; Mapperley or Saxondale, but that was the extent of it. Doctors at Mapperley Hospital most frequently treated patients with drink problems and managed them alongside patients suffering other forms of mental illness. There was no specialist treatment for alcoholism in place because the concept was not yet commonly understood. Thus individuals with alcohol problems often travelled to neighbouring cities to attend AA meetings, which were emerging in some parts of the country at this time. In the mid Fifties however, a Nottingham Fellowship was established through the efforts of self-proclaimed alcoholic George J., who gained sobriety by attending AA meetings in Leicester. Discovering that substantial benefits could be drawn from participation in AA, George J. held the first meeting at his home in Aspley Lane, Nottingham. In 1956, Nottingham had its first public meeting of AA at the Young Men's Christian Association (YMCA), Shakespeare Street. AA thereafter became an informal meeting society for recovering alcoholics whose primary purpose was to stay sober and help other alcoholics achieve sobriety. Many embraced the approach because it afforded a less judgmental view of their difficulties. As a member of AA recalled; *"Before that there wasn't any support. People were seen as drunks"*. [41] By 1960 up to twenty-five men and a few women, mostly drawn from the respectable working and middle classes, regularly met on Wednesday evenings. [42]

AA AND THE EMERGING MEDICAL RESPONSE

With little formalised medical help or treatment available for individuals experiencing difficulties with drink, the emergence of AA was a major step forward for those in need of help. As previously stated, GP involvement was patchy with a tendency to refer patients to hospital if they were tricky cases, or avoid treating them at all. Mapperley Hospital admitted more than any other hospital though specialist treatment for alcoholics was not available until 1962.

Patients were usually allocated to the hospital's acute wards. If detected, alcohol problems were frustrating to treat, with frequent relapses and admissions. They accounted for many of the 'revolving door' admissions (in 1957, 1310 patients accounted for 1638 admissions at Mapperley Hospital),[43] though it is almost impossible to determine with any accuracy how many were treated for alcoholism because no formal diagnosis was used until the mid 1960s.

Mapperley Hospital ©Alan Murray-Rust
(Licensed for reuse under the Creative Commons Attribution)

To impede investigation further, from 1963 and for reasons unknown, the diagnosis of patients admitted or discharged from the hospital was not supplied on hospital registers. The hospital's admission and discharge register of male patients, 1949-1966, provides summaries of the diagnosis of each male patient (the majority of whom were elderly) but contains no reference to any diagnosis that specifically mentioned alcohol.[44] Likewise the 'non-status' (voluntary) admission register, 1955-1962 provides no detail of diagnosis or treatment,[45] and the register of Death Notices identifies alcohol as the cause of death in only three cases between 1965 and 1968.[46] One case described the cause of death as 'alcoholism', another as 'chronic alcoholism' and the third defined the antecedent cause of death as 'alcoholic psychoses'. This lack of reference to 'alcoholism' among patients of the hospital suggests either a general lack of awareness of the disease and its progression in patients among doctors, or there being not much of a detectable local problem at that time. Nevertheless when alcoholism was considered a key factor in a patient's ill health, they might be exposed to all manner of treatments intended for the mentally ill. They could be sectioned if necessary and held down with 'liquid cosh' (heavy sedation such as chlorpromazine, one of a number of new drugs synthesised in the 1950s) as part of treatment for alcohol withdrawal symptoms.[47]

The medical response developed in a more determined way with the arrival of psychiatrist Alfred Minto, who had a particular interest in treating alcoholism and was approached to head up a planned new addiction unit at the hospital. Minto was a Scot and grew up in Aberdeen where subsequently he trained as a psychiatrist. He was a member of the Socialist Medical Association, which had campaigned for a National Health Service in the UK, and was active in campaigns against issues such as NHS charges, smoking, tuberculosis and adequate nutrition.[48] In his professional life he took a good deal of interest in the problem of drink. His views were shaped by his childhood experience of growing up in Aberdeen where he saw the impacts of poverty and unemployment first hand. His father was unemployed for ten years between 1928 and 1938, an experience that impacted significantly on family life, and was the fate of many at that time. Minto considered alcohol *"an escape in many people's lives."*[49] He worked previously in Middlesbrough where he had set up a small alcohol unit, on one occasion experimenting with the drug Antabuse, an aversion treatment, by giving it to eight male patients and having *"a little drink party"*. A number of the men had severe reactions, so he never repeated this type of group treatment again though maintained an interest in pharmacological treatments throughout his working life.[50] He was passionate about helping those on the margins of society. His perspective was thus; *"On no account should you assume a patient is doomed forever....You are admitted for six weeks and you are a bit better. You are in for six months and you are not a lot different, but you have lost contact with your family, your mates are now entitled to view you as pretty weird...so your social ties had gone."*[51]

In this, he joined the sway of psychiatrists who, in the post war period, adopted a more social view of mental illness. The hospital superintendent at Mapperley Hospital at that time, Duncan Macmillan, was a pioneer and champion of the social psychiatry movement.[52] This was an important new approach to mental illness and other pioneers included Erik Erikson, who discussed the influence of society on development (1950); Frederick Redlich who looked at the influence of social class on psychiatric conditions (1958); and Trigant Burrow, a pioneer of social causes of mental disorder who put forward 'Sociatry' as a name for the new discipline. The approach was instrumental in the development of 'therapeutic communities' which was a participative, group-based approach to long-term mental illness greatly influenced by Maxwell Jones, the army psychiatrist, who helped develop the concept.[53] Therapeutic communities utilised democratic, user-led forms of therapy; the central philosophy being that benefits could be derived by patients becoming active participants in their own and each other's treatment.[54] Mapperley Hospital was at the forefront of this post war development. The shift represented a belief that things had to be different and emphasised the need for inclusion in society, whether that meant providing homes or protecting the rights of the mentally ill. The move was in advance of antipsychotic medication drugs, which often have been credited with making this change possible, and in evidence in Scotland by 1945 (Dingleton Hospital on the Scottish borders) and England at both Warlingham Park, Surrey and Mapperley Hospital, Nottingham by 1952. Macmillan previously had been the medical officer for mental health at the local government health department. Whilst at the city health department he developed extraordinarily good relations with officers at the department. One result was that he and the senior mental welfare officer at the health department built up a team of social workers, paid for by the local authority, but working in and out of Mapperley Hospital. This was a most unusual move in the 1950s where a hostile gap often existed between hospital and local authority services.[55] In 1952 Mapperley hospital opened its doors and became renowned for running industrial rehabilitation schemes and encouraging frequent patient leave.[56] Macmillan also reduced compulsory admissions, blocking the use of long term compulsory orders to detain people in hospital and encouraging detention under Section 20 of the Lunacy Act, 1890 (a three day order which could be made by a social worker) in place of long term orders.[57] One of the first experiments in de-designated wards (which led to the 'informal' status of the 1959 Act) was carried out at the hospital.[58] These ideas were not entirely new however, their roots found in 'moral therapy' of the nineteenth century, which stressed 'work, reward and warm relations' in mental institutions.[59]

The regional alcohol treatment unit

Approval for a regional addiction unit was granted in 1962, with a unit formally established at Mapperley Hospital in 1964 at the behest of Sheffield Hospital Board. This followed the Ministry of Health memorandum; "Hospital Treatment of Alcoholism," (1962). The Ministry's guidance ran concurrently with The Hospital Plan of the same year.[60] Because psychiatrists at Mapperley Hospital were pioneering 'community care' at this time, alcoholism treatment followed suit.[61] The mode of treatment followed that tested in the 1950s by Max Glatt, a psychiatrist at Warlingham Park in Surrey. Glatt's experiments provided the blueprint for alcoholism treatment units and formed the basis of Ministry of Health's guidance on hospital treatment of alcoholism (1962).[62] His ideas endorsed the view of the BMA/Magistrate's Committee 1958-61, which emphasised the interface between medicine and criminal justice.[63] Glatt's model formed an important basis to the programme at Mapperley Hospital alcohol unit and there is evidence of some interplay between the two units. In hospital records, evidence suggested that the charge nurse at Mapperley's unit was seconded to Warlingham Park for *'the purposes of studying practice and technique'*.[64] The particularities of policy developments at Mapperley also corresponded with events in South London where Griffith Edwards, a leading psychiatrist who specialised in the area of addiction, actively became involved in trying to set up services for skid row drinkers, working closely with the Camberwell Council on Alcoholism, which had already laid some of the groundwork for opening a rehabilitation hostel.[65] But whereas many of the other alcohol units that developed in the 1960s and 1970s tended to respond to less chaotic sorts of alcoholic, with treatment often directed towards those from the middle classes, treatment at Mapperley developed principally in response to the homeless/vagrant drinker.[66]

It was intended to admit patients who had either drug or alcohol problems, though in the early days most admitted had alcohol problems. Drug addicts (mostly LSD users),[67] tended to be younger, and there were fewer of them and at any rate, Minto considered treatment for their drug use relatively ineffective. The unit operated as a ten-bedded unit from 'The Cottage', formerly the insulin treatment unit at the hospital.[68] Dr Minto was intent on forging good links with AA and other groups within the community. This meant any differences between AA and medicine over what constituted 'alcoholism' had to be cast aside in order to establish a unified response. AA ran weekly meetings on the unit and became involved in patient aftercare. Work for the new team at the unit involved admitting people for short episodes of treatment and returning them to the community soon after to begin the lengthy process of reintegration and rehabilitation. The unit was run in orderly fashion, with clear boundaries and rules. Group work was not well favoured though one concession was the weekly group where new patients had to tell their 'life story' to other patients. But despite the best efforts of staff, only half the patients made adequate progress, which led to further doubts about the merits of hospital care. A conscious decision therefore was made to admit only the 'long ill', the chronically ill, like the extreme case of the vagrant alcoholic, because he was most likely to benefit from such an intensive arrangement. Admissions were high but there was a quick turnaround. In reality there were tangible differences over conceptualisation, with AA's version of the addict being of stigmatised identity; a person of moral weakness and deviant, whereas the medical disease required some sort of cure and these differences eventually became a source of conflict between the agencies, though not for several decades.

Minto's work at the addiction unit occurred alongside heavy commitments at the hospital establishing new forms of provision in the community as well as a day unit for industrial therapy. At the industrial unit he aimed to bring about *bona fide* work opportunities for patients and was helped in this by fellow doctor, Dr Maurice Bawd, head of occupational health at Boots (the pharmaceutical company), and Father Douglas Brown, a monk at the Society of the Sacred Mission at Kelham. There was significant emphasis on gainful employment at the industrial centre and involved undertaking work for local companies, for example, Chambers pencils, and shoe work for a factory in Mansfield, but patients also made goggles for Olympic swimmers for Speedo as well as glitter balls for ballroom dances.[69] Though the length of the average stay was reduced, patients were quickly returned to the community, sometimes in the early days without adequate support to sustain improvements. The problem was exacerbated by overcrowding in the hospital for at that time there was approximately one doctor to every 300 patients. Between 1955 and 1959, admissions to the hospital rose exponentially from around 1100 admissions to over 1800 annually, and by 1969 admissions reached 2350 and were set to rise still further, though the authorised number of beds remained fairly static (in the region of 1000-1100 beds).[70] The lack of beds led to increased provision of day care and new programmes of patient discharge to the community. Minto was involved in the changes, charged with returning two hundred male patients back to the community. Between 1961 and 1964 in a novel move, he discharged patients not to special care hostels but ordinary, commercial lodgings. In interview he recalled; *"This started when a wife of a patient of mine who took in Irish navvies as lodgers asked if she could take in some of our patients. She recognised they needed a home. So we started farming out a few patients to this pretty thin accommodation... Later of course it was better because as we closed down the wards we had beds, mattresses and all sorts we could give. So we equipped these landladies for nothing!"* [71]

The move was not without its problems;

"The landlady got a sum of money from the DHSS and a sum from the local authority mental health services as well, which gave them a good income per patient..... We had to make sure that the patients weren't in any way ill treated or disadvantaged so what I did was employ three retired male nurses who could visit each of these houses on an absolutely regular basis.......so I claim therefore, very modestly, to be the legitimate father of the community psychiatric nurse in Britain".[72]

Many individuals had social and psychological difficulties including alcohol problems that required ancillary support. Local AA members helped this along as did a staff of unqualified social workers at the mental health department. Psychiatrists visited individuals in the lodgings and their own homes but the development nonetheless had immediate and considerable impacts. Though it added considerably to reintegration of the socially marginalised in the community it added inadvertently to the band of disenfranchised people visible in and around the city centre. The effect was to make the problems of poverty more transparent and alter public perceptions about the extent of the community's problem of drink.

The prominence of poverty

During the mid and late 1960s poverty became a prominent local issue. Nottingham's slums had achieved notoriety as the worst in England at this time. Many of the houses were rotten, damp, and lacked basic amenities. The programmes of St. Ann's and the Meadows were among the largest in Europe and involved the clearance of 25,000 houses. Many in the slum areas experienced a significant degree of social fragmentation as a result of the clearance programmes. Many opposed redevelopment and claimed the process destroyed communities.[73] Though the programmes were eventually stopped, many of the thirty thousand people who lived in the slum houses lost their homes, only to be re-housed on the new estates which replaced them. Drink became inextricably bound up with the anxiety about community fragmentation, poverty, as well as to concerns about the erosion of traditional ways of life. In the late 1960s, Nottingham was placed on the map as a centre of poverty by Ken Coates, a lecturer at Nottingham University, who in preceding years researched poverty in the St. Ann's area of the city. The research findings and the subsequent backlash from residents of the area, led not only to Nottingham gaining an unsavoury reputation, but stimulated action over conditions in the city. The background to Coate's work was mounting interest in the issue of poverty in the post war period. Social scientists, among them Peter Townsend and Brian Abel-Smith, brought attention to the issue in Britain.[74] Ken Coates, along with colleague Richard Silburn, sponsored by the Department of Adult Education at Nottingham University and the Workers' Educational Association (WEA), set out to study the issue in Nottingham.[75] The subsequent study found that residents of the inner city, former slum area, of St Ann's were suffering from a problem of poverty and apathy over conditions in the area. The authors suggested welfare services were failing to alleviate poverty and called the slum clearance programmes a failure. Local residents criticised the study for being conducted by 'outsiders' and blamed Coates for slurring the character of those living in the area. Nevertheless Coates' and Silburn's findings were widely broadcast via a BBC film documentary.[76] The film showed slum clearance as a good idea and a benefit to the people who lived in the area. But many people living in Nottingham believed that they had been used to deceive the British public, and many who lived in the area liked it, and did not regard it as a poverty stricken slum area. All the same, the episode left Nottingham's earlier reputation as a 'boom town' badly tarnished and was the trigger for initiatives to combat social deprivation.

MEDICINE AS PART OF SOCIAL CONCERN

Nottingham epitomised the problem of poverty, an issue already on the national conscience where plans were developed at government level for new social work agencies. These were to be of a scale and character 'hitherto only dreamed of,' with plans afoot for new community and family orientated services.[77] But Nottingham's problems required a sharp and speedy response in the aftermath of the media exposure, and so the community itself began to mobilise. In this regard it came to exemplify the era. It was one of significant social upheaval and, as political economist Francis Fukuyama observed, a time when change came *'not from any grand plan or economic imperative but as a result of ordinary people individually marching with their feet'*.[78] It was in this context and circumstances that alcoholism developed as a problem associated with one of a number of problems linked to homelessness, and the vagrant alcoholic emerged as the local *cause célèbre*. Homelessness and vagrancy first emerged as concerns of the late Sixties with one case in particular catching the local imagination; the case of Albert Wilson, a former seaman. A proud, respectable man, his roots were torn up in the wake of the massive redevelopment scheme of St Ann's. Unable to face the prospect of leaving St Ann's and being re-housed in one of the council estates on the outskirts of Nottingham, he started sleeping rough. Though befriended by a local clergyman, Canon David Keene, Albert declined offers to come in out of the cold and died from hypothermia in the winter of 1969/70. In an interview for the *Nottingham Evening Post*, his wife, Muriel Keene recalled how Albert had slept in doorways before making his outdoor home in the garage at the vicarage. She described how after he died, a lot of homeless people still knocked on the vicarage door and a scheme for giving out tokens so they could get a bed for the night at the Salvation Army hostel had to be worked out.[79] Canon Keene started holding regular meetings at the vicarage with social workers, probation officers and caring agencies and from thereon in, initiatives got underway in support of those who found themselves without a roof over their heads. New groups with self help ideals began to spring up, as well as new charitable organisations. Voluntary community action first developed in response to the problems in St. Ann's. The St. Ann's Tenants and Residents Association (SATRA) was set up in response to concerns that Nottingham Corporation's redevelopment plan for the district of St Ann's, were to be carried out without proper consultation with the 30,000 people involved. One of its leaders was Ray Gosling, the writer/broadcaster, who was the Association's chairman for fifteen years. Community historian Ruth Johns wrote of SATRA that its most important achievement came with its role in helping create a growing political self awareness of what could happen to communities without their consultation, its emergence marking the end of the 'age of accepting what was handed down'.[80] Canon Keene, at St Catherine's, let SATRA have the church hall for free and public meetings were held there so that local people might get to know more detail of the Council's development plans. SATRA also developed an off shoot, the St Ann's Care Group, which was established to assist elderly people living in appalling conditions and there were plans for a club, though SATRA members could not decide whether this should take the form of a 'boozing' club or work as a community centre. Other community groups also formed in the inner city areas at this time. Though often diverse, they were united in trying to address problems within the community. Among concerns picked up were the needs of young unmarried women, the mentally ill and homeless.[81] Some within these groups had fallen foul of drink and the issue was increasingly taken up by various church groups. The Sanctuary, an Outdoor Mission established in 1963 by Sister Elizabeth of the Little Company of Mary in the deprived area of Hyson Green, was intended to help the poor in the community and operated from a small room at 6 Marlborough Road. Because the problem of drink was identified as a major factor in the problems of the poor, the Mission expanded to provide a more comprehensive service and work soon integrated with AA. Another local endeavour was Nottingham Family First, established in 1965. A housing association, it focused on families and the needs of lone-parent families in the community. The Salvation Army (its founder William Booth was born in Sneinton, Nottingham in 1829), already well interwoven in the cultural fabric of the city, also began to focus on the problems of alcohol among the homeless in its care though this work was not formalised until the 1970s.

Alfred Minto, the psychiatrist at the addiction unit, was a willing participant in these community affairs along with other psychiatrists at Mapperley. Minto was initially involved in the release of mentally ill patients from the hospital and his interest grew from there. He wanted to widen support for individuals returning to the community. He instigated and helped establish the voluntary group Nottingham Help the Homeless Association (NHHA), and was also active within other community groups. Ken Coates, for instance, recalled Alfred Minto attending his Workers' Education Association (WEA) classes, and Ray Gosling the journalist/broadcaster who was involved with SATRA remembered him actively helping patients out in the community; "*I was nearly killed by a lodger with a brick. I rang up Mapperley and Minto answered. Police came and Minto needed 2 doctors to sign him away. A lot of people were fond of him, as we were of Duncan Macmillan*".

Minto strongly supported the 'self-help' concept advocated by AA and referred patients to AA meetings and other community groups on discharge. By this stage AA was well ensconced in the community, running weekly meetings at Friends Meeting House on Clarendon Street. Regular attendees were mostly derived from the respectable working and middle classes but the vagrant alcoholic, on account of his chaotic lifestyle, found support of this sort difficult to take up. On the basis of this, the vagrant was directed towards more intensive inpatient treatment at the addiction unit. The medical response thus began to develop a number of distinguishing features. It responded to drink as a social problem and encouraged take up of support in the community. Only the most complex and chaotic of alcoholic cases were taken into the hospital and only then for short intensive periods and for 'drying out' purposes. Such intervention necessitated finding ways of working effectively with the penal sector. The approach fitted well with developments occurring in the community and met the needs of the penal sector where there was a growing pressure to deal more effectively with the problems of drunken offenders. Probation officers at the local probation department found they received significant support from medical specialists at this time and relations between the agencies strengthened through close and frequent contact. For a period from 1965 to the early 1970s a group of probation officers met up once a month at the Coppice Hospital,[82] with consultant psychiatrists and psychologists for case presentations about offenders with addictive problems that probation officers found difficult to handle. John Harding, former chief of Inner London Probation Service (ILPS) was a probation officer in Nottingham from the mid Sixties recalled; "*Probation officers used to make referrals to the alcohol specialist, Dr Alf Minto. Probation officers could enlist the help of psychiatrists, with forensic interests or with knowledge of addictions to both drugs and alcohol. Psychiatrists were generous with their time in terms of seeing probationers and ex-prisoners and often at our request, and the local courts, be they magistrates or Crown Courts, commissioned psychiatric reports.*"[83] The events reinforced the targeting of habitual drunken offenders for specialist treatment at the local level. Though concern nationally over the habitual drunken offender had been rumbling since the early 1960s, the issues returned to the policy forefront again until the end of the decade because voluntary responses, chiefly over homelessness, began to impact on the national agenda.[84]

Conclusions

Local responses to wider policy developments over hospital treatment for alcoholics first developed along the lines of the model proposed by the Ministry of Health, but became highly receptive to local needs. Research carried out by social scientists in St Ann's Nottingham, played a considerable role in drawing attention to poverty as a significant local problem, which in turn led to responses to alleviate the problems of the poor and homeless. This had the effect of altering perceptions about what constituted the local problem of alcohol which, over the course of the 1960s, increasingly became defined as a problem of the vagrant or homeless alcoholic. The medical response to alcoholism that subsequently developed was influenced greatly by the ideas of self help, as promoted by AA, and the concept of social psychiatry which ultimately led to unified medical/community responses and initiatives that put Nottingham at the forefront of the national trend in 'community development'. This convergence between psychiatry and local community groups provided a framework for responding that was to last several decades, which helped sustain the view of the problem as one of vagrancy. Meanwhile at the national level responses to the issue of the vagrant alcoholic were slower, although pressure began to mount on government to respond to the broader issue of homelessness with the launch of the national housing campaigning group 'Shelter'.[85] This helped raise policy interest in homelessness, which in turn brought focus to the problem of the habitual drunken offender. There was increasing concern that existing policies towards persistent public drunkenness were regarded inappropriate and failing, which ultimately led to the 1967 Criminal Justice Act, section 91 and provided for the removal of imprisonment for the offence of public drunkenness and government calls for improved responses to the habitual drunken offender.[86] Section 91 of the Act was not to be activated however, until suitable community alternatives to imprisonment were available. As a consequence this section of the Act was not brought in until 1978 when, at least in some parts of the country, provision was put in place. This meant that, though Nottingham's medical response to alcoholism reacted to local concerns first and foremost, its response was compatible with the government's at the start of the 1970s.

Notes

1. V. Berridge and K. Loughlin, 'Smoking and the New Health Education in Britain 1950s-1970s,' *Am J Public Health* 95 (2005), pp. 956-964.

2. J.D. Pratten, 'The Development of the Modern UK Public House: Part 1: The Traditional British Public House of the Twentieth Century,' *International Journal of Contemporary Hospitality Management* 19, 4 (2007): pp.335–342.

3. J.D. Pratten, 'The Development of the UK Public House: Part 2: Signs of Change to the UK Public House 1959-1989'. International Journal of Contemporary Hospitality Management, 19, 6, pp.513 - 519

4. M. Neve, "A Commentary on the History of Social Psychiatry and Psychotherapy in Twentieth-Century Germany, Holland and Great Britain," *Medical History* 48 (2004), pp.407-412.

5. C. Webster, 'Psychiatry and the Early National Health Service: The Role of the Mental Health Standing Committee,' in *150 Years of Psychiatry, 1841-1991*, eds. Berrios G.E and H. Freeman (London: Royal College of Psychiatrists, 1991) pp. 103-4.

6. J. Greenaway, Drink and British Politics since 1830 (Hamps: Palgrave Macmillan, 2003), p.161.

7. Home Office, Offences of Drunkenness, (London: HMSO, 1962) p.3; Home Office, Criminal Statistics of England and Wales, (London: HMSO, 1962), p.9; M.C. Moss and E. Beresford Davies, A Survey of Alcoholism in an English County (Altrincham: St. Ann's Press, 1967).

8. Ministry of Health, Hospital Treatment of Alcoholism: Memorandum HM (62) 43; B. Thom, Dealing with Drink: Alcohol and Social Policy (London: Free Association Books, 1999), p.43.

9. Ministry of Health, The Treatment of Alcoholism; Memorandum HM (68) 37.

10. The Oxford Group was a non denominational Christian group which began life as 'The First Century Christian Fellowship' in 1908, but gained popularity as the 'Oxford Group' in the 1930s and as 'Moral Re-Armament' after 1938. See E. Kurtz, *Not-God: A History of Alcoholics Anonymous* (San Francisco: Harper and Row, 1979), pp.3-9.

11. Alcoholics Anonymous (New York: Works Publishing Company, 1939). The twelve steps are outlined in the glossary at the back of the book.

12. The web site of The General Service Board of Alcoholics Anonymous (Great Britain) Ltd. Available from http://www.alcoholics-anonymous.org.uk (Cited April 21st 2011). Last updated January 9th 2008.

13. Alan Sillitoe interviewed by Jane McGregor, London, July 2007.

14. Ken Coates interviewed by Jane McGregor, March 2008. Ken Coates died 27th June 2010 at the age of 79. Among other roles, including that of politician, he was Labour Party Member of the European Parliament from 1989 to 1999; he was the key animator of the Institute for Workers' Control, founded in 1968 and wrote publications on poverty, political philosophy and democratic socialism. He retained the role of special professor in the Department of Adult Education at the University of Nottingham until 2004.

15   R.I Johns, *St Ann's Nottingham: Inner-City Voices* (Warwick: Plowright Press, 2002) p.238. 'Shebeen' was a popular term for an illicit drinking party.

16   J.A. Giggs, 'Housing, Population and Transport,' in *A Centenary History of Nottingham*, ed. J.V. Beckett (Manchester: Manchester University Press, 1997), pp.457.

17   Ray Gosling interviewed by Jane McGregor, Nottingham, November 2008.

18   J.V. Beckett, ed., *A Centenary History of Nottingham.* (Manchester: Manchester University Press, 1997), p.519.

19   Nottingham Archive: CA/HE/2/1/37, "Annual Report of Health Services 1971."

20   J. V. Beckett, ed., A Centenary History of Nottingham, p.541.

21   J.A. Giggs, 'Housing, Population and Transport,' in *A Centenary History of Nottingham*, p.455.

22   J.R Gusfield, *Symbolic Crusade*, 2nd ed. (Chicago: University of Illinois Press, 1986), pp. 194-6.

23   K. Coates and R. Silburn, Poverty: The Forgotten Englishmen (Harmondsworth, Middlesex: Penguin, 1970), pp. 95-6.

24   The annual average figure of arrests was double that of the figure of the 1930s at 218: J.A. Giggs, 'Housing, Population and Transport,' in *A Centenary History of Nottingham*, p. 457.

25   'The 'forgotten' race riot' BBC News online, May 21st, 2007. Available from http://news.bbc.co.uk/1/hi/uk/6675793.stm   (Cited August 30th 2011).

26   C. Webster, *Understanding Race and Crime* (Berkshire: Open University Press: McGraw-Hill International, 2007), p.91.

27   'A Cry from the Streets,' Time Magazine, September 8th 1958.

28   Nottinghamshire Central Library, Local Studies Library: Oral History Collection project 'Making Ends Meet' transcript A87 e-I recorded 1982-84 for Nottinghamshire Libraries.

29   R.I Johns, St Ann's Nottingham: inner-city voices (Warwick: Plowright Press, 2002), p.238-9.

30   Nottingham Archive: Minutes and reports to the Council CA/TC 1/2/126

31   K. Coates and R. Silburn, *Poverty: The Forgotten Englishmen*, p.63.

32   Ray Gosling interview.

33   C. Langhamer, 'Adultery in Post-War England' *History Workshop Journal* 62 (2006), pp.86-115.

34   J. Newson and E. Newson, *Patterns of Infant Care in an Urban* Community (London: George Allen and Unwin, 1963).

35   Alan Sillitoe interview.

36   J. Warner, 'Historical Perspectives on the Shifting Boundaries around Youth and Alcohol. The Example of Pre-Industrial England, 1350-1750', Addiction 93, no. 5 (1998). Also P. Borsay, 'Binge Drinking and Moral Panics: Historical Parallels?' History and Policy 62 (2007); N. Dorn, Alcohol, Youth and the State: Drinking Practices, Controls and Health

(London: Routledge, 1983); E. Fossey, W. Loretto and M. Plant, 'Alcohol and Youth,' in Alcohol Problems in the Community, ed. L Harrison (London: Routledge, 1996); C. Griffin, Representations of Youth: The Study of Youth and Adolescence in Britain and America. Feminist Perspectives. (Cambridge: Polity Press, 1993); K. Gunthorpe, Between Dependency and Adulthood: The Treatment of Youth in British Politics, 1959-70. (Leeds 1995); V. Hey, Patriarchy and Pub Culture (London: Tavistock, 1986).

37 For an historical perspective on the concept of teenage: J. Savage, *Teenage: The Creation of Youth Culture* 1875-1945 (London: Vintage, 2008).

38 'Community development in this context refers to the changing relationship between ordinary people and people in positions of power, where people in the community take part in the issues that affect their lives. It starts from the principle that within any community, knowledge and experience can be channelled into collective action to achieve the communities' desired goals. For an overview of 'Community Development' see G. Craig, K. Popple and M. Shaw, Community Development in Theory and Practice: An International Reader (Nottingham: Spokesman, 2008)

39 For perspectives on the self-help concept see F. Lavoie, T. Borkman and B. Gidron, *Self-Help and Mutual Aid Groups: International and Multicultural Perspectives* (New York: Haworth Press, 1994); A. H. Katz, 'Self-Help and Mutual Aid: An Emerging Social Movement?' *Annual Review of Sociology* 7 (1981), pp. 129-55.

40 'Alcoholics Anonymous: They Are at Work Here in Notts,' Nottingham *Evening Post*, September 15th 1960; LINK UP East Midlands Intergroup (EMIG) magazine spring 1977; Nottingham and Leicester AA timeline, unpublished.

41 AA member interviewed by Jane McGregor, Nottingham, January 2008.

42 Information drawn from Nottingham and Leicester A.A. Timeline, unpublished.

43 D. Macmillan, 'Mental Health Services of Nottingham,' Journal of Social Psychiatry 4 (1958). Also S. Davies and S Payne, 'Patients Repeatedly Admitted to Psychiatric Wards: A Four-Year Follow-Up,' Psychiatric Bulletin 20 (1996).

44 Nottinghamshire Archives SO/HO/6/3/2/6: Admission and Discharge Register (males) 1949-1966.

45 Nottinghamshire Archives SO/HO/6/3/4/1: 'Non-status' (voluntary) admission register, 1955-1962.

46 Nottinghamshire Archives SO/HO/6/3/5/7-8: Death notices, June 1964-November 1967 and November 1967-September 1971.

47 Nick Tegedine, Director of Nottingham APAS, interviewed by Jane McGregor, Nottingham, September 2008.

48 J. Stewarts, *The Battle for Health: A Political History of the Socialist Medical Association, 1930*-51 (Aldershot: Ashgate 1999). The SMA (now Socialist Health Association) was established as a group of socialist medical professionals that strongly influenced Labour's policy on health in the 1930s and early 1940s, and influenced the setting up of the NHS.

49 Alfred Minto interviewed by Jane McGregor, Nottingham, October 2009.

50 A. Minto and F.J. Roberts, "Temposil; a New Drug in the Treatment of Alcoholism," *Journal of Mental Science* 106 (1960), pp. 288-95.

51 Alfred Minto interview.

52 L. Clarke, "The Opening of Doors in British Mental Hospitals in the 1950s," *History of Psychiatry*, IV (1993), pp.527-51.

53 M. Jones, *Social psychiatry. A study of therapeutic communities.* (London: Routledge and Kegan, 1952); M. Jones, *The Therapeutic Community* (New York: Basic Books Inc., 1953); M. Jones, 'Industrial rehabilitation of mental patients still in hospital.' *The Lancet* 271, no. 6950 pp. 985-986.

54 E. Shorter, A History of Psychiatry: from the Era of the Asylum to the Age of Prozac (Chichester: Wiley, 1997), pp. 190-236; S.L. Bloom, Creating Sanctuary: toward the Evolution of Sane Societies (London: Routledge, 1997), pp.92-96.

55 Duncan Macmillan House library archive: Nottingham No 3 Management Committee, The Pioneer Years in Mental Health 1948-70, (Nottingham: Mapperley Hospital, 1970), p.19.

56 Duncan Macmillan House library archive: Spring 1970 edition of the Newsletter of the National Association of Mental Health,

57 Wellcome Library, Special Collections GC/132/4, S.Sussman interview with Dr A. Minto. Psychiatry Interviews, 1988-1989. Tapes and transcripts of interviews conducted in 1988 by Sam Sussman with three Nottingham psychiatrists A.D. Douglas, E.D. Oram and A. Minto.

58 'Informal admission' was introduced in the Mental Health Act 1959. During the period a major turning point for mental health was the publication of the Percy Report in 1957. This stated that mental illnesses should be treated in a similar manner to physical illnesses, with a similar form of care. The Mental Health Act (1959) which followed allowed admissions to mental health units to be as informal as those to medical wards, and also made local councils responsible for the care of mentally ill individuals outside of hospital. These changes led to an increase in the number of psychiatry outpatients.

59 For a review of the history of Moral Therapy see L. Sederer, 'Moral therapy and the problem of morale' Am J Psychiatry 134 (1977), pp 267-272

60 Nottingham No 3 Management Committee, 'The Pioneer Years in Mental Health 1948-70,' p.19. This was in response to Ministry of Health, Hospital Treatment of Alcoholism: Memorandum HM (62) 43 and Ministry of Health, National Health Service. A hospital plan for England and Wales. Cmnd 1604. (London, HMSO, 1962). This aimed to separate the NHS into three parts – hospitals, general practice and local health authorities. The Plan approved the development of district general hospitals for population areas of about 125,000 and, in doing so, laid out a 10-year programme of hospital building.

61 S. Pile and N. Thrift, Mapping the Subject (London: Routledge, 1995), p.212; L Clarke, The Time of the Communities: People, Places and Events, (London: Jessica Kingsley, 2003), p.70.

62 M. Glatt, 'Treatment Centre for Alcoholics in a Public Mental Hospital: Its Establishment and Its Working.' *British Journal of Addiction* 52 (1955), pp.55-133.

63 B. Thom, Dealing with Drink; Alcohol and Social Policy, (London: Free Association Books, 1999), pp.37-39.

64 Nottingham Archives: Minutes of the Mapperley Hospital (House) Committee meeting January 1st 1964, p. 64: staff matters.

65 Thom, Dealing with Drink, pp.89-90.

66 Ibid, pp. 36-39.

67 LSD or Lysergic Acid Diethylamide is a hallucinogenic drug. It was synthesised in the 1930s. Its use as a psychedelic became popular among youth in the U.S, Britain and other parts of the world in the 1960s.

68 Insulin treatment was recognised treatment for schizophrenia and was not used to treat alcoholics at the hospital though elsewhere modified insulin therapy was occasionally used by doctors, with patients put into a partial coma.

69 Alfred Minto interview

70 Nottingham No 3 Management Committee, 'The Pioneer Years in Mental Health 1948-70.' Also J. Howat, 'Nottingham and the Hospital Plan: a follow-up study of long-stay in- patients', *British Journal of Psychiatry,* 135 (1979), pp. 42-51.This retrospective study supports the view that hospital discharge was keenly on the local agenda from the 1960s and met the proposals of the Hospital plan.

71 Alfred Minto interview

72 Wellcome Library Special Collections GC/132/4, S. Sussman interview with Alfred Minto.

73 R.I Johns, St Ann's Nottingham: Inner-City Voices, p.240.

74 B. Abel-Smith and P. Townsend, 'The Poor and the Poorest,' *Occasional Papers on Social Administration* 6 (1965).

75 K Coates and R. Silburn, *St Ann's: Poverty, Deprivation and Morale in a Nottingham Community* (Nottingham: Spokesman, 1967). This was followed in 1970 by K. Coates and R. Silburn, *Poverty: The Forgotten Englishmen* (Harmondsworth, Middlesex: Penguin, 1970).

76 Televised documentary, St Ann's, transmitted by Thames Television in 1969, directed by Stephen Frears. Available from http://video.google.com/videoplay?doc id=8063122702317512133# (Cited May 2011)

77 Report of the Royal Commission on Local Government (Redcliffe-Maud Report 1966-1969); The Seebohm Report of 1968, which took effect from 1970 in the form of 'The Local Authority and Allied Social Services Act.'

78 F. Fukuyama, The End of Order: SMF Centre for Post-Collectivist Studies Paper 3 (London: The Social Market Foundation, 1997).

79 'Bygones: Death of rough sleeper led to new charity' *Nottingham Evening Post*, February 25th 2010.

80 R.I Johns, St Ann's Nottingham: Inner-City Voices p.226

81 For detailed discussion of local responses see R.I. Johns, *Nottingham's Family First 1965-2005* (Nottingham: Family First Ltd, 2006).

82 The hospitals in Nottinghamshire were grouped under the Sheffield Regional Hospital Board. The area covered included Derby, Leicester and Lincoln in addition to Sheffield and Rotherham. The various hospitals dealing with mental health in the Nottingham area included Saxondale Hospital, Mapperley Hospital, St Ann's, St Francis, Coppice, Aston Hall, Balderton Hospital and Westdale Hospital, and grouped under the Nottingham No. 3 and Nottingham No. 4 Hospital Management Committees.

83   Personal communication, John Harding, August 2008.

84   Home Office, "Report on the 'Habitual Drunken Offender',"(London: HMSO, 1971); B. Thom, *Dealing with Drink,* pp.86-104.

85   Shelter was founded in 1966 by the Reverend Bruce Kenrick, who was horrified by the state of the tenements round his Notting Hill parish. 1966 was also the year that the BBC screened Ken Loach's film about homelessness, 'Cathy Come Home'. The film alerted the public, media, and government to the scale of the housing crisis.

86   Simple drunkenness never had carried imprisonment but non-payment of fines for the offence sometimes led to imprisonment.

3
MEDICAL RESPONSES TO THE VAGRANT ALCOHOLIC, 1970s

"For many years, the alcoholic has been drawn as a character on a bomb site with a bottle of "meths" stuck in his pocket. He has been ridiculed on the stage as the proverbial drunk with a red "hooter" propping up a lamp post, as someone everyone laughs at. He has been described as a person lacking in moral fibre, who has no will-power. For many years, metaphorically he has been swept under the carpet and not admitted to by any of his family, because of the stigma attached to his so-called weakness. How wrong this conception is!

(John Wodehouse, 4th Earl of Kimberley (1924-2002)
19th March 1975, House of Lords)

As recounted in chapter two, in the late 1960s psychiatrists at Mapperley Hospital joined community activists to define alcoholism as a problem of the vagrant/homeless, in response to a media slur that characterised Nottingham as a place of poverty. Into the 1970s, the local treatment approach continued on a similar path. Psychiatrists worked in an increasingly integrated way with the police as well the local probation department, and in consequence a thriving medical-penal alliance developed. This meant that during the early part of the decade, local and national approaches had relatively similar aims. At that time, government interest in the habitual drunken offender was re-awakened, for reasons outlined in this chapter, and culminated in the publication of the Home Office document, *Report on the Habitual Drunken Offender* of 1971. But the overlap between national and local responses was momentary and largely coincidental, for local policy owed more to the particular orientation of psychiatrists at Mapperley than to blind adherence to government policy. This point is most clearly demonstrated by the fact that when national discussion shifted towards a public health/population view of the problem, homelessness continued to inform local policy.

National policy developments

From the late 1960s there was renewed policy interest in the habitual drunken offender, but impetus was soon lost, not least because of government cuts. In 1971, in its *Report on the Habitual Drunken Offender*, the Home Office recommended a system of rehabilitative care to replace the existing penal approach and proposed the setting up of detoxification centres to which inebriates could be taken.[1] Then in 1973 the responsibility for dealing with habitual drunken offenders was transferred from the Home Office to the Department of Health and Social Security (DHSS), which offered funds to voluntary bodies to provide services for people with alcohol problems, with the aim of seeing established specialist hostels, detoxification centres and rehabilitation programmes. As suggested in chapter two, there was concern that existing policies towards persistent public drunkenness were inappropriate and failing, which led to the 1967 Criminal Justice Act, section 91. This provided for the removal of imprisonment for the offence of public drunkenness.[2] However, the section of the Act was only activated in 1978 by which time some provision was put in place. The idea that imprisoning habitual drunken offenders was expensive and ineffectual was not new. In 1879, for instance *The Habitual Drunkards Act* identified a similar need for 'retreats' for the 'reception, control, care and curative treatment of habitual drunkards'. No such retreats ever existed, but the *Inebriates Act* of 1898, which came after, called for the establishment of State or Inebriate Reformatories. Though a number were established, they were expensive to run and by 1921 all had closed. The idea of treatment replacing punishment was not restricted to the UK, but taken up by a number of European countries. Among them was Poland, which from 1956 had 'sobering-up stations' where a drunk could be taken by the police, examined by a doctor, bathed and put to bed. Czechoslovakia had similar facilities as did Russia. Sweden had a detoxification system, the last stage of which was a voluntary labour camp. Scotland also had a detoxification project, set up in Edinburgh between 1973 and 1975. This was an experimental project set up to determine the feasibility of detoxification centres in Britain. The results were promising, but the project had been and gone before a detoxification centre was set up in England. The first in England was established in Leeds in 1976 and a further centre was set up in Manchester. Various other detoxification projects started up including hostels, day centres and housing associations during the years 1977 and 1978. But in 1979 government 'cuts' made everything look vulnerable when the DHSS announced that the policy of implementing the recommendations of the habitual drunken offender working party would be discontinued. Protest from those most concerned led to an extension of the policy until 1981, at which point the policy was finally discontinued. But while the DHSS turned away from the problem, the Home Office returned to it because of concerns about high prison population levels. It had no power to set up detoxification centres however, because these were considered a health matter, so it developed plans for 'wet shelters', to keep alcoholics out of the way. Even so, although a centre of this type was established with Home Office funding in Birmingham in 1981, open overnight shelters for alcoholics never took off in a significant way.[3]

Other issues of importance in the 1970s included the identification of new target groups, which had implications for the treatment setting. Whilst at first government focused on treatment of alcoholics within hospital facilities,[4] it later urged for treatment to be based in the community.[5] This change in view of the problem was largely influenced by new medical research on alcohol, which turned attentions towards a wider outlook on the problem. The public health perspective, which regarded the problem of alcohol from the perspective of the whole population, received considerable attention in the mid 1970s following the publication of the World Health Organisation (WHO) report, *'Alcohol Control Policies in Public Health Perspective.'*[6] Kettil Bruun, a social scientist and WHO expert advisor, headed the research team whose subsequent report, which became known as the 'purple book', made a profound impression on the international discussion of alcohol control policies and research in the field.[7] The report presented the argument that changes in overall alcohol consumption had a bearing on the health of society. Its perspective was derived from the earlier research of Sully Ledermann (1956),[8] whose work suggested that total per capita alcohol consumption was related to levels of alcohol misuse. The report concluded there was a direct relationship between the proportion of heavy drinkers in a given population and the mean average consumption in that population. This meant a reduction in the former could only be achieved by a reduction in the latter. Although the report was initially criticised and took time to be taken up in policy terms in the UK as well as Europe, the approach eventually led to a focus on the interaction between alcohol, the environment and drinkers. Other influences at the international level at this time included the Lalonde report (1974), which stimulated new thinking about public health, whilst in the UK the public health agenda over drink was underlined by the publication of *Everybody's Business* in 1976, which implied individual and community responsibility.[9] Inevitably this new perspective led to different groups of drinkers coming under scrutiny. The drinking harms resulting from accidents in the home, child abuse, domestic violence, accidents at work, from motor vehicle accidents, criminality and public drunkenness all began to come under the watchful eye of medicine and other interest groups. Related to this shift, there was some modification of the concept of alcoholism, with the emergence of 'alcohol dependence' syndrome. The syndrome gained increasing acceptance within medical circles.[10] It was concerned with the narrowing in the repertoire of drinking behaviour and involved drink-seeking behaviour. Symptoms included increased tolerance to alcohol, repeated withdrawal symptoms, and avoidance of withdrawal symptoms by further drinking, a compulsion to drink, and reinstatement of the syndrome after abstinence. These elements were considered to exist in degrees and range in severity. The new syndrome fitted well within the context of the new population-based public health approach where various interest groups became involved and the alcohol sector began to widen. The syndrome's adoption in clinical practice was encouraged by government in its report *The Pattern and Range of Services for Problem Drinkers* (1978),[11] which recommended the full scope of professionals be involved in the identification and management of alcohol problems. The view was endorsed by the Royal College of Psychiatrists' (1979), who refuted past medical claims that 'alcoholism' was a small problem that could be left to specialists to treat.[12]

Nottingham: a medical-penal alliance over vagrancy

The previous chapter argued that in Nottingham treatment was set up to respond to alcoholics in a fashion that corresponded with the concerns of the local community. The resulting approach, which was overseen by psychiatrists at Mapperley Hospital, was community-based and relied on the support of AA and other voluntary groups. Good relations formed between the various local agencies and psychiatrists at the hospital and of note was the interaction between medicine and the local probation department, which looked to psychiatrists for responses to the homeless drinker because all too often he was trapped in the penal system, and defined as a habitual drunken offender.

The local approach was already firmly established when in early 1968 Dr Alfred Minto, the psychiatrist at the helm of the alcohol unit, departed to take up the position of superintendent at Rampton Secure Hospital, in the Bassetlaw District of Nottinghamshire. There were difficulties finding a suitable replacement and for a time developments stalled. A psychiatrist by the name of Dr W. McAdam temporarily oversaw the unit until a new specialist psychiatrist, Dr Bruce Ritson, was appointed in July 1968. Ritson had some pedigree, having studied at Harvard Medical School and worked with Professor Gerald Caplan, often described as the father of 'community mental health'.[13] Like many psychiatrists at that time, Ritson was drawn to Mapperley because of its pioneering work in social psychiatry and community care. On his arrival in Nottingham, Ritson took over and maintained the treatment regime established by his predecessor, Alfred Minto, which was based on the concept of alcoholism, the most widely held perspective in psychiatry at that time. The unit had strong links with AA, and the Fellowship ran groups there. During 1969, the inpatient unit was relocated to Porchester House, an internal hostel of Mapperley Hospital that had been vacated thanks to the increasing numbers rehabilitated into the community. This was a large building with a considerable number of inpatients. The staff comprised nurses, an occupational therapist, two social workers, a part-time psychologist and trainee medical staff including a registrar and senior registrar. Ritson continued the work of his predecessor by treating increasing numbers of patients at the outpatient clinic instead of the unit, which fitted well with the hospital's ongoing policy to reduce the length of inpatient stays. Most patients came from the Nottinghamshire area but a few came from further afield.[14] There were tenuous links with the General Hospital though these were not nearly as well defined as the links with the community.

Treatment at the unit had a primary goal of abstinence. Almost all the patients were significantly dependent on alcohol and bout drinking, which today might be construed as 'binge drinking', was not a common feature among the patient group. Jellinek's categories of 'alcoholism' were made use of, and most patients were considered either continuous dependent drinkers (had an inability to abstain) or had a 'loss of control' pattern.[15] Many patients were referred by GPs but a significant minority were homeless, and came from the courts as part of a probation order. All patients were voluntary, with a few seen on a domiciliary visit prior to admission. The treatment programme was both inpatient and outpatient, with active follow-up, sometimes involving spouse and family. A typical inpatient programme lasted approximately three to four weeks and was based on group therapy and the principles of the 'therapeutic community'. As stated in chapter two, this approach laid emphasis on patients being active participants in their own and each other's treatment as well as sharing responsibility for the daily running of the community. As treatment developed, strong links were forged between medicine and the penal sector. Links were already established with forensic services through the probation service and visits to prisons in Lincoln and Leicester. This was easy to achieve as the county probation service had a good reputation under a dynamic chief officer, Peter Paskell, who surrounded himself with a young graduate staff of men and women who were interested in multidisciplinary ways of working with other agencies around problems presented by offenders, both juvenile and adult. A number of his staff went on to make a name for themselves, among them Lord Herbert Laming, who went on to become chief inspector of the social services inspectorate.[16] Another high achiever on the team was John Harding, mentioned in chapter two, who became chief probation officer for the Inner London Probation Service (ILPS).[17] This group of probation officers became closely associated with the local psychiatric hospitals: Saxondale (formerly Sneinton Asylum), Mapperley; Balderton Hospital near Newark (an institution for offenders and those with learning disabilities); Rampton Hospital (a secure unit, and quite close to Mapperley); Coppice Hospital. Each hospital had its own geographical area of referral, so depending on which area and court, probation officers could enlist the help of psychiatrists with forensic interests or knowledge of addiction and refer offenders to the hospitals' outpatient clinics. Psychiatrists were generous with their time, seeing probationers and ex-prisoners and writing psychiatric reports at probation officers' or courts' request. They also engaged in group work and regularly met for case discussions with probation officers in the dining room of the Coppice Hospital.

Probation officers participated in regular discussions about alcoholism and addiction with two brother psychiatrists Frank and Brian Lake from the Clinical Theology Association (CTA) in Nottingham.[18] Frank and Brian Lake set up the CTA initiative in 1958, running seminars about working more therapeutically with individuals. Both brothers trained as doctors in Edinburgh. Afterwards Frank went to India to be a medical missionary and Brian became a ship's surgeon on the Atlantic run. Whilst in India Frank felt called to psychiatry, and Brian also felt attracted to the discipline and as part of his training took a clinical post at Warlingham Park Hospital in Surrey. In the 1960s, psychiatry was often seen by the clergy as a secular rival to their work but in this case Frank Lake married the two disciplines in a move that attracted a number of clergy to enrol in the seminars he was pioneering. The discipline became known as Clinical Theology and, from a base in Nottingham, teaching and clinical help were made available to the clergy. Seminars were established all over the UK, and a two-year course was offered. Very few of the clergy had any previous training in therapeutic work but within three years there were forty seminars around the country and one thousand clergy in training. The work began to penetrate into post ordination training and spread far beyond the confines of the Church of England, as people of other denominations and religions, as well as doctors, social workers, teachers, case workers, and many ordinary men and women became involved. The centre in Nottingham, 'Lingdale', was a hive of activity. Whilst Frank Lake later moved in new directions, the CTA transformed into the Bridge Pastoral Foundation, which today offers training in pastoral care to persons suffering from spiritual and emotional distress.[19] These events highlight the considerable interaction between professional groups and clergy at this time.

At the addiction unit Ritson also accepted referrals from the probation department and had a part-time liaison officer appointed to work with him and his team. There was much crossover of ideas especially as a number of probation officers were influenced by the 'Community Development' approach.[20] This offered theoretical underpinning for social and community work and focused on helping local neighbourhood groups to set and meet their own needs. Community work was taken to mean helping local people to decide, plan and take action to meet their own needs, often with the help of outside resources. In line with this approach, the probation officer John Harding joined forces in the late 1960s with the Council of Voluntary Service (CVS) and city mental health department to set up an unstructured kind of organisation called 'Friendship Unlimited'. The Council provided a rent-free disused brothel, which was refurbished with help from offenders and patients from the alcohol unit. It ran as a centre for the socially isolated and had a team of about twenty-five volunteers on a rota system. It took referrals from the addiction unit, which used the venue for weekly meetings between patients and their families, and referrals from the psychiatric hospitals, probation office and the CVS, and advertised in the free press. Its main attraction was a coffee bar, which acted as an introductory point for visitors. Although people were referred occasionally by social workers, the impetus for change came from the attendees themselves. The outreach and self help ethos of Friendship Unlimited was similar to Alcoholics Anonymous, making use of the process of helping others to provide the motivation to engage in self-help activities, and was run on non-hierarchal lines.[21] The ideas instigated were in advance of trends nationally, though developments in social work and the scale and extent of social work activity grew considerably following expansion of social work departments in 1971. It was the fusion of ideas between the probation department and medicine at this time that paved the way for further medical-penal initiatives.

A further local initiative at this time was a new probation hostel at 28 Addison Street. Intended to provide help to male offenders with alcohol problems, it marked a more formalised phase in the medical-penal alliance. It was operated by the Nottingham Bridgehead Association, a joint committee formed from the Diocesan Council for Social Aid and the Nottingham Area Association for the Care and Resettlement of Offenders. The house, near the city centre, provided accommodation for twelve male alcoholics and offered physical and emotional security for alcoholics during their initial rehabilitation. It was organised as a therapeutic community with resident involvement in its operation. Rules were kept to a minimum but it was a 'dry' hostel, with a strict 'no drinking' rule for residents. Residents were expected to pay a nominal charge for their board and find work. There were links to the addiction unit. The probation service appointed a liaison probation officer to work with the unit and the psychiatrist, Bruce Ritson, was a member of the Hostel Management Committee and regularly discharged homeless patients in need of longer-term rehabilitation to the hostel. He recalled; *"The homeless presented particular challenges for rehabilitation and that was a sphere in which working with other community-based facilities and agencies was most important. There was a lot of interest in the habitual drunken offender, decriminalising drunkenness and avoiding the revolving door of recurrent short term imprisonment. Joint plans for detoxification and rehab for this group was a matter of widespread debate"*. [22]

Whilst Bruce Ritson had been active in all the developments at this time, he left Mapperley Hospital in 1971, though the set up he had helped establish continued. Relations between the NHS and probation department remained intact but the alcohol unit operated for a brief period with locum cover. Then sometime later a Dutch doctor, Pierre Jacques Anthony Willems took over. Though his influence on the specialist unit was short-lived (he left in 1974), his stance involved establishing a full-blown therapeutic community run by the patients, with AA facilitating the group programme. Psychiatrists working in the speciality at this time valued groups as a means to assist patients in developing ways to cope with their addiction to alcohol and the approach crossed over with work from other areas ('Friendship Unlimited' and the hostel at Addison Street). The nature of group therapy on the unit was distinct, with no direction given from the therapist to group members. The group was allowed to use the influence of the group to aid individual recovery.[23] Like his predecessors, Willems believed short stay treatment was preferable over long stay care and engaged in research in this area.[24] He viewed alcoholism as 'socially infectious', similar to the way drug addiction was viewed at that time.[25] From this perspective treatment was a form of 'outbreak control'. He estimated there to be as many as two thousand alcoholics in Nottinghamshire, a far greater number than previously supposed, especially since only a small fraction were actually receiving treatment. In the Annual Report of Health Services, 1971, he wrote *"At this rate it will take over 40 years to treat the present population of alcoholics, disregarding those yet unborn."* [26]

Viewing alcohol from a public health perspective was not new, but the approach was revived in the 1970s. French philosopher and social theorist, Michel

Foucault, argued that at this time the medical gaze shifted from the individual to the community, a view with which others have concurred.[27] Diseases became located not just in individual bodies but in the social body, prompting development of population-based responses. Though within the international medical community this line of thinking saw interest grow in the relationship between total per capita consumption and the related harms to the population, this viewpoint had yet to gain momentum at the local level. Willem's concerns about the social spread of alcoholism were not picked up by local public health doctors, nor were they of much consequence to his colleagues at Mapperley. The Medical Officer of Health's annual reports for the years 1970-74,[28] and reports subsequent to 1974 contain little mention of alcoholism as a public health issue or any role in its treatment by public health physicians or general practitioners.[29] Referrals and admissions at the addiction unit remained fairly static with 140 patients treated from 1968 to 1971 at a rate of between 44 and 48 treated per annum.[30] Though referrals increased to an average of 100 per annum by the end of the decade, only half actually underwent treatment.[31] Some alcoholics may have been taken into care by the Salvation Army but supported withdrawal or detoxification, though part of the Salvation Army's provision within the large direct access hostels, was still in its infancy and its hostels could not have accommodated treatment of large numbers of drinkers.[32] At any rate there was confusion over the number of alcoholics in the city for a local survey of the period found only a handful of people sleeping rough, even though those involved in responding to alcoholism believed that the homeless made up a vital proportion of the 'alcoholic' population. This report from the *Nottingham Evening Post* highlighting their concerns;

> 'A recent survey found only a handful of people sleeping rough in the city but Ken Wilde thinks this hardly gives an accurate picture of the problem'... "They move around all the time and you could find a different number each night except for the regulars. One of the city's favourite skippering places is Huntingdon St depot where there are plenty of comfortable back seats to stretch out on if you don't mind keeping a lookout for the police or the depot attendant...Nottingham has a wealth of derelict houses to choose from and they provide homes for transient vagrants...they all have problems; drink or mental or both." [33]

Further plans to develop alcoholism treatment were stalled when in early 1974; Willems departed and took up post at Barrow Hospital in Bristol. He left behind an unruly unit; with other doctors at the hospital concerned its therapeutic community was anarchic. However, the unit had a loyal following from its nursing staff and they tried to persuade the authorities that they could run the unit without a doctor in charge. But the authorities would have none of it and the place closed for a year. In June the following year a suitable replacement was found, a psychiatrist by the name of Dr Philip McLean. He was to provide considerable continuity at the unit, remaining in post until 2010. McLean, like Ritson, was Edinburgh trained. He had had experience in specialist alcohol services in Edinburgh, and in Jamaica with Professor Michael Beaubrun and, unusually for a trainee then, in drug replacement therapy.[34] But the Edinburgh Unit had too many middle class drinkers for his liking and so, in relation to offering treatment in Nottingham, he was determined not to be highly selective but to take all drink and drug problems that came his way. He recalled that the approach was popular with colleagues at Mapperley: *"The other psychiatrists at Mapperley liked that as they had been treating down and out boozers after Willems left, and Nottingham had a lot of them."*[35] Whilst not believing psychiatrists to be the only people capable of modifying alcoholic behaviour, McLean believed that psychiatric training and experience best fitted the manifold problems that alcoholism posed during treatment. He was influenced by the model of Isaac Marks from the Institute of Psychiatry (London) about behavioural treatments of phobias and anxiety neuroses,[36] and by Milton H. Erickson (1902-80) a psychiatrist and hypnotherapist from the US, who was an important influence in psychiatry at that time.[37] McLean's favoured approach also centred on the behavioural, an approach that involved working with patients to encourage the substitution of desirable behaviour responses for undesirable ones.

Mapperley's was one of only thirteen units in the country at that time and McLean was the only specialist psychiatrist heading up one who had not worked in London. What attracted him most to the post in Nottingham was the apparent willingness of his predecessors to engage with 'down and outs'. Psychiatrists in the speciality generally were not inclined to assist the habitual drunken offender or homeless drinker. Nevertheless there were a few exceptions, as discussed previously in chapter two. In particular Nottingham's policy developments corresponded with developments in South London where Griffith Edwards, a leading psychiatrist who specialised in the area of addiction, became involved in trying to set up services for 'skid row' drinkers, working with the Camberwell Council on Alcoholism, which had already laid some of the groundwork for opening a rehabilitation hostel.[38] Nevertheless most ATUs tended to admit males (only one in five to one in three patients were female), in their forties and from higher social classes with reasonable levels of social stability.[39] The pattern of admission at Mapperley therefore was quite distinct. Like elsewhere, few female patients were admitted but male patients tended to be older, far less well educated and more likely to be unemployed than was typical.[40] This was due largely to the system of referral that operated between the unit and probation department where men were over-represented in the criminal justice system. The one or two women admitted to the unit tended to come from higher social classes. Though AA attempted a campaign to encourage women's attendance at meetings, women's attendance remained low throughout the era, as did their admission for treatment. Young people and teenagers were not admitted to the unit and, despite growing concern in the public sphere over youth and underage drinking, discussed in the next chapter, there was no provision for young people save for weekly AA meetings for young alcoholic boys at Lowdham Grange Borstal run by a probation officer, Mr Whittey, who had a particular interest in that area. McLean saw that there were medical obligations, as well as ethical reasons, to engage with those with extreme end drink problems. He was convinced that there was more in the way of physical peripheral neuropathy and Korsakov's Psychosis at that time and attributed this to patients' health problems not being detected early enough.[41] He recognised that this group of drinkers needed intensive rehabilitation and sought a collaborative treatment approach with others who were involved in responding to these drinkers in the community. He recalled: "*I recognised that there were far more drinking problems, like the street-drinkers, than ever got into alcoholism units elsewhere. So I decided I would take everybody and try and do something with everybody. There were reasons for that. Nottingham it seemed had a big population of homeless drinkers and...a fair reputation for homelessness and rowdiness.*"[42]

On arrival McLean found the addiction unit in chaos. There had been a succession of consultants and locums and none of them had lasted for a long time. The unit in the preceding years had been run by the patients as a 'Therapeutic Community', and was a shambles; graffiti strewn and so on. The unit was based in Porchester House, which is now demolished, and had eighteen beds for men and the same number for women. It was rarely full but was used as an inpatient 'drying out' or detoxification station. McLean had a rather more disciplined view of what it should be, however his involvement was to be half-time, despite having responsibility for the whole Trent Region, which had at that time a population of four million and covered Leicestershire, South Yorkshire, Nottinghamshire, Derbyshire and Lincolnshire, but excluded North Humberside. Deciding that the mainstay patient should be the homeless alcoholic he tried to devise more effective ways of treating them. They did not participate well in group psychotherapy so the unit dropped this to focus on specific medical responses such as detoxification (medically assisted withdrawal of alcohol). In addition, patients were offered a 'wash and brush up' service, hot meals and baths. McLean did not regard alcoholism as a psychiatric problem as such, but saw psychiatric problems arising from alcoholic excess. He understood the problems to be undoubtedly physical in origin (e.g. delirium tremens and fits) and their manifestations as being in the realm of disturbance of mental functioning.

These shifts in the focus of treatment at Mapperley coincided with a general shift and acceptance of the notion of 'alcohol dependence' in medical circles both in national and international spheres. Although the idea of an alcohol dependence syndrome gained ground during the 1970s its existence had been evident for many years.[43] The clinical description, as outlined earlier, was articulated first by the London based psychiatrist Griffith Edwards, a leading figure in the speciality.[44] McLean found this perspective useful as he set about establishing new treatments for the chronically dependent, believing this legitimised his interest in attending to the more 'physical' aspects of the alcoholic condition. Furthermore it allowed him to medically treat the most severe cases, whilst leaving the less complex cases to community groups such as AA. The introduction of the new treatments and methods however, sometimes had surprising consequences. On one occasion an antidote treatment inspired an illicit trade to develop in the community, mirroring problems encountered in treating drug dependent patients, who sometimes sold on their prescribed drugs. In the main however, this was a time when doctors could pretty much do as they saw fit; a time of significant clinical freedom, as McLean recalled; *"There was very little in the way of government, municipal or health authority involvement... Calling it an illness served to get the medical profession involved. So we [the medical profession] took hold of it and ran these units, and had a vested interest in not doing away with them"* [45]

An important decision for the unit's chaotic clientele was that McLean and his team wanted to ensure ease of access to treatment. A social worker was appointed from 1976 and the team ran outpatient clinics at St Ann's Hospital where people referred by GPs and other doctors came along, were assessed and admitted for 'drying out' or detoxification. Rehabilitation was a slow, gradual process and patients were encouraged to stay for long periods but with increasing freedom to come and go from the hospital. This changed the emphasis from short to longer stay in some cases, and put pressure on beds when patients stayed for sometimes weeks or months on the ward. But somewhat fortuitously the addiction unit benefited from additional NHS resources when monies were made available for refurbishment and expansion. This resulted from calls for more equal distribution of hospital beds in the regions. Trent Region had previously been the worst provided for in terms of health provision in England with average revenue expenditure per person lower than other regions. But the 1974 NHS reorganisation, which created an administrative tier, the Area Health Authority (AHA) with responsibility for a specific geographical population, encouraged expansion in local health care services. The hospital benefitted as a consequence and circuitously, the addiction unit did as well. What resulted was the transformation of Castle Ward (formerly the disturbed admission ward) to an admission ward where patients were assessed, dried out and, if warranted, sent for extended care to Porchester House, which was also refurbished and the number of beds reduced to twenty. Designed as two-bedroom and three-bedroom dormitories, this provided opportunities for re-socialisation and rehabilitation and was where AA ran regular meetings. On discharge the, mostly male, patients often went to Addison Street hostel where they could stay for a long time though for many, AA meetings were the only real source of aftercare.

Co-ordinating the response: the Nottinghamshire Council on Alcoholism

In the late 1970s drink problems were viewed increasingly under the broader definition of 'problem drinking' as public health thinking began to take influence. 'Problem drinking' was a term that viewed alcohol problems as psychological, physical or social problems that could exist in varying degrees of severity, be caused by acute intoxication, or at the other end of the continuum, by excessive consumption over a long period, which might cause a range of problems including 'alcohol dependence'. This newly adopted perspective led to calls for specialist and non specialist services, including GPs, to respond in a co-ordinated fashion to alcohol problems.[46] As such there was recruitment in Nottingham of a wider range of professions including nursing, social work, psychology and the probation service; groups for which training was required. But at the same time alcohol treatment was becoming ever more specialised, with those working in the sector expected to have highly expert knowledge, events that led a process of professionalisation, where the qualified were singled out from the unqualified amateurs. This state of affairs threatened to divide the sector and create disparity, for doctors did not see it within their remit to address the whole spectrum of problems. It was largely on these grounds that McLean, at the helm of Mapperley addiction unit, backed calls for a local Council on Alcoholism to co-ordinate the community response.

Regional councils of alcoholism developed from the national agenda. This increasingly placed focus on communities to take the brunt of responsibility for dealing with drink problems. The National Council on Alcoholism formed in 1962 and, aided by government grants from 1973, offered 'pump primed' grants to support the establishment of a network of councils across the regions that would work with health and the local authorities in tackling the problems arising from alcohol.[47] Nottinghamshire Council on Alcoholism (NCA) was formally established in 1975. The idea of a local agency with a focus on alcoholism was mooted in the 1960s by the medical officer at Players' cigarette factory, a testament to the fact that there was growing interest in alcohol as a health issue. Health and safety at work was a salient policy concern of the decade with legislation drawn up under the *Health and Safety at Work Act 1974*. The rapid growth of science funding, advances in industrial hygiene and epidemiology, coupled with industrial growth from the 1950s saw industry involved in health and safety issues, though drink and occupation were linked before this, during and after World War One. The local social work department also supported the idea of a local agency focused on alcohol, for it viewed drink as a matter of social concern. The need for better co-ordination of social services was emphasised by the Health Services and Public Health Act 1968, which came into force in 1971, which increased local authority powers to provide care services, and by the Local Authority Social Services Act, 1970, which established a single social services department in each local authority.

Once up and running, the NCA played a vital role co-ordinating provision of community services, education and prevention initiatives around the risks of alcohol. It also helped uphold the view that the local problem of alcohol was one of vagrancy and stimulated more development in that area. Many of the volunteers co-opted onto the Council's steering group as committee members were the original campaigners of the 1960s who highlighted the city's problems of poverty. They included local councillors, clergy, magistrates, retired police officers, social service staff, academics, psychiatrists and doctors from occupational health, as well as a significant number of recovering drinkers and adherents of AA. From the outset the NCA's role was one of co-ordinating local effort and disseminating information about alcoholism. George Lanagan was the person appointed to head up the new organisation. A recovering alcoholic, he had worked previously in London as a member of the organisation, Helping Hand,[48] and was part of an established group within the local AA fraternity who wanted to see developed more provision for drinkers. He saw the new organisation as having responsibility to '*convince society at large that the problem of alcoholism existed in Nottinghamshire*'.[49]

However only a few years later in 1977, Lanagan relocated to London having been promoted to the position of Deputy Director of the National Council. His successor, David Levell, was of a different kind of director. He observed a change in trend in appointments within the wider organisation; *"There was an old guard of directors. In many cases folk who had found their way in the AA, and they moved into it as a job. They were gradually supplanted by a younger professional group. In the main they were people who came with either health or social services credentials... This younger, newer breed of people formed quite a cosy club, forming ourselves a National Association of Director."* [50] Many within the network of Councils on Alcoholism were concerned about how the charitable sector was regarded and managed at this time. In light of this the new director, sensing he might need the support of the larger statutory organisations (NHS, social services, probation department), stepped up recruitment of key individuals from these organisations to the executive committee of the NCA. This afforded opportunities to consort with a diverse array of professionals, as well as with voluntary organisations within the region.

Because such a strong local commitment had already developed in relation to tackling the problems of the vagrant alcoholic, it was easy to set in motion new initiatives, and the NCA was an obvious vehicle for moving responses forward. Philip McLean of the addiction unit suggested this was always the local plan. It was intended that the alcohol unit do the treatment, and the Council on Alcoholism would concentrate on *"informing people, provide information, interact with the City Council, and push things along."* [51] The NCA henceforth developed as the hub of the local alcohol network. Members of the network regularly would meet to discuss initiatives for the local level. Plans were hatched for a detoxification centre along the lines of the Leeds detoxification centre (1976), and a Homeless and Vagrant Alcoholic subcommittee was set up, which put up all manner of ideas for local consideration. A lot of the work was carried out by volunteers. Work included the development of a drop-in centre, named 'The Sanctuary', run by the Mary Magdalen Foundation (MMF). There was also St Barnabas Church, where drinkers could knock on the door and be fed, and Emmanuel House, situated in Goose Gate in the city centre. The latter set up in 1976 by former head teacher and clergyman, Father Killeen, in response to concern over the extent of homelessness and alcoholism among Irish immigrant workers, as a consequence most of its clientele were middle aged men. Though the City Council gave Father Killeen a long term lease on a property to provide shelter, the initiative relied heavily on funds from the public (particularly the Catholic churches). Its 'dry' day centre was aimed at drinkers trying to combat their problems and attendees had to be clean and sober on the day. Other, more formal arrangements also developed at this time, including a second hostel for alcoholics on Woodborough Road, Nottingham.[52] Its costs were met by the DHSS and Nottinghamshire Social Services approved the scheme. This provided six single bed-sitters for men who are successful at 28 Addison Street but needed further rehabilitation. Most referrals came through the alcohol unit at Mapperley or the probation department. Further development came in 1979 when the Lord Mayor of Nottingham Council officially opened a new night shelter converted by the Nottingham Help the Homeless Association from a former police station in Canal Street. By the late 1970s, owing to the energy and commitment of the local network, two distinct types of provision were perceptible. These divided into specialist (medical) and non specialist (voluntary) elements. The alcohol unit and the medical experts at Mapperley had a dominant role in treatment and McLean accepted the new voluntary schemes and agencies as legitimate sources of patient referral. The non specialist agencies established roles in providing care pre- and post medical involvement. To ensure a flow of care between one agency and another, the network planned to compile a register of mutual clients. This was intended to facilitate follow up, though the idea was later dropped as it presented too many practical difficulties. Nonetheless, that the agencies considered the move indicates that a co-ordinated system was developing. This meant that as time went on and the agencies settled into easy relations, the NCA could pay attention to other community matters such as prevention and education concerns. The issue of youth drinking, which is taken up for discussion in chapter four, was an escalating source of local concern and formed part of a wider shift in concern about the contributions of delinquent youths to criminality in society.[53] On this issue, the NCA, on the advice and guidance of the National Council on Alcoholism, initiated a number of local education campaigns all the while emphasising the responsibility of the whole community to address the problems resulting from drink.

Conclusions

The decade saw a relative neglect of attention at the local level to the wider problems associated with alcohol and a continued focus on the alcohol problems of a few, notably extreme end cases. This contrasted with developments nationally where the problem was regarded broadly with the emergence of the public health/population approach. Though initially, and on the face of it, the local response was consistent with national policies over the habitual drunken offender, the approach was a response to *local* concerns, and the problem defined in *local* terms. The approach, which held that the extreme case of the homeless drinker was the chief population of concern, was reliant on the particular orientation of the specialist psychiatrists at Mapperley and its shared view with the local alcohol network, which comprised the penal and charitable sectors.

Notes

1   Home Office, *Report on the 'Habitual Drunken Offender* (London: HMSO, 1971).

2   Simple drunkenness had never carried imprisonment but non-payment of fines for the offence sometimes led to imprisonment.

3   J.R Hamilton, A. Griffith, B. Ritson, and R.C.B. Aitken. *Detoxification of habitual drunken offenders.* (Edinburgh: Scottish Home and Health Department, 1978). Also R. Smith, 'Alcohol and Alcoholism: The habitual drunken offender: everybody's fool, nobody's friend', *British Medical Journal* 283 (1981), pp 1251-1253.

4   DHSS Circular 16/71, *Development of Hospital Facilities for the Treatment of Alcoholism (London: HMSO, 1971).*

5   DHSS Advisory Committee on Alcoholism *The Pattern and Range of Services for Problem Drinkers,* (London: HMSO, 1978).

6   K. Bruun, M. Lumio, K. Mekela, L. Pan, P. Popham, R. Room, W. Schmidt, O. Skog, P. Sulkunnen and E. Osterberg, 'Alcohol Control Policies in Public Health Perspective,' (Helsinki: Finnish Foundation for Alcohol Studies; WHO Regional Office for Europe; Addiction Research Foundation of Ontario, 1975).

7   Kettil Brunn was the director of the Social Research Institute of Alcohol Studies, Finland, from 1955 to 1968. In 1971 he was awarded the Jellinek prize for alcohol research.

8   S. Ledermann, *Alcool, Alcoolisme, Alcoolisation* (Paris: Presses Universitaires de France, 1956).

9   DHSS, *Everybody's Business* (London: HMSO, 1976).

10 G. Edwards and M.M. Gross, 'Alcohol Dependence: Provisional Description of a Clinical Syndrome,' *British Medical Journal* 1 (1976).

11 DHSS, *The Pattern and Range of Services for Problem Drinkers,*

12 *Alcohol and Alcoholism: A Report of a Special Committee of the Royal College of Psychiatrists.* (London: Royal College of Psychiatrists, 1979).

13 Gerald Caplan, 1917-2008, was a world leader in the areas of preventive psychiatry and community mental health.

14 The region extended north to Sheffield and included parts of Lincolnshire and Derbyshire.

15 E.M. Jellinek, *The Disease Concept of Alcoholism* (Newhaven: Hillhouse Books, 1965). Jellinek identified five different types of alcoholism: *Alpha alcoholism*: psychological continual dependence on the effects of alcohol to relieve bodily or emotional pain. *Beta alcoholism*: polyneuropathy, or cirrhosis of the liver from alcohol without physical or psychological dependence. *Gamma alcoholism*: involving acquired tissue tolerance,

physical dependence and loss of control. *Delta alcoholism*: as in Gamma alcoholism, but with inability to abstain, instead of loss of control and *Epsilon alcoholism*: the most advanced stage of the disease, manifesting as dipsomania, or periodic alcoholism.

16   William Herbert Laming, Baron Laming, CBE, born July 19th 1936. Laming was chief inspector of the social services inspectorate from 1991 until 1998, worked as an advisor to the Local Government Association, and is a past President of the Association of Directors of Social Services.

17   John Harding was the final Chief Probation Officer of the Inner London Probation Service, which existed until March 2001 when it was succeeded by the larger London Probation Area. His interest in addiction endured and, in retirement from 2001-2007, he was Chair of the organisation Addaction.

18   Personal communication from Bruce Ritson, June 2008.

19   R. Dupuis 'Acceptance - Birth of CTA in the 60s,' in *British Pastoral Foundation* (Birkenhead: British Pastoral Foundation, undated).

20   Two initiatives of the era symbolised community development; a study group by the Gulbenkian Foundation in 1966 looked at the nature and future of UK community work, and as part of an anti-poverty strategy the Home Office developed the Community Development Projects in the late 1960s/early 1970s. See Caloste Gulbenkian Foundation, *Community Work and Social Change, A Report on Training* (London: Longman, 1968).

21   J. Harding, 'Helping the Socially Isolated,' *British Hospital Journal and Social Services Review* (1971), pp. 2142-3.

22   Personal communication from Bruce Ritson, June 2008.

23   For reading about the therapeutic communities see R. Haigh, P. Campling and J. Cox, *Therapeutic Communities; Past, Present and Future* (London: Jessica Kingsley Publishers, 1998).

24   P. J. A. Willems, F. J. J. Letemendia and F. Arroyave, 'A Two-Year Follow-up Study Comparing Short with Long Stay in-Patient Treatment of Alcoholics' *The British Journal of Psychiatry* 122, pp. 637-648 (1973).

25   This take on addiction was evident in drugs policy of the 1960s; V. Berridge and S. Bourne, 'Illicit Drugs, Infectious Disease and Public Health: A Historical Perspective,' *Can J Infect Dis Med Microbiol* 16 (2005), pp.193-196.

26   Nottingham Archive: CA/HE/2/1/37 Annual Report of Health Services 1971.

27   M. Foucault, *The Birth of the Clinic: An Archaeology of Medical Perception* (New York: Vintage, 1975); D. Armstrong, *Political Anatomy of the Body* (Cambridge: Cambridge University Press, 1983); D. Armstrong, 'The Rise of Surveillance Medicine,' *Sociology of Health and Illness* 17 (1995), pp. 393-404.

28   Local authority Medical Officers of Health posts were abolished after 1974 and the annual public health report lapsed until 1988 following re-organisation of the health service and local government.

29   Nottinghamshire Archives: Medical officer of Health's Annual Report of Health Services CA/TC1/2/126-134. For discussion of the demise of the MOH see J. Welshman, 'The Medical Officer of Health in England and Wales, 1900-1974: Watchdog or Lapdog?' *Journal*

of Public Health 19 (1997), pp. 443-450 and M. Gorsky, 'Local Leadership in Public Health: The Role of the Medical Officer of Health in Britain, 1872-1974,' *J. Epidemiol. Community Health* 61 (2007), pp. 468 - 472.

30   Nottingham Archive: CA/HE/2/1/37 Medical officer of Health's Annual Report of Health Services 1971.

31   Philip McLean interviewed by Jane McGregor, Nottingham, September 2007

32   Personal communication from Dean Logan, Salvation Army Addiction Service, 2008.

33   'Local survey on the homeless '*Nottingham Evening Post*, December 9th, 1972.

34   Medications available to treat addiction are called replacement therapies. Methadone, for example, is a replacement therapy used in the treatment of heroin addiction.

35   Philip McLean interview. Michael H. Beaubrun (1924-2002) introduced AA in the West Indies (1956) and founded the Caribbean Institute of Alcoholism and other Addictions, a leading institute in the training of advisers of alcoholism and drug addiction in the region.

36   I. Marks, 'Phobic Disorders Four Years after Treatment: A Prospective Follow-Up', *The British Journal of Psychiatry* 118 (1971), pp. 683-88. Marks was a founder Member of the Royal College of Psychiatrists and his early work included work on phobic disorders

37   See E. Rossi, ed., *The Collected Papers of Milton H Erickson's on Hypnosis* (New York: Irvington, 1974).

38   B. Thom, *Dealing with Drink; Alcohol and Social Policy* (London: Free Association Books, 1999), pp.89-90.

39   Ibid, p.57

40   Nottingham Archive: CA/HE/2/1/37 Medical Officer of Health's Annual Report of Health Services 1971.

41   Peripheral neuropathy is damage to the body's nerve tissue particularly the extremities. Korsakov's Psychosis is a type of dementia sometimes observed after chronic alcohol misuse – see glossary at the back of the thesis.

42   Philip McLean interview.

43   A similar medical view is presented in Thomas Trotter's 1804 account; *An Essay, Medical, Philosophical, and Chemical on Drunkenness and Its Effects on the Human Body with an Introduction by Roy Porter.*, ed. R. Porter (London; New York: Routledge, 1988).

44   G. Edwards and M.M Gross, 'Alcohol Dependence: Provisional Description of a Clinical Syndrome,' *British Medical Journal* 1 (1976), 1058-1061; G. Edwards, J. Orford, S. Egert, S. Guthrie, A. Hawker, C. Hensman, M. Mitcheson, E. Oppenheimer and C. Taylor, 'Alcoholism: A Controlled Trial Of Treatment And Advice.' *Journal of Studies on Alcohol* 38 (1977), 1004-31; G. Edwards, *The Treatment of Drinking Problems*, 2nd ed. (Oxford: Blackwell Scientific Publications, 1987), pp. 47-50.

45   Philip McLean interview

46   Royal College of Psychiatrists, *Alcohol and Alcoholism: A Report of a Special Committee of the Royal College of Psychiatrists*,(London: RCP, 1979), pp.126-127.

47   Royal College of Psychiatrists, *Alcohol and Alcoholism: A Report of a Special Committee of the Royal College of Psychiatrists*, (London: RCP, 1979).

48 Helping Hand was later renamed Turning Point, which still exists today as a major national charity working with those experiencing problems related to mental health and addiction.
49 APAS archive: Minutes of Nottingham Council on Alcoholism 2nd AGM October 3rd 1977.
50 David Levell interviewed by Jane McGregor, Nottingham, October 2007.
51 Philip McLean interview
52 By 1979, both 28 Addison Street and Woodborough Rd hostels were run under the auspices of Stonham Housing Association.
53 J. O'Connor, *The Young Drinkers* (London: Tavistock, 1978); The House of Commons Expenditure Committee, *Reduction of Pressure on the Prison System, England*, (London: HMSO, 1978); C. Clayson, 'The Role of Licensing Law in Limiting the Misuse of Alcohol,' in *Alcoholism: New Knowledge and New Responses*, eds. M. Grant and G. Edwards (London: Croom Helm, 1977).

4

YOUTH IN PUBLIC VIEW, 1970s

During the 1970s revived public health thinking on alcohol internationally and nationally, emphasised the importance of total consumption in populations. This perspective meant other groups' drinking, including women's and ethnic minorities', became targets of concern, yet it was anxiety about youth that proved the most persistent. This chapter explores the changing perceptions and realities that contributed to the problematising of youth drinking. Borne out of anxiety about the declining morality of youth, concern was first articulated when publicans expressed concern about rising hooliganism in the city in the mid 1970s. In an episode involving the consumer group Campaign for Real Ale (CAMRA), which called for longer pub hours, publicans alleged a new young hooligan element, visiting football fans, was causing drunken mayhem. As a consequence CAMRA's application for an extension of licensing was turned down by the local justices and Nottingham pubs stayed early closing. But the problem of youth and hooliganism was overstated. In reality there was little evidence of a growing problem; in fact, drunken disorder was declining.

National developments

Attitudes and controls over drinking shifted in the 1970s. On one hand, attitudes in relation to drinking became more relaxed. An Act in 1961 had introduced the right of appeal to quarter sessions. Then the 1964 Act restricted the discretion of magistrates in relation to applications for restaurants and residential licenses, and in 1969 the Monopolies Commission recommended a relaxation of the liquor licensing laws. Many regarded the existing licensing laws as archaic and called for further liberalisation of restrictions on drinking. But on the other, there were some, chiefly doctors, who called for restraint in the overall pattern and level of consumption because of the new public health perspective. The public health approach, as it took hold, led to more attention to drinking in society and saw particular groups, among them women and young people, periodically singled out. The media, reinforced by pressure groups and parliament, often were responsible for intensifying concern over a number of different groups.[1] The broadcast on television of the drama *Edna, the Inebriate Woman* in 1971 for instance,[2] served not only to intensify concern about homelessness, but women and drink. What significantly influenced perceptions about women's drinking at this time was the changing role of women in society. A rapidly rising national divorce rate contributed, thanks to the 1969 divorce reform laws, which allowed couples to break up simply by living apart. Women also won the fight to equal pay (the Equal Pay Act was passed in 1970), which for some women led to greater financial independence, and the Sex Discrimination Act of 1975 put an end to separate areas for different genders in public houses. Changes also occurred in cultural life as the country became more diverse, and the old patriarchal structures were reacted against. The consumer rights movement formed alongside a whole host of other social movements as interest in campaigning and the discourse of 'rights' took hold; in trade unionism, charities and voluntary organisations as well as single issue campaigns (feminism and environmental protection are examples). The movement was not about obtaining value for money, but about ensuring choice and fair dealing was offered to the poor, not just the affluent.[3] As a consequence, drinkers for the first time were supported by a consumer pressure group, CAMRA (the Campaign for Real Ale). It made demands for improved standards in the quality and price of drink, and also in the quality of UK public houses.

Ambivalent attitudes existed over the issue of alcohol consumption in society. Though some called for liberalisation there were fears about the consequences of the dramatic rise in drink consumption, which reflected both increased demand for drink and changes in the nature of supply. New markets sprang up on account of demand, whilst beer, wine and spirit consumption also rose. Other factors influencing events included the removal of retail price maintenance from alcoholic drinks in 1966, and supermarkets selling alcohol at a discount. Consumer tastes were also changing with imported beers and spirits becoming more popular, and advertising played an important role. The pub too faced changes, as landlords looked to attract new clientele as customer numbers fell. This was owing in part to competition from the new entertainment industry; clubs, discotheques and places offering food and night entertainment, which in turn caused brewers to move away from their core activities and sell off unprofitable houses.[4] The conflict of attitudes towards drink was well articulated in the debates surrounding the Erroll Committee report of 1975. This recommended lifting a number of restrictions on licensing. It proposed making on and off-licences easier to come by, reducing the age limit on drinking in licensed premises to 17 from 18 years, permitting hours of sale of alcohol to become more flexible and extending closing time to beyond

11pm.⁵ Though lively debates ensued, Erroll was subsequently defeated in 1976 however, similar proposals were approved in Scotland.⁶ The public were fairly divided over the issue; younger people generally favouring later closing, and older people more resistant.⁷ The medical lobby objected to the Erroll recommendations on the grounds that it was a move towards liberalisation, whereas it preferred to see prevention measures put in place. This was because doctors were concerned that drink problems were escalating. An estimated 91 people per 1,000 were classified as problem drinkers in England and Wales between 1962 and 1972, and deaths from cirrhosis of the liver were observed to have increased by a third, whilst admission rates to hospitals had also increased. There were also social concerns. Between 1958 and 1973, annual convictions for drunkenness also rose from 75,000 to 99,275 and on top of this there were concerns about the rising costs to industry through lost work hours due to drink.⁸

Nottingham: Changing realities and perceptions of the local problem

During the early 1970s Nottingham saw significant change in the community, much of it in line with national events. As discussed in chapter three, since the early 1960s management of the problems of alcohol had been in the hands of medicine. Then with the adoption of public health thinking on drink, considerably more problems than alcoholism became associated with drink including accidents, drink-driving, lost work hours, and criminal and anti social behaviour such as domestic violence and hooliganism. New ways of regulating drink behaviour also became available. The Road Traffic Act of 1962, for instance, introduced the possibility of alcohol analysis although no legal limit was set at that time.⁹ It led, however, to driving becoming a prominent local issue, despite the fact that Nottinghamshire rates of arrest for drink driving stayed relatively static throughout the period.¹⁰ By the mid 1970s drunken disorder and fights, once an accepted aspect of public drinking, also became much more of a problematised issue. Publicans declared drink related violence a growing problem and defined it invariably as a problem of youths and hooligans. Police, unlike local publicans, were not unduly concerned about youth at this time. Crime data showed no cause for concern, as arrest rates for drunkenness were falling.¹¹ From the police point of view the biggest problem remained illegal after-hours drinking, though this was controlled through periodic 'clean-up' operations, dealing with lock-ins or 'after-hours binges', where the landlord ushered out undesirables and unknowns and closed the doors with his regulars inside.¹² The reframing of drink as a problem of the whole community gave rise to concern about specific groups in the community, in particular women, ethnic minorities and most persistently, young people, and led to increased medical and penal surveillance over aspects of otherwise 'normal' drink behaviour. The situation thus led to a broadening of concern about the issue, where the more conventional problem drinker was responded to with medical care, whereas drinkers caught flouting the regulations, such as drink-drivers, tended to be criminalised. All the same there remained a tendency to neglect the many drinkers who did not break the rules but still drank too much.

WOMEN AND DRINK

Nottingham's lively night life was a major source of attraction for women. New light alcoholic drinks such as 'Babycham' (the trade name of a light, sparkling perry or pear cider) became popular, and were deliberately geared towards the female market. Yates' Wine Bar near the Old Market Square was a favourite local haunt, one of a number of bars designed to have more of an appeal to women. *"They had all these slogans on the walls to improve you - like 'The whiter the bread, the sooner you're dead,"* remembered the broadcaster and journalist Ray Gosling, about Yates' and its distinctive atmosphere.[13] One consequence of the development was greater criticism of women's consumption of drink. A report in the *Nottingham Evening Post* of the mid 1970s was typical of the type of concern roused. It featured local women *'so dependent they could not get through a day without a bottle'* and claimed women were drinking more because *'the stigma of going to pubs alone and being one of the boys'* was disappearing.[14] The Nottingham Council on Alcoholism (NCA), established in the mid 1970s and discussed in chapter three, also highlighted the problem. In an article of the *Nottingham Evening Post*, Mr Lanagan, the director of Nottinghamshire Council on Alcoholism, suggested women's drinking problems were not as noticeable as men's because *"they usually indulged in 'continuous tippling' at home rather than going out on 'benders'."* It was also suggested that as well as the advent of 'women's lib' leading to more women going to pubs, domestic stress and isolation/depression of women 'trapped' by children added to the problem.[15]

There were various factors influencing attitudes to women at this time. In Nottingham from the 1960s women outnumbered men within the workforce (though male unemployment throughout the period was below the national average).[16] Women also enjoyed status positions for the first time. In 1968 Nottingham saw its first woman Lord Mayor, Joan Case, and its first female

Chair of the County Council, Anne Yates.[17] The changes in role were tolerated to a point, although women, especially mothers, were singled out for criticism during the late 1970s when economic decline disproportionately affected full time jobs in traditionally male work and industries and led to a rise in local unemployment. As the economy shifted, dependence on women's earnings increased although many women continued to undertake most of the unpaid work in the home, and care for children or elderly relatives.[18] The *Divorce Reform Act* came into effect in 1971 and the main law on divorce, the *Matrimonial Causes Act* was passed in 1973, having impacts on women's behaviour. The changes in women's role in relation to family life coincided with bleak economic conditions; coal shortages and for many workers, the experience of the 'three-day week'; issues that impacted negatively on families and family life.[19] In addition there were changes in the cultural mix that affected many communities. Many post-war immigrants to Nottingham differed in race and religion to the established population, and bringing up children in a foreign country was a difficult task for parents wishing to embrace their new home whilst wishing also to pass on their cultural traditions to their children. These issues focused attention on women from different ethnic groups and drink was often just another 'stick' with which to beat them, as highlighted earlier in chapter two.[20] Another factor in focus, especially at this time, concerned the harms of drinking during pregnancy. This was owing to the recognition of a condition in babies called foetal alcohol syndrome (FAS). This marked a pattern of abnormalities that occurred in children born to alcoholic mothers, and caused much heated public and medical debate.[21] The so called 'tragic disorder' was discovered by scientists in the United States but resonated in Britain with broader social concerns about a perceived increase in child abuse as well as alcohol's deleterious effect on society.[22] Hence it was drinking *within* the home, not *outside* of it that provoked the most anxiety in relation to women and drink. Consequently CAMRA made efforts to encourage women into the public house, for this move had a number of perceived benefits. Many anticipated that women's presence would have a restraining effect on men's behaviour and bring a sense of inclusivity to the environment. The move was part of a wider public reaction to the erosion of traditional home life. With divorce and family break up bringing a threat of loss of private spaces for families (the home), the pub was viewed as a symbolic substitute.

Pubs, publicans and anxiety about youth

Concern about youth arose in society in the 1960s when the concept of adolescence was reworked as a distinct phase of life. Adolescence was commonly regarded by adults as a troubled period of life, and a decline of deference and what seemed a general lack of regard for the old social order affected age relations. Alcohol, illicit drugs, pop and rock music, and changing political attitudes were among the activities that signified a new problem of youth. In Nottingham anxiety over youth was articulated over a number of issues, including underage drinking. Concern was first articulated by publicans who became progressively more exercised about a problem of delinquency at night in the city centre. In 1975 the *Nottingham Evening Post* reported publican concerns. It called underage drinking "*the greatest social problem of our age*', and linked it to delinquency and crime, as well as marital problems and violence in the home in later life.[23] One of the reasons concern developed at this time, was that the nature and location of the drinks trade changed and the drink environment transformed. Traditional pubs faced losing the youth market to the bars and clubs that specifically targeted a younger clientele and allowed quite legitimate drinking until about two in the morning. On top of that there were takeovers, as well as closures, of a number of long established local breweries and following a 'merger mania' from the late 1950s, significant changes in the ownership and the running of pubs at the local level. It was change brought about by the Licensing Act 1961 that had most impact. The Act introduced a new kind of justices' licence for restaurants where the only test was the suitability of the premises. Before, the only way of obtaining authority to sell alcoholic drinks in a restaurant, was to obtain an on-licence of the kind held by hotels, inns and public houses. The relevant provisions of the 1961 Act were then consolidated in the Licensing Act 1964. This change entitled any restaurant to apply for a supper hours certificate allowing an additional hour for the sale and supply of alcohol after the end of normal licensing hours. The licensing justices had no discretion to refuse an application if they were satisfied that it related to a *bona fide* restaurant. The separate restaurant, residential and combined restaurant and residential licenses meant that the pub's share of the drink trade began to contract. The accumulative effect of these changes meant the pub's important place in the community was starting to be seriously challenged. Nationally, the shift was depicted in Christopher Hutt's book '*The Death of the English Pub*'.[24] The *Nottingham Evening Post* ran a number of nostalgic pieces about the city's old style pubs. In 1975, an article described the pub as "*an escape from economic collapse, rising crime rates and urban terrorism.*" whereas the new bars were "*soulless chromium plated; glass and concrete*".[25] Another article featured a woman called Ida Sadler, then in her seventies. She remembered staying over at her at her grandmother's house in West Street, Sneinton on Saturday evenings and watching the fistfights outside the Queen Adelaide while her mother, father, aunts and uncles toured the pubs in town. In later life she used to pop into Jallands in Hockley for a glass of port. "*It was really good plonk – after two glasses one could sing 'Rule Britannia' in any key and play arpeggios on the organ*".[26] There was a move to re-introduce regular "free and easy" sing songs in some pubs and working men's clubs.[27] Though the old guard generally regarded the changes with some scepticism, police found the new arrangements and hours of licensing favourable because they reduced the problem of pub 'lock-ins' although the 'shebeens' or blues parties that ran from houses around the Hyson Green and St Ann's areas of the city persisted.[28] Thus Police were broadly receptive of the move towards late night licensing of bars. A police officer, interviewed in the early 1980s, expressed the police point of view; "*A man can drink all he wants in a pub till half past ten and then move to a restaurant and have a meal with his drink. Because it's legal he's not tempted to go to the illicit drinking places.*"[29]

The new clubs and bars proved a popular diversion for the young. Quite a number of bars adopted American youth tastes in clothes, music and drink, for instance coke and lager.[30] Young people took up club going in greater numbers; a move that proved a sticking point for the publicans of traditional pubs for they lost out on the new trade. For this reason some raised objections to the granting of licenses for the new drinking venues. One case in point was an application to convert a warehouse in Masonic Place, Goldsmith Street in the city centre into a new pub and night spot for young people. The aim was to attract students from the nearby Trent Polytechnic. It was proposed that the first floor would have an area designated for a disco and restaurant, and a pub on the ground floor. Though a Justice's Licence to sell liquor was provisionally granted the application was opposed by several breweries. Spokesmen from Ansells, Bass and Home Breweries said there was no need for another pub in the area. Crucial to their argument was that the city already provided enough late-night entertainment.[31] A major concern of city centre publicans was that pubs, unlike the new bars, closed at ten thirty in the evening. Nottingham was behind the times on this issue as most towns and cities had moved to eleven o'clock closing. Most publicans, however, were reluctant to back pub goer calls for later closing, citing issues such as problems getting bar staff home after closing time and a potential rise in the price of beer in opposition.

CAMRA and the campaign over pub hours

The traditional pub was inextricably bound up with the old way of life, and its predicament, and declining customer base, reflected the social changes.[32] CAMRA, the organisation working on behalf of drinkers, appeared on the scene in 1971, and grasped the important connection between the pub and the people. The local branch was one of the first of the organisation.[33] Its members represented the views of mainly older drinkers though it also had a student contingent. It believed early pub closing created an uneven playing field between traditional pubs and the new clubs, and contributed to other drink related problems such as drink-driving, as people dashed from the city to catch last orders outside the city boundary. The organisation took up local concerns in a proactive way. First it took on the brewery industry's giants, campaigning to save local brewers from takeover. The large breweries were starting to take over smaller breweries in the region, closing them down or converting them to produce a local version of their premium beers. CAMRA launched its' 'Save our Shippo's' campaign (James Shipstones and Sons, a local brewery) when the Hull based giant, Northern Foods attempted a takeover of Shipstones. Shipstones fought off the bid but it subsequently agreed terms with Warrington brewers, Greenall Whitley a year later. The episode was important because it marked the beginning of a sharp decline in local brewing, from which it did not recover.[34] CAMRA also railed against pub name changes, and called for more inclusivity in pubs, before becoming involved in campaigning for longer pub hours.

The organisation launched its campaign to extend drinking hours in 1975. It called for early closing restrictions to be lifted from city centre pubs. CAMRA members pressed for 11pm closing in the city, at least at weekends. Members argued that eleven o'clock closing occurred in Derbyshire, Leicestershire and other parts of Nottinghamshire and Nottingham was being penalised, having 10.30pm closing.[35] The National Association of Licensed House Managers and Nottingham and Nottinghamshire National Union of Licensed Victuallers (NNLVA) did not back the move though, because from the outset its members objected. Nevertheless there were no objections from police and the application was supported by a three thousand name petition. Only days before the hearing in March 1976, 11pm closing had been agreed for the outlying districts of Carlton, Hucknall, Eastwood, Kimberley, West Bridgford and Arnold.[36] Despite this, the application for longer pub hours in the city centre was turned down by the Licensing Committee. In the main, police remained neutral on the issue, though reported no crime increases in areas with 11pm closing. The application was rejected principally on the grounds of the objections of the city centre publicans, who claimed longer hours would bring no benefits and aggravate the growing trend toward pub violence. The licensee of The Bell Inn in the Market Square expressed the NNLVA view that *"Until the mid-sixties violence occurred in just one or two pubs that were well known for it...Since then the atmosphere of disrespect for authority has accelerated to the extent that we are now in a situation that is getting a little bit out of hand...the city centre on Friday and Saturday nights is not a safe place to be"*.[37]

The perception that youth violence was on the rise developed nationally as well as locally, as previously discussed. The events played out over extended hours in Nottingham underscored concerns debated in Parliament at the time. The recommendations of the Erroll Committee Report (1972) concerned the relaxation of regulations over alcohol.[38] In fact there was a good deal of intertwining of local and national issues in the debates around licensing at this time. In part this may have been because two of the key actors in the national debate were prominent local figures. Kenneth Clarke, the Member of Parliament for the local borough of Rushcliffe, proposed a Private Member's Bill that passed through Parliament in 1976. National Chairman of CAMRA Chris Holmes, who supported Clarke's proposal, was a business studies lecturer at Nottingham's Trent Polytechnic.[39] The crossover and blurring of the issues was evident in local press coverage: *"Nottingham Licensing Committee turned down an application by CAMRA for an extension within the city's boundaries...But the extended hours issue could become irrelevant if a Private Member's Bill, currently passing through Parliament becomes law...put forward by Kenneth Clarke, Conservative MP for Rushcliffe and it already had its second reading unopposed...... [Mr Clarke's] Bill takes account of the major proposals in the 1972 Erroll Committee Report on licensed premises; that pubs should be allowed to open any time between 10am and midnight at the licensee's discretion..."*[40]

Clarke's Bill proposed that pubs should be allowed to open any time between 10am and midnight at the licensee's discretion and also proposed children should be allowed into pubs where a suitable separate room was available. But the public was divided and Clarke's proposals in 1976 met the same fate as both Erroll, as well as the local CAMRA campaign.[41] Clarke recalled; *"By and large the opposition was based on the idea that I was leading the nation to its alcoholic ruin...it was filibustered by a hard core of members who were wedded to the idea of extremely restricted hours on drinking; to protect us from the evils of drink."* [42] In the aftermath of both local and national events, the issue of later pub hours in Nottingham was temporarily placed on the backburner.[43] In some respects resistance to changed hours was higher in the aftermath of the campaign, and pubs in the city continued to close earlier than those in other areas for a further decade. Indeed, Nottingham ending up last but one to move to eleven o'clock closing in 1987 (Newcastle was the last).

The 'problem' of the hooligan

Events surrounding the CAMRA campaign put the spotlight on young people and drink, and identified it as an emerging problem of hooliganism. Where at the start of the decade it was relatively commonplace for young people to flout the age limit and buy alcoholic drinks in pubs, and the issue was largely overlooked, as time went by the issue provoked greater concern and came much more to the fore.[44] In 1975, at the height of the campaign for longer pub hours, a public conference was held about alcoholism, and the issue of youth drinking. This brought together local clergymen, parents, teachers and students to reinforce the perils of underage drinking.[45] Reporting on the conference the *Nottingham Evening Post* claimed, *"Underage drinking is a problem in Nottingham... and is set to increase the alcoholic population in the 1980s."*[46] Much of the concern stemmed from anxiety about the changes in the environment. Historian David Pomfret, who wrote of age relations in Nottingham in the inter-war period, documented a similar situation then. He suggested as new approaches to city life were developed, educated observers articulated their fears about the impact that the city had on the young, using instances of misbehaviour by the young as a reference to environmental conditions in the city.[47] More generally it has been characteristic of those defending the morals of the past to express outrage and perceive a threat from social change. It is also characteristic to blame the problem on youth.[48] It was certainly true that youth of the 1970s had opportunities to break free from the social restrictions of the past, whereas in the 1960s a night out likely constituted a trip to the pub, social club or bingo. New youth leisure activities, incorporating new forms of late night entertainment, provided an alternative to the pub. Ultimately whilst these changes were welcomed by the young, older members of the community complained that young people were monopolising the city centre and treating it as their exclusive domain. Publicans of city centre pubs and bars also came under increasing attack for the apparent rise in disorder. Poor pub management and lack of supervision were viewed as contributing to the predicament. Such was the perception of a new threat from youth disorder that calls were made to magistrates to stiffen penalties against street fighters.[49] During the last few years of the decade, concern about growing city centre violence was relayed frequently in the local press. The instigators were thought to be young and unruly outsiders. Newspaper coverage of the period largely took the view of local publicans and reported that pub violence was increasing. The view of local police however, which got rather lost in the media coverage, was that pub violence was limited to only a handful of pubs, well known for being unruly.[50] The 'problem' was levelled at football fans from other cities; fans from Derby, Leicester or even Stoke, as this report from the *Nottingham Evening Post* suggested; *"They turn off their homeward route and head for Nottingham because they think it is a swinging city where everything happens...They are the sort of people who abuse everything they touch. They are not here to enjoy a drink; they are here to consume alcohol until they are told to go."* [51] The problem was considered restricted to the city centre. Pubs on the outskirts were less affected by the phenomenon. The landlord of the Man of Trent pub on Clifton Lane told local reporters; *"There were that many customers in here at one time you could float a match on the spilt beer. There was more drunkenness then and more violence".*[52] And despite the altered perception, there is little hard evidence to suggest young people were drinking more problematically, or in different ways than before in the late 1970s.[53] Arrests for drunkenness were actually in slight decline, though Nottingham's rates remained higher than elsewhere in the region.[54] This suggests that the problem of drunken youth disorder was more a perceptual than actual change in young people's drink behaviour. Regardless, police were called on to respond to those flouting the rules and their tactics became progressively more heavy-handed. Hence by the 1980s the football hooligan and other wayward youth had become the 'face' of the local alcohol problem.

Conclusions

By isolating alcoholism as a problem of the few, attitudes to 'normal' drinking in Nottingham were at first relaxed. However, as new public health thinking affected the local level, new constructions of the problem began to emerge. Although some otherwise 'normal' drinkers, including women and ethnic minorities, were singled out for criticism, youth drinking emerged as the main problem. Nationally, concern about underage drinking was driven by national research. The Medical Council on Alcoholism indicated that there was a new problem emerging with a number of studies identifying large numbers of 13 and 14 year olds drinking, with many 16 year olds regularly flouting the law.[55] However later studies found no evidence that 'underage' drinking had either increased or decreased during this period, or much indication from the criminal statistics of the regularity with which the licensing legislation was breached.[56] Locally, the shift of concern from vagrant to young hooligan was aggravated by changes in the nature and location of the drinks trade and by changes in the social environment. Publicans first brought attention to the issue by using it to oppose CAMRA's call for longer pub hours. This move had important consequences for ordinary drinkers in the city for it put on hold for another decade, plans to extend licensing for city pubs. Concerns of the local level were more or less in line with national concerns of the period; especially with regard to rising alcohol consumption rates among certain groups in society, and resistance over extending pub opening times chimed with concerns about the recommendations of the Erroll Committee (1972). This was set up to review the liquor licensing system and recommending the lifting of a number of licensing restrictions, but was defeated at about the same time as the application for extended pub hours was rejected in Nottingham. The rejection of further change in relation to licensing marked a shift in the latter half of the decade towards tighter regulation of drink, and marked the start of a more determined effort by police to stamp out the problems of hooliganism and disorder.

Notes

1. R. Baggott, *Alcohol, Politics and Social Policy* (Aldershot: Avebury 1990), p.16.
2. 'Edna the Inebriate', a television drama transmitted by BBC as part of the Play for Today series, October 21st 1971.
3. M. Hilton, 'The Duties of Citizens, the Rights of Consumers,' *Consumer Policy Review* 15 (2005), pp.6-12. Also C. Crouch and R. Dore, *Corporatism and Accountability: Organized Interests in British Public Life* (Oxford: Clarendon Press, 1990).
4. J.D. Pratten, 'The Development of the UK Public House: Part 2: Signs of Change to the UK Public House 1959-1989,' *International Journal of Contemporary Hospitality Management* 19, 6 (2007): pp. 513-519.
5. The existing restrictions were originally introduced at the start of World War One.
6. In 1971 under the chairmanship of Christopher Clayton a Committee formed to review licensing in Scotland. The Clayton Committee report, as it became known, recommended longer opening hours and a special dispensation for to open for extended hours, were included in the Licensing (Scotland) Act 1976.
7. For health debate and public reaction on the licensing debate see D. Robinson, 'The Erroll Report: Key Proposals and Public Reaction,' *Addiction* 69 (1973), pp.99-104.
8. Hansard: *HL Deb 19 March 1975, 358, cc 775-819.*
9. Before this act was introduced successful drink driving prosecutions relied solely upon the subjective tests and observations of '*police surgeons*' and other evidence such as witness statements. The Road Safety Act of 1967 introduced the first legal drink driving limit in the UK. In the same year the breathalyser was introduced as a way of testing a person's blood alcohol concentration level at the roadside.
10. D. Cameron, *Liberating Solutions to Alcohol Problems* (London: Jason Aronson Inc, 1991), p.192.
11. Ibid p. 191
12. For discussion of police measures to deal with illicit drinking see Nottingham Central Library Local Studies Library, Oral History Collection project 'Making Ends Meet' 1982-84, Tape A87 f,
13. 'Two Town Mad', a televised broadcast for BBC Inside Out - East Midlands, transmitted on February 14th 2005.

14 'Women alcoholics', *Nottingham Evening Post*, September 30th 1975.

15 'Women drinking themselves to secret alcoholics', *Nottingham Evening Post*, January 20th 1976.

16 F. A. Wells 'Present Day Economic Structure,' in *Nottingham and its Region*, ed. K.C. Edwards (Nottingham: British Association for the Advancement of Science, 1966), pp. 363-404

17 S. Clements, 'Feminism, Citizenship and Social Activity: The Role and Importance of Local Women's Organisations in Nottingham 1918-1969', Nottingham: PhD thesis, 2008, pp. 258-267.

18 Changes in the role and status of women in Nottingham are examined by J. O'Neill in 'Family Life in the Twentieth Century,' in *A Centenary History of Nottingham*, ed. J.V. Beckett (Manchester: Manchester University Press, 1997), pp. 513-32

19 From 1965 Nottingham's voluntary organisation 'Family First' strove to tackle problems for families in housing, childcare, and neighbourhood centres.

20 J. O'Neill, 'Family Life in the Twentieth Century,' in *A Centenary History of Nottingham*, p.526.

21 K.L. Jones and D.W. Smith, 'Recognition of the Fetal Alcohol Syndrome in Early Pregnancy,' *Lancet* i (1973), pp.999-1001; K.L. Jones and D.W. Smith, 'Offspring of Chronic Alcoholic Women,' *Lancet* ii (1974), p. 349.

22 E. Armstrong and E. L. Abel, 'Fetal Alcohol Syndrome: The Origins of a Moral Panic', *Alcohol and Alcoholism* 35 (2000), pp. 276-282.

23 'AA meeting', *Nottingham Evening Post*, April 3rd 1975.

24 C. Hutt, *The Death of the English Pub* (London: Hutchinson, 1973).

25 'Pub entertainment in Nottingham,' *Nottingham Evening Post*, December 1st 1975.

26 'Nottingham pubs changed beyond recognition,' *Nottingham Evening Post*, April 7th 1978.

27 'Pub entertainment in Nottingham,' *Nottingham Evening Post* December 1st 1975.

28 After-hours drinking was referred to as an after-hours 'binge' in an article that discusses the demise of pub early closing in Nottingham in the late 1980s. 'Lock-in ends' *Nottingham Evening Post*, August 23rd 1988.

29 Nottingham County Library, Local Studies Library, Oral History Collection project 'Making Ends Meet' Tape A87 f.

30 Changing youth tastes are discussed in B. Stapleton and J. Thomas, *Gales: A Study in Brewing, Business and Family History* (Aldershot: Ashgate, 2000).

31 'New pub and night spot for young people to open,' *Nottingham Evening Post*, July 26th 1975.

32 There is a fairly substantial literature on the public house. Key texts include P. Jennings, *The Local: A History of the English Pub (Stroud: Tempus Publishing, 2007)* and S. Earnshaw, *The Pub in Literature.* (Manchester: Manchester University Press, 2000). For a local perspective see J.J. Rowley, 'Drink and the Public House in Nottingham 1830-60,'

Transactions of the Thoroton Society of Nottinghamshire 79 (1975) and G. Wright and B.J Curtis, *The Inns and Pubs of Nottinghamshire. The Stories behind the Names* (Nottingham: Nottingham County Council, 1955).

33 The local branch of CAMRA produced a local magazine; the *'Notts and Derby Drinker'*. It has been published since 1976. Derby pulled out of the venture due to financial losses and in 1984 it became the *Notts and District Drinker*, finally taking the title *'Nottingham drinker'* in the 1990s.

34 Hardy and Hansons was the last main local brewery in Nottinghamshire. Founded as Kimberley Brewery in 1832 it was taken over by Hardy's in 1857 and merged with another local brewer Hansons in 1930. It was taken over by Greene King in September 2006. Brewing ceased there on December 11th 2006 and transferred to Bury St Edmunds.

35 'Move to extend opening hours in Nottingham is launched by CAMRA,' *Nottingham Evening Post*, August 20th 1975.

36 'Court decision to extend licensing hours attacked,' *Nottingham Evening Post*, March 18th 1976.

37 Ibid

38 The Erroll report recommendations included extending opening hours, reducing legal age for purchase in pubs from 18 to 17 years of age, and allowing children under 14 into specially licensed pubs also serving food. See D. Robinson, 'The Erroll Report: Key Proposals and Public Reaction,' *Addiction* 69 (1974), pp. 99-104.

39 Kenneth Clarke interviewed by Jane McGregor, London, July 2007. Clarke's Private Member's Bill is discussed in R. Baggott, 'Licensing Law Reform and the Return of the Drink Question,' *Parliamentary Affairs* 40 (1987), pp. 501-16. Also D. Rutherford, 'The Drinks Cabinet: UK Alcohol Policy,' *Contemporary British History, 1743-7997*, 5 (1991), pp. 450-67.

40 'Controversy over extension of licensing hours,' *Nottingham Evening Post*, March 22nd 1976.

41 D. Robinson, 'The Erroll Report: Key Proposals and Public Reaction,' *Addiction* 69, 2 (1974), pp. 99-104.

42 Kenneth Clarke interview,

43 'Court decision to extend licensing hours attacked,' *Nottingham Evening Post*, March 18th 1976.

44 'AA meeting', *Nottingham Evening Post*, April 3rd 1975.

45 'Local drug and alcohol conference' *Newark Advertiser*, September 27th 1975.

46 'Underage drinking is a problem in Nottingham,' *Nottingham Evening Post*, July 1st 1975.

47 D.M Pomfret, 'Representations of Adolescence in the Modern City: Voluntary Provision and Work in Nottingham and Saint-Etienne, 1890-1914', eds. Jean-Luc Pinol and Richard Rodger, *Historical Urban Studies* (Aldershot: Ashgate, 2004).

48 S. Cohen, *Folk Devils and Moral Panics: The Creation of the Mods and Rockers*. 3rd edition (MacGibbon and Kee: London, 2002); N. Ben-Yehuda and E. Goode, *Moral Panics: The Social Construction of Deviance* (Oxford: Blackwell, 1994); T. Besley, *Counseling Youth:*

Foucault, Power, and the Ethics of Subjectivity (Rotterdam: Sense Publishers 2006), p. 143.

49 'Pub entertainment in Nottingham,' *Nottingham Evening Post*, December 1st 1975

50 'AA meeting', *Nottingham Evening Post* April 3rd 1975; 'Court decision to extend licensing hours,' '*Nottingham Evening Post,* March 18th 1976; 'Controversy over extension of licensing hours' '*Nottingham Evening Post*, March 22nd 1976.

51 'Clean up pubs campaign,' *Nottingham Evening Post, February* 2nd 1978.

52 'The pubs of Clifton' *Nottingham Evening Post*, February 3rd 1978.

53 'Opposition to alcohol rehab', *Nottingham Evening Post*, February 14th 1976; 'Book published about alcoholism,' *Nottingham Evening Post,* October 19th 1976.

54 'High levels of drunkenness,' *Nottingham Evening Post*, August 24th 1978. Also D. Cameron, *Liberating Solutions to Alcohol Problems*, (London: Jason Aronson, 1995), p.191.

55 The Medical Council on Alcoholism was established in 1967 with a view to the co-ordination of effort, the better understanding of alcoholism, its prevention and the treatment and after-care of alcoholics. It reported findings on a number of studies of the period. Other research from the period includes B. Stacey and J. Davies, 'Drinking Behaviour in Childhood and Adolescence: An Evaluative Review.' *British Journal of Addiction* 65 (1970), pp 203-212; J. Davies and B. Stacey, *Teenagers and Alcohol. A Developmental Study in Glasgow* (London: HMSO, 1972); A. Hawker, *Adolescents and Alcohol* (London: Edsal, 1978).

56 D. Lister Sharp, 'Underage Drinking in the United Kingdom since 1970: Public Policy, the Lane and Adolescent Drinking Behaviour,' *Alcohol and Alcoholism* 29 (1994), pp. 555-563; C. May, 'A Burning Issue? Adolescent Alcohol Use in Britain 1970-1991,' *Alcohol and Alcoholism* 27 (1992), pp. 109-115.

5

COMBINING DRINK AND DRUGS: ALCOHOL TREATMENT IN THE 1980s

At the beginning of the 1980s concern about alcohol had shifted to the young drunken hooliganism in the community, but the focus of concern of doctors and the network of alcohol agencies continued to be the older homeless alcoholic. This situation saw medicine out of step not only with the views of the local community, but with national government. Government faced a new drugs epidemic at this time, as well as an emerging problem of HIV/AIDS. The circumstances caused political attention to shift away from alcohol and the lack of interest in alcohol treatment left developments in many parts of the country at a virtual standstill. Yet in Nottingham the issue of alcohol remained an important policy concern and local provision expanded. This divergent situation was made possible when monies meant for drugs misuse were used in addition to tackle problems of drink. Alcohol provision also improved with better co-ordination, which came as a result of health policy changes, in particular in the area of health planning in the NHS. These conditions provided the means by which Nottingham was able to develop as a centre specialising in responses to the homeless/street drinker. Increased collaboration helped facilitate the rise of the local hostel sector and culminated in the development of an innovative project, the Handel Street wet centre, the first centre of its kind in England. But for all the advances of the local alcohol network over the course of the decade, an observable shift occurred since police moved on to tackle the emerging problem of youth disorder, an issue in which medicine was not involved.

National policy developments

The combined issues of drug misuse and HIV effectively knocked alcohol off the policy agenda during the 1980s. New trade routes opened from South West Asia (Iran, Pakistan, and Afghanistan) during the early part of the decade meant cheap heroin supply became more readily available, and contributed to an escalation in illicit drug use in Britain. There was a marked increase in heroin use but with geographical differences, heroin use being slower to spread in the East than in the West of the country.[1] Britain, so government believed, was in the throes of a 'new' drug problem. The Conservative government consequently introduced the central funding initiative (CFI) in 1985. This aimed to stimulate the setting up of services outside of London and integrate services for drug users into the mainstream. Part of this move involved partnerships and the setting up of drug problem planning teams. Planning teams involved different disciplines and agencies and were set up with the expectation they should work together to deal with drug misuse.[2] Then in the mid 1980s HIV/AIDS added to concern about drugs to bring radical changes to British drug policy.[3] HIV virus was discovered among drug users in Britain in 1985. Its transmission was thought to be caused by the sharing and re-using of syringes contaminated with HIV-infected blood.[4] Major reports on drugs and AIDS followed as did funding, to the tune of £17 million, for the development of drug services. Needle exchanges, widespread health education and drug treatment were made available in order to keep HIV levels low.[5] These developments impacted upon the size and nature of the UK drugs sector, and the majority of drug services established after the CFI of 1985 benefitted from annual allocations of specific grants.[6]

In contrast to the issue of drugs, the UK alcohol sector suffered a lack of policy interest and with that a lack of government funding. The approach to drink was similar to that of drugs, and concerned with lessening the harms with associated drinking. This meant there was importance placed on the provision of alcohol education and intervention early in an individual's drinking career. The concept of alcoholism was seriously challenged; no longer was drink regarded as a problem of the few, but the harms of alcohol, to greater and lesser degree, understood to affect the whole of society. As the population or public health approach took hold, there was a focus on reducing 'problem drinking'. The approach required broad responses, and prompted a need for a system of joint planning to co-ordinate community health and social care, as was the trend in health policy of the mid to late 1970s.[7] The DHSS document *Drinking Sensibly* (1981) called for responses from primary care and the community to support the new emphasis. This saw the Royal Colleges play key roles, linking the national and local levels through education, training and networking.[8] They undertook surveys to establish the number of problem drinkers in the population and attempted to standardise the measurement of alcohol consumption. Subsequently this led to the adoption of a 'unit' system of measurement in the UK. A report *'Alcohol and Alcoholism'* (1979), and three subsequent reports by the Royal Colleges legitimised the use of the unit system, defined as 10 millilitres or approximately 8 grams of ethanol, with different guidelines developed for each gender.[9] This led to recommendations for 'sensible' levels of drinking; up to 21 units a week for men and 14 per week for women, 21-49 units a week and 14-35 units a week respectively considered 'hazardous' drinking, and above 49 for men and 35 units for women being dangerous. However there was some doubt to the dependability of these figures, which were reportedly 'plucked out of thin air'.[10] Nonetheless the approach was legitimised by the medical scientific community who sought to present a consistent message in the face of powerful alcohol advertising and growing drink industry strength.[11]

Throughout the period there was also increasing medical acceptance of 'controlled' or 'moderate' drinking; an approach to drinking that emphasised moderation rather than abstinence. This issue was debated by the international research community for a number of decades.[12] Many in the alcohol research community were becoming convinced that changes to drinking patterns from excessive to moderate patterns could be achieved through behavioural approaches to treatment. The concept fitted well with the new concept of problem drinking and led to developments in treatment where doctors absorbed the new, broader definitions into the medical perspective and modified treatment.[13] As a consequence, controlled drinking programmes became an integral part of treatment in many UK treatment centres.[14] In some areas, Community Alcohol Teams (CATs) emerged, designed to offer direct service in the community and advise GPs and primary care workers on identifying and managing alcohol problems. Despite this there continued to be resistance from GPs as some still regarded the issue as specialist treatment. This, coupled with the fact that the target group was becoming more diverse, meant it became more difficult to allocate patients to suitable treatment.[15] Much of the work was farmed out to voluntary organisations, which added to the sector's growth.[16] Whilst this brought greater diversity it also fragmented the sector.[17] On top of this, the arrival of the 'contract culture' at the end of the decade had impacts on government and local authority funded services, creating competition between agencies.

Nottingham and the impacts of national policy change

Despite the policy changes nationally, alcohol treatment in Nottingham remained relatively unaffected and unchanged. This was partly because psychiatrists at Mapperley still dominated the local treatment arena and regarded alcohol as a specialist area. They held a particular view of the problem, perceiving alcoholism and homelessness as worrying local predicaments. Local policy also remained unchanged because drug misuse was not an especially obtrusive problem in Nottingham at that time, unlike in London and a number of other major cities. The reason why drug problems did not escalate in the social realm, according to McLean the director of the addiction unit at Mapperley, was that the liberal prescribing policies were adopted in the treatment of heroin addiction. Individuals addicted to heroin were prescribed bigger doses and more liberally in Nottingham than in London, where prescribing was limited to 35 milligrams of methadone and limited to detoxification. He claimed the approach he took in Nottingham prevented the boom for about another two years."[18] It was his view that it was only in the mid to late 1980s that drugs misuse really hit Nottingham. At that time a local drug prevalence study identified 170 Class A drug misusers in the city. The study suggested a relatively static number of addicts in the city, the greatest concentration of addicts being in the inner city residential areas, in neighbourhoods fringing major suburban shopping centres, and several council estates. Analysis also established significant links between drug use and deprivation, unemployment and crime.[19]

Though the problems of drugs and drink were viewed as patently different entities, treatment for drug and alcohol dependency was combined at Mapperley Hospital. This meant that additional funds from government to treat drug misuse were spread across the addiction service for the benefit of all patients, including the problem drinkers. Doctors played a vital role in keeping alcohol on the local policy agenda as McLean admitted; *"Birmingham, Leeds and Newcastle; these were regional units like us but gradually for them it became drug misusers and homelessness. We kept the focus on homelessness but also on treating drinkers."*[20] Stressing the importance of alcohol locally, the addiction treatment unit underwent a decisive name change in 1984 to reflect this dual aspect and was renamed Nottingham Alcohol and Drug Team (NADT). The name change emphasised the importance of drink over drugs. The new name marked a shift away from the 'hospital' and a focus on the 'team', as well as away from 'addiction' and 'alcoholism'. The letter 'A' in 'NADT' (Nottingham Alcohol and Drug Team), referred to alcohol, and was placed before the letter 'D', which referred to drugs. This was a deliberate move to emphasise the importance of alcohol against the dominating force of central government and the national focus on drugs.[21] Thus when NADT received the third largest CFI allocation in the country and gained considerably from a subsequent allocation in 1988, doctors used the occasion to bolster alcohol provision as well.[22]

Because of these decisions, alcohol treatment at the local level was relatively unaffected by changes in government funding at this time though by contrast changes within the NHS influenced co-ordination and decision-making to some extent. Following the Griffith report of 1983, general managers were introduced into the health service, a shift that significantly curtailed doctors' clinical autonomy and power of influence in terms of health planning. Coupled with this there were changes in the area of strategic planning. Where the 'area' tier had the major share of responsibility for health planning and policy in the NHS re-organisation of 1974, this was abolished in the early 1980s and decision-making devolved to the local level or district area authority (DHA).[23] Health care planning teams (HCPTs), which constituted one of the distinctive features of the re-organisation in 1974, became important in relation to local planning and policy.[24] Policy documents pressed for collaboration between health and local authority officers, and joint planning teams were formally set up across the NHS towards the end of 1983/early 1984.[25] Requirements to work together were no guarantee of success however, and health policy makers often viewed the process as nothing more than a mechanism for information sharing.[26] As a result of these modifications, a working party was set up in Nottingham to establish a joint planning team for substance abuse (JPTSA).[27] This was fully functioning by 1987 and provided a multidisciplinary and multi-agency forum for discussion about aspects of services related to the problems of substance abuse. It also acted as the local health authority's drug dependency advisory committee. It liaised with the Regional Drug Advisory Committee, County Council Alcohol, Drugs and Solvent Forum, the Mid Trent Clinical area meeting and District AIDS Advisory Committee, and considered joint finance proposals. The joint planning team consisted of six representatives from Nottingham Health Authority including Philip McLean, the psychiatrist from the addiction unit at Mapperley, as well as representatives from Nottinghamshire County Council social services and the education and leisure (youth and community) department. There were also representatives from the police, probation, the Family Practitioner Committee, Nottingham Community Health Council, the Association of District Councils and representatives from the voluntary sector. The group had quarterly meetings and submitted annual reports. In its lifetime the group undertook specific work including a drug prevalence study, a lifestyle survey, which raised the prominence of the local problem of alcohol abuse, and importantly supported expansion not only of drug treatment but alcohol provision.

The JPTSA provided means to work collaboratively. As a result, close bonds between agencies were formed, though 'partnerships' were not commonly referred to at the time. It was a forum where local agency staff could meet and pull together rather than act simply as rivals for the same 'pot' of funds.[28] From around 1988, an additional Regional Drug Advisory Group formed, which was a council-led forum on alcohol and drugs. Together, the various policy and planning groups operated until the national structure changed in the 1990s and Drug Action Teams (DATs) were introduced. In conjunction, a regional alcohol co-ordinator worked on behalf of the county council and organised regional activities and developments. He was involved in local (district) level commissioning to some extent, but involvement tended to vary from district to district. He had a small pot of funds and was automatically involved in bidding processes for national development grants.[29] Opportunities for the voluntary sector to compete for additional funds and contracts meant the sector went from strength to strength. Hence by the end of the 1980s, not only had the nature of planning and co-ordination of local alcohol provision altered substantially, having come a long way from the informal style of the 1960s and early 1970s, but the nature of the voluntary sector had started to change.

IMPROVED CO-ORDINATION AND DEVELOPMENTS IN THE COMMUNITY

Paradoxically, the combined effect of the national policy move towards drugs, the introduction of new monies to that area, and changes to health service planning and management helped strengthen alcohol treatment at the local level. The most tangible benefits were in the areas of policy co-ordination and inter-agency collaboration. When a system of joint planning between the health authority and local authority was introduced, plans were hatched to extend community provision and involve other health and social care professionals. The move was in line with the national drive.[30] Whereas in many areas community alcohol teams were introduced with the explicit aim of encouraging GPs to become involved in alcohol treatment, a community alcohol team was not developed in Nottingham. In fact few local GPs became involved with the issue because many still regarded alcoholism as the preserve of the specialist psychiatrist. Instead a new outpatient clinic, John Storer Clinic, was established in 1985. It shared a building with the Nottingham Council on Alcoholism, which had moved from Mansfield Rd and changed its name to Alcohol Problems Advisory Service (APAS).

John Storer Clinic was situated on Park Row in the city centre and offered treatment and detoxification from alcohol and drugs on an outpatient basis. It was overseen by Philip McLean and other staff from the addiction unit at Mapperley. The clinic served four counties. There were only about forty clients with drug problems in total across the four counties, so the work became heavily orientated towards alcohol. McLean wanted community psychiatric nurses to visit people in their homes and pushed the nursing establishment to allow this and eventually they gave way. The first instalment of government funding for drug treatment was spent on community facilities and employing community psychiatric nurses and social workers. Social workers were able to work more effectively with families, often making home visits though sometimes arranging to see families at the clinic. A social worker from the clinic also ran surgeries at the night-shelter on Canal Street. This initiative, a good example of the close links and collaboration between agencies at this time, developed after concerns about safety in the night-shelter threatened to force it to close. At the time the whole enterprise was run by one paid member of staff who was supported by a handful of young volunteers. The situation, according to Ira Unell, who worked at John Storer Clinic as a social worker at the time, was 'a catastrophe waiting to happen'. A plan was subsequently hatched among the alcohol treatment network to get it on a sounder basis. Because neither the city nor county council would give further funding the local alcohol network advised that it close down. Within weeks of closing there were complaints from the police and local councillors. It stayed closed for 4-6 months but eventually the council gave money to open it up again. It was on a sounder basis from this time on, helped by the support of staff from the John Storer Clinic, who started to go there early in the morning one day a week to screen people for alcohol problems, see people that had been inpatients previously or had gone back there for aftercare.[31] There was also much co-operation between the clinic, local agencies and the inpatient unit at Mapperley. For instance, drinkers were often taken to the probation hostel on 28 Addison Street after they were dried out at Mapperley addiction unit. Staff at the hostel would take care of them, and saw that if they 'fell off the wagon,' and their condition necessitated it, they were taken to the clinic or back to the hospital to be dried out again.

After that the community side expanded and APAS became more involved in delivering services, as well as continuing its co-ordination role, and began to offer counselling training to volunteers as well as running a no-alcohol pub for its clientele. 'The Amethyst Club' ran on a Tuesday evening in the building. McLean became chair of APAS at this time and developed around him a tight knit group of key individuals from the alcohol network. The group pretty much did what it liked; there was no interference from others outside of the local alcohol policy network. APAS continued in its vital role in co-ordinating the activities of the local alcohol network until it was superseded in this role in some ways in the late 1980s by the Hostels Liaison Group (HLG), which was established to bring the hostel sector together and became an institution in its own right. Housing associations Macedon and Family First were the first to be involved but most of the voluntary agencies belonged to the group eventually. HLG was initially intended as a meeting of people interested in homelessness, either on the health and social services provision side or statutory housing side. From 1986 it received funding from the Council through the joint funding initiative. This provided the funds to pay for a resource worker. It subsequently attracted further funding to pay for a peripatetic worker to cover when staff at the other hostels were sick or on leave and formally became a provider of services in 1989, providing overarching provision such as mental health and resettlement services.[32]

The changing nature of homelessness and break-up of the medical-penal alliance

In many respects the local commitment to the homeless was in keeping with the concerns of wider society in the 1980s. This issue is discussed at some length in the next chapter but briefly, when Margaret Thatcher became Prime Minister in 1979, the Conservative government pursued economic, social and housing policies that exacerbated the homelessness situation in the country. The decline of the large-scale manufacturing industry hit some groups particularly hard, affecting poorly qualified young men by cutting off their traditional route into work (apprenticeships or unskilled labour). One consequence was that youth unemployment grew dramatically. Less well understood was why youth homelessness and mobility increased in the 1980s. It is likely that a number of interconnected public policies, including a significant reduction in the social security protection given to unemployed people, particularly affected young people. In what has been described as government's 'social experiments with youth,' benefit entitlement was withdrawn from the majority of 16 and 17 year olds. These factors, compounded by increased youth unemployment, low wages and the inadequacy of the legislative safety net, all served to discriminate against the young person.[33]

In response to the growing concern about youth and rising crime, crime prevention strategies were developed that were oriented towards strengthening communities and restoring informal surveillance and control of crime. Over time the 'crime prevention' approach was replaced by the 'community safety' approach so that by the late 1980s/early 1990s, there was growing collaboration between police, local authorities, health authorities, transport authorities, housing associations and local businesses, all of whom were intent on making the local community a safer place to be.[34] Increasingly this meant responding to the apparent 'problem of youth'. Hence as the decade progressed, police attention shifted from the older street drinker to concerns of the wider community, issues such as street crime, violence and drug misuse. The change in policy stance formed part of a wider move in urban policing towards 'quality-of-life offences' and involved the removal of unwanted groups such as beggars and drug-users from city centres.[35] Medical interest through this transition period remained fixed on the problems of the older homeless drinker and the police move ultimately led to the dismantling of the local medical-penal alliance in relation to managing the problem of drink. The reason why the medical perspective remained intact and largely unchanged was because the approach had become the mainstay approach of psychiatrists at Mapperley. High rates of mental illness persisted, particularly in Nottingham's inner city areas.[36] Though some had believed the housing programmes of the late 1960s/ early 1970s would relieve the burden of mental illness by improving the quality of the built and living environment, this was patently not the case. For this reason psychiatrists continued to exert pressure over issues like homelessness and poor housing, as they saw these factors as contributing to mental illness.[37]

The rise of the hostel sector and development of the 'wet' project

Though this decade marked the beginning of the end of the medical-penal alliance, one issue over which they remained united was over the need for a place for persistent drunks. For medicine this was because it was envisaged that such a place could afford opportunities to engage chronic drinkers in interventions to reduce the damage of heavy and persistent drinking and so improve their health, whereas for police it was about keeping persistent drunks off the streets and out of sight. A long standing problem of urban areas, there had been renewed impetus to tackle the problem with successive national reports recommending that help and treatment should be provided by psychiatric and social services rather than through the criminal justice system.[38] From 1973 the responsibility for dealing with habitual drunken offenders was transferred from the Home Office to the DHSS.[39] Under the Housing Act of 1977 local authorities were obliged to secure long term accommodation for those in priority need and the DHSS offered funds to voluntary bodies to provide alcohol services such as specialist hostels, detoxification centres and rehabilitation programmes.[40] The DHSS first supported the development of two centres; the Leeds Detoxification Centre, which opened in 1976 and a detoxification unit at the Withington Hospital in Manchester, which opened two years later. These made it possible for drunken offenders to be taken for treatment by the police rather than remain in police cells. In 1981, the Home Office funded a centre in Birmingham that opened overnight for drinkers but by the mid-

1980s there was growing recognition that chronic drinkers found it difficult to abstain from alcohol. A response to the problem was the creation of 'wet' projects with the idea being to allow drinking on the premises. Their aim was to encourage more moderate drinking and less dangerous substitutes in order to promote better health and more stable lifestyles. In the mid-1980s, the first of this type of project, the Heavy Drinkers Project, was established in Manchester by Peterloo Housing Association, and in 1986, Wernham House in Aberdeen was set up by the Aberdeen Cyrenians. The first wet day centre in Scotland opened in Dundee in 1978 and in England the first opened in Nottingham in 1991 though others subsequently developed in London, Brighton, Oxford, Leicester and Manchester.[41]

DEVELOPMENT OF THE HOSTELS LIAISON GROUP (HLG)

The background to developments in Nottingham was that in the late 1970s and early 1980s, the churches gave very large funds to Macedon Housing Association, a registered social landlord, founded in the 1970s. On top of that statutory funding for the housing association expanded. The city council provided considerable funds and there were rent subsidies, which meant Macedon expanded from one small hostel to a significant number of properties. It became responsible for more than half a dozen hostels, had flats and house-shares and grew exponentially over the next five years. Surrounding cities had very few facilities for the homeless and so, before very long, Nottingham became a magnet for the intransient. By the end of the 1980s, between Macedon, Nottingham Help the Homeless Association and a supported landlord scheme, there was thought to be about two thousand homeless lodged in the city. This was a lot when compared to neighbouring cities Derby, Mansfield, Lincoln, Leicester and other surrounding areas.[42] According to McLean, the issue was positive on one hand because Nottingham became known as a city specialising in the management of homelessness, but it also had its downside; *"Nottingham built up this provision and was known throughout the country as the place to go for a homeless hostel. Now that's a double edged sword because on one hand it is good and gives you a reputation and on the other it attracts criminals and vagrants and drug takers."*[43]

As concern grew about the extent of homeless drinkers in Nottingham, there were discussions within JPTSA from the late 1970s regarding establishing some sort of detoxification centre in the city. At the time Canal Street night-shelter was facing increasing criticism for tipping drinkers out of the hostel on to the streets during the daytime. A subgroup of the JPTSA was tasked with looking into the issue.⁴⁴ It first considered setting up a detoxification centre along the lines of a centre in Manchester.⁴⁵ Plans were soon thwarted however because the health authority was reluctant to fund the project. Undeterred, one of the local hostel charities, Nottingham Help the Homeless Association (NHHA), stepped in and shaped plans into something more radical. Its ideas were helped along in 1989 by a health authority decision to establish an Alcohol Strategy Working Group (ASWG) to consider the implications of the circular *HN89 (4): Alcohol Misuse*.⁴⁶ The circular emphasised the social impacts of alcohol misuse and gave considerable emphasis to multi-agency partnerships between national and local initiatives. This group, made up of members of the local treatment alliance, became the vehicle through which ideas for a detoxification and counselling route for drunken offenders came to fruition.⁴⁷ The proposal was that drinkers would be provided with day provision where they could spend time during the day. This would be a place to 'keep them out of harm's way' but also somewhere where they could access support for their problems. Plans included provision for new hostel accommodation as well as a day centre. Because of previous concerns about difficulties managing the night shelter, the health authority and local authority took time to warm to the idea of the project being run by a voluntary sector organisation. It was not until the Hostel Liaison Group (HLG) entered the arena that either authority agreed to fund the project.⁴⁸ As briefly mentioned earlier, the HLG was a local partnership set up in 1981 with funding from the city and county councils to support voluntary sector agencies working with homeless people. An umbrella organisation for all homeless services it provided training, information and organised things like homeless watch surveys and fostered close links among the local authority housing and social services departments, health services and the probation service, consequently co-ordinating responses to homeless people.

HANDEL STREET DAY CENTRE: THE 'WET' PROJECT

At the same time as the wet centre was proposed, there was some media interest on the homeless 'problem' in the city. According to Ira Unell, the NHS addiction service representative for the HLG, resources to fund the project were only found after the BBC decided to do a three part television series on homelessness in Nottingham. *"It was Nottingham; the city of homelessness". The council was extremely unhappy about this and worried about the angle that this is where the dossers come and gather."* ⁴⁹ Concern about the problem had led to an earlier initiative involving the creation of a new homeless nurse post, which was taken up by a community psychiatric nurse based at Mapperley Hospital. The work became too much for one person however and soon there was discussion of health input into the new 'wet' project. It was largely on the back of the interest and offer of support from doctors at Mapperley that the authorities agreed to support the initiative.[50] Chief Executive of the Council, Peter McKay, told local newspaper reporters that medical experts were willing to provide training and advice insisting; *"We have Mapperley Hospital behind us on this project"*[51] Premises for the proposed day centre were initially identified on Canal Street adjoining the night shelter, which had moved from temporary accommodation to its site on Canal Street, but in the end, premises were secured on Handel Street in Sneinton because that was where most of the drinkers used to collect. Opening in 1991 the wet centre offered individuals free food, laundry, showers and access to benefits. By the mid 1990s a former district nurse, Caroline Thompson, developed a healthcare clinic there. Much of the work involved attending to rotten feet and wounds and helping individuals better manage their drinking. There was also a medical clinic run by a GP by the name of Dr Michael Varnam.[52]

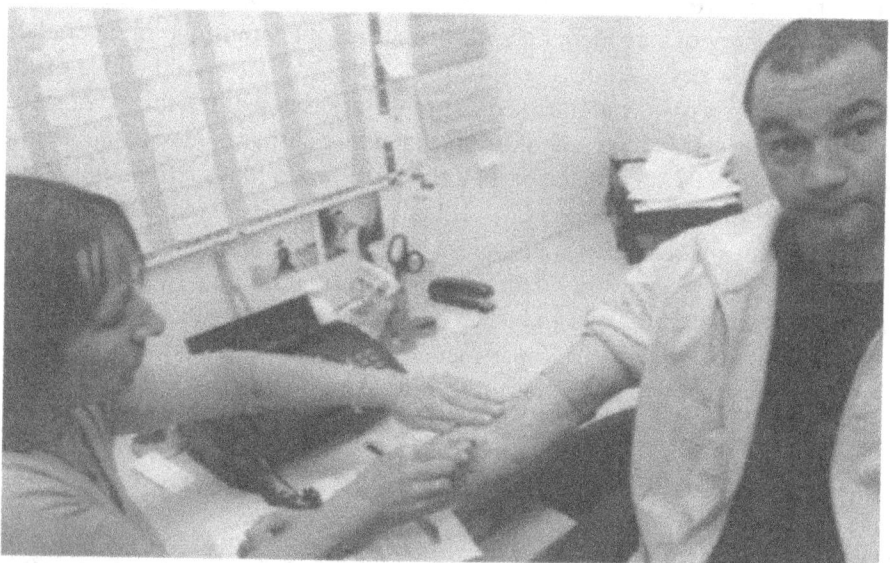

Handel Street nurse-run health clinic © Framework

There was a wet room for street drinkers and also daytime activities. The room had benches around three walls, windows high up on one wall, and a drain grid in the centre of the room. The centre catered for up to twenty five clients at any given time. Alcohol could only be consumed in the wet room, with no restriction on the amount that could be brought into the centre.

An advice session at Handel Street © Framework

Though the style of project was not taken up extensively elsewhere in the country and penal measures such as extensive use of police cautioning schemes, and other more cost effective in terms of dealing with drunken offenders, were commonly developed instead,[53] the day centre was an important feature of the local treatment scene. In the 1990s due to local government re-organisation, the City Council, rather than the County Council, funded the project.[54] It also developed as a project of the Rough Sleepers Initiative (RSI). This was an initiative by the government's Rough Sleepers Unit (RSU), supported by both Conservative and New Labour governments of the 1990s, and designed to accommodate homeless people with emergency hostels. Voluntary sector organisations were funded directly by government to provide services and central government took the unusual step of funding directly as it had little confidence in local authorities to address the problem of rough sleeping.[55] As a result the wet project was able to expand to include a five bed hostel at 77 Raleigh Street, which was intended as a long-stay wet hostel. Street drinkers continued to be the core group of the wet project but they began to see many more people who were using illegal drugs, which presented considerable challenges in terms of health and safety, legal and management issues. Also in the 1990s, both Macedon Housing Association and Nottingham Help the

Homeless Association went on to develop their work with older homeless people, developing 32 Bentinck Road, accommodation exclusively for people aged over 55, as well as Albion Supported Housing and Sneinton Hermitage, now called Michael Varnam House, both of which accommodated a significant number of older people. In the late 1990s, the two organisations, Nottingham Help the Homeless and Macedon, were often fighting for funding and pitched against each other so the idea of merging these two together was proposed. The merger was in 1999 and the new organisation became known as Framework, and was officially launched in 2000. In early 2011 it was announced that Handel Street day centre would be closing and it was subsequently decommissioned by the City Council. Yet over the years Handel Street had become a major provider of services, extending its remit to include tenancy support, welfare advice, education and training and having up to 80 people visit the centre each day. [56]

Conclusion

The local treatment response of the 1980s continued to emphasise the older, street drinker where nationally the issue of drink was taken up more broadly. Also where the UK alcohol sector in general faced financial and resource problems as a result of changed government priorities, the decision to divide monies meant for drugs between alcohol and drugs meant the emphasis on alcohol was not only maintained but enhanced at the local level. Improved co-ordination and experience of working together on joint bids helped partnerships develop among the alcohol network, and a shared interest in the issue of street drinking saw the local sector become a leading light in this particular area of alcohol treatment. By the end of the 1980s however, tangible shifts in the balance of power occurred and the nature of the sector was changing. The hostel sector, having united under the umbrella organisation HLG, emerged the stronger player. The police meanwhile began to disconnect from the issue of street drinking as their role and involvement in managing street drinkers became reduced and the issue became a less visible problem on the streets. Instead their attentions began to fix upon youth disorder, which is the focus of chapter six. The decade consequently marked the beginning of the end of the alliance between medicine and police over drink and the beginning of a new phase in policing where tough new measures were introduced to remove undesirables from the streets.

Notes

1. J. Strang and M. Gossop, *Heroin Addiction and the British System Volume I: Origins and Evolution* (London: Routledge, 2004), p.104.

2. V. Berridge, AIDS *in the UK: The Making of Policy, 1981-1994* (Oxford: Oxford University Press, 1996), pp. 94-95.

3. A. Mold, *Heroin: The Treatment of Addiction in Twentieth-Century Britain* (DeKalb, Illinois: Northern Illinois University Press, 2008), pp. 128-142.

4. For overview of HIV policy, V. Berridge *AIDS in the UK: The Making of Policy, 1981-1994*.

5. A. Mold and V. Berridge, 'Crisis and Opportunity in Drug Policy: Changing the Direction of British Drug Services in the 1980s,' *Journal of Policy History* 19 (2007), pp. 29-48; The Central Funding Initiative is also the subject of a chapter in their book; A. Mold and V. Berridge *Voluntary Action and Illegal Drugs: Health and Society in Britain Since the 1960s* (Basingstoke, Hamps: Palgrave Macmillan, 2010); R. Lart, "Drugs and Health Policy," in *Drugs: Policy and Politics*, eds. R. Lart, P. Higate and R. Hughes (Maidenhead: Open University Press, 2006), pp.92-112; S. MacGregor, *Drugs and British Society: Responses to a Social Problem in the 1980s* (London: Routledge, 1989); S. MacGregor *Drugs Services in England and the Impact of the Central Funding Initiative* (London: ISDD, 1990).

6. G. Stimson, 'AIDs and Injecting Drug Use in the United Kingdom, 1987–1993: The Policy Response and the Prevention of the Epidemic' *Social Science & Medicine* 41 (1995), pp.699-716.

7. B. Thom, *Dealing with Drink; Alcohol and Social Policy* (London: Free Association Books, 1999), pp. 193-95.

8. DHSS, *Drinking Sensibly*, (London: HMSO, 1981); DHSS, *White Paper: Promoting Better Health* (London: HMSO, 1987). See also R. Baggott, *Health and Health Care in Britain* (London: Macmillan, 1994), p.204.

9. Royal College of General Practitioners, *Alcohol: A Balanced View. Reports from General Practice 24*, (London: Royal College of General Practitioners, 1986); Royal College of Physicians, *A Great and Growing Evil: The Medical Consequences of Alcohol Abuse*, (London: Royal College of Physicians, 1987); Royal College of Psychiatrists, *Our Favourite Drug*, (London: Tavistock, 1979).

10. Richard Smith, one of the medical experts from the Royal College of Surgeons involved in setting the unit system recommendations, years later made comments to *The Times* newspaper suggesting the drink limits had been 'plucked out of the air;" *The Times*, October 20th 2007.

11. B. Thom, *Dealing with Drink: Alcohol and Social Policy*, pp.128-129.

12. While a few reports of controlled drinking outcomes had occasionally appeared in the scientific literature before 1962, most commentators date the beginning of the controlled drinking controversy to the publication that year of a paper by British psychiatrist D.L Davies, 'Normal drinking in recovered alcohol addicts', *Quarterly Journal of Studies on Alcohol,* 23 (1962), pp. 94-104. In this paper Davies reported that, in the course of long-term follow-up of patients treated for 'alcohol addiction' at Maudsley Hospital in

London, seven of the 93 patients investigated had subsequently been able to drink normally for periods of seven to 11 years after discharge from hospital. Other notable studies on the topic include the US study of M.B. Sobell and L.C. Sobell, 'Alcoholics Treated by Individualized Behaviour Therapy:One Year Treatment Outcome,' *Behav Res Ther* 11 (1973) ; followed by their 'Second Year Treatment Outcome of Alcoholics Treated by Individualized Behavior Therapy: Results,' *Behav Res Ther* 14 (1976) ; Also D.J. Armor, J.M. Polich and H.B. Braiker, 'Rand Report: Alcoholism and Treatment,' (1976) ; and G.R Caddy and S.H Lovibond, 'Self-Regulation and Discriminated Aversive Conditioning in the Modification of Alcoholics' Drinking Behaviour,' *Behaviour Therapy* 7 (1976), pp.223-300.

13 N. Heather and I. Robertson, *Controlled Drinking*, (New York: Methuen, 1981); N. Heather and I. Robertson, *Problem Drinking: The New Approach* (Harmondsworth: Penguin Books, 1985).

14 The increasing acceptability of controlled drinking programmes was highlighted in a survey carried out by Nottingham based researchers H. Rosenberg, J. Melville, D. Levell and J. E. Hodge, 'A 10-Year Follow-up Survey of the Acceptability of Controlled Drinking in Britain,' *Journal of Studies on Alcohol* (1992), pp. 441-446.

15 This shift influenced a movement in the United States and UK towards matching clients to treatment. See L. Lindstrom, *Managing Alcoholism: Matching Clients to Treatment* (Oxford: Oxford University Press, 1992).

16 J. Kendall and M. Knapp, *The Voluntary Sector in the United Kingdom* (Manchester: Manchester University Press, 1996); A. Mold and V. Berridge, 'Crisis and Opportunity in Drug Policy: Changing the Direction of British Drug Services in the 1980s,' *Journal of Policy History* 19 (2007), pp.29-48.

17 P.M. Strong, 'Doctors and Dirty Work - the Case of Alcoholism,' *Sociology of Health and Illness* 2 (1980); B. O'Hagan, *The History of UK Charity*, (London: PNN Online, 2001).

18 Philip McLean interviewed by Jane McGregor, August 2007.

19 J.A Giggs, P. Bean, D. Whynes and C. Wilkinson, "Class a Drug Users: Prevalence and Characteristics in Greater Nottingham," *British Journal of Addiction*, 84 (1989), pp.1473-80.

20 McLean interview

21 Personal Communication: Philip McLean, October 2008.

22 Philip McLean interview

23 For discussion of changes in the health sector see T. Rathwell, *Strategic Planning in the Health Sector* (London: Routledge, 1987).

24 The planning teams were widely established throughout England and covered five basic client groups; the elderly, mentally ill, children, learning disabilities and maternity/family planning.

25 DHSS, *Care in Action* (London, HMSO, 1981). A majority of team members were doctors. Community health councils (CHCs) also had a representative but there was considerable variation between regions. For further reading; W. Kearns, K. Murray-Sykes and P. Mullen, 'District Planning Teams in England,' *Public Health* 96 (1982), pp. 86-95 and B. Thom, *Dealing with Drink*, pp. 193-195.

26 T.A. Booth, 'Collaboration between Health and Social Services: A Case Study of Joint Care Planning, *'Policy Polit* 19 (1981), pp.23-49; T. Rathwell, *Strategic Planning in the Health Sector*, p.9.

27 APAS archive: Executive Meeting Minutes, September 23rd 1981.

28 Personal communication: McLean, October 2009.

29 Personal communication: Nick Tegedine, Director of APAS (formerly NCA), October 2009.

30 DHSS document, *Sensible Drinking* (London: HMSO, 1981).

31 Ira Unell interviewed by Jane McGregor, April 2008.

32 Claire Grainger, Chief Executive of HLG, interviewed by Jane McGregor, July 2011.

33 D. Killeen, 'Housing and income' in *Youth Policy in the 1990s. The way forward*, eds. J. C. Coleman and C. Warren-Adamson (London: Routledge, 1992).

34 The community safety approach is sometimes defined as preventing, reducing or containing the social and environmental and intimidating factors that raise the level of fear of crime or affect people's quality of lives. It includes preventative measures that contribute to crime reduction and tackle anti-social behaviour.

35 This subject is comprehensively dealt with by M. Raco, 'Remaking Place and Securitising Space: Urban Regeneration and the Strategies, Tactics and Practices of Policing in the UK,' *Urban Studies* 40 (2003), pp.1869-1887.

36 J.A Giggs, "Mental Disorder and Ecological Structure in Nottingham," *Social Science and Medicine* 23 (1986), pp. 945-961; J.A. Giggs, 'Ethnic Status and Mental Illness in Urban Areas,' in *Health, Race & Ethnicity*, eds. T. Rathwell and D. Phillips (London: Routledge, 1986), pp.137-174; J.A. Giggs and D.K. Whynes, 'Homeless People in Nottingham,' *East Midlands Geographer* 11 (1988), pp.57-67.

37 For reports on mental health and homelessness see G. Harrison, 'Residence of Incident Cohort of Psychotic Patients after 13 Years of Follow Up' *British Medical Journal* 308 (1994), pp.813-816. Also D. Kingdon, 'Implications of Social Policy,' in *Homelessness and Mental Health*, ed. D. Bhugra (Cambridge: Cambridge University Press, 1996), pp. 267-295.

38 Home Office, *Report on the 'Habitual Drunken Offender'*, (London: HMSO, 1971) and Home Office, *Working Party on Vagrancy and Street Offences Working Paper*, (London: HMSO, 1974). P. Archard, *Vagrancy, Alcoholism and Social Control* (London: Macmillan 1979).

39 DHSS circular 21/73. This dealt with community services for alcoholics.

40 The following reports had some bearing on developments; *The Pattern and Range of Services for Problem Drinkers. Report by the Advisory Committee on Alcoholism*, (London: HMSO, 1978); The House of Commons Expenditure Committee, *Reduction of Pressure on the Prison System, England*, (London: House of Commons, 1978); *The House of Commons, Third Report from the Home Affairs Committee, Session 1979-80: Deaths in Police Custody, (16 June),* (London: House of Commons, 1980).

41 M. Crane and A.M. Warnes, 'Wet Day Centres in the United Kingdom: A Research Report and Manual,' (Sheffield: Sheffield Institute for Studies on Ageing, University of Sheffield on behalf of The King's Fund and Homelessness Directorate, 2003).

42 Ibid

43 Philip McLean interview

44 The group comprised members of APAS, Probation and Police Services Nottinghamshire Association for Mental Health and Nottingham Help the Homeless Association (NHHA) and was chaired by Philip McLean from the Nottingham Alcohol and Drug Team.

45 B.D. Hore, 'The Manchester Detoxification Centre,' *British Journal of Addiction* 75 (1980), pp.197-205; N. Kessel, B.D. Hore, J.D. Makenjuola, A.D. Redmond, C.J. Rossall, D.W. Rees, T.G. Chand, M. Gordon and P.C. Wallace, 'The Manchester Detoxification Service. Description and Evaluation' *Lancet.* 1 (1984), pp.839-842.

46 Philip McLean's personal collection of letters and minutes: Report of Alcohol Strategy Working Group, February 20th 1989.

47 Philip McLean's personal collection of letters and minutes: Minutes of meeting; JPTSA: Alcohol Strategy Working Group, July 11th 1989.

48 Philip McLean's personal collection of letters and minutes: Letter from Clerk of the County Council and Chief Exec A. Sandford, November 13th 1989.

49 Ira Unell interview

50 Philip McLean's personal collection of letters and minutes: Letters from NHHA dated May 27th 1988, August 9th 1988, November 14th 1988 and June 1st 1989, Memorandum from the Estates Officer dated August 17th 1989; Memorandum from the Principle Welfare Rights Officer and Principle Officer (Homelessness and Accommodation), June 21st 1989.

51 'Handel Street day centre for homeless drinkers opened', *Nottingham Evening Post*, February 14th 1990.

52 Michael Varnam was involved in the project from the start. He died in April 2006. The hostel was subsequently renamed 'Michael Varnam House' with the overall project, 'Michael Varnam Service'.

53 K. Smith, *Wet Day Centres for Street Drinkers,* (Sheffield Institute for Studies on Ageing, Community Sciences Centre, 2004); M. Crane and A. Warnes, 'Wet Day Centres in Britain,' *Drug and Alcohol Findings* (2005), pp.24-29.

54 Parliament approved reorganisation in 25 counties. The subsequent process of restructuring occurred between 1995 and 1998

55 In 1997 the incoming Labour government created the Social Exclusion Unit (SEU), situated within the Prime Minister's Cabinet Office, to prioritise the key social issues. Rough sleeping was selected as a high priority and the RSU was created, headed up by a 'homelessness tsar'.

56 In 2010, its final full year of operation, a total of 1,163 individuals utilised Handel Street and its extensive services.

6

'DRUNKEN YOBS AND AGGRESSIVE BEGGARS': THE 1980s

Community and medical views of what constituted the local alcohol problem became more divergent during the 1980s. Whereas the older homeless drinker continued to be important to psychiatrists and others working in the alcohol treatment sector, the problem for police switched fully to youth. A day of mass arrests in the summer of 1980 of skinheads, punks and habitual drunks in Nottingham's Old Market Square signified the new approach and behind the new framing lay a growing consensus that exposure of young people to the destructive dangers of the streets turned them into hooligans. Factors fuelling concern about young people at that time included social unrest, high youth unemployment, a new pattern of youth mobility and homelessness, and an emerging problem of drugs misuse. Concern reached new heights in the late 1980s, when Government moved to relax licensing restrictions (the Licensing Act 1988). This brought the prospect of 'all day' drinking, and caused considerable unease, especially over the likelihood of the situation increasing the extent of underage and youth drinking. But though many pubs stayed open during the afternoons following the Act's introduction, there was no indication that the drinking public was going overboard, or any sign of unruly mobs, as was feared by some pub landlords. Consequently, and in somewhat of an ironic twist, the unpredicted outcome bolstered radical plans to turn Nottingham into a '24 hour' city.

National developments

Government gave considerable attention to so called 'normal' drinkers because of an increase in overall alcohol consumption.[1] The main driver of this increase was not from beer drinking, which remained at similar levels to the 1950s, but from increased consumption in other forms, including cider and perry, spirits and wine. Increasing alcohol consumption in women from 1978 to 1985 was reported, with the drinking patterns of women more closely resembling men's.[2] Yet conversely, consumption among working class males declined during the same period,[3] because duty on beer rose, as did value added tax (VAT). In addition, a social life beyond the pub began to emerge. Improvements in housing helped break the association between poor housing and heavy drinking, and television persuaded many to stay at home.[4] Home consumption became a real alternative to visiting the pub and this shift saw 'take-home' sales of beer increase. Take-home sales rose from five per cent of total sales in 1960 to twelve per cent by 1980, with supermarkets accounting for about half of all sales.[5] In response to these changes, the drinks industry improved their pubs to maintain sales and introduced keg beer (draught and canned) supported by national advertising campaigns. Changes in the law encouraged the growth of supermarkets and brewers saw off-sales as an alternative market, investing in off-licenses, distilleries and soft drink producers. Pubs meanwhile responded by offering a wider choice of drinks and food. Food accounted for a greater share of turnover, so much so that alcohol sales represented just under two-thirds of total pub spending by the end of the 1980s.[6] Pub ownership also changed. A growing trend was for breweries to run their pubs directly, employing a salaried manager. Most such breweries controlled hundreds of pubs in a particular region of the UK, whilst a few spread nationally. The beer selection in tied houses was mainly limited to beers brewed by that particular company. But in 1989 the Monopoly and Mergers Commission declared that brewers owning tied retail outlets were operating a complex monopoly. As a result that same year Parliament issued the Supply of Beer (Tied Estate) Order and The Supply of Beer (Loan Ties, Licensed Premises and Wholesale Prices) Order. The Beer Orders, as these were commonly known, restricted the number of tied pubs that could be owned by large brewery groups in the UK to 2000, and required large brewer landlords to allow 'guest' ale to be sourced by tenants from someone other than their landlord. The industry responded by creating spin off pub-owning companies or 'pubcos'[7], from the older brewing-and-owning companies (notably Allied Lyons, Bass, and Scottish & Newcastle) though many breweries were absorbed by larger companies in the food, hotel or property sectors.[8] At the same time, the number of customers was falling, so the competition between major suppliers was much fiercer.[9] More policy changes came at the end of the 1980s with a move that relaxed restrictions on licensing. The Licensing (Restaurant Meals) Act 1987 provided for the sale of liquor without the restriction of normal licensing hours and hours were extended the following year (Licensing Act 1988), allowing pubs to remain open in the afternoons. Traditionalists opposed the move, but others hoped it would allow a more leisurely approach to drinking. These changes entirely transformed the drink industry.

Given the considerable changes in the drink milieu, it is surprising that UK *per capita* alcohol consumption remained unremarkable in comparison with other countries of a comparable size and income level at that time, and well below historic levels such as those in the eighteenth or very early twentieth century.[10] This made the growing concern about underage and adolescent drinking all the more surprising. Though a succession of 'moral panics' amplified in the popular media led to public concern about an 'epidemic' of alcohol misuse by young people, the research evidence did not sustain this popular supposition, for the pattern of youth drinking actually altered very little in the period and a succession of studies indicated the normality and moderation of alcohol consumption among the age group.[11] Nevertheless the issue added to a series of other 'crises' about young people, including concern over the rising level of illicit drug use among young people, and a correlating rise in crime.[12] Adding to the woes, a new pattern of youth mobility and homelessness emerged, linked to political and social changes of the era.[13]

When Margaret Thatcher became Prime Minister in 1979 the new Conservative government increased value added tax (VAT) to nearly double its previous rate. Then in 1981 taxes were put up despite a recession. At the same time government also introduced successive benefit cuts which reduced the eligibility of young people to claim state assistance. These policy shifts, coupled with high levels of unemployment, which peaked at three million between 1979 and 1983, hit the 18-24 age group especially hard.[14] The government's second term of office was punctuated by periods of major industrial action, most notably the Miner's Strikers of 1984-5. The strikes against pit closures became symbolic of the battle between the trade unionist movement and Government's free-market programme and ended bitterly, with many coal mining areas becoming scenes of social devastation, as pit after pit in different parts of the country was closed down. Often mining was the only real employment in those areas. But the impact of the strike went beyond the miners and their communities. With the decline of manufacturing so began the process of restructuring regional economies and the transformation of the structure and nature of the UK economy, which increasingly placed importance on the service sector.[15] It was during this period of economic turmoil that headlines proclaimed that an epidemic of youth violence had begun. This view prevailed especially after riots in a number of UK cities, including London, Liverpool and Nottingham erupted in 1981. Sparked by racial issues, these saw young people on the defensive. A subsequent report on the issue, the Scarman Report, found racial disadvantage 'a fact of current British life'.[16] Then a wave of nationalist support was prompted by the Falklands Conflict, fought in 1982 between Argentina and the UK over the disputed Falkland Islands in the South Pacific. The war resuscitated a sense of antagonism towards foreigners interfering in British interests. Patriotism spilled over to the football terraces, with followers of the England national football team especially unwilling to accept the country's new international positioning; economically outstripped by emerging nations and defeated war enemies, especially after the British Government revived images of empire and triumph in war. Hooliganism accordingly was about defensive patriotism in the face of wider national decline but also the drunken hooligan was a fitting scapegoat for the disorder of the times.[17] Much like earlier versions of the 'hooligan', the 1980s version was characterised as working class and 'trouble'.[18] Football stadiums became identified as a place where fights could easily take place and youths from working class housing estates of the major cities identified as those most likely to stir up trouble. Though the new version was closely associated with drunken violence, the level to which drink actually contributed to the violence of the era remains difficult to determine. Nevertheless, this did not deter government, which introduced the Sporting Events (Control of Alcohol etc.) Act in 1985. This prevented drunken entry into a football ground, the consumption of alcohol within view of the playing area, consumption during the restricted period or in rooms within the grounds and even, in particular cases, on coaches, trains and motor vehicles travelling to a designated football match but the legislation only applied to football; there was an absence of restrictions in other sports including cricket and rugby.[19]

Nottingham: alcohol as a problem of young outsiders

Nottingham, in many respects, reflected the spirit of the 1980s. From the very beginning of the decade anxiety about young people was mounting. Marking this, more than one hundred arrests were made in one afternoon in July 1980 in the city centre. Skinheads, mods, rockers, punks and habitual drunks, all habitués of the Old Market Square, were arrested. Police responded to complaints about the *"unedifying spectacle of alcoholics lurching about drinking wine and cider and... lying on the bench urinating or vomiting in their stupor... and a litter of skinheads lying about the Council House steps."*[20] Nottinghamshire's Chief Constable, Charles McLachlan, said the problems signified *"a deterioration of standards which we have seen over the past decade or two... for which there is no easy answer."*[21] He was replying to complaints that it was unsafe to walk through the city centre not only after dark, but during daylight working hours. The problems are not peculiar to Nottingham, but apparently causing concern throughout the country, particularly in the larger conurbations. On the question of drunkenness, there were 479 arrests for drink offences in the city in the previous year (1979) but police believed arresting them did not necessarily solve the problem. The real question, they said, was what to do with these 'unfortunate' people.

Habitués of Old Market Square and the city centre

© Paul Fillingham and Christopher Richards

A particular view materialised over the course of the decade that young people, especially young 'outsiders', were the basis of the local alcohol problem. This had much more to do with an increase in visibility than it had to do with an actual increase in the size of the problem for in truth, the burden of responsibility for the rise in alcohol related problems should have been shouldered by adult drinkers in the community.[22] The increase in visibility of youth in the public domain was largely connected to new patterns of behaviour in this age group. At this time a new phenomenon, 'circuit drinking,' became a trend among young people that was widespread throughout the UK. This involved them congregating in large groups in the city centre rather than meeting in their 'local.' Drinking often started and finished in the popular city drinking circuits.[23] Where young people's consumption was seen to shift out of the 'private' sphere of family life and into public spaces; it added to existing concerns about youth.

Other factors affecting perceptions of youth included unemployment, homelessness and increased mobility. Unemployment levels were high at the local level and hit the 18-24 age group particularly badly.[24] In addition a new pattern of youth mobility emerged. This not only affected towns and cities in the UK but a number of European countries and some US states as well. The reasons remain uncertain but illicit drug use likely played a role.[25] The outcome was that in urban areas young people began to constitute the 'street people' and like other street people, they sparked anxiety. In particular, working class youth behaving in this way were looked upon as drifting and avoiding responsibility. In the early 1980s there were also fears that homelessness was a problem on the increase.[26] One local survey, carried out in September 1986 attempted to identify the baseline homeless population. From March 1985 to April 1986 over 1800 households were accepted as homeless; a fifty per cent increase on the previous year, and a total of 530 single homeless people were recorded.[27] It was feared that the young made up a significant proportion of this category. A study conducted two years later in 1988 found approximately 2,000 homeless seeking shelter within statutory and voluntary sector agencies in the city. About one-third of the homeless population were travellers/itinerant and under 30 years old.[28] Hostel workers speculated that the major reason for the increase in young single homelessness was stress in the nuclear family as a result of unemployment and poverty, and that young people were often escaping home because of violence, incest, parental alcohol and drug related problems and divorce. Young people in the homeless/itinerant category also were thought to be using illicit drugs, which led the police to deal with the problem of 'street people' in a more forceful way. But drug misuse was more widespread among young people in any case by the mid 1980s. In an interview conducted during the period, one police officer attributed this to the fact that *"the price [of heroin] has come down so much that it almost equates with a bottle of spirits."*[29] All these issues thus contributed to the growing perception that growing numbers of young people were out of control, hostile and dangerous.

Football and riots: intensified responses to youth

It was in this climate that a new kind of youth behaviour emerged in society, epitomised by a new kind of lawlessness. This was most consistently associated with football, where an atmosphere of aggression and violence materialised.[30]

This largely stemmed from a 'fear of the mob' mentality provoked by the governmental approach of the day specifically with regards to Falkland Islands but also over the troubles in Northern Ireland. Many commentators have argued that the mass media also played an important role in amplifying the occurrence and significance of football hooliganism. Indeed the issue became part of the circulation wars of the 1980s, when English tabloid newspapers became increasingly xenophobic in their coverage of foreign cultures. To that extent hooliganism within football was about confronting 'outsiders'. As such, football became something of a focus for the expression of racist sentiments among some young fans.[31] Whilst football hooliganism was not a feature of fans of the local clubs, Notts County and Nottingham Forest, the mass terrace affrays and running streets battles in the late 1970s and early 1980s did give rise to anxiety about visiting drunken fans.[32] As a consequence police numbers increased at football matches and crowd control measures were put in place for the first time.[33] Rising street disorder after football matches saw police attention turn to the management of busloads of fans from towns and cities like Mansfield, Sheffield, Doncaster and Derby. A television documentary *Saturday's Match*, in 1982 and featuring a Nottingham Forest home match showed the changes to policing practices and highlighted the increasing use of mounted police at football matches.[34]

Policing Notts County © North East Photographic Record

RIOTS AND OTHER HOSTILITIES

In another television documentary *'Under Pressure,'* aired in 1982, Nottinghamshire police were seen taking a hard line against groups of young troublemakers and rioters in the city.[35] Much of the trouble occurred around the 'Monkey Run' as licensees referred to the area around Bridlesmith Gate, in the city centre, where crowds of people tended to move from one pub to another. Publicans called for action, calling on city magistrates to use their powers to ban drunken hooligans from pubs in the area.[36] This response came only months after fights broke out on the streets in August 1980 when black youths were attacked by white youths.[37] Later copycat riots occurred in July 1981, and were imitated in other areas of the country (Liverpool and Notting Hill). Witnesses recalled rampaging mobs on Alfreton Road and Radford Road, with shop windows boarded up and premises set on fire, and police officers protecting themselves with dustbin lids.[38] In 1985/6 further disturbances took place after street searches by police caused widespread anger.[39] The riots added to concern about young people and city centre violence. They, like the threat of football hooliganism, provoked a strong police presence on Friday and Saturday evenings and the use of mounted police in the city centre at weekends. Yet these were not the only influences. The Miner's Strike of 1984 also contributed to the introduction of mounted police in the city centre. When flying pickets from other areas descended on Nottingham during the strikes and clashed with their colleagues, horses played a major role in dealing with the disputes and mounted units were deployed from several forces.[40] Local justices were unhappy about the move and called for the Council to get tough on the granting of licences instead, complaining that Nottingham had "...*the unique and unenviable reputation...of being the only city where mounted police have been used to keep public order at night-time on a regular basis*" [41] The police's reliance on using military style tactics to combat drunken disorder at that time met considerable public disapproval and confidence in them was at an all time low. This put police on the defensive, especially as during the period 1987/88 there was a sharp increase in late night disorder and arrests for drunkenness. Though not especially high, they were higher than any other period in the decade. Consequently, though many believed the use of mounted police was an intimidating way to keep law and order, police continued to use horses at weekends.

Courting youth: a U-turn on approach

In the mid and late 1980s though there were complaints about the antics of young people, many pub landlords still wanted to attract them in through their doors because the expansion of places to drink other than pubs, and the equally significant expansion of places to buy drink to consume at home, saw pub sales shrink. To compete some pubs tried harder to appeal to the younger crowd.

Often these pubs were redesigned as open plan to attract what the trade called a 'one drink visit'. Seating often was taken out altogether, and hi-tech games replaced traditional pub games. Doormen were installed to regulate customer flow outside some of the larger venues,[42] and quite a lot of public houses were bought up and run as managed pubs.[43] This led the local branch of CAMRA to claim that the large brewers' policy was to 'kill the public house'. This was a mirroring of national concerns about the power of the brewing industry that eventually led to both the Monopolies and Mergers Commission report and the 'Beer Orders' Act in 1989.[44]

Another factor affecting pubs was the price of beer, which began going up. Ale was seen as a diminishing market and pint prices rose as a result. Local brewery products had always been cheaper than the nationals, but the price of a pint of 'local Bitter' went up in 1980 by as much as 37 per cent in some cases (inflation was running at 16 per cent). Local ales from Home Brewery, Kimberley and Ansells in particular saw significant price increases.[45] The ale market was also affected by brewery closures and takeovers, and the economic recession, which was also beginning to bite, leading to job losses in some of the local breweries. For instance local brewer's Hardys and Hansons at Kimberley closed their bottling stores with a loss of twenty-one jobs because bottling had become unprofitable. Regional brewers faced an uncertain future, particularly after the national brewer's began re-introducing a range of cask beers with a regional identity in a bid to switch consumer preference away from the regional's products. Then there was the threat from canned take-home beer to consider.[46] A report in the *Notts and Derby Drinker*, the local CAMRA magazine, drew attention to the issue; *"A large number of beer adverts have started to appear over Nottingham heralding the arrival of CANVA (Real Value)...At first glance it appears this is a new organisation that sponsors lowering of their beer prices but on investigation it is the work of Whitbread, who wants you to buy their cheap canned take home beer."* [47]

Not only did pubs adopt new styles of refurbishment, in many cases pub names changed. The local branch of CAMRA was concerned that the city was losing its traditional pub names especially as some had historical significance. Shipstones was accused of being the worst offender and Whitley, the Warrington-based brewing giant which took over Shipstones in 1979 was accused of not taking into account local sensitivity. According to one local expert on Nottingham pub names, twenty-six pubs had lost their old names in little over four years.[48] In its local magazine CAMRA frequently bemoaned the fact. It described the New Wellbeck pub in the Victoria Centre being renamed 'Fitzroy's, as looking more like *'a boutique than a boozer with a blight of plastic foliage and Art Deco style,'* and suggested the Hole in the Wall on Shakespeare Street and its *'pink and grey décor, Venetian blinds and sparse seating'* gave it the appearance of a place *'... purchased from Habitat.'* [49]

CAMRA also was concerned with the rapid disappearance of good locals from the city centre pubs like the Crystal, which was regarded as an important part of the Nottingham scene. Its future looked uncertain, and there was planning in place for its conversion to shops which many feared would mean the death knell for the area, especially in the evenings when all the shoppers had gone home. But not all pub owners were in a state of inertia about the problem. Some began concentrating on a new marketing approach. An old Music Hall on St James' Street, which ran down its final curtain in 1913 and had stood as a derelict shell ever since was converted to a new drink venue in October 1983. The Old Malt Cross, as it was called, opened its doors again fully restored to its former glory, complete with a stage featuring regular entertainment, making it an unusual addition to the city's drinking scene. Other pubs mimicked the look of nightclubs. 'Pumps' for example, which was the new name given to the Exchange on the Poultry, by the side of the Council House in the Old Market Square. Two illuminated Shell petrol pump lamps in the entrance give a clue to the pub's title. The atmosphere was more akin to a plush nightclub than a pub and accentuated by bouncers on the door. It was designed to appeal to the younger set and provide a new and exciting venue. Pub and club owners completely overhauled former cinemas, social clubs and music halls to provide for a new customer base, the youth market. Premises near the Trent Polytechnic, located just north of Nottingham city centre were frequently chosen because they were likely to attract students living nearby. In the early 1980s an estimated extra six thousand students were anticipated when the Polytechnic applied for university status.[50] Combined with growing student numbers at Nottingham University, the presence of students in the drinking scene was considerable. As a result the city centre became an increasingly attractive proposition for businesses keen to target the reasonably affluent youth and student markets and by the end of the decade, effectively saw a wholesale move in location of the drinks trade to the city centre. Typical of these new venues were The Video Disco Bar, which became the Nottingham Palais' response to the growth of alternative dance music, screening pop videos to hundreds of young drinkers; Zhivago's, New York New York discotheque, Harvey's Bar, and the Variety Club on Radford Road, all of which were designed to appeal to affluent young people. Some instigated strict door policies that excluded male groups, underage drinkers, and drunkards, and many of the clubs began to employ doormen. Clubs towards the end of the decade catered specifically for the 'yuppie' contingent, whilst a small minority of bars gained reputations for permitting underage drinkers.[51]

  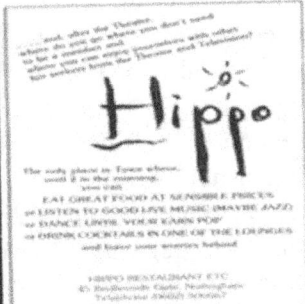

Local and national moves on licensing

The changes in the local drink scene resulted in a social trend for people to go out later at night. They tended to flock to the city centre, especially at weekends, which fuelled demand for later pub closing at 11pm. Unlike the 1970s when pub landlords generally opposed the move, they noted that on Friday and Saturday nights they got a lot of young people in, and their next stop was often a nightclub. Since the cost to get in to a nightclub was between three and five pounds and the drinks were more expensive, many saw there was a market in that area. In 1985 pub regulars were asked if they wanted longer licensing hours. City's magistrates considered the idea at a special Brewster Sessions meeting on March 8th that year. They wanted a flavour of public opinion. A group of local breweries and more than 20 private landlords had put forward a request for closing time to be switched from 10.30 to 11 pm on Fridays and Saturdays. A petition from nearly 5000 customers supported the proposal. As in the mid 1970s, the Licensed Victuallers Association (LVA) was afraid it would lead to more violence at closing time but the group calling for change argued that the basic reason was the pattern of trade had changed. The pubs are particularly busy on Fridays and Saturdays and the surrounding borders all closed at 11pm. The switch would benefit cinemas, restaurants and theatres and get people over the danger of using their cars to move on to a pub which served until later hours, they said.[52] But no change in licensing hours came as a result of this move, at least not without more ado. The City of Nottingham Licensing Justices decided not to grant an application for 11pm pub closing on Friday and Saturday nights, a situation that left Nottingham and Newcastle as the only two places in the country denied a modest relaxation of licensing laws. All three of the local breweries were in favour, local and national tourists backed the idea, police had no objections and many argued it would put an end to the scramble to leave the city in order to get late orders in adjoining areas. But as it was, the Justices were swayed more by concerns of city centre LVA activists who opposed longer hours of work for fear their staff would demand monetary compensation. [53]

Yet only a year later, in 1986, the issue came back to the fore. A motion backed by Rushcliffe Borough Council urged magistrates to change the licensing hours at weekends so the city could fall in line with the rest of the county. This was triggered by havoc caused by people rushing out of the city centre, which was thought to be getting worse especially in the surrounding villages of Ruddington and Gotham. Rushcliffe Borough Council was urged to call for the same closing throughout Nottinghamshire after violent attacks including one on Gotham's village policeman which led to four youths being charged with serious assault on a police officer.[54] This time, two local breweries; Shipstones and Home Brewery, petitioned regulars at pubs in the city centre to gain support for later drinking hours. Posters backing the move went up in more than three hundred pubs in the city and the Clerk to the licensing justices invited views from the public. The application, heard on 5th February 1987, was supported by the East Midlands Brewers Association and the regional LVA, who wanted *"to stop 'drinking-against-the-clock' and Le Mans style rush from one pub to another to get an extra half hour"*.[55] In the end, two applications were considered by the Licensing Committee. The first was from East Midlands Licensing Association, supported by Nottingham, Gedling and Rushcliffe Councils and a second application was backed by Nottingham Playhouse and the Barton Bus Company.[56] Notice of opposition was given by the National Association of Licensed House Managers, representing ninety members in Nottingham. All objections were finally overlooked when on 23rd February 1987, Guildhall licensing magistrates granted applications giving landlords the option to call time at 11pm Monday to Saturday and Shire Hall Magistrates granted extensions from Monday to Thursday bringing pubs in line with new city hours. CAMRA greeted the decision as *"victory for common sense"*,[57] though it brought a mixed reaction from pub managers, some of whom feared it would exacerbate city centre violence.[58]

The local decision to extend pub hours in the city in the spring of 1987 was no doubt influenced by changes to licensing nationally. Together with the slightly less ambitious Licensing (Restaurant Meals) Act 1987, the Licensing Act 1988 represented the first serious challenge to the framework of the Licensing Act 1964. The Act represented a substantial change to the licensing law applicable in England and Wales. The Licensing Act (Restaurant meals) 1987 applied to parts of licensed premises used as restaurants but the 1988 Act affected pubs more generally.[59] It gave pubs the option to stay open all day until 11pm and was widely regarded as a step forward in the liberalisation of alcohol licensing due to its removal of afternoon drinking restrictions. The changes ensured legal afternoon drinking in 125 of the city's licensed premises and meant restaurants or pubs which had part of their premises set aside for meals and a 'supper hours certificate' could sell alcohol for 13½ hours continuously from 10.30 in the morning until 12 midnight, Monday to Saturday. On Sundays alcohol sales were legal from 12 noon until 11.30pm. The requirement was that drink accompanied a substantial meal. The changes were broadly welcomed, celebrated as the time when the 'lock in' became history. However some publicans steadfastly resisted operating under extended hours. Publicans, especially those who ran pubs around the Old Market Square stoutly refused to do the 'continental thing', turning the Square into *'a plaza of drinking palaces with tables and umbrellas to match'*.[60]

The big city makeover

A watch was kept on the change to the drink environment and its effects. A reporter of the *Nottingham Evening Post* spent time absorbing the atmosphere in the city at night and reported back that;*"Youths hang out in gangs of up to 16... The social scene is really one of a revolving pub crawl...The old Market Square serves as a focal point. I saw drunkenness but no violence... no mass battles with police ... the situation in Nottingham is under control."*[61] Police monitored drink related crime to ascertain whether any upsurge in problems followed the changes. Though many city centre publicans feared the hooligan element would be enticed by all-day drinking, there were positive early signs that the lifting of restrictions on licensing had little effect on crime as there was no dramatic increase even after football matches.[62] Crime data for the period suggests the rate of arrests for drunkenness went into decline, for though arrests peaked prior to the licensing changes (1987/88), afterwards and until they end of the decade they fell into quick decline.[63] Police were given extended powers under the Licensing Act 1988 to monitor licensed premises and object to licensing applications and renewals.[64] The Act also increased the number of licensing sessions from one per annum to seven, affording magistrates more opportunities to revoke licenses, a shift that satisfied police that the instruments of the Act would ensure and put pressure on licensees to keep their establishments in order. The city centre was now increasingly regarded as a more effectively managed domain, a situation that provided the Council with fresh impetus and wherewithal to attempt to revive the jaded local economy. Thus in the late 1980s the city embarked on a period of extensive modernisation, with the Council specifically encouraging entrepreneurialism in its tourist and night entertainment trade.[65] The move, a trend noticeable in a number of major UK cities in the late 1980s, afterwards led to a proliferation of large fashionable bars, pubs and clubs in Nottingham's city centre. However fear about city centre disorder and violence in the city was never far away. One of the issues affecting the situation and highlighting Nottingham's problems in this regard was change in the way crime was reported. Before the 1980s, very little data had been systematically collected in England and Wales on offences not reported to, or recorded by, the police. However, in 1982, following the lead set in the United States a decade earlier, the Home Office carried out the first British Crime Survey (BCS),[66] a survey of households across England and Wales, which clearly demonstrated that only a minority of incidents that are recognized as 'crimes' by their 'victims' end up in the official statistics.[67] The BCS has been repeated many times since and become as important as police-generated statistics on crime. One drawback to the approach was that subsequent reporting of local crime figures by the mass media gained the city a reputation for disorder, which threatened to put off tourists and new business. This was one of the reasons why Nottingham signed up to the Safer Cities initiative when it was announced in 1988. The initiative belonged to a set of initiatives under the 'community safety' approach that had gained favour at around this time,[68] its aims to reduce crime, reduce fear of crime, and establish safer cities where economic enterprise and community life could flourish.[69] In consequence to the initiative, police helped the Council move things forward by cranking up their 'clean up' operations, removing the young homeless and beggars out and away from the city centre and backing the development of Handel Street wet centre, envisaged as a dumping ground plus better alternative to the streets.[70]

Considerable efforts by the Council helped create the right conditions for enterprise to flourish. Nottingham joined the 'English Cities Marketing Group' along with twelve other cities in order to promote the city as a holiday destination. The Council's popular 'away break' weekends featured in the scheme and Lord Young, the then Secretary of State for employment, singled it out, praising it for its job-creating potential.[71] The late night entertainment sector initially centred round the Old Market Square area but began to extend to the previously run down area of the Lace Market area.[72] The policy of the

Council at this time was to encourage the letting of properties to avoid the city centre becoming a ghetto of empty buildings. People who sought to rent these were often small businesses, sometimes linked to Nottingham's Trent Polytechnic. The Polytechnic had a very active art and design section which spawned many new businesses such as printers, clothes and fashion designers including Paul Smith, who started in this area. The large warehouses and factory buildings were used during the daytime for small businesses and at night-time the larger spaces between the buildings were taken over as licensed premises by entrepreneurs operating as independents. Initially the breweries were not interested in these areas. The Council persuaded the local justices to adopt a fairly open-minded approach to dealing with licensing applications. This resulted in an increase in 'Special Hours Certificates' for venues fulfilling the local criterion, requirements that involved the venue providing music, dancing and food, employing door staff and meeting the requirements of the Licensing Act as well as health and safety standards.

As a result of the lenient approach, the development of new forms of licensed premises was rapid and licensing magistrates were soon criticized for being too lenient in relation to handing out licences. But licensing magistrates hit back, calling on the Council to clamp down on night club licences, and slammed the behaviour of young people for the growing incidents of crime and violence in the city centre at weekends. In a letter to the city's chief executive Michael Hammond, the clerk to the city justices said the Council needed to get tougher with regard to granting entertainment licences; *'the committee feel the public at large will have to pay the price in the end and the city's reputation will be impaired by further public order difficulties. The city council is asked to examine all applications for public entertainment licenses equivalent to the former music and dancing licences, with care.'*[73] Meanwhile it was estimated that up to 30,000 were on the streets after the pubs closed on Friday and Saturday nights, leaving a situation where according to the local newspaper; *'Nowhere in the UK is there such a concentration of licensed outlets, propriety clubs, late night drinking establishments terminating at midnight as there are in the central square mile of Nottingham'*.[74]

Conclusions

The problem of drink, as seen from the perspective of the local community especially the Establishment, began to mutate from a problem of vagrancy to an issue of youth during the 1980s. Crime, homelessness and dereliction affected the way public drunkenness was viewed and these became important factors in the reconstruction of the problem of drink as one of youth. Additionally, drugs became a more important issue for police at the local level with government interest in that area intensifying, this issue eventually causing the break-up of the medical-penal alliance over drink. Drink and drunkenness were less of an actual problem than they were perceived to be, particularly in the younger age groups for throughout the period youth consumption of alcohol remained low and relatively stable. Drunkenness also played less of a part in local disorder than was supposed, with arrest rates for drunkenness lower than the rates recorded for the 1970s and going into steep decline towards the end of the decade, indicating perhaps that the concern up to this point had been connected to the introduction of the Licensing Act, 1988 and fears over the prospect of all day drinking. But the surprising finding that the drinking public had not gone overboard with the introduction of extended drinking hours brought unexpected opportunities, and in the last few years of the decade the Council set about turning Nottingham into a '24 hour' city. From this point forward, young people became important to the success of the night-time entertainment economy, a realisation that prompted a turnaround of approach by the Council, a situation that would cause conflict between it and the police in their transactions over the night-time economy, as discussed in chapter eight.

Notes

1 DHSS, *Drinking Sensibly* (London: HMSO, 1981).For patterns and prevalence of drink see L. Smith and D. Foxcroft, *Drinking in the UK: an exploration of trends* (York: Joseph Rowntree Foundation, 2009).

2 G.C. Dunbar, and D.D Morgan, 'The changing pattern of alcohol consumption in England and Wales 1978–85', *British Medical Journal Clinical Research Edition*, 295 (1987) , pp. 807–10; K.M. Fillmore, *When Angels Fall – Women's Drinking as Cultural Preoccupation and as a Reality* (New York: Guildford Press, 1984).

3 T.R. Gourvish and R.G. Wilson, *The British Brewing Industry 1830-1980* (Cambridge: Cambridge University Press, 1994), p.457.

4 J.D. Pratten, 'The Development of the UK Public House: Part 2: Signs of Change to the UK Public House 1959-1989' *International Journal of Contemporary Hospitality Management* 19 (2007), pp. 513-519.

5 T.R. Gourvish and R.G. Wilson, p. 457. See also Brewers' Society, *Statistical Handbook* (London: Brewers' Society, 1980).

6 J.D. Pratten, 'The Development of the UK Public House: Part 2,' pp. 513-519.

7 A 'pubco' is a company involved in the retailing but not the manufacture of beverages, while a pub chain may be run either by a pubco or by a brewery. If the owning company is not a brewery, then the pub is technically a 'free house', however limited the manager is in his/her beer-buying choice.

8   J.D. Pratten, 'The Development of the Modern UK Public House: Part 3: The Emergence of the Modern Public House 1989-2005' *International Journal of Contemporary Hospitality Management* 19 (2007), pp. 612-618.

9   T.R. Gourvish and R.G. Wilson, p.558; C. Lewis, 'The Future of British Brewing: Strategies for Survival,' *Strategic Change* 10 (2001), pp.151-61.

10 J.A. Spring and D.H. Buss, 'Three centuries of alcohol in the British diet,' *Nature* 270, no. 5638 (1977), pp. 567–572.

11 D. Lister Sharp, 'Underage Drinking in the United Kingdom since 1970: Public Policy, the Law and Adolescent Drinking Behaviour,' *Alcohol and Alcoholism* 29 (1994), pp. 555-563; C May, 'A Burning Issue? Adolescent Alcohol Use in Britain 1970-1991,' *Alcohol and Alcoholism* 27 (1992), pp. 109-15; R. Room and M. Järvinen, *Youth Drinking Cultures: European Experiences, 13* (Aldershot, Hamps, Ashgate, 2007), p.5.

12 The total number of drug offenders more than doubled over the period 1982-92, with offenders under the age of twenty-one accounting for about half the increase - Statistical source: Home Office Statistical Bulletin 30/93.

13 For literature on homelessness in the era: J. Wardhaugh, *Sub City: Young People, Homelessness and Crime* (Aldershot: Ashgate, 2000); S. Hutson and M. Liddiard, 'Youth Homelessness: Marginalising the Marginalised?' in *Towards a Classless Society?* ed. H. Jones (London: Routledge, 1997), pp. 96-120; S. Ruddick, 'Modernism and Resistance: How ' Homeless' Youth Subcultures Make a Difference,' in *Cool Places: Geographies of Youth Cultures*, eds. G. Valentine and T. Skelton (London: Routledge, 1998), pp. 344-362.

14 N. Pleace and D. Quilgars, 'Youth Homelessness,' in *Young People, Housing and Social Policy*, ed. J Rugg (London: Routledge, 1999), p.93-108.

15 This sector involves the transport, distribution and sale of goods from producer to consumer, as may happen in wholesale and retail, or may involve the provision of a service, such as entertainment.

16 The Brixton disorders, April 10th-12th 1981: *Scarman report: report of an inquiry* (London, Home Office, 1981).

17 For literature on football hooliganism: E. G. Dunning, P. Murphy and J. Williams, *The Roots of Football Hooliganism* (London: Routledge, 1988); S. Frosdick and P. Marsh. *Football Hooliganism.* (Devon: Willan Publishing, 2005). J. Williams and S. Wagg, *British Football and Social Change*, (Leicester: Leicester University Press, 1991).

18 The term 'hooliganism' came into common usage in 1898 when gangs of rowdy youths in London during August bank holiday celebrations resulted in more than usual number of arrests for drunken disorder and fighting. For literature on the hooligan: G. Pearson, *Hooligan. A History of Respectable Fears* (London: Macmillan, 1983); G. Pearson, 'Victorian Boys. Here We Are! [1983],' in *The Subcultures* Reader, eds. K. Gelder and S. Thornton, *The Subcultures Reader, Alcohol and Addiction* (London: Routledge, 1997), p.266;

19 T. Collins and W. Vamplew, *Mud, Sweat and Beers, a cultural history of sport and alcohol* (Oxford: Berg, 2002), p. 87.

20 'Bid to clean up city centre of nuisances,' *Nottingham Evening Post*, July 3rd 1980.

21 Ibid

22 Consumption was thought to have risen by as much as 44 per cent in the East Midlands during the 1980s; D. Cameron, *Liberating Solutions to Alcohol Problems* (London: Jason Aronson, 1995) pp.180-181; E. Goddard and C. Ikin, *Drinking in England and Wales in 1987* (London: HMSO, 1988). Older drinkers were more likely to be arrested for drink driving as well as experience alcohol related health conditions such as liver disease and alcohol related psychosis.

23 This national trend is reported on by Gofton, L,. 'On the town: Drink and the 'new lawlessness,' *Youth and Society* 29 (1990): pp.33-39; F. Coffield and L. Gofton, *Drugs and Young People* (London: Institute for Public Policy Research, 1994) p.10.

24 J.A. Giggs, 'Housing, Population and Transport,' in *A Centenary History of Nottingham*, ed. J.V. Beckett (Manchester: Manchester University Press, 1997), p.453.

25 A US study found the problem was associated with a wide variety of problems including depression, prostitution, and drug use; G. L. Yates, R. Mackenzie, J. Pennbridge and E. Cohen, 'A Risk Profile Comparison of Runaway and Non-Runaway Youth.,' *American Journal of Public Health* 78 (1988), pp.820-821.

26 Nottingham Homelessness statistics, 1981-1999, Housing Aid, Nottingham City Council. Local homelessness data does not include information about age until the 1990s.

27 *Notts Welfare Rights Newsletter*, April 1987; 'Single and Homeless' survey. Part of a report by the Bishop of Sherwood's Inquiry into Housing.

28 J.A. Giggs and D.K. Whynes, 'Homeless People in Nottingham,' *East Midlands Geographer* 11 (1988), pp. 57-67; D.K. Whynes, 'Mobility and the Single Homeless,' *Area* 23 (1991), pp. 111-118; D.K. Whynes and J.A. Giggs, 'The Health of the Nottingham Homeless,' *Public Health* 106 (1992), pp. 307-14.

29 Nottingham Central Library, Local Studies Library: Transcript of A87 e-I from the Oral History Collection project 'Making Ends Meet' recorded 1982-84 for Notts Libraries. Tape A 87 side g.

30 J. Muncie, *Youth and Crime: A Critical Introduction* (London: Sage, 2004) pp. 3-8

31 S. Wagg, 'Playing the past: the media and the England football team' in J. Williams and S. Wagg (eds) *British Football and Social Change* (Leicester: Leicester University Press, 1991). See also J. Kerr, *Understanding Soccer Hooliganism* (London: Routledge, 1994)

32 Nottingham Forest Football Club is an English professional football club based at the City Ground in West Bridgford, Nottingham. Notts County Football Club is the oldest league football club in the world, formed in 1862.

33 S. Frosdick and P. Marsh. *Football Hooliganism*. (Devon: Willan Publishing, 2005), pp.135-6 & 180. In 1989 it was usual for Nottingham Forest to have about 150 police officers in the ground.

34 Televised programme, 'Saturday's Match' was the fifth in a series of six films, showing preparations being made for a match by police. Transmitted by Central Television in 1982.

35 Another televised series by Central Television, 'Under Pressure,' was broadcast in 1982.

36 'Pub violence', *Nottingham Evening Post*, January 30th 1981.

37 A. Simpson, *Stacking the Decks: A Study in Racial Inequality in Council Housing in Nottingham*, (Nottingham: Nottingham and District Community Relations Council, 1981),

pp. 289-290; J.A. Giggs, 'Housing, Population and Transport,' in *A Centenary History of Nottingham*, ed. J.V. Beckett (Manchester: Manchester University Press, 1997), p.455.

38 Nottstalgia, 'The Nottingham Riots' (2008), available from http://nottstalgia.com/forums. (Cited July 8th 2011).

39 J.T. Benyon and J. Solomos, *The Roots of Urban Unrest* (Oxford: Pergamon Press, 1987) p.9; Nottingham Chief Constable's Annual Report, 1981.

40 For reading on the 'Miner's Strike'; M. Adeney, *The Miner's Strike 1984-5: Loss without Limit* (London: Routledge, 1986); R. Winterton and J. Winterton, *Coal, Crisis, and Conflict: The 1984-85 Miners' Strike in Yorkshire* (Manchester: Manchester University Press, 1989); S. McCabe and P. Wallington, *The Police, Public Order, and Civil Liberties: Legacies of the Miners' Strike* (London: Routledge, 1988).

41 'Crime increase blamed on too many nightclubs,' *Nottingham Evening Post* April 22nd 1987

42 L. Gofton, 'Folk Devils and the Demon Drink: Drinking Rituals and Social Integration in North East England,' *Drogalkohol* 12 (1988), pp.181-196.

43 'Notts businessman sells large leisure and pub empire,' *Nottingham Evening Post*, January 27th 1984; *Notts and Derby Drinker* Jan 1984 1, 1.

44 The Supply of Beer (Tied Estate) Order 1989 and The Supply of Beer (Loan Ties, Licensed Premises and Wholesale Prices) Order 1989, commonly known as the Beer Orders.

45 Notts and Derby Drinker, January 1980, 23.

46 R. Barrow, 'Beer Can History,' *Off License News* December 12th 1985. Relaxation of the licensing laws in the 1960s and the introduction of the ring-pull in 1967 meant more supermarkets sold alcohol. Sales increased in the UK, accounting for 81 per cent of all packaged beer in the take-home market by 1985.

47 *Notts and Derby Drinker*, February 1984 1, 2.

48 'Nottingham's lost pub names,' *Nottingham Evening Post*, August 3rd 1984.

49 *Notts and Derby Drinker*, February 1985 2, 2.

50 **Nottingham Regional College of Technology** was granted polytechnic status in 1970. The official name change to Trent Polytechnic took place in 1988. It gained university status in 1992.

51 The term 'yuppie' (short for "young upwardly-mobile professional") refers to a phenomenon of the 1980s and early 1990s. It was a term for financially secure, upper-middle class young people in their 20s and early 30s looking to advance socially and economically.

52 *Nottingham Evening Post*, February 8th 1985.

53 *Notts and District Drinker,* 2, 3 (1985)

54 'Junior health minister, Edwina Currie, challenged to look into claims that poverty is a major cause of ill health and premature death in Nottingham,' *Nottingham Trader* November 5th 1986

55 'Two breweries petition regulars at pubs,' *Nottingham Evening Post*, January 24th 1987; 'Bid to standardise licensing hours,' *Nottingham Journal* 10, January 30th 1987.

56 'Applications adjourned,' *Nottingham Evening Post*, February 5th 1987.

57 CAMRA had tried since 1976 to bring Nottingham's hours in line with other cities and had campaigned throughout the 1970s on this issue as discussed in chapter four.

58 'Chief constables give evidence,' *Nottingham Evening Post*, February 21st 1987.

59 D. Hobbs, P. Hadfield, S. Lister and S. Winlow, *Bouncers: Violence and Governance in the Night-Time Economy* (Oxford: Oxford University Press, 2003) p. 78.

60 The law stipulated beer could not be served outside unless it was with waiter service and customers were seated

61 'Thousands questioned about bangers, booze and smokes' *Nottingham Evening Post*, June 16th 1988.

62 'Afternoon drinking receives positive response,' *Nottingham Evening Post*, May 6th 1987; ' Landlords and police remain cautious as extended drinking hours come into force' August 23rd 1988; 'Fears unfounded,' August 31st 1988; and 'Nottingham Pubs need to apply for licence extensions over the holiday period,' December 2nd 1989.

63 'Fears unfounded,' *Nottingham Evening Post*, August 31st 1988.

64 In addition to previous arrangements, certain groups and individual members of the community had the right to apply to the magistrates to issue an order obliging licensees to close their pubs during the afternoons if staying open was causing a nuisance.

65 This is based on the level of coverage of the issue in the local press at this time (c.1987/8)

66 M. Hough and P. Mayhew *The British Crime Survey: First report* (London: Home Office, 1983)

67 M. Maguire, 'Crime data and statistics' in *The Oxford handbook of criminology*, 4th Edition eds. M. Maguire, R. Morgan, R. Reiner, (Oxford: Oxford University Press, 2007), p.242.

68 As discussed in chapter five, the 'community safety' approach involved preventative measures that aimed to reduce crime and tackle anti-social behaviour.

69 N. Tilley, *The prevention of crime against small businesses: the safer cities experience. Crime Prevention Unit Series Report No. 45* (London: Home Office Police Department, 1993).

70 The 'clean up' operation aimed to exclude those considered to be undesirable elements. Specific references to police operations are found in articles of the *Nottingham Evening Post*, 'High rise tenants claim drunken destitutes making lives a misery.' 2nd June 1989, and 'Day centre a 'dumping ground,' 14th February 1990.

71 'Joins English cities marketing group,' *Nottingham Arrow*, 109 October 1986.

72 L. Crewe and J. Beaverstock, 'Fashioning the City: Cultures of Consumption in Contemporary Urban Spaces' *Geoforum* 29 (1998), pp. 287-308; S. Tiesdell, 'Tensions between Revitalization and Conservation: Nottingham's Lace Market 'Cities 12 (1995), pp. 231-41.

73 'Crime increase blamed on too many nightclubs, '*Nottingham Evening Post*, April 22nd 1987.

74 Ibid

7

POLITICISATION AND FRAGMENTATION: ALCOHOL TREATMENT IN THE 1990s

With Government promoting ideas of community safety and emphasising the reduction of harm related to episodes of heavy drinking and intoxication, alcohol was shaping up as a policing and youth issue in the community. Yet in the treatment arena, responses largely remained focused on the few, and stayed firmly a health matter. As a consequence, the treatment arena was significantly affected by sweeping changes in the wider sphere of health and social policy, particularly with regard to new ways of procuring and funding provision. Additionally the sector was subjected to more formal procedures and greater direction from the centre. These changes formed part of a new 'top down' approach and had impacts not only on implementation but local relations. This chapter examines the changes taking place in health care by examining one specific local event; the arrival of a new private clinic, 'The Nottingham Clinic'. This was a test case for a new type of NHS public/private finance initiative, and is used here to illustrate the substantial changes and impacts on local treatment arising from the major changes underway in UK health and social care policy.

National policy development

Government concentrated little on alcohol treatment *per se* during the 1990s, focusing instead on drug misuse.[1] With little government interest the alcohol treatment sector therefore looked to medicine and other expert groups for direction. Expert advisory groups such as the Royal Colleges and groups like the 'New Directions in Alcoholism' group were influential at this time. The New Directions group promoted psychological perspectives of 'problem drinking', and was originally formed in the mid 1970s as a forum for people who had an interest in controlled drinking as a treatment goal for people with alcohol problems. It consisted of practitioners and researchers from the alcohol field. By the 1990s controlled drinking programmes established as an important element of treatment and moderation, as opposed to abstinence, an acceptable end goal of treatment.² This approach was compatible with the 'community safety' approach which developed as a way of tackling troublesome behaviour in communities. Alcohol was beginning to be shaped by economic and political processes in ways that saw it viewed as a problem not of the few but of the many, and a problem of anti-social behaviour. To that extent, responses borrowed from the drug and criminal justice sectors, such as models of harm reduction were put in place.³ These concerns are discussed extensively in chapter eight, which highlights the processes affecting society.

These issues, nevertheless, affected the way the alcohol treatment sector engaged with drink problems and led to the establishment of more community-based services. But what impacted upon the nature of treatment sector the most during the 1990s were changes arising in the wider sphere of health and social policy. In 1988, the Prime Minister Margaret Thatcher (1979-90) announced that the NHS would be reviewed, and what followed was the most significant cultural shift the NHS had experienced since its inception; the introduction of the so-called internal market. This was first outlined in the 1989 White Paper, *Working for Patients*,⁴ which passed into law as the *NHS and Community Care Act* (1990) during John Majors' time in office (1990-97). This Act kick-started a range of successive health and social care policies that encouraged the development of a competitive market designed to improve value for money within service delivery. One by-product of this competition was that services delivered by different organisations often worked in isolation as they competed directly against each other to secure service contracts.⁵ The former tasks of the District Health Authority (DHA) of purchasing and providing services were separated and instead they began to focus on purchasing health care for the populations they served. Alongside DHAs, GP fundholders purchased a limited range of services for their patients and under these arrangements both the DHAs and GP fundholders negotiated contracts to provide services of specified cost, quantity and quality of care.⁶ In addition, and initially out of concern about the level of public debt, pressure to change the standard model of procurement of public services arose. Government promoted the idea that private provision could be provided at no cost to the public and argued that a single private sector organisation should take responsibility for most aspects of service provisions. It thus duly set about making the NHS, as the identified public body in this circumstance, publicly accountable for essential aspects of health provision. Initially, most public-private partnerships were negotiated individually as one-off deals. However the Conservative government of John Major introduced the first systematic programme of private finance in 1992, which aimed at encouraging public-private partnerships.⁷

The changes in the way services were procured affected the alcohol sector profoundly. Services, be they non-statutory or statutory, found they were forced to compete for funding. And some areas of the sector, conspicuously residential care services, were especially hard hit. This was because local authorities were called on to develop strategies and services to respond to alcohol problems in local communities. Residential services, which had developed in the UK since the 1960s, typically were run by the charitable and private sectors and many operated from large country houses, where addicts would go for respite and rehabilitation. Many of the first wave rehabilitation centres in Britain were based on the principles of the therapeutic community (TC). By the late 1970s a number of Christian-based houses began to develop a more hard-edged, confrontative approach to the interactions between residents and staff.[8] The concept-based therapeutic communities accounted for almost half of the 250 residential rehabilitation beds for drug and alcohol addiction in the UK. These developments were, at least to start with, the result of the enthusiasm of a group of progressive psychiatrists; most of whom had been charged with the running of hospital-based addiction units and were inspired by their contact with American TCs, notably, Phoenix House. However by the 1980s, the influence of social psychiatry as well as the anti-psychiatry movement had put pay to direct medical involvement and the tools were now in the hands of lay practitioners and former addicts.[9] But the influence of the TC residential rehabilitation centre was also starting to wane, reflected in similar changes across Europe, and for broadly similar reasons. They were slow to adapt to the changing demography and struggled to compete with community-based services.[10] The backdrop to the situation was that in 1983, the British Government embarked upon a major central government funded pump priming initiative to establish a national network of drug treatment services, residential rehabilitation services were unable to secure more than 10 per cent of the new money, with the lion's share, 56.2 per cent, going to community services.[11]

What is more, the residential sector had grown significantly over the decades and was proving hard to sustain. For alongside the TC residential centres, a small number of Minnesota Method treatment centres had developed since the 1970s.[12] Broadway Lodge was one of the first, and opened in Weston-Super-Mare in 1974. Others, including Castle Craig Treatment Centre in Peeblesshire, Scotland opened in the mid and late 1980s.[13] Some delivered treatment for a whole host of addictions; eating disorders, gambling, alcohol and drugs. Then during the late 1980s and early 1990s, events in the US had impacts in the UK. US health insurance companies, though accustomed to paying for inpatient alcohol treatment programmes, began to refuse to fund patients in long stay, high cost treatments.[14] Because of this some private companies, many of which operated inpatient programmes of the Minnesota Model type, exported the model to other countries, including Britain. At the same time many of the existing residential rehabilitation centres in Britain, though operating for years under previous health and social care funding arrangements, began to adapt their programmes in light of health policy changes. These changes led to residential services adapting, improving treatments or risk fading away.[15] The model of treatment offered by the new Minnesota Model style inpatient units mostly were based on the disease concept of alcoholism, the treatment goal of abstinence and the principles of AA.[16] The Priory Hospital in North London, a private hospital specialising in the treatment of addiction which became well known as the rehabilitation centre of the famous, was bought by an American healthcare company at this time. Opening in 1986, it exemplified the new approach. Clinics and hospitals of this type had programmes that often consisted of an intensive inpatient stay of some weeks starting with detoxification followed by some or all of the following elements: group therapy, didactic lectures, use of recovering addicts or alcoholics as counsellors, multi-professional staffing, a therapeutic milieu, work assignment, daily reading groups, life history exposition, attendance at AA meetings, and recreational and physical activity. For those in the sector who had been moving responses towards tackling problem drinking over the last few decades, this new trend in inpatient alcoholism treatment was seen as a setback; a revival of an outmoded concept.

Nottingham: new developments versus established norms

Nottingham, in the policy climate of the late 1980s, exemplified these changes in the treatment sector. Around this time, Nottingham Health Authority made an unexpected move and announced there was going to be a new inpatient facility in the locality. The venture was going to be jointly funded by it and a private company, Regency Park. This was to be a test case in public-private finance (PFI). The new inpatient unit became known as the Nottingham Clinic. Most unusually, and this is where it differed from many of the other new treatment clinics and hospitals in the UK, it had the appearance of private healthcare yet represented free at source treatment to NHS patients.[17] The decision for the health authority not only to fund patient beds at the Nottingham Clinic but to enter into some sort of financial partnership was presented to the local treatment sector as a done deal, a *fait de compli*. Most in the existing treatment sector knew nothing about it. Ira Unell, a social worker from the local NHS alcohol and drug team recalled; "*Nobody knew, not even the people from public health who are employed by the health authority and who were on the committee. It came as a shock. The first time we heard about it, the deal was already signed.*"[18]

Up until this point the Nottingham Alcohol and Drug Team (NADT) had been the sole provider of inpatient treatment in the area. It was one of only a handful of the old regional hospital inpatient units still standing. Specialist alcohol services by this time had become a highly variable patchwork of provision. Services were often poorly coordinated and afforded low priority by planners. Regional units had become smaller with a more local focus, and many lost key functions such as training and research and development. NADT had experienced significant changes over time and now operated more on a city than countywide basis than previously, but remained a popular centre of referral for local health authorities including Lincolnshire and Derbyshire, and receiving additional referrals from some fundholding GPs.[19] Over time, the inpatient unit, outpatient and day services, now under the banner of Nottinghamshire Healthcare Trust, had joined forces with the forensic service within the Trust to form the Addiction and Forensic Directorate.[20] David Levell, the former director of the voluntary organisation, APAS, was appointed manager to the new directorate and psychiatrist Philip McLean, the clinical director of the drug and alcohol team.[21] A second community-based team was set up within a former Maltings at Mansfield, in the north of the county, to cater for people living at that end of the county.[22] The inpatient unit at Mapperley continued to provide assessment and facilities for detoxification, though GPs were increasingly expected to engage in the treatment of the problem drinker and models of shared care were developed, so the specialist staff from NADT could assist GPs in treating drinkers in the community.

Shared care most often involved the provision of outpatient or home detoxification with assistance from the GP, who became involved in prescribing detoxification regimens, whilst specialist community nurses visited patients in their homes. For service elements such as residential input or day care, local authorities looked to the non-statutory/voluntary sector where a plethora of different services had developed since the 1960s. The nature of the alcohol sector had altered substantially since its beginnings, with a greater mix of community provision as well as input from a wider range of professions and lay practitioners, mostly constituting volunteers and former drinkers. Because the sector had become so diverse GPs, especially fundholding GPs, were increasingly cautious about advising patients on treatment options. Since the 1980s, doctors in the UK had moved from a relatively protected position within the NHS, where clinical autonomy, social status and involvement in local health politics had been the norm, to a context in which the practice of medicine radically changed. One of their biggest concerns that affected clinical decision-making was a fear of being sued. The 'contract culture' and the new, but limited purchasing role of fundholding GPs played a significant part in the shift.[23] One consequence of this more cautionary approach of doctors that affected the alcohol treatment sector involved controlled drinking programmes and the viability of the approach as a treatment option for problem drinkers. Abstinence-based residential care providers were keen to amplify the concern because their own methods and position were also under some threat. A tug-of-war effectively broke out in 1992 when Castle Craig Treatment Centre in Scotland instructed lawyers to look into the question of liability in relation to controlled drinking arguing that; *"If such a body advocates the continued use of alcohol, albeit at a reduced 'controlled' level without advising the client to abstain completely until liver damage has been ruled out, then that body may well be liable."*[24] Because of this, GPs became more cautious about the services they referred patients to, or in the case of fundholding GPs, purchased under extra contractual referral (ECR) arrangements.

Birth of 'The Nottingham Clinic'

It was at the time of health policy upheaval and with question marks over the quality and efficacy of available treatments that one of these new style inpatient treatment centres emerged in Nottingham. Paradoxically, the move coincided with the publication of the Department of Health 1989 alcohol circular, which advised that the broad aim of government was to draw attention to well co-ordinated responses in harm prevention, reduction and treatment.[25] It advised that districts should take a single multi-agency approach so that services and resources could be more efficiently and effectively utilised to assess and meet local needs. The formation of local multi-agency groups to develop district alcohol strategies was supported nationally by both the Faculty of Public Health Medicine and the Health Education Authority and internationally by the World Health Organization's Regional Office for Europe.[26] At a meeting held in London with the directors of the Councils on Alcoholism, Department of Health representatives were unambiguous; *"We do not, in line with most current thinking, accept that alcohol abuse is, of itself, a medical condition and would strongly argue against heavy reliance on medical or quasi-medical models of response as the single plank of a local strategy."*[27] It was therefore surprising that Nottingham Health Authority focused on inpatient detoxification and quasi-medical intervention at this time, apparently against policy line.

The Nottingham Clinic was the brainchild of property developer Bob Beckett. A former alcoholic and benzodiazepine addict, he was admitted to hospital following an extended drinking binge. He recovered in a private London Minnesota Method clinic in 1987 after which he managed to stay abstinent. Determined to advance the Minnesota Method as the best way of treating addiction, Beckett subsequently went on to establish private Minnesota residential facilities in London. It was in 1988 that he approached a friend of his, Jim Lester, Broxtowe MP, and asked for an introduction to Nottingham Health Authority chairman.[28] He also involved Lord Mancroft, a fellow addict and Minnesota convert, and member of the all-party Parliamentary Committee for the Misuse of Drugs, in persuading the health authority that a new addiction treatment clinic was a good idea.[29] Lord Mancroft subsequently became deputy chief executive of the Clinic. This gained him the attention of politicians, with Keith Joseph, the former health secretary, keeping a close eye on developments.[30] For reasons unknown, the health minister of the time, Kenneth Clarke, who was MP for the Nottingham borough of Rushcliffe, was not informed or involved with the venture.[31] Nevertheless, Bob Beckett claimed he had backing from the top. In an interview for the *Nottingham Evening Post* in 1993 he proudly declared he had backing from the Prime Minister, Margaret Thatcher, claiming he had a letter from her about the time they signed the agreement with the health authority.[32]

The problem for the health authority was finding suitable business arrangements, for it was imperative that the authority's arrangements were sanctioned by the Department of Health. After a lot of wrangling, the health authority opted for a partnership arrangement. The purpose built clinic was registered in February 1988.[33] Based on Ransom Road in the St Ann's area of Nottingham, the facility had twenty-four beds, sixteen of which were available to private patients with the money helping to pay for NHS patients' treatment. It was opened in 1990 and received a favourable reception, especially from GPs and the criminal justice sector. The director of the Clinic, Adrian Lee, a former alcoholic, predicted; "*In five to six years time there will be six to ten modules [sic] like the Nottingham Clinic*". However there was considerable concern about it from other quarters, especially in terms of the legality of the move and whether or not a public body like the NHS could enter into such a financial partnership. When a draft document concerning the partnership between Regency Park (Beckett's company) and the health authority was sent to the Department of Health for approval, the two parties were already tied into a contract and had already spent £50,000 setting up the Clinic. Nottingham Health Authority owned the building, which it bought for £560, 000 for which the Clinic paid rent. Profits were to be divided between the health authority and the private company although the scale of these was unclear. In addition, the health authority was given access to eight beds for use by health authority residents. But just days before signing the partnership agreement the authority received a letter from the Department of Health, which clouded the legality of the arrangement. This moved the scheme from a low profile initiative with government backing, to a very public dispute about the conduct of a public body, the NHS.[34]

The Nottingham Clinic © Priory Group

This followed the district auditor carrying out a survey of the Clinic. This did not view the financial arrangements favourably; the auditor Kevin Chidgey stating in his report that the authority had *'fallen far below the standards expected of a public body'* having spent £1.8 million on a scheme that was supposed to be of no cost to the public.[35] The auditor advised the health authority who he said were faced *'with a salvage operation'* to *'unscramble the void agreement'*. On the basis of his report, the Department of Health ordered Nottingham Health Authority to stop funding the Clinic.[36] Nottingham Health Authority persisted for a while with the existing arrangements but over the following year tried to carve out an alternative agreement. No sooner had doubts about the legality of the agreement and validity of the project been expressed, than they were in the public domain. Throughout 1992-3 the press had a field day over the affair.[37] The BBC investigated the circumstances; the television programme *East Midlands Today* heavily criticising both the Clinic and Nottingham Health Authority.[38] It claimed that the health authority was spending almost half a million pounds a year on the Clinic. The programme also claimed the Clinic was coming under the scrutiny of private health insurers such as BUPA, who were not prepared automatically to agree in the future to cover treatment costs at the Clinic. In March 1993 *Private Eye* carried an article suggesting that a further auditor's report to the health secretary Virginia Bottomley had criticised the arrangement between the private company and Nottingham Health Authority; the auditor had again questioned the lawfulness of the agreement. Nottingham Health Authority issued a statement that the auditor report had substantial inaccuracies and asked for its withdrawal, but by this stage questions were being asked in Parliament.[39] John Heppell, MP for Nottingham East, put down a Commons motion asking whether the Secretary of State for Health would establish an inquiry into the establishment of the Nottingham Clinic and enquired whether the arrangements for the sale of the NHA share of the Clinic were in hand.[40]

One former Nottingham Health Authority official explained to me in the course of the research for this book that Nottingham Health Authority eventually withdrew from the partnership arrangement with the Clinic. The official suggested the authority had no option but to set aside the agreement because it was void. If they wished to continue with an access arrangement it could not be as a legal partner. In consequence, a new arrangement was constructed giving the health authority access to places at the Clinic on an item of service basis, but not exposed to the full implications of the Partnership Act (1896) provisions. An agreement set out the terms under which payments would be made to the Clinic for taking authority referrals and effectively shifted the revenue risks substantially back to the private company. The terms were then shared with a firm of commercial solicitors engaged by the authority who were asked to prepare a formal agreement between the authority and clinic that essentially was a purchasing arrangement.

Several months later the matter was settled when the health authority's partnership was dissolved and the Clinic sold to the Priory Hospital Group for an undisclosed sum.[41] The district auditor gave his full approval for the sale, and the Clinic became a provider under contract to NHS like all the other providers at this time. In a press release Nottingham Health Authority announced; *"The Nottingham Health Authority is pleased to announce that it has concluded the sale of its share in the Nottingham Clinic partnership....We are pleased that this successful joint venture with private industry has resulted in the development of a business eagerly taken up by the private sector market. The considerable proceeds from the sale are being re-invested in the Nottingham Healthcare Unit for a new pilot project developing sector based mental health services in the community."*[42] Bob Beckett, the original owner of the Nottingham Clinic, later reframed this as an episode when a pilot project of the era of the provider-purchaser split had threatened the psychiatric community.[43] He went on to found the UK Advocates (UKA) in the early 2000s, a charitable campaign group dedicated to helping alcoholics achieve lasting sobriety. This called for action to address what it regarded as serious shortcomings in the treatment of alcohol dependents, arguing that; *"Government policy has failed to recognise the difference between a problem drinker and an alcoholic who has a disease."* [44]

Impacts on the local treatment arena

Despite initial controversy over its financial arrangements, the Clinic managed to overcome its hesitant start and successfully moved to actual operation. The Clinic had a high level of occupancy by NHS patients from the very beginning but initially attracted few private patients. They accounted for less than a third of patient stays in 1990/91 although two thirds of beds were designated for them. Some believed British health insurance schemes were influenced by their American counterparts, who refused to pay for this form of treatment on efficacy grounds. The low level of private interest was also likely influenced by the high costs, which were between £8-10,000 per inpatient stay. The Clinic's success depended on GPs referring patients for treatment. In an interview given to the journal *General Practitioner* in 1990, Keith Sykes, the local health authority's secretary suggested the acid test was whether or not the Clinic won 'the hearts and minds' of GPs.[45] The city's doctors were, in consequence, encouraged to refer patients to use the new facilities, and indeed it became a popular place of referral, especially among fundholding GPs. Furthermore, the Clinic accepted referrals from the courts, which led to opportunities for probation officers, and solicitors, acting on behalf of an individual, to make a referral for assessment and the potential for individuals to receive treatment instead of a prison sentence.[46] Duty psychiatrist schemes were set up to detect the type of offender for whom treatment, rather than punishment, was regarded as the way to stop them re-offending. The opportunities for courts to prescribe 'a cure rather than a punishment' saw the Clinic immediately grab national headlines, especially as other medical treatment services planned to follow suit.[47] The resident judge at Nottingham Crown Court gave a ringing endorsement of the Clinic to the press; *"If there is nothing wrong with an individual who commits a serious offence, then to prison he must go...but if there is a psychological reason for the offence, and the offender is motivate...I would always consider sending him there [Nottingham Clinic]."*[48]

MODES OF TREATMENT AND THEIR EFFECTIVENESS

The negative and positive media coverage of the Clinic saw the existing specialist NHS alcohol treatment provider, NADT, overlooked for a time by policy makers. At this time the decision-making process about service provision was in the hands of bureaucrats and health officials. A 'top down' approach was the order of the day. Decisions made at national level were cascaded down from regional to district levels, leaving doctors' power of influence over planning this, and other medical specialisms, severely diminished. It therefore was unsurprising that the Clinic's presence on the local treatment scene was the cause of some resentment among other service providers. Other agencies, especially the NHS inpatient team at Mapperley were angry at not being consulted about the setting up of the Clinic and questioned the local need for it.[49] Since the new clinic represented something of a return to old models of treatment, many in the local treatment sector were unhappy that the health authority seemingly would endorse it. But in the immediate aftermath of the controversy over the initial development and financing of the Clinic, it and the other NHS provider, the Nottingham Alcohol and Drug Team (NADT, an amalgam of the inpatient unit at Mapperley plus NHS outpatient and day care) found both their models of care were to come under scrutiny. Local health commissioners wanted to evaluate the two approaches with respect to effectiveness as well as value for money. In essence, each treatment provider was expected to demonstrate its overall worth. In policy terms, the focus on evaluation and treatment outcomes formed part of a much broader drive towards evidence based medicine (EBM). EBM had recently emerged as an approach to aid decision making, which became the defining approach to health in the 1990s. It formed part of a drive towards the internationalisation of research, and the growing influence of evidence as a determinant of practice, rather than relying on doctors and policy makers to make the 'right' decisions on behalf of patients. The evidence based approach became the dominant culture within medicine and health care and provided policy makers with means to determine the potential usefulness of different types of provision.[50] Some local authorities developed outcome-based contracts under compulsory competitive tendering (the mandating of competitive tendering for specified services).[51]

So in 1991 the local health authority asked public health physician and local GP, Denise Kendrick, who worked within the Department of Public Health Medicine and Epidemiology at Nottingham University, to engage both the local inpatient treatment providers in an evaluation study. What was proposed was a retrospective cohort study comparing a group of patients from the Nottingham

Clinic, with two groups from the NADT. The reason NADT had two groups as compared to the Nottingham Clinic's one, was that some patients at NADT followed a treatment goal of abstinence whilst others followed a treatment goal of reduced alcohol consumption, otherwise known as modified (controlled) drinking. The outcomes measured included whether individuals achieved their stated goals, saw improvements in biochemical measurements (for example, liver function) and whether individuals saw improvements in the quality of their lives. Attrition rates or those dropping out of treatment, were also recorded and compared.[52] Both services agreed to take part but Philip McLean of the inpatient unit at Mapperley thought some important issues had been overlooked in the planning. He argued the health authority was not comparing like with like. He recalled in interview that *"The Nottingham Clinic was being offered as some kind of choice.... would you like to go to a half decent hotel for four weeks and be looked after and taken care of, or would you like to go and talk to somebody about coming to terms with your alcohol problem.."* [53]

In terms of what the two services offered, NADT inpatient unit mainly provided detoxification. The rest of the service, its outpatient unit and day care facilities, provided community support including home detoxification as well as abstinence and controlled drinking programmes. The approach was not fixed to a particular conceptual framework, though the ideas of alcohol dependence and problem drinking were generally understood to form its conceptual basis. Detoxification was a key feature of treatment for its mainstay patient, which remained the street drinker. Patients admitted to the inpatient unit at the hospital were for the most part physically dependent on drink, and often in a seriously deteriorated state of health, experiencing withdrawal symptoms such as black outs or DTs (delirium tremens), which were managed by prescribing medication and around-the-clock nursing care. The Nottingham Clinic had some similarities in that it too emphasised inpatient care at first, with the same emphasis on managing patients' withdrawal symptoms. Where it differed was that acceptance of the notion of alcoholism formed an important part of the treatment regimen. It followed the route set in the US, offering a means to abstinence through a process of group therapy, family counselling and AA, with follow up and aftercare in the community.[54]

A year long period of evaluation of the two services ensued. After this a report was produced, which became known locally as the 'Kendrick report'. It concluded that; *'...the Minnesota Model did not provide any greater health gain than less intense forms of intervention such as those provided by the DHA addiction services'*.[55] Of 45 cases studied at the Nottingham Clinic, seven achieved their goal. This compared to a success rate of 18 out of 43 cases at NADT.[56] The findings chimed with US studies that found that whilst health insurance companies were convinced by the efficacy of these forms of inpatient treatment, there was little evidence to suggest inpatients fared any better than outpatients.[57] One outcome at the local level as a consequence of the findings of the Kendrick report was that the Regional Drugs Advisory Committee recommended the findings be widely circulated around the region and made a point of discussion between planning managers, fundholding GPs and psychiatrists.[58] But in actual fact the report was left to gather dust in a cupboard somewhere inside the Nottingham Health Authority headquarters. It only resurfaced at a much later date, around 2002 is Philip McLean's recollection, when a new incumbent in the Health Authority was going through a cupboard and found it full of Kendrick reports.[59] At any rate, in the aftermath of the report, the health authority continued to buy beds for NHS patients from both the inpatient units regardless. This only caused further tensions between both providers.

The episode suggests additional factors were guiding commissioning and decision-making at this time. Following these events, Philip McLean of the NADT, became increasingly disillusioned with the alcohol sector especially the politics of it. He regarded the health authority decision to continue funding the Nottingham Clinic as criticism of the service provided by NADT, which he was responsible for as director, and hence he regarded this as a personal slight concerning his abilities to deliver a professional service. But when removing himself from the frame, he could also see that specialist psychiatry was beginning to 'run out of steam.' He recalled, *"There were no new alcohol treatments, no new medicines, acamprosate [a drug used to reduce cravings] popped up in 1990s, but was a damp squib. Other people were attacking the medical hegemony in alcohol services by advocating psychological treatments, which I always saw as a good thing, but to actually get the thing set up, that was difficult,...how to set up and move more towards the approach of controlled drinking and establish a proper programme."*[60]

From the mid 1990s, McLean relinquished his hold over alcohol treatment at NADT and became more focused on treating drug misuse, which was timely because out there in the public arena Government was starting to accentuate the links between drug misuse and crime and pushing for more drug users to be treated. McLean stopped overseeing the management of the alcohol service after 1998. He initiated the recruitment, and endorsed the subsequent appointment, of a new consultant psychiatrist by the name of Neil Wright, who had previously worked in Leicestershire. Neil Wright was a protégé of psychiatrist Doug Cameron, a protagonist of the controlled drinking approach, based in Leicester. Though a psychiatrist by training, Neil Wright was a psychologist in all but name. He found his medical training; *'so diagnostically driven'* that he *'ran out of enthusiasm for that game'*. His approach was driven by a *'fascination of grappling with how people pursue pleasure and get it wrong.'*[61] When he first arrived in Nottingham he found the approach of NADT stale. He found patients too willing to take the *'hapless victim role'* and felt there was too much of a revolving door effect. He believed inpatient admissions had become an easy fallback position; and patients too ready to accept inpatient treatment. In the early years Wright's compromise position was to offer community medical detoxification to *'lure people into day care'*.[62] Over the course of the next few years however, he undertook a radical overhaul of the service and set about deconstructing the NHS treatment approach, gradually weaning patients and GPs from referrals for inpatient treatment and encouraging the take up of community treatment. His approach was far more akin to the 'community safety' approach peddled by government, with its aim of reducing harms related to heavy drinking and intoxication.[63] Where it differed from national policy however, was that the service continued to emphasise one specific group, older drinkers, especially older street drinkers, as opposed to tackling the broad range of drink problems that existed in the community. Wright was quite radical in establishing ways of weaning street drinkers from drink. He opted to experiment with weaning as opposed to detoxifying patients using prescribed medication, and alongside this development he instigated programmes of controlled drinking.[64]

From 1999, with the help of Caroline Thompson, a nurse who had been employed for a significant number of years by the health authority to work with the homeless within the hostel sector, and working closely with Framework Housing Association, he tried out his ideas of 'weaning' on chronic drinkers living in the hostels. He explained that working with drinkers in this particular context meant he could do *'quirky things like tell them to have another drink if they looked a bit shaky'*. He was adamant that getting them to stop was rather missing the point and did not improve their relationship with drink.[65] He and Thompson subsequently published their early experimentations in a sector journal and became well known for their experimental approach as a consequence.[66] One of their published papers outlined a typical case that underwent the weaning process;

> *"A 28-year-old male living in a hostel for homeless people with alcohol problems asked staff for Chlordiazepoxide. He had a 10-year history of extreme alcohol-related problems. ....At the time he presented, he*

was consuming up to 6 litres of strong cider daily and experiencing withdrawal symptoms on waking-up...... staff suggested he drink his cider more slowly that day. Thereafter he repeatedly requested cider and 275 ml was given on occasions when his [breathalyser reading] had declined by any measurable amount since his last drink.... He breathalysed negative at the start of the third day, and was not exhibiting alcohol withdrawal symptoms. He was therefore given no further cider and congratulated on completing his detoxification...... he remained abstinent from alcohol for 5 months."[67]

As a consequence of these early experiments, weaning became an important component of treatment, though remained controversial. Local members of Alcoholics Anonymous and staff at the Nottingham Clinic voiced concerns about the approach being unethical; some going as far as calling it cruel and amoral. They also questioned whether NADT utilised the weaning process on 'real' alcoholics, meaning those that fitted the definition of alcoholic/alcohol dependent.[68] Nevertheless weaning became a popular component of treatment over time and controlled drinking, an established norm. Its availability as a treatment option did little to reduce hostilities between the two treatment providers, NADT and the Nottingham Clinic, and put pay to any sort of combined approach.

Conclusions

The decade thus ended with the local treatment sector on the defensive and at variance with one another. The NADT finally debunked the notion of alcohol dependency and promoted the idea that even the most extreme problems with drink could be brought under control, whilst the Nottingham Clinic, though outwardly had a fresh new look, revived the old approach of alcoholism as disease. The model it followed offered no prospect of a return of control over drinking, for the disease's effects over mind and body permanently diminished ability to be in charge. For the problem drinkers seeking treatment at this time some benefits must have been derived from the increased range of choice of treatment. However for some, the lack of consistency among treatment providers must have been an encumbrance. That the local treatment sector behaved in such an introspective fashion for much of the 1990s, and was over-involved in health policy developments of the centre, meant that it failed to keep pace with, and respond to, events nearer to home in the public realm. For in this sphere both locally and nationally, drink was becoming entangled with the issues of public disorder and crime. Here the new 'Community safety' approach was increasingly becoming more important than treatment.

Notes

1. Department of Health, *Tackling Drugs Together: A Strategy for England 1995-8*, (London: HMSO, 1995). Department of Health, *Task Force to Review Services for Drug Misusers. Report of an Independent Review of Drug Treatment Services in England*, (London: HMSO, 1996). Department of Health, *The New NHS: Modern and Dependable* (London: HMSO, 1997); Cabinet Office, *Tackling Drugs to Build a Better Britain: The Government's Ten-Year Strategy for Tackling Drugs Misuse* (London: HMSO, 1998); Home Office, *Crime and Disorder Act* (London: HMSO, 1998).

2. H. Rosenberg, J. Melville, D. Levell and J. E. Hodge. 'A 10-year follow-up survey of the acceptability of controlled drinking in Britain.' *Journal of Studies on Alcohol*, 53 (1992), pp. 441-446.

3. B. Thom, *Dealing with drink; alcohol and social policy* (London: Free Association Books, 1999), pp. 214-219.

4. Department of Health, *Working for Patients*, Cm. 555 (London: HMSO, 1989).

5. R. Klein, *The New Politics of the NHS: From Creation to Re-Invention* (Oxon: Radcliffe Publishing, 2006), p.162; C. Ham, *Health Policy in Britain* (Hamps., New York: Palgrave Macmillan, 2004), pp. 40-49; T. Ryana, L. Webb and P.S. Meierc, 'A Systems Approach to Care Pathways into in-Patient Alcohol Detoxification: Outcomes from a Retrospective Study ,' *Drug and Alcohol Dependence* 85 (2006), pp.28-34; G. Thornicroft, "The NHS and Community Care Act,1990: Recent Government Policy and Legislation," *Psychiatric Bulletin* (1994), pp.13-17.

6. C. Ham, Health *Policy in Britain* (Hamps., New York: Palgrave Macmillan, 2004), p. 41.

7. D. Gaffney, A. M. Pollock, D. Price and J. Shaoul, 'The Private Finance Initiative: NHS Capital Expenditure and the Private Finance Initiative expansion or Contraction?' *British Medical Journal* 319 (1999), pp. 48-51.R. Klein, *The New Politics of the NHS: from Creation to Re-Invention* (Oxon: Radcliffe Publishing, 2006), p.237; H. Jones and S. MacGregor, *Social Issues and Party Politics* (London: Routledge, 1998), p.99.

8. F.W. Wilson, 'Spiritual therapy in the therapeutic community' in P. Vamos, D. Brown ed. Proceedings of the 2nd World Conference of Therapeutic Communities: *The Addiction Therapist, Special Edition* 4 (1978), pp. 204-205.

9. Anti-psychiatry emerged in the 1960s and questioned the fundamental assumptions and practices of psychiatry. The term was first used by the psychiatrist David Cooper in 1967 in his book, *Psychiatry and Anti-Psychiatry* (London: Paladin, 1967).

10. R. Yates *Out From the Shadows*. (London: NACRO, 1981); R. Yates, 'A brief moment of glory: the impact of the therapeutic community movement on the drug treatment systems in the UK', *International Journal of Social Welfare*, 12, 3, pp. 239-243.

11. S. MacGregor, 'Promoting new services: The Central Funding Initiative and other mechanisms' in: J Strang, M Gossop, ed. *Heroin Addiction and Drug Policy: The British System*. (Oxford: Oxford University Press, 1994), pp. 259-269.

12. The Minnesota Model developed in Minneapolis, US in the late 1940s. It drew on ideas from AA. Founders insisted patients attend to the details of daily life, tell their stories, and listen to each other. The model drew heavily on the concepts of the therapeutic community and mutual aid.

13 Unpublished report by D. Cameron, University of Leicester, December 12th 1991.

14 D. Chapman Walsh, R. Hingson, S.J. Merrigan, S. Morelock Levenson, A. Cupples, T. Heeren, G.A. Coffman, C. Becker, T. Barker, S.K. Hamilton, T. McGuire and C.A. Kelly, 'A Randomized Trial of Treatment Options for Alcohol-Abusing Workers,' *The New England Journal of Medicine* 325 (1991), pp.775-782.

15 '12-Step Centres; Improve Treatments and Standards or Fade Way,' *Addiction Counselling World* 1992.

16 C.C.H. Cook, 'The Minnesota Model in the Management of Drug and Alcohol Dependency: Miracle, Method or Myth? Part I,' *British Journal of Addiction* 83 (1988), pp. 625-34; C.C.H. Cook 'The Minnesota Model in the Management of Drug and Alcohol Dependency: Miracle, Method or Myth? Part II,' *British Journal of Addiction* 83 (1988), pp. 735-748.

17 Health policy change including PFI is discussed in I. Greener, *Healthcare in the UK: Understanding Continuity and Change* (Bristol: The Policy Press, 2009); C. Ham, *Health Policy in Britain* (Hamps., New York: Palgrave Macmillan, 2004); C. Ham, *Management and Competition in the New NHS*, (Oxford: Radcliffe Medical Press, 1994); R. Klein, *The New Politics of the NHS: From Creation to Re-Invention* (Oxon: Radcliffe Publishing, 2006).

18 Ira Unell interviewed by Jane McGregor, Nottingham, April 2008.

19 Referrals could be made under a process of 'extra contractual referral' or ECR.

20 Nottinghamshire Healthcare Trust was a fourth wave Trust, established in 1993-4.

21 Philip McLean interviewed by Jane McGregor, Nottingham, August 2008.

22 Philip McLean interview

23 J. Allsop, 'Medical Dominance in a Changing World: The UK Case,' *Health Sociology Review* 15 (October 2006), pp. 444-457. Also R. Dingwall, 'Litigation and the Threat to Medicine,' in *Challenging Medicine*, eds. J. Gabe and D. Kelleher (London: Routledge, 1994), pp. 46-64.

24 APAS archive: Letter circulated to alcohol service from solicitor's Hill Dickenson Davis Campbell acting for Castle Craig Clinic, Peeblesshire, dated 6th May 1992. Circulated by Merseyside Regional Health Authority.

25 DH Circular: HN (89) 4: Alcohol Misuse: Prevention and Local Co-ordination.

26 The Faculty of Public Health Medicine of the Royal College of Physicians. UK Levels of Health: First Report, (London: RCP, June 1991); Health Education Authority. Health Education Authority response to the health of the nation (Health Education Authority, October 1991); WHO Regional Office for Europe. Targets for health for all. Targets in support of the European Regional Strategy for Health for All. (Copenhagen: WHO, 1985)

27 Philip McLean Collection of Private Papers: Minutes of Meeting of Association of Directors of Councils on Alcohol representatives with DH officers, March 16th 1989.

28 Broxtowe lies to the west of the City of Nottingham.

29 'Addiction clinic set to open,' *Nottingham Evening Post*, March 28th 1990.

30 Ibid

31 Kenneth Clarke interviewed by Jane McGregor, London, June 2007.

32 'Bitter row rages over city clinic', *Nottingham Evening Post*, June 25th 1993.

33 'Deal: we could not pull out,' *Nottingham Evening Post*, March 18th 1990; 'Bitter row rages over city clinic', *Nottingham Evening Post*, June 25th 1993.

34 'Bitter row rages over city clinic', *Nottingham Evening Post*, June 25th 1993.

35 The District Audit Service of the Audit Commission: District Auditor Report (K.F Chidgey), March 1993

36 Ibid

37 '£1.8m spent illegally on drug clinic,' *The Guardian* July 2nd 1993; 'All tied up in Notts,' *Private Eye*, June 18th 1993; 'Colour section', *Private Eye*, July 1st 1994;'Notts unravelling,' *Private Eye*, July 2nd 1993; 'Inquiry call over £1.8m clinic bill,' *Nottingham Evening Post*, June 11th 1993; 'Plan one-sided, says auditor, 'report is re-written,' *Nottingham Evening Post* June 25th 1993; 'Clinic - MP says 'put patients first,' *Nottingham Evening Post*, 28th June 1993.

38 'East Midlands Today' (BBC Midlands), broadcast August 25th 1992.

39 'All tied up in Notts,' *Private Eye*, June 18th 1993

40 HC Written answers: 6, 228, c375W, July 12th 1993.

41 'City's clinic for addicts is sold,' *Nottingham Evening Post,* November 11th 1993.

42 Nottingham Health Press Release: *Nottingham Clinic Sold to Priory Hospital Group*, October 25th 1993.

43 Posted comment by B. Beckett in relation to article, 'Rehabs Work: Research on Success,' *Addiction Today*, November 17th 2008. Available from http://www.addictiontoday.org/addictiontoday/2008/11/rehabs-work-research-on-success.html [Cited 4th May 2011].

44 'Campaign welcome parliamentary report exposing serious failings in treatment for alcohol dependents across England', *Medical News Today,* May 21st 2009.

45 J. Feinmann, 'Addiction Centre Breaks New Ground,' *General Practitioner*, November 23rd 1990, p.45.

46 '*Nottingham Evening Post*, August 24th 1991.

47 'If I don't drink, I won't offend,' *The Independent*, August 23rd 1991.

48 Ibid

49 'Pioneering scheme causes deep divisions,' *Nottingham Evening Post*, June 25th 1993.

50 Brought to prominence by D.L Sackett and colleagues in the early 1990s, evidence based medicine developed through all parts of health care: D.L. Sackett, W. Rosenberg, J. Gray, R.B. Haynes and W.S Richardson. 'Evidence Based Medicine: What It Is and What It Isn't.' *BMJ* 312 (1996), pp. 71-2.

51 Compulsory Competitive Tendering (CCT) in UK context; J. D. Smyth, 'Competition as a Means of Procuring Public Services: Lessons for the UK from the US Experience,' *International Journal of Public Sector Management* 10 (1997), pp.21–46; J. Lawler and

E. Harlow, 'Postmodernization: A Phase We're Going Through? Management in Social Care,' *British Journal of Social Work* 35 (2005), pp.1163-1174.

52 Philip McLean Private Collection of Papers: Letter dated September 5th 1991 from Denise Kendrick, Department of Public Health Medicine and Epidemiology.

53 Philip McLean interview

54 Nottingham Clinic brochure (undated, circa 1990), p.1.

55 D. Kendrick, *An Evaluation of Treatment for Patients with Alcohol Problems. NHS Addiction Services and the Nottingham Clinic* (Nottingham: Nottingham Health Authority, 1991).

56 Ibid

57 D. Goodwin, 'Inpatient Treatment of Alcoholism - New Life for the Minneapolis Plan,' *New England Journal of Medicine* 325 (1991), pp. 804-806. Goodwin reported that of the studies examined in 1991, 27 studies showed no advantage of inpatient programmes whilst only one study showed advantages.

58 Philip McLean Private Collection of Papers: Trent Health: Summary of Evaluation reports, (undated), p.2.

59 Philip McLean interview

60 Ibid

61 Neil Wright interviewed by Jane McGregor, Nottingham, March 2008.

62 Ibid.

63 B. Thom, *Dealing with Drink; Alcohol and Social Policy*, pp.218-219.

64 'Weaning' was a practice that commanded support in the 18th and early 19th century. By the mid 19th century the temperance movement developed a strong influence over the conceptualisation of habitual drunkenness and widened its condemnation of spirit drinking to all forms of alcoholic beverages, so weaning became more difficult to justify as a helpful intervention. See R. Porter, 'The Drinking Man's Disease: The 'Pre-History' of Alcoholism in Georgian Britain,' *British Journal of Addiction* 80 (1985), pp. 385-96.

65 Neil Wright interview

66 N. Wright and C. Thompson, 'Withdrawal from Alcohol Using Monitored Alcohol Consumption: A Case Report,' *Alcohol and Alcoholism* 37 (2002), pp.344-346. From the 1970s advocates of controlled drinking saw 'weaning' as a central issue with which to challenge their opponents. Even in the 1990s, many predicted weaning individuals from drink using alcohol rather than prescribed medication would be doomed to failure.

67 Ibid

68 Caroline Thompson interviewed by Jane McGregor, Nottingham, April 2008.

8

'LIBERTY'S' AND LICENSING: RESPONSES BY THE POLICE IN THE 1990s

From the early 1990s medicine, and the rest of the local alcohol treatment sector, was out of step with the concerns of the community, where a major drug crime problem was developing. By the late 1990s Nottingham had gained the media status 'gun capital of Britain,' and its reputation as a weekend break destination and place to work and study was seriously undermined. Alongside this another development was taking place. Disorder connected to the night-time economy was growing, and presenting police with problems. Police, in response, called for more resources to tackle the growing problem, but for government the issue was eclipsed by concern about drugs and serious crime. The actions of the City Council at this time only exacerbated the problem with its plan to enlarge the local night-time leisure industry, for its liberal approach to licensing resulted in an over-abundance of pubs and bars in the city. Taking matters into their own hands, police pursued a policy of objecting to new licenses in a bid to stall this development. But their approach was upended in 1996 when magistrates overturned police objections to the granting of a licence to Nottingham nightclub, 'Liberty's.' This landmark case not only provided momentum for the development of the wider UK night-time economy, but proved the catalyst for intensified criminal justice responses to youth drinking.

National developments

Nationally during the late eighties into the 1990s, as briefly mentioned in the previous two chapters, the community safety approach became important at a time when crime and drugs became significant policy concerns and as changes occurred in the social milieu. Young people at this time were beginning to engage in the night-time leisure scene and the drinks industry took advantage by becoming more geared towards the wants and aspirations of youth. Widespread drug use and an observed trend of the 1980s that involved young people converging on city and town centres meant they had become more visible to the public eye, as had their risky behaviours.[1] The approach to curb troublesome behaviours often involved closed circuit television, or CCTV. This was a significant part of the police arsenal, and used as a means of monitoring behaviour in public spaces. Police also engaged in efforts to eradicate nuisances from the streets, which often entailed the removal of beggars and the drunk and disorderly. In addition efforts were made to design out crime by transforming disused and derelict parts of cities into safe and accessible public spaces.

Fear of young people, which extended from the 1980s, was palpable in the public arena and meant there was almost unremitting concern about young people throughout the 1990s. In relation to drink new epithets emerged. The 'lager lout' replaced the 'football hooligan' and a female equivalent, the 'ladette', also appeared. Essentially a female version of the 'lad' where drinking and watching football were dominant pastimes, the ladette was associated with the 'Britpop' music of the era and the drink scene.[2] These changes contributed to a tendency noted by researchers, for young people of both genders, to drink for the singular purpose of getting intoxicated.[3] This shift was thought to be linked to the 'rave' culture. The illicit 'rave' culture of the 1980s moved to the mainstream in the late 1980s/early 1990s and shifted from an act of the rebellion to a mainstream activity.[4] The early rave scene was largely about indulging in weekend binges of drugs such as ecstasy and cannabis, and alcohol was antithetical to its ethos. But in contrast, the new mainstream rave culture saw drink and drugs used together. Stimulant drugs like cocaine also were popular in this new scene as were 'alcopops' and bottled lagers.[5] Alcopops were the drinks industry's response to the declining youth market. The first was launched on the British market in June 1995. Just over a year later there were about eighty alcopops on the market, ranging from alcoholic lemonades, colas and strawberryades to alcoholic soda waters.[6] Public concern about the new drinks helped launch a voluntary code of practice by the alcohol industry.[7] Nevertheless there was a subsequent increase in drink consumption among youths, with surveys reporting the average consumption of young adolescents (11-15) rising from 5.3 units per week in 1990 to 10.4 units in 2000. Over three quarters of those aged 16-24 reported frequent visits to the pub.[8]

The liberalisation of licensing also continued unabated, a move that was part of a broader move to de-regulate controls over trade in Britain.[9] As stated in chapter six, the Licensing Act of 1988 allowed afternoon drinking in public houses during weekdays.[10] All day Sunday opening followed in 1995, marking the beginning of an important shift in approach to licensing. From 1995, children were allowed into pubs (though young people aged 14 plus were already allowed in pub bars). The law only applied to the bar area and was intended to encourage a more responsible attitude to drinking and cater for families. Drink was also a significant economic issue in the 1990s. With the advent of the free market, there was unease over the extent of cheap European beer available in the UK. This was exacerbated by people selling French beer brought back from France. Known as 'booze cruises', these jaunts across the waters were a significant feature of the 1990s. The problem was also associated with organised criminals involved with outlets at night clubs, off licenses, working men's clubs and illicit drinking dens.[11] The situation led the Chancellor of the Exchequer, Kenneth Clarke, to freeze the duty on beer in 1994 and announce that Britain had to fall in line with European neighbours in relation to tax on alcoholic beverages. Clarke also cut tax on whisky, the first chancellor to do so for about one hundred years. Clarke's successor and member of the incoming New Labour government, Gordon Brown, followed suit, pursuing roughly the same policy, either freezing or raising duty in line with inflation to avoid lost revenue from alcohol and tobacco.[12]

Eighteen years of Conservative government came to an end in 1997. As the country geared itself for a general election that year, the issues of drugs and crime moved to the political foreground. New Labour, like the Conservatives, focused on crime and disorder, and became particularly exercised about drugs. John Major's Conservative government drew up an initial drug strategy in 1996; *'Tackling Drugs Together'* and when New Labour formed the new government in 1997, it developed its own national strategy, *'Tackling Drugs to Build a Better Britain'*, published in 1998. After this alcohol was overshadowed by drugs in policy terms, although New Labour pledged to review licensing policy. It proposed various licensing regimes for alcohol, including that public entertainment and late-night refreshment be combined. The new system aimed to clarify the purposes of alcohol licensing. It intended to transfer responsibilities from licensing justices to local authorities, and separate the licensing of premises serving alcohol from the licensing of persons responsible for them. It also sought to introduce clearer standards for the operation of premises and criteria to guide the granting, refusal and revocation of licences. Its proposals recommended the giving of additional powers to police to close down disorderly premises, and sought to clarify legal restrictions on alcohol sales to minors, and longer opening hours including 24-hour opening. The drinks industry, which had lobbied strongly for reform, carried much influence within government at this time, especially since it had a major role in reviving the UK economy.[13] This particular move was kick-started by central initiatives that saw some local authorities given more scope and powers to develop their economies.[14] At the same time 'core cities' were identified under the 'Core

Cities Initiative,' including Birmingham, Bristol, Leeds, Liverpool, Manchester, Newcastle, Nottingham and Sheffield. These cities worked with the Office of the Deputy Prime Minister (ODPM), the Treasury, and the Departments of Trade and Industry, Transport and Culture, and Media and Sport, to build capacity within the UK economy.[15] One of the few areas where cities managed to boost their respective economies was in the night economy although problems soon emerged in the form of public order difficulties. In some areas however, growth of the sector was impeded by licensing restrictions. Commonly, later hours could not be granted unless the applicant could prove by a process known as 'cumulative impact' that its presence and activities would not contribute to crime and disorder in the area. This approach proved a convenient panacea and enabled some authorities to take a strong stance against alcohol related disorder, although police were often accused of being 'needlessly obstructive' and the principle faced increasing challenge.[16]

Nottingham's changing drinking scene

In the late 1980s and early 1990s, as discussed in chapter six, Nottingham City Council instigated a move to turn Nottingham into a thriving modern European city. This involved embracing the idea of the '24-hour city' and encouraging growth of its night leisure industry. Nottingham was one of the first to embrace the concept.[17] Much effort was made to attract young people to the city, and a particular focus was the development of a lively night-time entertainment scene. But before any of this could happen, a major 'clean up' of the city took place. This saw street beggars and the homeless reduced to '*a problem of street cleaning,*'[18] and it was around this time that the Council got behind plans for the Handel Street 'wet' centre'.[19] Further to this, a byelaw to prohibit the consumption of alcohol on the streets was considered, similar to one introduced in Coventry.[20] The Council also joined up in 1991 to the 'City Challenge Initiative', which focused on city renewal. It was one of eleven local authorities that took part.[21] The initiative helped fund the development of a new day centre for young people, which developed through consultation with the health authority and local authority. The project, Base 51, was much like the Handel Street Wet Centre in that it proved a means by which the police could crackdown on the 'undesirables' on the streets. Base 51 was modelled on 'The Door', a revolutionary youth centre in New York. Opening in 1993, it undertook work with young people. Its work with the young homeless was expanded in 1996/7 when funding was secured for a housing worker. Later, a support worker was funded under the 'Rough Sleepers' Initiative'; another central government initiative of the period, which developed in response to the increasing numbers of homeless and mobile young people in Nottingham city centre at that time.[22] Although young people were not allowed to sleep at the project they were put in contact with a range of agencies that could find them accommodation. Basic facilities such as showers, lockers and laundry were available on site however, and a café offered a three course meal for under £1.[23]

Alongside the clean up measures, massive effort was put into marketing the city as a tourist stop and weekend break destination.[24] Growth in the number of hotels resulted, with increasing numbers capturing the weekend break and conference market. This development benefitted the night-time leisure industry, which became a great success. An article of the *Sunday Telegraph* (1993) highlighted the growing reputation of Nottingham's nightclub scene; *"Nottingham has more pubs in its square mile than any other town in Britain... In recent years it has taken over Manchester as the fashionable place to be, with an estimated 30000 revellers travelling into the area during a weekend.*[25]

Another development that helped the local economy at this time was the creation of new jobs and businesses. Increasing numbers of young professionals came to live and work in the city, sparked by a trend in city living. The Inland Revenue was one of several major employers to move to the city but there was also a growth in the number of service industries; banking, insurance and food and drink that pitched up at this time. The two Universities, Nottingham and Nottingham Trent, and the Queen's Medical Centre, also contributed significantly to the population of young people in the city, not just in terms of students but because they were leading employers in the city. In addition to these changes and as opportunities arose, the Council encouraged redevelopment of parts of the city such as the run down area of the Lace Market, which was turned into an area of offices and new bars. Up until this time, the area mostly consisted of derelict warehouses. Once the industrial centre, it declined after the First World War. Though the area faced demolition in the 1960s, a combination of listing, conservation activism and private investment in the 1990s turned the area back into a vibrant city quarter.[26] Individual entrepreneurs tended to invest in the area and the Council were keen to offer support. Tim Coulson, former Head of Food and Licensing at the City Council, described the ease by which club owners got things off the ground; *"The individual entrepreneur would open up a night club, put in a ticket booth on the door, have doormen, insert a bar, get a DJ in, have a big dance floor and that was it. Go to the court, get a licence. The policies were largely not about looking at the need for licensed premises but looking at the demand generated by business. Businesses could apply for a license and expect to get it unless somebody, usually the police, objected vehemently."*[27]

THE END OF THE PUB AND LOCAL BREWING AND THE ARRIVAL OF CHAMELEON BARS

As a consequence the Lace Market became quite a Mecca for small independent clubs, restaurants and bars. The Council believed they would provide a shopping environment that would attract shoppers from afar. Very few properties provided the 2,500-3000 square feet needed at ground floor level for bar and pub operations, so where suitable opportunities arose, the Council's planning department played an important role in granting planning and change of use consent. Licensing magistrates also played a role in helping 'unusual' buildings secure future economic use. Hence, buildings such as old cinemas and banks secured licences and were brought back to economic use.[28] Whilst some regeneration effort was imaginative and made use of former buildings, there was also a rise in the number of somewhat faceless 'theme' bars. CAMRA and private landlords were unhappy about the changes in the drink environment, because the new bars posed a threat to more traditional pubs.[29] In fact for many their introduction in the local drink scene represented the end of the traditional pub. The pub's demise was marked with a local exhibition in 1994, and in a book published in1995 that celebrated Nottinghamshire's drinking past, local pubs and brewing traditions.[30] The change was indicative of the power of the large national companies in the brewing industry at this time. Local brewery Shipstones, for instance, was shut down by Greenalls, a large national brewer, and Home Brewery, another local brewery at Daybrook, was bought out by Scottish and Newcastle.[31] Home Brewery's demise was observed with a minute's silence on the instruction of the Lord Mayor of Nottingham, Barrie Parker, at a council meeting in June 1996.[32] CAMRA declared Nottingham *"no longer a brewing city,"*[33] and the *Nottingham Evening Post* demanded to know what went wrong; *"The city should today be a brewing centre to match Burton-on-Trent or even Munich. Until 1978 we had three independent breweries providing us with the cheapest beer in mainland Britain. What went wrong? ...We have nothing to thank these national brewers for – they've given us high prices and ruined our pubs..."*[34]

The pub chain J.D. Wetherspoon made a conciliatory gesture however, playing on the idea of the 'community pub', a replacement for the 'local'. The Wetherspoon chain adopted a policy of low pricing and provided large barn-like pubs serving cask conditioned beers. Tim Martin, the company's founder, who had been a student in Nottingham, claimed to have got inspiration from Nottingham's pubs for the Wetherspoon concept. Referring to the author George Orwell's imaginary pub *'Moon under Water'*, he was quoted as saying a pub should have *'cheap beer, good conversation, motherly barmaids and an architecture that had the solid comfortable ugliness of the 19th century*".[35] City centre bars on the other hand, tended to have a wider range of designer beers and catered for the young contingent.[36] At the Cyberpub in Lower Parliament, for example, drinkers could use the Internet as they sipped their chilled beers. Customers could be served alcoholic drinks for most of the day. This and others such as Fothergill's, Café Metz, Keans Head, Limelight and Fat Cats were some of the countless 'chameleon' bars now occupying the city centre. They fell somewhere between pubs, restaurants and café bars. In addition there were multiple café/bars such as Café Uno Rouge and a number of city centre restaurants, which operated a variety of concepts from 10 am - late night. A high proportion of their turnover was food.

The new 'chameleon' bars emerged as a result of loopholes in the licensing laws that allowed for late night drinking in restaurants and clubs provided meals were eaten on the premises. This followed the series of liberalising changes in licensing that had occurred since 1961, outlined in earlier chapters. As the night economy expanded in the 1990s, this new type of bar began to proliferate, taking advantage of extended hours under the 'Special Hours Certificate' licensing arrangement. Under the Licensing Act 1964, the standard permitted hours for the sale of alcohol terminated at 11pm from Monday to Saturday and at ten thirty on Sundays. If a pub or bar wished to extend the hours of licensing, it had to obtain a Special Hours Certificate.[37] This effectively replaced the normal permitted hours license, allowing sales of alcohol until 2am. In order to get the certificate, one had to apply to the local licensing justices who, before granting the licence, had to be satisfied that a Public Entertainment Licence (PEL) granted by the local authority was in place, and assured that the sale of alcohol was ancillary to music and/or food.[38] In some areas of the UK the more ambitious local authorities actively reinterpreted existing restrictions by removing time limits on PELs. In order to do this, some pub chains brought in industry legal teams to convince the justices that they were offering a new type of venue, something different from a pub or discotheque. If successful, it meant the old restrictions need not apply.[39] Nottingham, as highlighted at the start of the chapter and discussed shortly, was to feature as the location of a landmark case concerning this issue.

Marketing alcopops: impacts on youth behaviour and the drink scene

The marketing of new drinks, the so called alcopops, and the commercialisation of the 'rave' scene in the 1990s, were changes that influenced youth behaviour considerably. The club scene established in the 1990s was derived from the rave scene of the 1980s and occurred as the rave became more of a mass phenomenon.[40] A huge circuit of commercial raves developed after the liberalising of licensing hours (Licensing Act 1988) allowed for rave-style clubs with all-night dancing. These changes contributed to a tendency all over Britain for young people to drink for the singular purpose of getting intoxicated.[41] Illicit drug-taking (ecstasy and cannabis were popular) became *de rigueur* and a new pattern of intoxicant use - weekend binges - began to take form. Drink also became submerged in the new dance culture of the club scene as youth '*came home and raved like they had in Ibiza*'.[42] On top of this, alcopops and other forms of alcohol including beer were introduced along with stimulant drugs like cocaine to the club scene.[43] For many, the hedonistic weekend lifestyle was an escape from the working week.[44] Alcopops were especially popular with women, and getting dressed up and going out was a major part of the way of life for young people in cities across the UK, especially in places like Nottingham, Leeds, Newcastle and Manchester.[45] Introduced in Britain in 1995, alcopops fed into an already changing drinking pattern among young people. There was an explosion of brands and types of drinks from alcoholic fruity mixes to buzz drinks that contained herbal stimulants. Some have argued that the drinks industry was under direct competition from the illicit trade in drugs at this time and made a calculated move to infiltrate the drug and dance culture.[46] Indeed some alcopops had names with hidden drug meanings. Measures were in the form of 'shots', a reference to 'shooting up' or injecting, whilst drink names included 'K', a slang term for ketamine, and 'Ice', drug jargon for methamphetamine. With eye catching advertisements the drinks industry lucratively captured the youth market.[47]

Another characteristic of the era was that the notion of 'youth' began to extend its boundaries. As a consumer culture developed there was a growing tendency by the media and advertisers to appeal to a wider range of consumers. In order to capture older consumers, marketers came up with the term 'middle youth' to describe people in the late twenties to early forties age bracket who wanted to avoid the trappings of middle age. These individuals tended to favour youthful leisure interests like clubbing, drugs and fashion. As a result, 'youth' became detached from a specific generational group. The term, which had been associated with young men and 'trouble' up until this point, also became detached from gender, as women became increasingly visible in the night-time economy.[48] In the highly commercialised new drink setting it became increasingly common for groups of young men and women to head out for a night out in the city centre on Friday and Saturday nights. It was in this environment that two 'new' cultural phenomena arose. The first was the 'lager lout'. This was a media contrivance that emerged in the mid to late 1980s and like the tag 'hooligan', captured the violent behaviour of the working class male when engaged in drunken brawls.[49] The second, the 'lad', was set up in opposition to what was seen as the 'feminisation' of the drink scene. He was portrayed also as football loving and beer obsessed but not associated particularly with violence. A local man recalled the behaviour of the archetypal local 'lad';

> *"There has always been a kind of pub crawl approach in Nottingham. But where before it was pints, people thought it cool to have shots as well... the doubles, triples, shots and bottled beers. And more people accessing foreign holidays such as a lads' week in Majorca or a Club 18-30s, affected the way they drank. They would come back from holiday and do it when they got home."*[50]

Women also behaved differently in the new drinking scene.[51] The changes in the labour market saw women take to the scene in greater numbers and on top of that the 1990s saw the rise of the 'ladette' culture. The ladette phenomenon emerged in the popular press around the mid 1990s and was initially associated with beer swilling, hard partying young women from the world of 'celebrity'.[52] Though at first pint-drinking was central to the ladette identity that representation broadened to include women who drank excessive amounts of wine or fashionable cocktails.[53] The shift was matched by a move by the drinks industry to entice women into the new bars.[54] The so called 'feminisation' of the drinks scene was a clear signifier that women were increasingly playing an important part in the new drinking scene. In Nottingham's Waterfront bar, for example, there were improvements to the lighting as well as an addition of '*a decent wine list and pot pourri in the ladies' loo*'[55] Newspapers and comfortable sofas were other features brought in, for women who preferred not to have to go to the bar, and there were areas designated for quiet chatting. An article of the *Nottingham Evening Post* claimed at that time that, "*Just about all the city bars are realising that what women want is the sound of George Michael, a glass of chardonnay and a designer salad with low fat dressing.*"[56] Women as a consequence, became a major source of interest to the media in the late 1990s and early 2000s for their antics in the drinks milieu, the spectacle of drunken women seemingly having a profound and destabilising effect on the rest of society.[57] Nationally, the proportion of young women aged 16-24 exceeding the sensible weekly limit more than doubled from 15 per cent in 1988/89 to 33 per cent in 2002/03. The proportion of women exceeding the weekly sensible daily limits rose from 10 per cent in 1988/89 to 17 per cent by 2002/03.

Drugs and the intensification of police concern over drink disorder

The interlocking by police of the issues of drugs and alcohol came about at a time when Nottingham ranked top in the crime polls. In 1989 police started to see the symptoms of crack cocaine around Radford, St Ann's and The Meadows. The emergence of an inner city culture of violent disorder associated with the illicit drugs trade was identified in an early 1990s report of the Home Office.[58] This coincided with the reporting in the national press of a spate of violent episodes, which contributed to the view that Nottingham was a violent and dangerous place. One prominent case was that of 19-year-old Lloyd Robinson from St Ann's who was beaten to death by a gang called the Meadows Posse in 1993. Four years later, Shane Thompson, 19, from St Ann's, was also beaten to death. One of the main factors influencing this development was the introduction of crack cocaine, a cocaine derivative, in some parts of the city. The gangs controlling the drug activity at first centred around the music scene but their conflicts soon extended to controlling the local drugs trade.[59] The arrival of the Jamaican 'Yardies' in the 1990s is thought to have significantly contributed to the problem. 'Yardie' was a name given to someone recently arrived in the UK from Jamaica and meant 'back yard', meaning 'back home'. Yardies, typically men in their twenties or thirties, tried to assimilate into the community by becoming involved in drug-related activity.[60] Whilst Jamaican street life had been imitated in some areas of Nottingham since the 1960s in clubs, bars and house parties, some of the entertainment venues of the 1990s also became used for crime. Over time the presence of violent gangs was felt and the number of shootings rose dramatically.[61] As a consequence, criminal justice responses were stepped up, and armed police replaced mounted police in some areas of the city as organised criminals took control of the drugs trade.[62]

For those involved in the illicit drugs trade there were huge profits to be made, especially those who infiltrated the local night-time economy. Ecstasy and amphetamine or 'speed' were already part of the culture of legal and illegal local raves, with security often organised by violent local gangs.[63] Ecstasy sales were booming in the city's club scene where people from London, Manchester, Sheffield, Leeds and Birmingham came to enjoy the hedonistic nightlife.[64] Bouncers/club doormen controlled the traffic of drugs going into some clubs and it was only after national media exposure of the problem of doormen in the mid 1990s that police and the City Council got anywhere near on top of the problem. The investigations of television reporter Donal MacIntyre, who went undercover in Nottingham as a bouncer, initially exposed the doormen's activities. His investigations were subsequently reported on television as a two part ITV *World in Action* programme in 1996. Thereafter, the Council introduced compulsory training and registration of doormen before entertainment licence could be granted or renewed. The first batch of pub bouncers graduated from a training course in door management at Clarendon College in Nottingham and other implemented strategies included police checks, to weed out bouncers with a history of violence.[65]

These issues took considerable attention away from other areas of policing as police were called on by government to reduce Nottingham's high drug crime. As mentioned earlier, a national drugs strategy was first outlined in *'Tackling Drug Misuse'*, published in 1985. This was followed by the Conservative government's *'Tackling Drugs Together'* in 1995 and New Labour's *'Tackling Drugs to Build a Better Britain'* in 1998, which was a ten year strategy.[66] As a result of the 1995 and 1998 strategies, as both endorsed the approach, Drug Action Teams (DATs) or Drug and Alcohol Action Teams (DAATs) were put in place across the country. From as early as 1995 Nottinghamshire had two teams; a county DAAT, Nottinghamshire County Drug and Alcohol Action Team, and a city DAT.[67] DATs typically had senior representation from the criminal justice sector, health, social services, prisons and other areas including customs and excise, to ensure the strategy was delivered locally. The role of DATs was principally to ensure local agencies co-ordinated the local approach and worked together.[68] Both the 1995 and 1998 strategies singled out drugs crime as a major issue with the 1998 report in particular, instigating a move towards criminal justice approach responses to drugs. This emphasis by government had important consequences for Nottingham where it became of the utmost importance to crack down on drug crime. Mike Trace, the government's Deputy Anti-Drug Coordinator or deputy 'drug tsar', stated that at that time Nottingham was important to the success of the national drugs strategy. He later recalled *"It was the violence. Nottingham seemed one of those cities. The DATs had to get it right."* [69]

The drugs/drug crime issue not only was the main focus of Nottinghamshire Police, but meant there was a shortfall in funding and resources in relation to more crime and disorder in the city. Paul Winter, the local area commander at that time, argued it was a perennial issue resulting from the city's distinctive geography. He explained that though the city was a core city, it was one of the smallest. Hence, he said, Nottingham lost out because *'with critical mass comes funding, and the ability to do more.'* [70] When calls for additional resources fell on deaf ears, police sought other means by which to argue for extra resources and hit on the issue of alcohol disorder, and made use of the local press to stress their case. In a *Nottingham Evening Post* article of 1995 that carried the headline 'Alcohol causes twice the crime as illicit drugs,' police reported that, of an overall policing budget of around £100 million, it cost Nottinghamshire £31 million a year to police problems associated with drink. This compared with about £16 million for offences related to drugs, they said. They also highlighted that in the first seven months of 1995, 4400 assaults were recorded locally of which the majority were estimated to be alcohol related.[71]

The case of Liberty's nightclub and the relevance of the principle of need

Having to focus on drugs and gun crime and having no additional resources, meant police ended up relying heavily on 'arms length' ways to manage the disorder in the night-time economy such as routinely objecting to licences when any new club applied for one. This approach singled Nottingham out because other police forces in places like Leeds and Manchester tried to work with, not against, their respective night-time economies.[72] In these other areas, police often would be lobbied by local politicians and business leaders and if they did obstruct licence applications, they were often castigated by magistrates for being needlessly obstructive and for holding back city centre regeneration by adhering to *'a dated and puritanical mandate.'*[73] The approach of police in Nottingham was accordingly awry with other forces at that time.

Increasingly police in Nottingham found they were at odds with the City Council over the night-time economy. The Council's laissez-faire approach to licensing saw the night-time economy boom and flourish. When pubcos and owners of the numerous chains of pubs, bars and restaurants offered to turn grand but redundant civic buildings into wine bars, the Council generally assisted them, and eased them through the process of applying for a licence. Police held that the largest sized drink establishments posed the greatest opportunity for disorder to break out, and wanted to see a restriction in their number. As mentioned, the key tactic used by police at this time to contain disorder at night was to object to new licence applications. They usually based their objections on the grounds that new premises would add to the level of disorder. Their objections generally carried sway, but in 1996 in a move that had far reaching consequences, magistrates unexpectedly overturned police objections. Police practice was designed to limit the number of licensed premises in some areas of the city, areas that were near-saturated with bars. Police were the main enforcers of licensing legislation, and developed the practice of objecting to new licences back in the late 1970s when concern about a hooligan element first arose. Persistent concern about disorder during the rioting and hooliganism years of the 1980s and more recent concern about drugs and drunken disorder in the nightclub scene, left police with little reason to alter their routine. By objecting to new licences when they arose, police aimed to prevent the licensed trade from taking advantage of loopholes in the law, if it could be shown that crime and disorder and/or public nuisance were a significant concern in a given area. Commonly, no later hours were granted unless the applicant could prove that they would not contribute, by a process known as 'cumulative impact', to crime and disorder in that area. The approach was a convenient solution that enabled police to gain political capital from being seen to take a strong stance against alcohol-related crime and disorder.

A magistrate could reject an application on the grounds that the area did not require or need another drinking establishment. This principle of 'need' was important in licensing. Whilst the principle did not appear in the legislation, mention of what can be termed need or demand is found in a late fifteenth century statute governing the conduct of alehouses.[74] Despite the fact that magistrates did not have to find need or demand in order to grant a licence, they could refuse an application if they found that there was no need/demand for the premises applying to be licensed. The Home Office had considered dropping this principle on a number of occasions since the 1970s because it was anticompetitive. The process was temporarily arrested in the mid-1980s with strong concerns over alcohol-related problems expressed by criminal justice and medicine. In the 1990s increases in alcohol-related problems led to stricter controls on numbers of outlets, while social and commercial pressures for liberalisation prompted relaxation of controls. It was the principle of need that formed the basis for objection to the granting of a late night licence to Liberty's nightclub and saw Nottingham play a prominent role in the area of licensing policy in the late 1990s.[75]

The main supporters of the police approach in Nottingham were the existing pub operators because it helped remove the threat of new competition. Most discotheques and late night sites were run by individual entrepreneurs, but companies arriving in the late 1980s picked up discotheques cheaply and were intent on doing things differently. Some operators sought out warehouses to form premises in which customers could drink, eat and dance (the so called 'chameleon bars'). Sometimes they brought in a team of lawyers who specialised in licensing to assist them in the licensing process. One such team of lawyers was local firm Poppleston Allen. It specialised in licensing related to drink and public entertainment. Up until this time, Poppleston Allen found little work in Nottingham and dealt mostly on a national basis.[76] However Jeremy Allen, one of the firm's solicitors, was approached in 1996 to undertake some work for a new nightclub in Nottingham called 'Liberty's.' At this time Nottingham was a city where it was very difficult to get licenses and police opposition to late night licensing was well known. Many in the licensing trade were of that view, which is in all probability why the operators of Liberty's sought out expertise from a national licensing team of lawyers such as Poppleston Allen.

As was the usual practice, when Liberty's case was heard by the justices, police objected to the licence application. As was their practice, they provided statistics to support the assertion that if Liberty's nightclub was granted a licence, the disorder problems in the area would be made worse. They detailed the amount of violence that occurred in the area and the number of people admitted to hospital with drink related injuries. However, the Poppleston Allen team representing Liberty's were highly adept at putting a case together. Their *modus operandi* involved using the team to find out what the local problems were, reading the papers, walking around the town and finding good witnesses. One of the advantages, as Jeremy Allen saw it, was that as a national firm, the clerks advising the magistrates would think if they ruled and were wrong, the case would be taken up to the High Court or to appeal, so they treated the national firms more carefully because of that.[77] Without doubt the approach took both the police and the magistrates off guard and as a result, Liberty's was granted its licence, though the police immediately took the case to appeal but the judge turned them down stating *'Liberty's would be a positive contribution to law and order and to the public good.'*[78]

The case was credited for exposing the way in which police opposed licensing applications, and the way licenses were dealt with by the licensing authorities. Magistrates feared that if they became more difficult, they could lose their role in licensing. For at this time Government appeared to want to de-regulate and be of the view that councils might be more lenient. The Liberty's case thus set a precedent. It influenced what happened elsewhere in the country and acted as a 'green light' to expansion of the UK night economy.[79] Not long after the Nottingham ruling, the Home Office Working Group on Licence Transfers (1996) recommended that the issue of 'need' be dropped from licensing. Subsequent to that, the lately elected New Labour government announced it wanted to modernise the liquor licensing system. It established a government review of licensing in May 1998, with the promise of a White Paper. The Better Regulation Task Force Report, published later that same year in July, suggested the administration of licensing be moved from licensing justices to local authorities. In early 1999 the Justices' Clerks' Society published its *Good Practice Guide* which, among many other things, required licensing committees to abandon need or risk loss of the jurisdiction.[80] Whilst the government appeared committed to abandoning the concept, it still required primary legislation.[81] Commentators have argued that the removal of need was vital in changing drinking culture and expanding the market place; with social scientist Dick Hobbs, who has written extensively on the subject suggesting it represented *'the removal of the last remnants of the old municipal restraint and control strategies'*.[82]

Intensification of police responses to alcohol

The UK night-time economy was fast developing as a place *'built on cheap drinking establishments'* by the late 1990s.[83] The Liberty's case not only had contributed importantly to national policy developments in this area, but had serious consequences for Nottingham. The most significant was the huge increase in the number of late night drinking venues. By 1997, Nottingham city centre bars and clubs could cater for upwards of 62,000 people. Its late night capacity, the bars and clubs that closed at 2 am, had already reached 24,000 and the number was expected to climb further.[84] For police this meant increasingly high levels of weekend drunken disorder, a dilemma that contributed considerably to intensified police responses to alcohol.

One area that typified the problem was the Lace Market area near the city centre and Hockley, where the young professional crowd and certain groups of students most often congregated. The area was a fine example of urban regeneration, having close relations and a sense of community between the commercial businesses that developed there.[85] Between 1997 and 1998 millions of pounds were invested in the area with new bars, examples including Lloyds No. 1 bar in Carlton Street, the Revolution and Wax bars in Broad Street and Berlin's at the bottom of Hockley. Hockley was also home to nightspot 'Brown's', and the Market Bar as well as a licensed bar at the cinema. City planning chairman, Councillor Alan Clark announced this quarter of Nottingham *"an up-and-coming area"*. [86] But even with the manifold advantages brought to many by the night-time economy, a growing number of people in the local community, especially older people, were put off from coming into the city centre at night. Young people too, especially those from middle class families, were put off from coming to Nottingham to study because of its reputation for crime and disorder. The situation worsened when a trend towards city centre living kicked in. In the Lace Market, loft conversions often fetched up to nearly £½ million; but the worsening levels of disorder put those prices in jeopardy.[87] The threat was perceived as one of drunken and anti social behaviour. The result was a culture clash between the different groups of young people. Tim Coulson, head of licensing at the Council recollected; *"There was this group who bought property and expected to have a luxury apartment with nice views across the city and be able to walk out of their front door for a nice al fresco- scene, not step over urine and vomit and drunken people."*[88]

This was, in many respects, a return to more reactionary attitudes in relation to the 'problem' of nightlife; where the issue was connected to the entertainment of the 'lower orders' and needed containing.[89] Many of the youths in the night-time economy were students from Nottingham Trent University, which was based in the city centre. Many more students than had previously been the case came from working class backgrounds. The situation came about as a result of a government push for a fifty per cent increase in student numbers. This shift resulted in huge growth in student numbers and also student accommodation. A lot of it was built in the city centre, which ultimately meant greater student take up of the city's night-time entertainment.[90] Facing rising complaints Nottingham City council conducted a study into the impact of student inundation. The results found that in some parts of the city more than fifty per cent of the population were students.[91] The Council responded to criticisms by employing a city centre management team but this had little immediate impact.[92] By the end of 1998, 15 per cent of Nottingham centre's 1565 commercial properties were devoted to food and drink and a 1997 survey of comparable cities showed only Newcastle had a higher proportion of outlets.[93] By 8-9 o'clock in the evening, bars shifted into late night economy mode. The pattern most prominent, especially at the weekends, was for young people to buy drink from a supermarket or off-license on the way home, have a drink at home to liven themselves up and come into the city centre using the buses and taxis, already having consumed alcohol. A typical night out consisted of going to a bar like Yates' en route and towards the end of the evening, around midnight, going to a nightclub and staying there until about two or three o'clock in the morning. The cost of disorder after a 'good night out' was rising; violence and disorder in the city centre increased from 1409 incidents in 1998 to 1559 in 1999. Over the same period woundings were up by 160 per cent, common assault by 145 per cent and violent disorder increased 80 per cent. Meanwhile the number of licensed premises had risen from 209 in 1995 to 356 in 2000 and the capacity of bars, pubs and clubs in total had risen to 111,000.[94]

Conclusions

Nottingham played an important role in terms of development of the UK night-time economy, which developed in a more *laissez-faire* way following the landmark licensing case in 1996 of Nottingham nightclub, Liberty's. The episode, and the city at that time, reflected the tensions inherent in policy involving drink. On the one hand, developments in Nottingham were a sign of the need for modernisation of the licensing system (the subsequent dropping of the principle of 'need') and on the other, reflected the intrinsic problems of the market-led approach for Nottingham's burgeoning night-time economy had unintended consequences on the local community and the police. As the number of bars and clubs in the local night-time leisure scene multiplied, alcohol contributed progressively to the problem of night-time disorder, a situation that saw police responses to drink intensify.

Notes

1   F. Coffield and L. Gofton, *Drugs and Young People* (London: Institute for Public Policy Research, 1994), pp. 13-14.

2   These shifts in youth drinking are explored in M. Martinic and F. Measham, *Swimming with Crocodiles: The Culture of Extreme Drinking* (Abingdon, Oxon: Routledge, 2008)

3   K. Brain and H. Parker, *Drinking with Design: Alcopops, Designer Drinks and Youth Culture*, (London: Portman Group, 1997); K. Brain, H. Parker and T. Carnwath, 'Drinking with Design: Young Drinkers as Psychoactive Consumers,' *Drugs: Education, Prevention & Policy* 7 (2000), pp. 5-20; C. May, 'A Burning Issue? Adolescent Alcohol Use in Britain 1970-1991,' *Alcohol and Alcoholism* 27 (1992), pp.109-115; H. Parker and L. Williams, 'Intoxicated Weekends: Young Adults Work Hard-Play Hard Lifestyles, Public Health and Public Disorder,' *Drugs: Education, Prevention and Policy* 10 (2003), pp. 345-367.

4   BBC Radio 4 programme: 'Sorted for E's and Whizz', October 4th 2007. Also F. Measham, 'The Decline of Ecstasy, the Rise of 'Binge' Drinking and the Persistence of Pleasure,' *Probation Journal* 51 (2004), pp.309–326.

5   F. Coffield and L. Gofton, *Drugs and Young People*, pp. 13-14.

6   M.A. McKibben, 'Letter: More Alcopops Have Come on Market since Study Was Done,' *BMJ* 313:1397 (1996).

7   Portman Group, *Code of Practice on the Naming, Packaging and Merchandising of Alcoholic Drinks*, (London: Portman Group, 1996).

8   R. Room and M. Järvinen, *Youth Drinking Cultures: European Experiences, Volume 13* (Aldershot, Hamps: Ashgate, 2007), p.5; P. Jennings, *The Local: A History of the English Pub* (Stroud: Tempus Publishing, 2007), p.223.

9   J. Greenaway, 'Calling Time on Last Orders'.

10 This was the first time afternoon drinking had been allowed since 1915.

11 Nottingham Drinker Sept/Oct 1994 (CAMRA magazine).

12 Kenneth Clarke interviewed by Jane McGregor, London, July 2007. Also Nottingham Drinker Nov/Dec 1994.

13 R. Baggott, 'A Modern Approach to an Old Problem? Alcohol Policy and New Labour,' *Policy and Politics* 38 (2010), pp. 135-152. Also M. Plant and M. Plant, *Binge Britain* (Oxford: Oxford University Press, 2006).

14 Local Government Commission for England (LGCE) reviewed the administrative structure of non-metropolitan areas in the 1990s, recommending some areas be set up as single-tier unitary authorities (UAs). This is discussed in J. Fenwick and M. Bailey, 'Local Government Reorganisation in the UK: Decentralisation or Corporatism?' *International Journal of Public Sector Management* 12 (1999), pp. 249-261.

15 M. Parkinson, *Cities and Regions: Institutions, Relationships and Economic Consequences. The Evidence Base*, (Liverpool: European Institute for Urban Affairs, John Moores University on behalf of the Core Cities Working Group, 2004).

16 D. Hobbs, P. Hadfield, S. Lister and S. Winlow, *Bouncers: Violence and Governance in the Night-Time Economy* (Oxford: Oxford University Press, 2003), p.80; P.M. Hadfield, *Bar Wars: Contesting the Night in Contemporary British Cities*, p.51.

17 The Civic Trust, *Nightvision: Town Centres for All*, (London: The Civic Trust, 2006), p.9.

18 'Street Drinking', *Nottingham Evening Post*, October 29th 1994.

19 'Handel Street day centre for homeless drinkers opened', *Nottingham Evening Post*, February 14th 1990.

20 T. Oc and S. Tiesdell, *Safer City Centres: Reviving the Public Realm*, Edited by Environmental Studies (London: Paul Chapman, 1997), pp. 219-220. This made it an offence to continuing to drink alcohol when asked to desist.

21 Among the aims of 'City Challenge' were plans to support strategies that attracted outside investment, created an enterprise culture and developed locally-devised plans that benefited local residents and all those with a stake in the area.

22 Personal communication from the Chief Executive of Base 51, Janet Lewis, September 2008. The Rough Sleepers Initiative (RSI) was a government-funded programme introduced from 1990 onwards by both Conservative and Labour governments. There were three

phases of the initiative lasting from 1990 until 1999. Until 1997 the RSI was concentrated on London but thereafter was extended to 36 other areas in England.

23 'A New Drop in Health Centre for Young People in Nottingham,' *The Independent*, June 15th 1993.

24 *Notts Industrial and Commercial Review*, October 1990 (supplement of the *Nottingham Evening Post*).

25 'Nottingham the fashionable place to be,' *Sunday Telegraph*, August 15th 1993.

26 *Nottingham Regeneration and Investment Magazine*, (Nottingham: 3Fox International Ltd, 2008).

27 Tim Coulson, former Head of Food & Licensing and Alcohol Lead Officer, Nottingham City Council interviewed by Jane McGregor, July 2007.

28 'Massive upsurge in demand for premises for pubs/café bars,' *Notts Commercial Property Weekly* (supplement of the *Nottingham Evening Post*), July 16th 1996,

29 *Notts and District Drinker* 6. 4 (1992); *Nottingham Drinker* May/June 1995 (name change for CAMRA magazine); 'LVA concerned about close of country pubs,' *Nottingham Evening Post*, June 3rd 1995; 'Notts pubs are celebrating their pulling power,' *Nottingham Evening Post*, June 15th 1995; 'Faceless theme bars threaten local brewers,' *Nottingham Evening Post* July 18th 1995; 'More Nottingham alehouses set to be turned into theme pubs,' *Nottingham Evening Post*, August 1st 1995; *Nottingham Drinker*, Autumn 1995.

30 G. Wright and B Curtis, J., *The Inns and Pubs of Nottinghamshire. The Stories behind the Names.* (Nottingham: Nottingham County Council, 1995). There was an exhibition on same theme; 'A Century of Nottingham Brewing at the Brewhouse Yard', 1994.

31 Shipstones was independent until its takeover by Greenalls in 1978. Home Brewery saw a takeover by Scottish &Newcastle Breweries in 1986.

32 *Nottingham Drinker* 15, August 1996.

33 *Nottingham Drinker* July/August 1995.

34 'Faceless theme bars threaten local brewers,' *Nottingham Evening Post*, July 18th 1995.

35 *Nottingham Drinker* 26, June 1998.

36 'More Nottingham alehouses set to be turned into theme pubs,' *Nottingham Evening Post*, August 1st 1995.

37 P. Jennings, *The Local: A History of the English Pub* (Stroud: Tempus Publishing, 2007), pp.226-227.

38 P.M. Hadfield, *Bar Wars: Contesting the Night in Contemporary British Cities* (Oxford: Oxford University Press, 2006), p.41.

39 Ibid pp. 51-52.

40 BBC Radio 4: 'Sorted for E's and Whizz'. October 4th 2007. Also F. Measham, 'The Decline of Ecstasy, the Rise of Binge Drinking and the Persistence of Pleasure,' *Probation Journal* 51 (2004), pp.309–326.

41 F. Measham, 'The Decline of Ecstasy, the Rise of Binge Drinking and the Persistence of Pleasure,' Also H. Parker and L. Williams, 'Intoxicated Weekends: Young Adults Work Hard-Play Hard Lifestyles, Public Health and Public Disorder,' *Drugs: Education, Prevention and Policy* 10 (2003), pp. 345-367.

42 BBC Radio 4: 'Sorted for E's and Whizz', October 4th 2007. The programme made a link between the emerging binge phenomenon of the 1990s and the trend towards holidaying in the Mediterranean island of Ibiza, known as the capital of the international rave scene.

43 F. Coffield and L. Gofton, 'Drugs and Young People,' (London: Institute for Public Policy Research, 1994), pp.13-14.

44 P. Chatterton and R. Hollands, *Urban Nightscapes: Youth Cultures, Pleasure Spaces and Corporate Power* (London: Routledge, 2003), pp. 114-16.

45 Alcopops proved especially popular with women and made Britain the biggest alcopop market in Europe. 'Ladette Culture Puts Britain Top of the Alcopops,' *The Telegraph*, April 2nd 2003. Also *Alcopops Factsheet*, (London: Alcohol Concern, 2001).

46 M. McKibben, *Pop Fiction? The Truth about Alcopops* (London: Alcohol Concern 1996); S.J. Blackman, *Chilling Out: The Cultural Politics of Substance Consumption, Youth and Drug* (Maidenhead: Open University Press, 2004), pp. 80-1.

47 Alcopop sales tripled between 1995 and 1996, but the instant success of the early alcopops brought a swift backlash. The Portman Group, set up by UK drinks producers to tackle social responsibility issues to do with alcohol, subsequently produced a voluntary code of practice on the promotion and packaging of alcoholic drinks in light of criticism; Portman Group, *The Portman Group Code of Practice on the Naming, Packaging and Merchandising of Alcoholic Drinks*, (London: Portman Group, 1996).

48 B. Osgerby, *Youth Media* (London: Routledge, 2004), p.56.

49 L. McDowell, *Redundant Masculinities?: Employment Change and White Working Class Youth* (Oxford: Blackwell Publishing, 2003), pp.203-4.

50 Local man interviewed by Jane McGregor, Nottingham, November 2007.

51 M.A. Smith, *Sex, Gender and Power: The Enigma of the Public House* (Hebden Bridge: Lambert Print & Design, 2003); G. Hunt and S. Saterlee, 'Darts, Drink and the Pub: The Culture of Female Drinking,' *Sociological Review* 35 (1987), pp. 571-601.

52 The British TV and radio presenter Zoë Ball was the personification of the ladette; her hard-drinking, hard-partying antics contributing to the identification of that culture in the mid to late 1990s.

53 The word 'ladette' entered the Concise Oxford Dictionary in 2001 as '... *young women who behave in a boisterously assertive or crude manner and engage in heavy drinking sessions.*' Some argued that the ladette is one of only a very few female 'folk devils' to have emerged in British society. Jackson and Tinkler suggested that the ladette shared similarities with the 'modern girl' or 'flapper' of the 1920s, arguing that what led to the labelling of women in this way was women occupying space outside the domestic sphere. C. Jackson and P. Tinkler, 'Ladettes and Modern Girls: Troublesome Young Femininities,' *Sociological Review* 55 (2007), pp.251-272.

54 J. Greenaway, 'Calling Time on Last Orders,' pp.181-196.

55 'Trendy bars in Nottingham trying to attract women,' *Nottingham Evening Post*, September 14th 1998.

56 Ibid

57 Institute of Alcohol Studies, *Factsheet: Women and Alcohol*, (Cambridge: IAS, 2008).

58 Personal communication: Philip Bean, January 2009. P. Bean and Y. Pearson, 'Crack and Cocaine Use in Nottingham in 1989/90 and in 1991/92' in Mott, J., ed. *Cocaine and Crack in England and Wales, Research and Planning Unit Paper 70*, (London: HMSO, 1992)

59 'City of Guns, Drugs and Murder Hires a Reputation Manager,' *The Telegraph*, October 13th 2005.

60 For more detailed discussion see J. Davison, *Gangsta: The Sinister Spread of Yardie Gun Culture* (London: Vision Paperbacks, 1997) and also; J. Ferrell and N. Websdale, *Making Trouble: Cultural Constructions of Crime, Deviance, and Control* (New York: Aldine de Gruyter, 1999).

61 BBC News Online, 'Who Are the Yardies?' June 19th 1999. Available from http://news.bbc.co.uk/1/hi/uk/371604.stm [Cited September 14th 2011].

62 I. Hardill, D.T. Graham and E. Kofman, *Human Geography in the UK* (London: Routledge, 2001), pp. 229-30.

63 Amphetamine or 'speed' was a main drug of choice in Nottingham. It was alleged to be derived from the days of the miners, who used to help keep them awake on the long shifts. Amphetamine also gained popularity in the 1980s as a drug of recreational use.

64 C. Fellstrom, *Hoods: the Gangs of Nottingham* (Lancs: Milo Books, 2008), p.68.

65 'First batch of pub bouncers graduate,' *Nottingham Evening Post*, October 20th 1997.

66 A. Mold, *Heroin: the Treatment of Addiction in Twentieth-Century Britain* (DeKalb, Illinois: Northern Illinois University Press, 2008), pp.147-8.

67 Personal communication: Kate Davies OBE, former North Notts DAAT Co-ordinator, August 2009.

68 R. Hughes, R. Lart and P. Higate, *Drugs: Policy and Politics* (Maidenhead: Open University Press, 2006), p.103.

69 Mike Trace interviewed by Jane McGregor, April 2009. Trace was UK Deputy Anti-drug Coordinator 1997-2001.

70 Local area commander, Paul Winter, interviewed by Jane McGregor, Nottingham, October 2007. Paul Winter since has been promoted to Chief Inspector for Communities for Mansfield and Ashfield Police.

71 'Alcohol causing twice the crime as illicit drugs,' *Nottingham Evening Post*, May 25th 1995.

72 P.M. Hadfield, *Bar Wars: Contesting the Night in Contemporary British Cities* (Oxford: Oxford University Press, 2006), pp. 39-80.

73 D. Hobbs, P. Hadfield, S. Lister and S. Winlow, *Bouncers: Violence and Governance in the Night-Time Economy* (Oxford: Oxford University Press, 2003), p.80; P.M. Hadfield, *Bar Wars*, p.51.

74   This was followed in 1552 by the introduction of a statutory system for the licensing of alehouses. Any two justices had full discretion in the issuing of new licences (which were subject to annual renewal).This statute is considered to be the first 'licensing act' and formed the basis of the UK licensing system. R. Light and S. Heenan, 'Controlling Supply: The Concept of 'Need' in Liquor Licensing,' (Bristol: University of the West of England 1999).

75   For discussion of the principle of need; P. Jennings, *The Local: A History of the English Pub* (Stroud: Tempus Publishing, 2007), pp. 217 -218.

76   Jeremy Allen interviewed by Jane McGregor, Nottingham, November 2007.

77   Jeremy Allen interview.

78   Ibid

79   The case is discussed in J. Nicholls, "Liberties and Licenses: Alcohol in Liberal Thought," *International Journal of Cultural Studies* 9 (2006), pp. 131-51.

80   R. Light and S. Heenan, *Controlling Supply: The Concept of 'Need' in Liquor Licensing*, (Bristol: University of the West of England 1999), pp 4-5 & pp.37-47.

81   The *Good Practice Guide* could only encourage licensing committees to limit 'need' to a consideration of whether premises would become as numerous as to produce problems of disturbance and disorder.

82   Transcript of BBC 1 Panorama programme 'Cldnt Give a XXXX 4 Lst Ordrs.' Also D Hobbs, 'The Night-Time Economy,' in *Alcohol Concern Research Forum Papers* (London: Alcohol Concern, 2003); D. Hobbs, P. Hadfield, S. Lister and S. Winlow, *Bouncers: Violence and Governance in the Night-Time Economy* (Oxford: Oxford University Press, 2003); D. Hobbs, S. Lister, P. Hadfield, S. Winslow and S. Hall, 'Receiving Shadows: Governance and Liminality in the Night-Time Economy.' *British Journal of Sociology* 51 (2000), pp. 701-717.

83   M. Roberts, 'From Creative City to No-Go Areas – the Expansion of the Night-Time Economy in British Town and City Centres,' *Cities* 23 (2006), pp. 331-338.

84   Memorandum submitted by Stephen Green, Chief Constable of Nottinghamshire Police to a Select Committee on Home Affairs, December 13th 2004.

85   J. Shorthose, 'Nottingham's De Facto Cultural Quarter; the Lace Market, Independents and a Convivial Ecology,' in *City of Quarters: Urban Villages in the Contemporary City*, eds. M. Jayne and D. Bell (Aldershot: Ashgate Publishing), pp. 149-162; S. Tiesdell, 'Tensions between Revitalization and Conservation: Nottingham's Lace Market,' *Cities* 12 (1995), pp. 231-241. Also *Nottingham Evening Post* July 16th 1996, *Notts Commercial Property Weekly Supplement*.

86   'Bar wars set to break out in Nottingham,' *Nottingham Evening Post*, January 21st 1998.

87   *Property for Life Monthly Newsletter*, April 2004.

88   Tim Coulson interviewed by Jane McGregor, Nottingham, July 2007.

89   D. Talbot, *Regulating the Night: Race, Culture and Exclusion in the Making of the Night-Time Economy (Re-Materialising Cultural Geography)* (Aldershot: Ashgate Publishing Ltd, 2007), p.2, & pp.71-84. Also A. Lovatt and J. O'Connor, 'Cities and the Night-Time Economy' *Planning Practice and Research* 10 (1995), pp. 127-134

90 Paul Winter (local area commander) interview.
91 'Problems of a high student population,' *Daily Telegraph* June 14th 2003, article reported the findings of the local DAAT.
92 In a Strathclyde university survey, Nottingham was placed bottom in a survey of 189 towns and cities due to its crime rate, *The Guardian*, January 13th 1997.
93 '15% of Nottingham centre's commercial properties devoted to food and drink,' *Nottingham Evening Post*, December 16th 1998.
94 'Drink and crime,' *Nottingham Evening Post*, May 9th 2001.

9

'CLDT GIVE A 4XXXX FOR LST ORDRS': THE NATIONAL/LOCAL PROBLEM OF BINGE DRINKING

"Public binge drinking is not a Nottingham problem. It is a British problem" [1]

After the Liberty's case recounted in the previous chapter, Nottingham's night-time economy grew rapidly, as did those in many other UK cities. For police this meant the problems of night-time disorder persisted. As the situation worsened Nottinghamshire's Chief Constable, Steven Green, spoke about Nottingham's aggravated problem of drink disorder in the media, together with a television documentary about 'binge drinking'. In the glare of publicity, Nottingham quickly became a flashpoint for national policy developments over drink. The episode represented a key policy moment, for Green's actions occurred at a time when '24 hour' licensing was debated in Parliament. Government used the ensuing crisis to push through its proposals for licensing reform, arguing a reduction in licensing restrictions would end 'bingeing to catch last orders,' whilst Nottingham gained notoriety as the 'Binge Capital of Britain,' and gave definition to binge drinking as a problem of youth disorder.

National developments

When New Labour came to power in 1997 it pledged to re-examine licensing laws but no move was made on this until the 2001 election. The feature of their campaign involved sending out a text message at 10 pm on the Saturday before the election, on the mobile phones of young voters and students that read, *'Cldnt gve a 4xxxx for lst ordrs? Thn vte Labr on thrsday 4 extra time'*. The tactic was intended to play to young voters, though was hastily played down because critics saw it as an irresponsible and inconsistent move.[2] After that the newly formed Department of Culture Media and Sport (DCMS) duly set out government proposals in the policy document *'Time for Reform: Proposals for the Modernisation of Our Licensing Laws'*, and during the course of 2002-3,

Government set about reviewing drinking laws.[3] Plans to liberalise licensing thus went forward, though many in the alcohol sector opposed the move and cited evidence that indicated more controls were needed rather than fewer, to make any impact on reducing alcohol-related harms.[4]

The move was set against a backdrop of changing leisure and drinking patterns among youth, as outlined in previous chapters.[5] The changes were largely to do with shifting market forces that helped establish a mainstream culture of drug taking and drinking among youth.[6] By the late 1990s there was widespread anxiety about drugs and drug-related crime in British society which saw Government sufficiently exercised to put a national drugs strategy in place.[7] At that time the UK had among the highest levels of recreational drug use in Europe, with drug problems steadily worsening.[8] The drugs strategy aimed to reduce the supply of illegal drugs, increase the numbers in drug treatment, and reduce drug-related crime. It was implemented by the National Treatment Agency (NTA), set up in 2001 as a special health authority and working with both the Department of Health and Home Office to increase the capacity and effectiveness of treatment of drug misuse in England.[9] Among the aims of the NTA was to ensure that money spent on responses to drugs met the needs of local people. To enable this to happen, the NTA set up nine regional teams to provide guidance and support to Drug Action Teams (DATs). DATs were local consortiums that brought together representatives of all the local agencies involved in tackling the misuse of drugs including primary care trusts, local authority, police and probation services. There were 149 DATs established in England from the mid 1990s covering all local authorities. The NTA regional teams monitored their performance. Some DATs included alcohol in their remit and were known as DAATs. The police were key players in this and combined the curbing of drugs supply with the potentially contradictory role of channelling drug-using offenders into treatment. The 1998 Crime and Disorder Act established partnerships between the police, local authorities, probation service, health authorities, the voluntary sector, local residents and businesses. These crime and disorder partnerships were intended to work to reduce crime and disorder in their area. They were expected to establish the levels of crime and disorder problems in their area, and to consult widely the views of local people before devising a strategy to tackle priority problems.[10] Government also introduced the *Anti-Social Behaviour Strategy* (2002), which provided new powers to help police and community safety partners tackle low-level crime and disorder.[11] Moreover the *Police Reform Act 2002* introduced community support officers to address public demands for a greater, more visible police presence on the streets.

Developments in Nottingham (2000-2004)

At the beginning of the 2000s, drugs and crime were important precursors to concern about drink, their significance explaining why police brought the issue of binge drinking into view. At the time Nottingham was dubbed the UK 'gun crime capital' after a spate of high profile murders linked to organised gangs involved in UK wide drug distribution.[12] These problems were politically salient in the late 1990s, first as the general election loomed and afterwards, as Government drew up its national drug strategy.[13] Because of this Nottingham became a place of some import in relation to the national approach to drugs. The regional office of the National Treatment Agency (NTA) was established at the Government Offices in the East Midlands (GOEM), in Talbot Street, a location just off the city centre. It reported directly, and on a monthly basis to the Prime Minister, Tony Blair, about the state of play in the city. The regional offices of the NTA were set up to oversee implementation of the national drugs strategy. The city Drug Action Team (DAT) worked closely with the local Crime and Disorder Reduction Partnership (CDRP), and there was a good deal of interplay between politicians, the local policy network, and the media over drugs and crime.[14] Mike Trace, the UK Deputy Anti Drug Co-ordinator, whose role it was to develop and oversee the implementation of the national drugs strategy saw Nottingham as having an important position in relation to drugs policy during that period; *"Nottingham, Bristol and Birmingham were not doing too well. These cities were massively political, and of particular concern"*.[15]

During those early years of the 2000s, Nottinghamshire Police faced important targets to reduce drug crime. Resources were progressively channelled to the problem of gun and drugs crime even though drunken disorder in the night-time economy persisted as a troublesome distraction. Around this time there was a change in leadership for Nottinghamshire Police. In 2000 the force's chief constable, Colin Bailey, retired. He was succeeded by Steven Green, a moderniser who aimed to transform the force. Green began his police career in 1978, following a short career as an army officer. He spent the majority of his police service with North Yorkshire Police before moving to Staffordshire as an assistant chief constable. At the time of his arrival in Nottingham, the city was blighted by gun crime. The problems escalated when serious organised crime peaked between 2002 and 2004. Police had to deal with several high-profile killings including the drive-by murder of teenager Danielle Beccan in 2003.[16] Government gave its backing to reducing gun crime, introducing a mandatory five year minimum jail sentence for anyone caught in possession of an illegal firearm at this time.[17] Green meanwhile set about establishing several major operations to tackle the root causes of the problem in order to reduce the misuse of firearms across the city, for which later he was credited with achieving a significant reduction in crime across Nottinghamshire, reducing it to its lowest levels in twenty years.[18] Under Green's watch a series of initiatives developed to tackle the problems. Nottingham's Operation Stealth was formed in 2002. The team involved recovered more than 300 firearms and thousands of rounds of ammunition between the years 2002 and 2004. Also at this time police intelligence identified that Nottingham city centre was circled by several 'open' drugs markets which operated in the Sneinton, St. Ann's, Meadows and Radford districts. The supply and misuse of Class A drugs in these districts not only had a corrosive effect on the local communities but significantly affected the city centre, fuelling high levels of acquisitive property crime and drug-related anti-social behaviour, such as street begging. Police took a number of additional steps including developing new operations to challenge street dealing and related criminality, disrupt the drugs markets, improve community confidence in local policing and improve police visibility.[19]

Police visibility was an issue particularly in the city centre, where as few as eight police officers could be on duty at night,[20] a situation that the Police Federation branded totally inadequate.[21] However it was largely owing to the Government's focus on targets such as those to reduce gun crime that led to the numbers of police in the city centre becoming much reduced. At this point, Green cleverly made use of the media to draw attention to the issue. During 2003/4, as the pressures on police mounted, he was provoked into a political row when he claimed his force was *"struggling to cope"*.[22] From thereon in Green used the issue of city centre disorder, and problems resulting from late night drinking, as a way to drum up extra resources. Already known for his anti-reform stance over licensing, he hit back in the media at government plans for 24-hour licensing, declaring the concept his *"idea of hell"*.[23] As the problems of resourcing escalated, he became increasingly vociferous about the problems in the night-time economy, which was burgeoning.[24]

Significantly, Steven Green's arrival in Nottingham coincided with a change in leadership at Nottingham City Council. The Council's outgoing leader, Graham Chapman, had been the major driving force behind the Council's vision of a '24-hour' city. Chapman, leader from 1996 to 2000, had been an enthusiast of late night licensing, believing that many of the problems facing the night-time economy could be ameliorated by extended licensing. But after Chapman stepped down there were several changes of face at the Council, with Chapman first succeeded by Brian Parbutt (Labour), and then Jon Collins (also Labour), in 2003. These changes occurred at a time when there was a groundswell of concern about developments in the night-time economy. Though leisure had become big business, there was concern that the city should not turn into "*a 24 hour party*' or '*equivalent of a rave*".[25] By this stage – 2002/3 – there were more pubs and clubs than ever before. In 1995 Nottingham had 209 bars and pubs within one square mile of the city centre, and by 2000 it had 368, an exponential rise.[26] As highlighted in chapter eight, the situation was exacerbated by the fact that the city accommodated significantly more students by this time, many of whom were regulars on the nightclub scene.[27] The *Daily Telegraph* noted the advantage this gave Nottingham, pointing to students' enormous spending power. Furthermore Nottingham had up to 100,000 visitors each weekend night and was a hugely popular destination for stag and hen parties. Football also swelled the numbers of young people in the city, particularly on Saturdays and some weekday evenings. This all added up to more young people, mayhem and disorder on the streets, particularly at weekends. So much so that by 2002 East Midlands Ambulance Service estimated five per cent of all emergency calls involved alcohol, with the percentage rising to 50 per cent on Friday and Saturday nights.[28]

TOWARDS TACKLING THE PROBLEM OF CITY CENTRE DISORDER

During the late 1990s police had begun to map where disorder was most concentrated in the city which was why, in the early 2000s, they were able to connect the emerging disorder problem with a new phenomenon of 'binge drinking'. Disorder generally followed national trends with reported incidents rising significantly; from 1409 incidents in 1998 to 1829 in 2000, up by nearly 30 per cent.[29] In 2001 police explained to reporters of the *Nottingham Evening Post*, that the problem was one connected to large groups of people drinking and moving from one place to another, who got involved in binge drinking.[30] Initially police efforts to curb night-time disorder only involved the Council in a very limited way. This was because partnership work between the two authorities was still at a very early stage.[31] Even so, police toyed with the idea of putting a levy on city centre clubs to pay for the extra officers, whilst the Council considered a rise in business rates as a way of dealing with the rising cost of street cleaning.[32] As highlighted in the previous chapter, this measure belonged to a move toward 'purification' of public spaces, which saw an increase in the surveillance of people as well as public spaces.[33] On city centre streets, police received information about crime from closed circuit television (CCTV) operators, as well as municipal wardens. In pubs and clubs, bouncers and licensees were expected to be vigilant and play a similar role. State-of-the-art cameras on poles were installed in Nottingham in the late 1990s and mobile

CCTV vans were an extra weapon in the police's arsenal to help in the clamp down on alcohol- related violence.[34] As a consequence of all this surveillance, Nottingham ended up with a reputation as one of the most heavily surveyed places in the UK, outside London.

Police also introduced a number of new criminal justice initiatives. In the street for instance, if revellers broke the ban on drinking alcohol in the city centre they faced the threat of arrest. A by-law, based on the Coventry by-law, was brought in during 2000. This banned people from drinking in specified open places. When the regulation was first introduced police could only confiscate alcohol from open-air drinkers. Then they gained powers of arrest in the Old Market Square, the Castle area, parts of Hockley and the canal banks. The by-law was soon updated to speed up the process of introducing bans in new areas, which made it easier for the Council to tackle other trouble spots if they emerged. Areas covered by the Council displayed signs indicating the extent of the no-drinking zones. Police were given the power to confiscate alcohol from street drinkers but drinkers could only be taken to court if an offence had been committed. In the first six months of 2001 there were 54 warnings and 12 prosecutions related to drinking in the designated area.[35] Under the new regulations contained in the *Criminal Justice and Police Act 2001*, the Council had to consult with the police, parish councils and license holders before designating areas. Licensed areas outside pubs and street cafés were exempt from the laws, but licensees had to ensure that the areas were properly licensed and the areas where drink could be consumed were clearly defined. The combined measures led to a better monitored and clearer view of the local situation, and provided a basis from which police could justify their demand for more resources.[36]

In 2001 Nottinghamshire Police successfully secured funds for a county-wide short term government project. The new project was supervised and evaluated by Professor Mike Maguire from Cardiff University and ran concurrently with a Cardiff based project, the Task Project.[37] This was **the prototype for later police initiatives at the national level over drink**. It involved the setting up of a special 'night clubbers' patrol (otherwise known as the alcohol-related violence project) and formed part of Operation Shield, a Home Office funded initiative.[38] The extra officers boosted the number on patrol on the city's streets on Friday and Saturday nights when thousands of revellers poured into the city centre.[39] Traditionally two shifts of officers covered the city from 2 pm to midnight and 10 pm to 7.30 am. Cover was usually at its thinnest when one shift of officers ended at midnight with the city still full of revellers. The additional police officers were intended to double the number on patrol, though the numbers on duty still remained comparatively low when contrasted with other areas of the UK.[40] Inspector Paul Winter, charged with developing the 'night clubbers' patrol, explained that the initiative was about targeted policing and *'pouring uniforms into areas where there were historically high levels of violence and drunk and disorderly.'* It was also about supporting the work being done at Nottingham's Central Police Station, which involved dedicated licensing officers reviewing incidents at licensed premises. In cases of concern, officers often would go and speak to the premises owner or licensee and try to agree some kind of an action plan for improvements to bring about better management and lower levels of violence and disorder.[41] The Nottingham initiative provided additional licensing officers, a database of detailed management information and targeted the policing of trouble 'hot spots'.

Additionally, alcohol arrests referral workers, drawn from the local NHS specialist alcohol treatment service, Nottingham Alcohol and Drug Team (NADT), provided assessment and support to arrestees. The *modus operandi* of the arrest referral scheme was about making use of the fact that people in custody are a captive audience. For some people getting arrested proved a reality check, and talking to a referral worker was enough to make them think again. Referral workers tried to engage with the sort of long term problematic drinkers that were getting health issues associated with it. Nottingham's arrest referral scheme was the first to use qualified nursing staff employed by the NHS. This meant they were screened and assessed in the custody suite rather than somebody writing a letter on their behalf to the local alcohol service, which also cut down on bureaucracy.[42] As a result of the Home Office initiative there was considerable activity in relation to alcohol. Leaflets, beer mats, posters and tee-shirts were distributed as part of a marketing campaign and radio adverts were played on a local commercial radio station before Christmas. A shopping centre campaign ran for seven days in the summer and campaigns also ran at local student fresher fairs. A total of 1,783 people were interviewed by an arrest referral worker and given advice or referred to treatment services. In addition 83 door supervisors completed door supervisors training. Licensing officers made over 1,100 visits to licensed premises in Nottingham and Nottinghamshire over the project period, conducted regular meetings with known 'high risk' premises, and were involved in developing local pubwatch schemes. In totality 104 special policing operations ran over the duration of the project during which 261 arrests were made for violent crimes, whilst 2,204 visits were made to licensed premises.[43]

Though the initiative was relatively successful the police overtime budget was used up and it was unclear whether the force would be able to commit similar amounts of funding to the project again.[44] For a time, police therefore were forced back into the position of opposing license applications to 'keep a lid' on the drink disorder problem. This move was less effective than before. Following the 1996 Liberty's landmark case and the removal of the licensing principal of 'need', magistrates rarely refused late night licenses. Because of this Steven Green frequently turned up in person at licensing hearings in order to emphasise that the police wanted to see the expansion of licensed premises stopped. Nevertheless, the situation remained difficult for police, for activity in the night-time economy was booming. By early 2004 the situation had not improved, despite police having put in place further strategies to tackle drink disorder. From the police point of view the problem was a case of 'too little and too late'. From this point onwards, Nottinghamshire's Chief Constable Steve Green propelled Nottingham's disorder problems into the media spotlight and the issue of binge drinking took centre stage.[45]

That Green took this step was unusual. Most chief constables kept out of the limelight, but Green was not media-shy. Kenneth Clarke, MP for the local borough of Rushcliffe in the south of the city, noted this tendency having worked with Green over local constituency matters. Though Clarke had a lot of time for Green, he recalled that he used to appear on *'far too many programmes'*, that he *'loved publicity far too much.'* In fact Clarke advised him not to have anything to do with television programmes like Panorama.[46] Not heeding the advice, Green co-operated with the BBC, making a documentary about Nottingham's problems with drink disorder in March 2004. His outspokenness undoubtedly played an important part in the decision of documentary makers to come to Nottingham in the first place. Liz Bloor, the producer of the BBC's Panorama programme suggested that they chose to come to the city because of the forthright way Steve Green the chief constable had tackled licensing issues in the city.[47]

The Panorama programme, *'Cldnt Gve a 4XXXX for Lst Ordrs,'* was broadcast on 6th June 2004.[48] It portrayed Nottingham has having played a defining role in the success of the UK night-time economy. Nottingham was chosen by the programme makers because it was where the drinks industry had taken on and defeated *'one of the most feared liquor licensing regimes in the country.'*[49] In his opening gambit the programme's reporter, Andy Davies, introduced many of the main actors in this policy arena. One such individual was Jeremy Allen, the national licensing solicitor whose Nottingham based firm, Poppleston Allen, had previously triumphed in the licensing case of "Liberty's" nightclub in 1996.

The case was held as a victory for the free trade and key moment in determining how UK city centres developed. Others involved in the programme from the policy arena included Dick Hobbs, a leading academic on the night-time economy, Mark Hastings from the Beer and Pub Association; Richard Caborn, the Minister for Sport & Tourism; Julie Kirkbride MP, the Conservative Shadow Secretary of State, Culture, Media & Sport; Don Foster MP Lib Dem Shadow Secretary of State, Culture, Media & Sport and Colin Drummond, an expert in addictive behaviour from St Georges Medical School, London. The programme used CCTV footage from cameras operated by Nottingham City Council, which put the spotlight on young clubbers. In the documentary Nottingham city centre represented the state of play in the UK, which was shown in chaos. It tapped into circulating concerns at that time over the Government's proposals for the reform of licensing. Green, for example, argued that the people most in need of policing could not get it because police officers who should be on the outer city estates, on the inner city estates or in the suburbs, had been taken out of those areas because of the problem of binge drinking in the city centre. He argued that the **risk period for police would get longer with the introduction of 24-hour licensing and that the resource consequences would become greater;** *'we're going to finish up with if, we're not careful, a 24 hour version of what we've got now, and that is my idea of hell.'* [50]

Green's very public stand over both licensing and the 'menace' of public drinking was very well timed, coinciding with public debate over the issues in the run up to licensing reform. From this time, and as events testify, drink developed as an urban youth problem of national scope. The programme showed, with devastating effect, what the city was dealing with in the aftermath of licensing policy decisions and the dropping of the principle of need. The programme makers spent a night following the emergency services as they struggled to deal with 50,000 drinkers on the square-mile drinking circuit of 356 bars. They portrayed the young drinkers as part of the constituency courted by the government three years previously with the text message: *Cldnt gve a 4XXXX for lst ordrs? Thn vte Labr on thrsday 4 extra time'*. The programme drew attention to how lawyers specialising in licensing had sprung up to assist the big pub operators in opening more bars and showed drunken young women on their way to and from nightclubs; a feature that emphasised that women had returned to the forefront of concern. **But** probably the most notable aspect of the programme was Steven Green's stand against the drinks industry, for he accused the industry of *'effectively selling a drug'*, saying that the selling of drinks for £1 each, or two for the price of one, was *"a blatant inducement towards binge drinking"*.[51]

National and local convergence over 'binge drinking'

Within days of the documentary being aired on television the media fixed upon Nottingham as a centre of binge drinking and depravity. In an article of the *Sunday Times* soon after, Nottingham was described as in the vanguard of the binge drinking trend;"*The proliferation of bars in city centres means binge drinkers can throw up, fall down, urinate and get into fights any place they feel like. Nottingham.... is at the forefront of this unlovely trend....*"[52]

Henceforth Nottingham was synonymous with 'binge drinking' and known as the 'Binge Capital of Britain'.[53] This episode represented a key policy moment; a moment that saw not only national and local concerns combine, but the police define the most recent of UK drink problems. There was a strong public view that Britain was in the grips of a new crisis. Some saw it as the re-emergence of a time-honoured British pattern of drinking, whilst others viewed the problem as a new cultural phenomenon involving young people and the night-time economy.[54] An important issue of debate in the public domain at the time was whether an increase in the availability of alcohol could have dire consequences on British society. The interim report on alcohol, first published in September 2003, originally had a passage on the effects of extended drinking hours in the draft which preceded publication. Later this was missing.[55] There was no reference to drinking hours in the final report published in March 2004 either. In a *Sunday Times* article published on the day the Panorama programme was aired in June 2004, a source close to the Government's strategy unit was reported as saying that the Department for Culture, Media and Sport (DCMS) was worried about the licensing bill *'going down the tubes'* if the wrong thing was said.[56] The final report proposed measures to tackle alcohol-related disorder in town centres. It also proposed a clampdown on irresponsible promotions by the drinks industry. Several of the experts who had advised the Government believed it had failed to take heed of their advice, and were critical of its failure to highlight the dangers of alcohol. They were disappointed by the emphasis on the idea that alcohol-related problems only affected a small minority. What is more, the 24-hour drinking policy was thought to have split the Cabinet. David Blunkett, the Home Secretary, expressed serious concerns over longer drinking hours but he was over-ruled by the DCMS, which was responsible for licensing law.[57]

Intent on keeping licensing reform on track, Government, in the thick of the drink crisis, seized the opportunity to declare licensing reform the best way to prevent binge drinking. Prime Minister Tony Blair, claimed binge drinking *'a new British disease',* which only licensing reform could prevent by bringing to a halt the rush to catch last orders and encouraging the adoption of European drinking styles.[58] In July 2004 nightly news reports on the problem reported a 'summer blitz' by the Home Office on drink-related disorder. A few months later (November 2004) ministers demanded a serious crackdown, blaming drunken yobs for half of all violent attacks. Coverage centred heavily on the problem of the 'British disease'; Tony Blair was prompted, in his speech at the Labour Party conference in Brighton, to promise to extend powers of on-the-spot fines to deal with binge drinking.[59] An analysis of newspaper coverage of the issue between 2003 and 2006 conducted by Chas Critcher, an academic from the field of communication, concluded that binge drinking was initially played up, as well as defined, by Government itself, in order to present its reforms in favourable terms. Critcher examined newspaper sources of the period and came away with the view that the 'primary definers', those describing or expressing an opinion on the issue, were politicians, mostly from Government but also the Opposition.[60] After that came the police, who stressed the criminal aspects of binge drinking and public order. Only after that came 'medical authorities' and the drinks industry, in terms of contributing to definitions of the problem. Campaigning groups and the national bodies such as Alcohol Concern, the Institute of Alcohol Studies, and drinks industry's body the Portman Group, rarely were sources at this time. Television played an important role in playing up the problem during the crisis, with Granada's television series '*Booze Britain*' and other televised programmes confirming drink as a major urban public disorder matter.[61] Newspaper strap lines made reference to an earlier English crisis, the eighteenth century 'Gin Crisis' at this time.[62] Though the use of images in shaping views on drink was not new, the ubiquity of communication technology at this time, such as television and the internet, significantly impacted upon policy making; its effect, something along the lines of 'if it looks bad on television, it must be a problem', forming part of the policy process.[63]

Gin Lane (William Hogarth)

'Binge drinking' was subsequently taken up in the Cabinet Office report *'Alcohol Harm Reduction Strategy for England'* in 2004, where the concept was defined in terms of criminal justice. Health harms were not emphasised, much to the dismay of the health lobby though the strategy featured a central role for the drinks industry and targeted a particular group - youth.[64] With crime and disorder strongly peppering its theme, the strategy arrived in 2005 at the height of the debate and in advance of the Licensing Act (2003).

© Jonathan Cleave, Arts University College Bournemouth

Conclusions

According to many, the national alcohol strategy was misdirected because it failed to address the root cause of the problem, which was Britain's drink culture.[65] Although consumption increased markedly amongst young people between 1990 and 2006, the shift was only part of the story. An important and overlooked problem was the issue of rising UK *per capita* consumption. The average units of alcohol consumed by men and women in Britain had increased since the 1990s, with estimates suggesting that more than 10 million people were consuming over the recommended daily limits.[66] Nottingham's crisis over drink therefore signified the changes in British society. From the late

1990s public drinking became a prominent local issue as changing realities saw police increasingly connect the problem of public disorder to the booming night-time economy. Steven Green's role in the whole affair was essentially that of campaigner, for as well as using the issue of night-time disorder to ease a problem of police under-resourcing, he was strongly against government plans for longer drinking hours.[67] The Panorama programme, 'Cldnt gve a 4XXXX' saw Nottingham reflect the emerging national problem, and the episode represented a key policy moment. The crisis that irrupted advanced particular perspectives of the 'problem', defining it as one of youth disorder. The episode showed the importance of alliances, between the police and media for example. Furthermore campaigns, as run by the police and Government, showed their influence on policy developments. Possibly the most interesting finding however was that individuals proved to be important in relation to the policy process. Steven Green's role in bringing the issue of binge drinking to the fore suggests the role of individuals is much wider, and arguably more important, than generally is supposed. Though the role of individuals has been noted as having influence *inside* government circles (policy entrepreneurs, for instance), this episode, which played an important part in shaping responses to binge drinking, showed that those *outside* government influence the policy process also.

Notes

1. '50,000 drinkers on a square mile drinking circuit of 356 bars,' *Nottingham Evening Post*, June 4th 2004.

2. House of Commons: Debate on the Address [First Day] June 20th 2001. The Government Minister Tessa Jowell later played this down in the press. 'Jowell: we got it wrong on 24hr drinking,' *Independent on Sunday*, August 28th 2005.

3. Department of Culture Media and Sport, *Time for Reform: Proposals for the Modernization of Our Licensing Laws*, (London: DCMS, 2001).

4. See T. F. Babor, R. Caetano, S. Casswell, G. Edwards, N. Giesbrecht, K. Graham, J. Grube, P. Gruenewald, L. Hill, H. Holder, R. Homel, E. Osterberg, J. Rehm, R. Room and I. Rossow, *Alcohol: No Ordinary Commodity: Research and Public Policy*. (Oxford: Oxford University Press, 2003); R. Room, 'Disabling the Public Interest: Alcohol Strategies and Policies for England,' *Addiction* 99 (2004), pp.1083-1089; M. Marmot, 'The Rising Tide of Alcohol,' *Addiction* 99 (2004), p.1090; T. Chikritzhs and T. R. Stockwell, 'The Impact of Later Trading Hours for Australian Public Houses (Hotels) on Levels of Violence,' *Journal of Studies on Alcohol* 63 (2002), pp. 591-599.

5. This trend is documented by L. R. Gofton, 'Folk Devils and the Demon Drink: Drinking Rituals and Social Integration in North East England,' *Drogalkohol* 12 (1988), pp. 181-196; L. Gofton, 'On the Town: Drink and the New Lawlessness.' *Youth and Policy* 29 (1990), pp. 33-39.

6   F. Measham, 'The Decline of Ecstasy, the Rise of Binge Drinking and the Persistence of Pleasure,' *Probation Journal* 51 (2004), pp. 309–326;F. Measham, 'Play Space: Historical and Socio-Cultural Reflections on Drugs, Licensed Leisure Locations, Commercialisation and Control,' *International Journal of Drug Policy* 15 (2004), pp.337-45; H. Parker, 'The Normalization of Sensible Recreational Drug Use,' *Sociology* 36 (2002), pp. 941-964; H. Parker, F. Measham and J. Aldridge, *Illegal Leisure: The Normalization of Adolescent Drug Use* (London: Routledge, 1998); H. Parker and R. Newcombe, 'Heroin Use and Acquisitive Crime in an English Community,' *The British Journal of Sociology* XXXVIII (1987), pp. 331-350. H. Parker, R. Newcombe and K. Bakx, *Living with Heroin: The Impact of a Drugs Epidemic on an English Community* (Milton Keynes: Open University Press, 1988); H. Parker and L. Williams, 'Intoxicated Weekends: Young Adults Work Hard- Play Hard Lifestyles, Public Health and Public Disorder,' *Drugs: Education, Prevention and Policy* 10 (2003), pp.345-367.

7   Cabinet Office, *Tackling Drugs to Build a Better Britain: The Government's Ten-Year Strategy for Tackling Drugs Misuse* (London: HMSO, 1998).

8   P. Reuter and A. Stevens, *An Analysis of UK Drug Policy*, (London: UK Drugs Policy Commission, 2007). The number of dependent heroin users in England increased sizeably from an estimated 5,000 in 1975 to 280,000 in the mid 2000s.

9   For more discussion on the role of DATs see K. Davies and J. Barnard, 'Working with Other Agencies,' in *Care of Drug Users in General Practice: A Harm Reduction Approach*, ed. B Beaumont (Abingdon, Oxon: Radcliffe Publishing, 2004), pp.157-176.

10 Information about Crime Reduction Partnerships is available from the Home Office web site http://www.crimereduction.homeoffice.gov.uk/partnerships2.htm [Cited May 2011].

11 T. Oc and S. Tiesdell, *Safer City Centres: Reviving the Public Realm*, (London: Paul Chapman, 1997), pp.198-221.

12 Carl Fellstrom deals comprehensively with the issues of serious organised crime in Nottingham at this time; C. Fellstrom, *Hoods: The Gangs of Nottingham* (Lancs: Milo Books, 2008). For an overview of the pattern of crime at this time see K. Coleman, C. Hird and D. Povey, *Home Office Statistical Bulletin: Violent Crime Overview, Homicide and Gun Crime 2004/2005, Supplementary Volume to Crime in England and Wales 2004/2005*, (London: HMSO, 2006).

13 Cabinet Office, *Tackling Drugs to Build a Better Britain: The Government's Ten-Year Strategy for Tackling Drugs Misuse* (London: HMSO, 1998).

14 Personal communication; Kate Davies OBE, former DAAT Co-ordinator, Nottinghamshire County, November 2009.

15 Mike Trace interviewed by Jane McGregor, April 2009. Trace was the UK Deputy Anti Drug Co-ordinator from 1997-2001.

16 'Woman killed defending her shop', *BBC News online*, September 30th 2003. Available from http://news.bbc.co.uk/1/hi/england/nottinghamshire/3152588.stm [Cited September 20th 2011].

17 Possession of an illegal firearm received a mandatory five year prison sentence from January 2004. This was in addition to new laws in the Anti-Social Behaviour Act to combat the misuse of air weapons and imitation firearms. Offences involving firearms (other than air weapons) increased by two per cent in the year to March 2003, a dramatic slowdown

compared to the 34 per cent increase the previous year. See 'Blunkett confirms five-year jail term for gun possession.' *The Independent*, January 6th 2003.

18 '*Policing in Nottinghamshire*' Local Police Summary 2007; Nottinghamshire Police, 'Crime Continues to Fall in Nottinghamshire,' *Engaging: Stakeholder Bulletin* (November 15th 2007).

19 *Report of Nottinghamshire Police: Nottingham Crime and Disorder Reduction Partnership* (Nottingham: Nottinghamshire Police, 5th February 2004).

20 Drink and crime,' *Nottingham Evening Post*, May 9th 2001.

21 Nottingham had more than 20 officers on patrol at weekends in the 1980s, according to the Police Federation chairman Brian Burdus; 'Drink and crime, '*Nottingham Evening Post*, 9th May 2001).

22 'City's recent history of murders' *BBC News online*, October 11th 2004. Available from http://news.bbc.co.uk/1/hi/england/nottinghamshire/3732706.stm [Cited September 26th 2011].

23 Licence law reforms could be 'hell' *BBC News online*, June 4th 2004. Available from http://news.bbc.co.uk/1/hi/programmes/panorama/3766637.stm [Cited March 26th 2010].

24 Licensing proposals were still being debated in Parliament. The Licensing Act 2003 came fully into force on November 23rd 2005.

25 'Out-going leader's vision is of a 24-hour city,' *Nottingham Evening Post*, March 15th 2002.

26 *Nottingham City Centre Problem Profile* (Nottingham: Nottinghamshire Police, 2005). Licensed capacity (combined occupancy of licensed premises) rose from 61,378 to 10, 8258 between 1997and 2004, representing a rise of 76% over the period. The capacity at 2 am equated to 37, 000.

27 At this time there were in excess of 50,000 students in attendance at the two universities, Nottingham Trent and the Nottingham of Nottingham.

28 'Problems of a high student population,' *Daily Telegraph*, June 14th 2003.

29 Ibid

30 'Drink and crime,' *Nottingham Evening Post*, May 9th 2001.

31 'Out-going leader's vision is of a 24-hour city,' *Nottingham Evening Post*, March 15th, 2002.

32 'Drink and crime,' *Nottingham Evening Post*, May 9th 2001.

33 There exists a body of work that critiques the role of CCTV in relation to the moral regulation of public space. See for example M. Levine, *Side and Closed Circuit Television (CCTV):Exploring Surveillance in Public Space* (Lancaster: University of Lancaster, 2000); J. Bannister, N. Fyfe and A. Kearns, 'Closed Circuit Television and the City,' in *Surveillance, Closed Circuit TV and Social Control*, eds. C. Norris, J. Moran and G. Armstrong (Aldershot: Ashgate, 1998).

34 Mobile CCTV vans were used in Operation Shield, a Home Office project to tackle alcohol related violence. See 'City centre a violent place,' *Nottingham Evening Post*, March 14th 2002.

35 'Drinking in the street,' *Nottingham Evening Post*, September 11th 2001.

36 T. Oc and S. Tiesdell, *Safer City Centres*, pp.218-219.

37 M. Hopkins and M. Maguire, *Targeted Policing Initiative- Reducing Alcohol Related Violence in Nottinghamshire* (Cardiff: Cardiff University, May 2002). According to Mike Maguire (personal communication: March 2009) a final version of the report was not written up but the findings were incorporated into a chapter of a book; M. Maguire and M. Hopkins, 'Data Analysis for Problem-Solving: Alcohol and City Centre Violence.,' in *Crime Reduction and Problem-Oriented Policing*, eds. K. Bullock and N Tilley (Devon: Willan, 2003), pp.126-153. A similar initiative is reported by A. Deehan, E. Marshall and E. Saville, *Police Research Series Paper 150: Drunks and Disorder: Processing Intoxicated Arrestees in Two City-Centre Custody Suites* (London: Policing and Reducing Crime Unit Research Home Office, Development and Statistics Directorate 2002). Also M. Hopkins and P. Sparrow, 'Sobering Up: Arrest Referral and Brief Intervention for Alcohol Users in the Custody Suite,' *Criminology and Criminal Justice* 6 (2006), pp. 389-410.

38 Operational Shield Project funded by £1.2 million Home Office grant.

39 'Drink and crime,' *Nottingham Evening Post* May 9th 2001.

40 Coventry, by way of example, which was of similar size to Nottingham, had about thirty officers on city centre patrol.

41 Paul Winter interviewed by Jane McGregor, Nottingham, November 2007.

42 Paul Winter interview

43 M. Maguire and M. Hopkins, 'Data Analysis for Problem-Solving: Alcohol and City Centre Violence.' in *Crime Reduction and Problem-Oriented Policing*), pp. 126-53.

44 'City centre a violent place,' *Nottingham Evening Post*, 14th March,2002.

45 Paul Winter took up post as local area commander for the city centre on January 1st 2004.

46 Kenneth Clarke interviewed by Jane McGregor, London, July 2007.

47 '50,000 drinkers on a square mile drinking circuit of 356 bars,' *Nottingham Evening Post*, June 4th 2004.

48 BBC 1, Panorama programme, *Cldnt Gve a 4XXXX for Lst Ordrs?* Television documentary broadcast on June 6th 2004.

49 Transcript of BBC 1, Panorama programme, *Cldnt Gve a 4XXXX for Lst Ordrs?* Available from http://news.bbc.co.uk/nol/shared/spl/hi/programmes/panorama/transcripts/xxxx.txt [Cited September 20th 2011].

50 Ibid

51 Ibid

52 'Labour concealed its doubts over 24-hour drinking initiative,' *Sunday Times*, June 6th 2004.

53 'A Tale of Two Cities,' *The Observer, Review section* May 22th 2005, pp. 1-2; 'Nottingham Grabs a Piazza of the Action,' *The Times*, April 3rd 2007, p.16.

54 For discussion of the ' new culture of intoxication' see F. Measham and K. Brain, 'Binge Drinking, British Alcohol Policy and the New Culture of Intoxication,' *Crime Media Culture*

1 (2005), pp. 262-283 ; G. Valentine, S. L. Holloway, M. Jayne and C. Knell, 'Drinking Places: Social Geographies of Consumption,' (York: Joseph Rowntree Foundation, 2007).

55   *Alcohol misuse: Interim Analytical Report* (Prime Minister's Strategy Unit, 2003).

56   'Labour concealed its doubts over 24-hour drinking initiative,' Sunday Times, June 6th 2004.

57   Ibid

58   'On the Streets of Binge Britain,' *The Observer*, Sept 5th 2004.

59   Ibid

60   C. Critcher, 'Moral Panics and Newspaper Coverage of Binge Drinking,' in *Pulling Newspapers Apart* ed. B. Franklin (London: Routledge, 2008), pp.154-162.

61   'Booze Britain', a fly-on-the-wall television series produced by Granada Television documenting the binge drinking culture of various towns and cities in the UK.

62   For example G. Hinsliff and M. Bright, 'Britain: A Nation in Grip of Drink Crisis,' *The Observer*, November 21st 2004; 'Binge Drink Panic Mirrors Hogarth's Gin Craze,' *Observer* September 9th 2007.

63   Some theorised that a type of 'mediacracy' developed particularly in relation to news media. The media was seen to outpace Government in terms of public influence and its propensity to dictate the direction of policy on headline issues. See D.L. Altheide, 'The Impact of Television News Formats on Social Policy,' *Journal of Broadcasting & Electronic Media* 35 (1991), pp.3-21

64   Cabinet Office, *Alcohol Harm Reduction Strategy for England* (London: Prime Minister's Strategy Unit 2004), p.7.

65   Joseph Rowntree Trust, *Drinking in the UK: An Exploration of Trends* (York: JRF, 2009). Department of Health estimates indicated that over two-thirds of young men and three-quarters of young women continued to drink within the sensible drinking guidelines. Also the British Crime Survey (BCS) 2006 suggested that, with the exception of 2003/04, the number of alcohol-related violent offences has decreased every year since 1995.

66   Alcohol was 65 per cent more affordable in 2007 than in 1980, accounting for only 5.2 per cent of household spending compared with 7.5 per cent in 1980. Women remained less likely than men to drink and continued to consume less. However, studies of the trends over the last 15 to 20 years have indicated a narrowing of the gender gap, with the drinking behaviour of women moving towards that of men; Joseph Rowntree Trust, *Drinking in the UK: An Exploration of Trends* (York: JRF, 2009), and Office of National Statistics *Psychiatric Morbidity among Adults Living in Private Households* (UK: ONS, 2000).

67   J. Greenaway, 'The Politics of Drink: Research on New Labour and Alcohol 1997-2005,' in *PAC Conference,* (York, 2008).

10

UK ALCOHOL POLICY: NATIONAL-LOCAL INTERACTION

The final chapter of the book draws together some conclusions about what can be learnt from documenting the recent history of drink and drink policy from the perspective of the local dimension. The most significant thing perhaps is that whilst it showed that doctors and activists in Nottingham brought together local, national and international developments in the treatment of alcoholism in order to tackle the city's alcohol problems, the problem itself was defined narrowly and for a lengthy period as the extreme case of the 'homeless alcoholic', a problem not of personal, but of societal inadequacy. From the 1960s, street drinking, in its shifting forms, was the core definition of local policy, and reflected a desire at the local level to do something about social deprivation in the city. Looking at the changing situation from a geographical as well as an historical perspective, helped show how a conceptual space was created over time by governing authorities and authoritative voices, in which the place and meaning of intoxicants was mapped out.[1] Moreover, studying a location in this way detected the surfacing of 'policy by geography', an idea that suggests specific areas, whilst working within government constraints, draw on their various capacities, including formal and informal networks, to adapt and innovate.[2] The approach to street drinking led to local schemes for community care becoming established that persisted when national policies hid a failure to deal with social ills and moved in new directions and devised methods that medicalised the problem and marginalised the alcoholic. The local approach continued to be sustained when national directives moved towards a public health/population based approach in the 1970s, and survived in the form of local resistance to the centrally-forged agenda, and an absence of government interest in alcohol in the 1980s, when national attention was diverted to HIV and drugs. In fact Nottingham's core approach remained intact right up to the early 2000s, when national and local policy collided over 'binge drinking', the newest soubriquet for street drinking. Since that time, national and local responses to alcohol have remained interconnected although there are signs locally that the persistent concern about deprivation is returning to the fore. In 2008 a local consultant in public health medicine described the problem in Nottingham as having *"a social gradient'*, and described the city's high rate of alcohol related hospital admissions as deprivation-linked.[3] Police also linked the problem to *'the social end of housing'*,[4] as did a fairly recent report of the Nottingham's Crime Reduction Partnership (CDP), which concluded that the common denominator locally may be deprivation and the wider issue of social exclusion".[5]

The approach used in this book also helps reveal how policies on drink were based on the intoxicating effect of the income that could be derived from alcohol. It highlights that as alcohol consumption became liberalised from restriction, policies of regulation operated that allowed access to society's elite spaces for the 'civilised' consumption of alcohol, but relegated the 'problems' of drink and denied access to these spaces to other groups; the young, women, the socially inept, for fear of the destabilising effect on society. This moral discourse is captured in modern-day etchings 'Binge Lane' and 'Pub Street' (see opposite and overleaf) by British artist Enoch Sweetman, which emulate William Hogarth's Gin Lane and Beer Street. The drawings, created for the Society of Independent Brewers, convey the message that drinking in pubs is socially proper, whilst buying cheap alcohol from supermarkets and drinking it on the streets are the ways of the socially inept.[6]

Binge drinking: a national problem?

Binge drinking remains of concern because many UK drinkers regularly consume alcohol at levels in excess of UK guideline limits; a binge most often defined as the consumption of 5 or more standard drinks in a single drinking occasion. One reason people are drinking more is thought to be the availability of low-cost alcoholic beverages. For this reason government currently is considering the introduction of a minimum price per unit of alcohol as a means to reduce UK alcohol consumption. A recent report by Hagger *et al* suggested the public are largely sceptical of the introduction of a minimum price per unit alcohol-pricing policy, but believe such a policy would be acceptable if introduced as part of a wider strategy to curb alcohol consumption.[7] But strategies to curb consumption may not be as necessary as they were considered several years ago because although UK consumption increased by 40 per cent between 1970 and 2007,[8] per capita consumption appears to be falling again. Recent figures suggest men and women of all ages are slowly curbing their excesses. Recent data from the Office for National Statistics (ONS) suggest that heavy drinking is falling, abstinence is rising, and young people are leading the drive towards healthier patterns of drinking.[9]

Etching by artist Enoch Sweetman ©SIBA

Enoch Sweetman ©SIBA

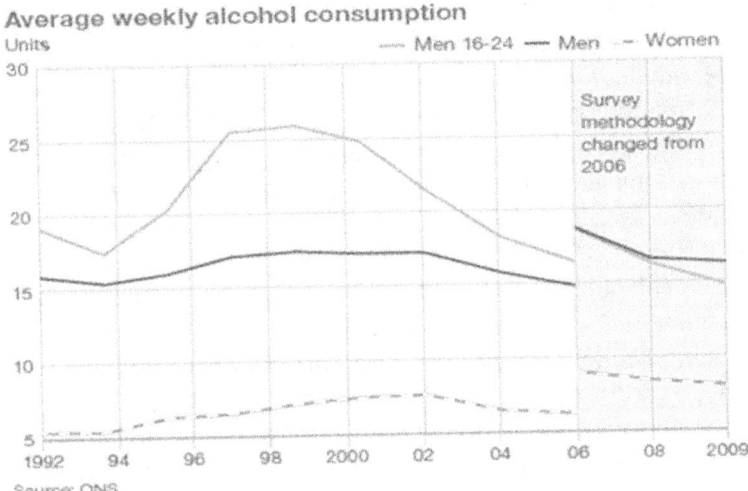

The ONS figures tally with data of the British Beer and Pubs Association (BBPA), which show that alcohol sales peaked in 2004 but have fallen by 13 per cent since. The recent shift in consumption levels is not that unexpected. Historically, sales of alcohol have tended to rise and fall with the economy; recent examples include the recessions in the early 1980s and 1990s, which were coupled with a slump in drinking. It appears that the current economic downturn is having a similar effect, as during the period 2008-2009 per capita alcohol consumption in the UK fell by six per cent. Consumption per head rose 0.6 per cent in 2010, but was still 11% lower than in 2004 when a decline in consumption began.[10]

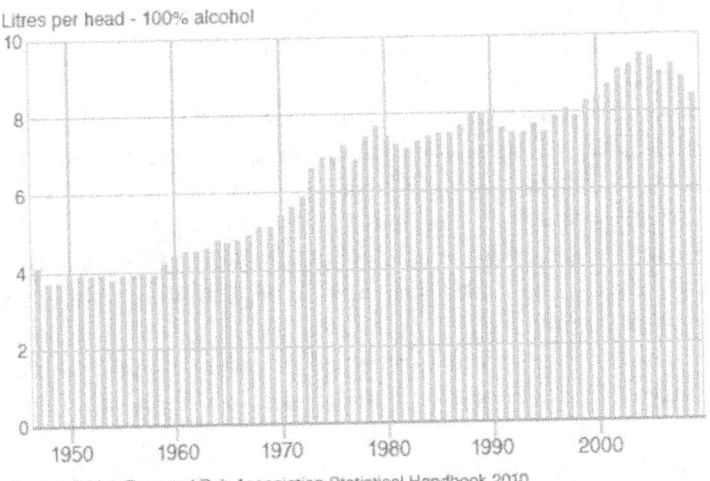

Some argue that the decline in consumption came about because the concept of 24-hour drinking never properly took off, pointing to the average pub only opening 24 minutes longer after 11pm last orders was abolished.[11] Others argue that the decline in consumption was as a result of the negative publicity and headlines that made out Britain was out of control. According to promoters of this view this set a new tone for alcohol reporting and led people to moderate their behaviour because of a new kind of social stigma around being drunk. Whatever the reasons for the recent decline in population consumption, hospital admissions for alcohol-related problems remain high, a situation that prompted the Department of Health recently to advise that government alcohol policy should ensure alcohol becomes less affordable permanently, not just during the current downturn, the department's concern being based on the assumption that alcohol consumption will rise again once the economy picks up. This point was also stressed recently by Alcohol Concern, which pointed to the 10 million people currently drinking above the government's recommended level, and 1.6 million thought to be alcohol dependent. This concern is underscored by mortality rates for alcohol-related deaths, which though recently showing a decrease – a fall from 6,769 in 2008 to 6,584 in 2009, remain 20 per cent higher than figures for 2001 (5,477).[12]

CHANGING FACE OF THE PROBLEM

One of the most obvious changes to occur has been to do with the transformation of the face and character of the problem drinker. Over time a perceptible shift occurred that saw the problem drinker first as the older alcoholic then the young binge drinker. In addition there had been increasing focus on women drinkers. Concern about youth and women, in truth, has been rumbling away since the 1960s. The moral code that existed in the immediate post-war period was broken down by a process of social change. The shift was formalised by legal changes in the 1960s. Abortion and homosexuality became legal, capital punishment was abolished, and measures were taken to improve the position of women. The authority of age was overthrown and, in its place, there was an emphasis on youth. Young people took their leave of the leisure pursuits of their parents and took up interests of their own. Alcohol, illicit drugs, pop and rock music, and changing political attitudes were among the activities that put a strain on age relations and signified a new problem of youth. Successive measures that saw licensing restrictions lifted also helped a trend in youth drinking. In 1961 there was provision made for late night drinking in restaurants and clubs. The change was first made in London in 1949 but extended in 1961 to the whole country. Pub hours were slightly extended and there was more flexibility permitted in the setting of the hours of drinking. In 1964 an Act promoted growth in the number of off-licenses, which facilitated their appearance in food shops. In addition the abolition of Resale Price Maintenance in 1964 encouraged home drinking. This had a big impact for in 1951, there were 26,200 off-licenses but by the late 1970s, the figure had risen to 41,100. Drink consumption rose dramatically from 1960s to end of 1970s. This was partly a reflection of demand for drink but also an issue of supply. Supermarkets began selling at a discount following removal of retail price maintenance and consumer tastes changed; imported beers and spirits became more popular as did advertising. The 1980s saw the youth market's potential rocked by high unemployment. Commentators from the commercial sector even speculated whether 'the commercial and cultural centre of gravity' needed to shift up to the middle age group. Meanwhile pub hours were extended (Licensing Act 1988), allowing pubs to remain open in the afternoons during weekdays. Despite the predictions, for many young people the 1990s turned out to be a time of relative prosperity,[13] a tendency which saw British youngsters feted by marketers, who noted that young people had developed 'a new consumption and success ethic', generated by economic growth.[14] This view influenced the drinks industry's marketing approach of the mid and late 1990s, a time when the 'consumer culture' took hold. But only a few years later in the early 2000s, at the height of debates over 24-hour drinking, youth were the face of the new drink problem and the scourge of British society.

Women also featured heavily in the commentary on binge drinking. Early on this took the form of attacks on the 'ladette' culture. Then policy makers and the media suggested that the panic over young women in town centres was unjust and young women were being demonised unfairly when the problem lay with middle age, professional women who drank excessively.[15] Often viewed in the past as a comparatively civilised form of drinking, women's drinking habits have come under attack because national statistics show this group, and middle class, middle aged women in particular, are drinking more frequently and more heavily.[16] Yet in the introduction of the book it was pointed out that women's drinking has emerged, diminished and re-emerged as a focus of concern at different historical moments. From the early twentieth century when a new critique of alcohol evolved, which pointed to increasing female insobriety as a factor in infant mortality; to the 1960s and 1970s and concern about the 'hidden harms' of women's alcohol abuse on infants and family life, attacks on women's drinking have occurred when women's position and roles in society have altered. Concern about women, and the debate about who is, and is not, a problem drinker looks set to continue. This has led some to query whether the UK's policy of encouraging supposedly civilised European café bar and home-based drinking whilst demonising working class adult 'problem drinking', was the right one. Britain at present is one of the heaviest alcohol consuming countries in the world and has a lower than average percentage of non-drinkers.[17] Current alcohol trends and the focus on binge drinking may challenge some of the lasting stereotypes about problem drinking and may even make us ponder on why we have been so eager to demonise young people. But there still exists resistance on the part of policy makers to recognise that consumption patterns never stay static, but go down as well as up.

Local-national interaction and the policy process

The core proposition of this book is that in the early 2000s the national problem of 'binge drinking' became linked to Nottingham. Even in a centralised state such as the UK, the capacity for local actors and implementers to define the problem and to take initiatives that diverge from those at the national level, has been considerable. Yet studies of the policy process often emphasise only the processes of national policy making and neglect the important role of local definitions of a problem and their persistence despite national policy change. Such a 'national-centric view' overlooks the interplay between levels yet as this case study illustrates, the local dimension can and does influence national policy, and *vice versa*. Nottingham's responses to drink drew on long standing local themes and issues, but also drew on national and international ones; the binge crisis being a good illustration of the interplay. Police used the problem of binge drinking disorder to draw attention to a local resourcing issue, yet we now know the problem was overstated, for in fact the level of binge drinking in Nottingham was not far off the national average during the 'binge crisis'. Figures indicate 20.3 per cent of the population over the age of sixteen were binge drinking compared to 18.2 per cent nationally; statistics which do not justify the city being singled out at that time.[18] This suggests other issues were at play affecting local-national relations and Nottingham's role in shaping national policy at this time, which are brought to the fore next.

EXPLANATIONS OF THE FREQUENT SEPARATION AND OCCASIONAL UNITY BETWEEN LOCAL-NATIONAL POLICY

The mainstay local problem, defined by both the local community and by doctors as one of vagrancy and homelessness, was pushed aside by police in the 1990s who redefined the predicament as one of youth. Nevertheless doctors and others in the local alcohol sector remained preoccupied with the homeless drinker, even though national and local responses got closer together again. The pattern observed of frequent separation and occasional unity with the national perspective can be explained by the fact that local policy was influenced to a great extent by local community concerns. Hence when the issues that were important locally became important nationally, greater unity was observed between local and centre; though of course the national definition was exposed to, as well as influenced by, a myriad of factors that the local level was not.

When one looks across the whole study period from the 1950s to the present, the first time policy perceptibly converged was the 1960s, when national and local concerns over poverty and homelessness combined. At that time housing conditions in many British cities were substandard and homelessness was linked to housing shortages. A series of policies from the late 1960s onwards focused on the problems of deprivation in inner city areas. The media played a significant role in amplifying the problem, which resulted in homeless people attracting significant public sympathy. The BBC television film 'Cathy Come Home', for example, helped draw attention to the issue and mobilised voluntary impulses that led to the establishment of new voluntary organisations such as the national organisation, 'Shelter.'[19] The response in Nottingham to homelessness at that time, as nationally, relied extensively on voluntary action and mutual aid, and was likely triggered by events at the centre where street homelessness received national attention because it was such a visible signifier of wider social problems such as poverty and housing shortage. The focus on street people nevertheless shifted the focus of national alcohol policy towards the habitual drunken offender. In the early 1970s this shift saw an interface developed between medical and criminal policy with the Home Office report on the 'Habitual Drunken Offender' in 1971 and subsequent Criminal Justice Act 1972, which empowered police to take persons who were drunk and incapable or disorderly to a medical centre for alcoholics.[20] Nottingham's response, as detailed in chapter two, was in keeping with this centre view, though developments resulted not from blind adherence to central authority but through a local desire to address social inadequacies.

The next time policy started to converge was when a fear of crime arose in the social realm in the 1980s. Economic decline, social unrest and high unemployment, especially among young people, were problems apparent in the public sphere. The Conservative government of the time characterised the core problem in society as crime and disorder. It introduced in 1988 the 'Safer City Initiative' following a number of earlier crime prevention initiatives to cut crime. These sought not only to create safer cities, but to provide opportunities for economic enterprise and community life to flourish.[21] There followed another government scheme in 1995, the 'CCTV Challenge' initiative; which led to the installation of closed circuit television cameras (CCTV) in many UK city centres. Crime and anti-social behaviour developed as a major political concern after that and was a strong theme of political campaigns in the general election of 1997, with New Labour pledging to be *"tough on crime and tough on the causes of crime"* in its party manifesto.[22] Concerns in Nottingham mirrored those of the centre at that time. It had a particular struggle with high crime and extensively installed closed circuit television cameras as a counter-measure. This led to it becoming one of the most heavily surveyed places in the UK, a situation that in all probability heightened concern over the scope and magnitude of the problem.[23] CCTV formed part of a rise in 'surveillance society' and had consequences on everyday life.[24] It and new communication technologies such as the Internet meant public life was ever more scrutinised. This development had impacts on the speed with which governments became aware of, and responded to, public problems; Nottingham's high levels of surveillance providing valuable 'evidence' of a new problem of binge drinking, the surveillance footage often forming the basis of news stories and commentaries on 'proper' behaviour in public spaces.[25]

SOCIAL PSYCHIATRY'S ROLE IN SHAPING THE LOCAL RESPONSE

Looking now to what first shaped the Nottingham view of the problem of drink; a lot can be made of the fact that it pioneered a form of psychiatry - social psychiatry. The approach had a humane, patient-centred meaning and involved care that was administered outside the asylum in the community. This fitted well with the community response to poverty that emerged in the city in the 1960s. The influence of internationally renowned psychiatrist, Duncan Macmillan, who pioneered 'open door' and community care policies in the late 1950s and 1960s plus the influence of a group of émigré doctors from Germany, Austria and other European countries who had knowledge of social psychiatry and psychoanalysis and applied it to their work, had a huge impact on hospitals' policies. Macmillan regarded the community care approach as a means by which to prevent frequent readmission of patients who previously would have had prolonged admissions. The approach was intended to raise morale and the status of both patients and staff, with custodial care replaced by a new therapeutic and social relationship between doctors and patients.

So it was that community care developed as a central feature of treatment for problem drinkers at the local level.[26] Psychiatry was able to innovate, as well as fit in with the demands and events of the local community because at that time the place of medicine within the state was not particularly centralised. This meant local variance could develop over policy to tackle mental illness.[27] The adoption of a community approach meant co-operation was fostered between the hospital and the local community.[28] Alfred Minto, the psychiatrist charged with setting up the original addiction unit at Mapperley, worked tirelessly with, and on behalf of, the local community. This meant that responses from psychiatry became meshed with ideas from the community (self help, and mutual aid) plus the voluntary sector, criminal justice and social care sectors to form a unified local approach, though in later years this fragmented. Nevertheless the long-term preservation of the policy of treating the vagrant alcoholic is evidence of the existence of a determined local treatment culture. Over time the treatment culture was maintained because psychiatrists coming to work at the addiction unit at Mapperley subsequently were drawn to the hospital because of its involvement in community care and commitment to the social side of mental illness. In the allied sectors of criminal justice and social care, an equivalent idea was available for professionals to respond to; this being the idea of 'community development'. The commitment to community responses coupled with little movement in the constituency of actors and networks in Nottingham over time, meant the treatment approach persisted for a long time in relatively unhampered style.

Medical autonomy also goes some way to explaining the mechanisms that kept the local model on its original course. The 'doctrine of clinical autonomy' was an issue at the heart of early NHS policy and had implications for the relationship between policy makers at the centre and clinical decision makers at the local level.[29] The centre's lack of authority over clinical decisions could often confer positive advantages in certain circumstances. It meant that local alcoholism treatment was shaped by the pioneering effort of local psychiatrists at Mapperley Hospital rather than rigidly having to stick to a clinical pathway envisaged by the Ministry of Health. In fact medicine maintained its favoured approach without any outside interference until the 1990s when it faced increasing challenge by the centre and from competing views, such as the treatment paradigm of the private sector treatment centre, The Nottingham Clinic. Nevertheless by this stage medicine was somewhat 'path dependent'; its traditions had become self reinforcing and its approach increasingly narrow.[30] What maintained its dependence on this path mostly was resistance to outside interference. The local approach was exposed to a sustained challenge from the 1980s onwards because national policy had an explicit aim to change practice. Co-ordination of the local approach was at first of an informal and kind, but with the advent of the Nottinghamshire Council on Alcoholism (NCA) in the 1970s, which was a regional arm of the National Council on Alcoholism, the local level became not only better connected to the national level but more organised. The NCA had a mediating or brokering role which helped the different local groups stick to their original objective. By the late 1980s, the NCA's co-ordinating role was much reduced however, affected by wider changes including the contract culture of the NHS, and the new 'managerialism' introduced into health and social care. This change brought a new tier of policy makers to the local level and a trend towards a whole community/ public health approach. This meant that from the 1990s the local level lacked the kind of mediation necessary to pacify competing local groups, and as a result tensions became more apparent as groups jostled for dominance. This eventually gave rise to a rift between medicine and police over what constituted the local problem, and ultimately led to separate responses.

The detectable shift in relative autonomy at the different levels of policy making around the late 1980s and early 1990s with escalating central control exerted on the local level also included a reduction in the level of clinical autonomy for doctors within the NHS. At the national level there was a push for more central co-ordination, even from the sector itself, and there were calls from bodies like Alcohol Concern for a national strategy for alcohol. In addition to this shift there was also one in the way responses to alcohol and other health problems were formulated, with an internationalisation process developing in the world of research, and the introduction of evidence based practice in medicine, and policy.[31] These shifts had significant impacts on the character of national policymaking, which took a more top-down approach from this time. First under the arrangements laid out in the Community Act 1990, local social service authorities took coordinating responsibility as 'lead agency' and were charged with conducting 'needs assessments' and funding appropriate levels of care to individuals in the community presenting with problems. Then by the mid 1990s a national system of policy coordination was put in place. This involved regional alcohol co-ordinators having input and the Drug and Alcohol Action Team (DAAT) approach. This phase of policy co-ordination was pivotal, being a period during which local variation became much reduced.

THE RISE AND ROLE OF THE CRIMINAL JUSTICE SECTOR

Police concern about binge drinking in Nottingham's night-time economy in the early 2000s and the subsequent involvement of Nottingham's Chief Constable in the national policy debate were circumstances that helped bring local and national policy together. Stephen Green expressed his concerns publically, which led to Nottingham representing the new trend in binge drinking just as Government began a process of overhauling UK licensing laws (Licensing Act of 2003). The fact that Green emerged as a key player in the binge drinking crisis suggests there is an important role for individuals, sometimes called 'product champions' or 'policy entrepreneurs.' It suggests that in the policy process influence remains dispersed throughout the system of policy making; that individuals *do* have power to influence the policy process, despite it seeming a far less personality-driven process than in the past. Though there is relatively little written about this, a recent case study from the academic field of environmental policy suggests a personal desire to influence policy, and effort in doing so by focusing particular attention on the power centres of the time (central government), plus status and being in the right location, are all factors which may help individuals influence policy in important ways.[32]

Alcohol was firmly on the political agenda after the above-mentioned events. The criminal justice sector's involvement in policy over drink was seen as justified at the time because statistics suggested over one-third (37%) of offenders had an existing problem with alcohol use, a similar proportion (37%) had problems with binge drinking and 32 per cent of offenders had violent behaviour related to their drinking.[33] Hence, though the main driver of the reforms had been a commercial one, government justified its reforms on the grounds that they would combat alcohol-related crime and anti-social behaviour. As a consequence, criminal justice developed as a new and important frame for national alcohol policy. Health was notably absent from policy discussion at this time and policy over alcohol developed a strong criminal justice flavour (*Alcohol Harm Reduction Strategy for England*, 2004).[34] Having jostled for dominance, the medical lobby, which for so long had promoted public health responses to alcohol, seemed to lose the fight, and its influence in policy making circles for the time being at least, became somewhat diminished.

Since that time, there has been more of a balance between the two approaches and calls from various quarters to deal more effectively with alcohol's hidden harms. This means that whilst policy appears to be continuing along the lines of the community safety/criminal justice approach, there have been more attempts of late to integrate public health measures. A recent example of this has been the Liberal-Conservative coalition's unveiled plans to set a minimum price for alcohol in England and Wales. Government said banning shops and bars from selling drinks for less than the tax paid on them would cut crime and set a 'base price' for the first time. Many health campaigners were behind the move though were disappointed by the minimum prices set, arguing that

Government was too lenient with the drinks industry over the issue; the Royal College of Physicians arguing that the proposed minimum prices were too small a step likely to have no impact on the vast amount of cheap drinks sold in supermarkets.[35] Doubtless health campaigners, the criminal justice sector and the drinks industry have a lot invested in the way issues are debated in public, but it is probably right to 'call time' on 'Binge Britain' and to adopt policies based on a more nuanced understanding of the problems and benefits of drink instead.

CHANGING REALITIES

The point just made leads to another important issue, which is that perceptions and definitions of the problem of drink have been altered by changing realities. In the aftermath of the Second World War, British society was changing fast. The 1960s saw greater diversity in society, challenges to the system of social class and changes in gender roles. With social and legislative changes came behaviour changes that affected most aspects of everyday life. The leisure scene reflected the changes, especially the public house. Though the pub still played an important role in the lives of many in the late 1950s, it was not fashionable with the young. This all started to change however, when the 1961 Licensing Act's tidied up and amended existing laws and kick-started a dramatic move towards liberalisation. The 1961 Act made provision for late night drinking in restaurants and clubs. The changes were first made in London in 1949 but following the introduction of the 1961 Act, were extended to the whole country. Then in 1964 a subsequent Act promoted growth in the number of off-licenses, which facilitated their appearance in food shops. In addition the abolition of Resale Price Maintenance in 1964 encouraged home drinking. These shifts had important consequences for the drink scene. Changes in Nottingham reflected this, with new bars and restaurants appearing that pulled in the young crowd, as most likely happened up and down the country in towns and cities. Following on in the 1980s, there was a further lifting of restrictions in 1987 which saw intoxicating liquor able to be served with meals in restaurants. Then in 1988 mid afternoon drinking in a public house was allowed on a weekday in England and Wales; this latter shift signposting the way to development of the night-time economy in the 1990s.

The developments in the physical and social environments meant that the relationship between young people and city space began to change. Young people became more visible for one thing; as witnessed by the trend in 'circuit drinking' and in their habit of congregating in city centre spaces.[36]

This development led to opportunities for the commercial sector so that by the 1990s Nottingham's city centre, like many UK city centres, had developed into a leisure space for the young. These changes contributed significantly to the rise in concern about youth disorder. Evolving from the separation of youth from the leisure activities of older adults in the 1960s 'youth bashing' developed as a national obsession. Here, Nottingham reflected the new obsession, and its reputation for crime was the catalyst for responses that majorly influenced national developments. The emphasis on surveillance in the early 1990s placed great focus on the issues of crime and disorder and here again, Nottingham reflected the times. It operated city 'clean ups', where undesirables, the itinerant and intoxicated young, were removed from the streets or else hidden from view; in preparation for the city's transformation into a thoroughly modern city, a 'playscape' for the excesses of consumerism and youth. [37]

Since the early 2000s when bingeing on alcohol erupted as a major problem of society, things have notably changed. Since those heady days of the consumer boom the local situation, as nationally, has been hard hit by the economic downturn. On the alcohol treatment front the most significant local shift has been a move by medicine away from the homeless drinker. Instead there has been emphasis on tackling the significant burden of alcohol consumption of the wider community. Nationally and locally in the arena of treatment, drug and alcohol have been viewed as comparable or equivalent issues, and the drive has been about 'recovery'. At around the time of the global crisis, a new recovery movement emerged in the UK. Many of the instigators of the movement were from the UK residential rehabilitation sector, and adherents of AA. They were concerned about the direction of UK drug treatment policy at that time, where it seemed there was an over-emphasis on getting people into treatment, rather than 'off' drugs. Many of the campaigners and lobbyists being AA followers, viewed recovery as a permanent process without culmination, and this led to a renewed focus on abstinence. Recovery since this time has been taken up by government. First as a theme in the New Labour drug strategy, Drugs: Protecting families and communities (2008), which promised a radical new focus on services 'to help drug users to re-establish their lives'. Then the theme was echoed in the Drug Strategy 2010, and most recently in the National Treatment Agency's consultation document 'Building Recovery in Communities.'[38] The shift to recovery and abstinence may well reflect, be indicative of, these more sober, economically-turbulent times.

The aforementioned shifts have had serious implications for the local level with the homeless sector bearing the brunt of the changes and seeing responses to the homeless scaled back. The dropping of concern about the homeless drinker by health culminated in early 2011 in the forced closure of the wet centre at Handel Street after it was decommissioning by local health and social care commissioners. The move prompted Framework Housing Association, the organisation behind the wet centre, to retaliate with a well orchestrated media campaign. Despite this, funding for the issue of homelessness has been seriously cut back. Framework has since organised high profile fundraising campaigns including one called the 'Big Sleep Out campaign'. This sets out to challenge the people of Nottingham to give up their beds to sleep out in the city centre for one night. The development coincides with the release of new figures that show homelessness in Nottingham rose by 80 per cent in 2010. It is likely that local activists will continue to campaign over the issue for the foreseeable future.

Another concern looming large locally is the threat of yet another youth crime crisis. This follows copycat riots that broke out in August 2011 in Nottingham, Birmingham, Liverpool and Bristol after several nights of rioting in London. Most of the incidents that occurred in Nottingham took place in the St Ann's area of the city. Trouble began when missiles were thrown at a marked police car by a gang of young people. After that youths rampaged through the area, attacking a police station, damaging cars and setting light to a container of tyres. In a second night of rioting in the city, five police stations were fire-bombed and violent disorder spread to extensive areas of the city with groups of masked and hooded youths causing violent disturbance, criminal damage and arson. Like the copycat riots in the city in the 1980s, the episode provoked debate about whether the rioters belonged to a criminal, feral underclass or were victims of the economic blight getting their own back on the rest of society.[39] Nationally the riots proved a watershed moment for social policy, a warning that urgent action was required to tackle racial disadvantage and distrust in the police. Since then the London School of Economics announced it will be working on the first empirical study into the rioting and looting.[40]

Conclusion

In drawing conclusions about drink and responses to it over time, one can point to trends in drinking patterns coming and going, and consumption rising and falling. These fluctuations make abundantly clear that the UK does *not* have a fixed drinking culture, that 'Binge Britain' is not a permanent state. The fluctuations in UK drinking patterns are inextricably bound up with changing economic and social conditions and because the vast majority of people in

Britain consume alcohol, this permits drink to act as some sort of social barometer, and reflect something of the times. Drinking, whether *en masse* or individually, reflects the state of our health and well being.

Examining the recent history of UK alcohol policy has exposed some important issues for the makers of current and future policy. It has shown how much policy is, for example, brought about not so much on the basis of carefully assembled scientific evidence, but as historian James Nicholls aptly put it, by means of persuasion, power and consensus. Politicians and the public make decisions based upon values, personal interests and prejudices as well as countless other factors, so that 'evidence' ends up becoming, as Nicholls would have it, '*the servant of other forms of persuasion.*'[41] The problem for government is that concern about drink, and other issues of public interest such as crime, has intensified with the emergence of surveillance technologies and new modes of communication. Greater scrutiny and surveillance of public spaces played an important role in magnifying the problem of Binge Britain on the streets. It distorted perceptions; most of the public made their acquaintance with binge-drinking via television and the newspapers and the media controlled how we saw it, by creating the images and texts that shaped perceptions of the phenomenon, and gave new definition of the problem. But lest we forget, though the media projected the crisis, behind it were a series of organisations, professional bodies and pressure groups that fed information and statistics, and pursued agendas which reflected their own views on politics and society.

Studying the recent history of alcohol from the point of view of the local dimension has provided an opportunity to observe and document not just the key national developments affecting British attitudes to drink, but more subtle changes and nuances over time in the social context and in everyday life. From this position, one observes a number of trends over time, one of the most important being a need of society to scapegoat certain groups, in order that the rest of society are freed from blame and granted license to drink. On the policy front, a pattern of kneejerk reaction emerges whenever consumption goes up; a circumstance where panic frequently sets in, when the problem is linked to social class. Studying policy change from the local viewpoint also has unearthed gaps between what was intended by national government and what was implemented in policy terms, a circumstance that sheds some light on the interplay between the different levels of policy. This is an aspect of the policy making process about which little is actually known so in that respect this book's account of national and local events and processes adds to the emerging body of evidence that identifies how 'problems' for government evolve as part of a social process involving interaction between international, national and local dimensions. As others have pointed out, it is not so much the *dimensions* of a problem but the *definitions* of it, which are most in need of analysis.[42] Shifts in policy are often brought about by a general acceptance of new definitions of the problem, emerging from the local dimension. Examination of the local therefore teaches us that above all else, no matter how divorced from the local dimension policy making often appears, in the end, and in borrowed words, "All politics is local."[43]

Notes

1   A. McShane and J. Kneale, 'Histories and geographies of intoxicants and intoxication – an introduction,' *Social History of Alcohol and Drugs*, 25 (2011), pp.6-14.

2   P. Hadfield, S. Lister and P. Traynor. 'The Orientation and Integration of Local and National Alcohol Policy in England and Wales.' (London: AERC, 2009).

3   *Nottingham Evening Post*, 'Teenagers want QMC drink unit,' 29th November 2008.

4   Paul Winter (Local Area Commander) interviewed by Jane McGregor, Nottingham, October 2007.

5   Policing and Public Safety: Crime and Anti Social Behaviour Report 18th March 2008.

6   Sweetman's 'Binge Lane' saw the gin of the 18th century replaced by a trolley of cheap drinks. Drunken tramps, fighting youths and schoolgirls outside an off-licence named 'Beer Gin Booze', while 'Pub Street' (a second painting based on Hogarth's Beer Street not shown here) showed a collection of overweight bourgeois drinking pints of ale in a much more sedate environment. These etchings were commissioned by The Society of Independent Brewers (SIBA) and are reproduced with full permission from former SIBA chairman, Peter Amor.

7   M.S. Hagger, A.J. Lonsdale, R. Baggott, G. Penny, and M. Bowen, *The Cost of Alcohol: The Advocacy for a Minimum Price per Unit in the UK*, (London: AERC, 2011).

8   Office for National Statistics, *Over a third of adults exceed regular daily drinking Limit* (Newport, UK: Office for National Statistics, 2007).

9   General Lifestyle Survey (formerly the General Household Survey), *Smoking and Drinking, 2009* (London: ONS, 2009).

10 British Beer and Pub Association, *Statistical Handbook 2011* (London: BBPA, 2011).

11 'Why is alcohol consumption falling?' *BBC news magazine*, February 15th 2011.

12 NHS Information Centre, *Statistics on Alcohol: England, 2011* (London: The Health and Social Care Information Centre, 2011)

13 J.C Coleman, *Youth policy in the 1990s: the way forward* (New York: Routledge, 1992) pp.207& 225.

14 B. Osgerby, Youth media (New York: Routledge, 2004), p. 26.

15 Headlines such as; 'Alcohol abuse: middle class women are new bingers, *Daily Express*, October 4th 2011; 'Why middle class women are dying for a drink,' *Daily Mail*, June 3rd 2010.

16 General Lifestyle Survey (GLF), formerly General Household Survey, *Smoking and drinking, 2009* (London: ONS, 2009).

17 Institute of Alcohol Studies, *Alcohol Consumption and Harm in the UK and EU* (St. Ives: IAS, 2010).

18 Alcohol Needs Assessment Research project, Department of Health (2004).

19 K. Loch, "Cathy Com Home, (UK; BBC, 1966). This was followed by a later film; T. Kotcheff, "Edna, the Inebriate Woman." (UK: BBC, 1971).

20 Home Office, "Report on the 'Habitual Drunken Offender'," (London: HMSO, 1971); **Criminal Justice Act 1972 (c.71).**

21 T. Oc and S. Tiesdell, *Safer City Centres: Reviving the Public Realm*, (London: Paul Chapman, 1997), pp.76-81.

22 New Labour's Manifesto, 1997.

23 T. Oc and S. Tiesdell, *Safer City Centres*, pp. 218-219.

24 The implications of surveillance are discussed in D. Lyon, *Surveillance Society: Monitoring Everyday Life* (Buckingham: Open University Press, 2001).

25 G. Palmer, 'The New You: Class and Transformation in Lifestyle Television,' in *Understanding Reality Television*, eds. S. Holmes and D. Jermyn (London: Routledge, 2004), pp. 173-190.

26 L. Clarke, 'The Opening of Doors in British Mental Hospitals in the 1950s,' *History of Psychiatry* 4 (1993), pp.527-551. Also S. Davies and S. Payne, "Patients Repeatedly Admitted to Psychiatric Wards: A Four-Year Follow-Up," *Psychiatric Bulletin* 20 (1996), pp.342-344.

27 M. Neve, 'A Commentary on the History of Social Psychiatry and Psychotherapy in Twentieth-Century Germany, Holland and Great Britain,' *Medical History* 48 (2004), pp.407-412. Also M. Gorsky, 'Public Health in Interwar England and Wales: Did It Fail?' *Dynamis* 28 (2008), pp.175-198; J. Lewis, *What Price Community Medicine? The Philosophy, Practice and Politics of Public Health since 1919* (Brighton: Wheatsheaf, 1986).

28 Nottingham No 3 Management Committee, 'The Pioneer Years in Mental Health 1948-70,' (Nottingham: Mapperley Hospital, 1970). The issue of émigrés at Mapperley was discussed by Alfred Minto during interview, Nottingham, October 2009.

29 R. Klein, *The New Politics of the NHS: From Creation to Re-Invention* (Oxon: Radcliffe Publishing, 2006), pp.62-64.

30 The concept of path dependence is explored in J. Mahoney, 'Path Dependence in Historical Sociology,' *Theory and Society* 29 (2000), pp. 507-548.

31 Shifts in medical autonomy are discussed in S. Harrison and W. I. U. Ahmad, 'Medical Autonomy and the UK State 1975 to 2025,' *Sociology* 34 (2000), pp. 129-146.

32   F.J. Convery, 'Making a Difference - How Environmental Economists Can Influence the Policy Process - a Case Study of David W Pearce,' *Environmental and Resource Economics* 37 (2007), pp.7-32.

33   National Probation Service, *Working with alcohol-misusing offenders – a strategy for delivery* (London, HMSO, 2006).

34   Cabinet Office, *Alcohol Harm Reduction Strategy for England* (Prime Minister's Strategy Unit, HMSO, 2004), p. 7.

35   'Minimum alcohol price levels planned by coalition,' *BBC News*, January 18th 2011.

36   L. Gofton, 'On the Town: Drink and the New Lawlessness', *Youth and Society* 29 (1990), pp.33-39; L. Gofton, 'Folk Devils and the Demon Drink: Drinking Rituals and Social Integration in North East England,' *Drogalkohol* 12 (1988), pp.181-196.

37   P. Chatterton and R. Hollands, 'Theorising Urban Playscapes: Producing, Regulating and Consuming Youthful Nightlife City Spaces,' *Urban Studies* 39 (2002), pp.95-116; P. Chatterton and R. Hollands, *Urban Nightscapes: Youth Cultures, Pleasure Spaces and Corporate Power* (London: Routledge, 2003).

38   Home Office, *Drugs: protecting families and communities* (London: HMSO, 2008); National Treatment Agency, *Building recovery in communities; A consultation for developing recovery-orientated framework to replace Models of Care* (London: HMSO, 2011); Home Office, The drug strategy, 'Reducing demand, restricting supply, building recovery: supporting people to live a drug-free life' (London: HMSO, 2010).

39   'Rioters in Nottingham damage vehicles,' *BBC News*, August 9th 2011; 'Hiding under her hood: The smirking 11-year-old girl in 'large scale riot rampage' refuses to apologise,' The Daily Mail, August 11th 2011.

40   'Reading the Riots study to examine causes and effects of August unrest,' The Guardian, September 5th 2011.

41   J. Nicholls, Alcohol policy comment: determinants, influences and the media, Alcohol Policy UK, March 28th 2011. Available at http://www.alcoholpolicy.net/2011/03/alcohol-policy-comment-determinants-influences-and-the-media.html [Cited October 6th 2011].

42   V. Berridge, *Opium and the People: Opiate Use and Drug Control Policy in Nineteenth and Early Twentieth Century England* (London: Free Association Books, 1999), p. xxix.

43   The phrase "All politics is local" was coined by former Speaker of the US House of Representatives, Thomas Phillip O'Neill, Jr. (December 9th 1912 – January 5th 1994).

REFERENCE SOURCES

References are divided under documents, reports and guidelines and printed sources.

DOCUMENTS

Nottinghamshire Archives

CITY COUNCIL RECORDS

CA/TC 1/2/124-135 Minutes and reports to the Council, 1970 - 1974
CA/CE 1/1-24 Minutes and reports to the Council, 1974 - 1997
CA/HE/2/1/26-34   1960 - 1968 (1969 missing) Annual reports of the Medical Officer of Health
CA/HE 2/1/36-38 Annual reports of the Medical Officer of Health, 1970 - 1972
CA/HE 4/6 Agendas, minutes and reports from the meetings of the Nottingham Health and Welfare Committee, 1990
CA/HE 4/7 Circulars issued by the Department of Health and Social Security, 1970 - 1971
CC HE/1/1/38-50   1960 – 1972 Nottinghamshire County Council: Annual reports of the Medical Officer of Health

MAPPERLEY HOSPITAL RECORDS

SO/HO/6/3/2/6 Discharge and Transfer Register (males), 1949-1966.
SO/HO/6/3/4/1 ‹Non-Status› (voluntary) admission register, 1955-1962.
SO/HO/6/3/5/7-8 Death Notices, some including detailed patient notes, 1964-1971.
Mapperley Hospital (House) Committee minutes 6th July 1955-6th March 1963
Mapperley Management Committee minutes 3rd April 1963 - 4th March 1970
Minutes of the Mapperley Hospital (House) Committee meeting 3rd July 1963, 4th December 1963, 1st January 1964, 4th March 1964 and 7th October 1964.
Mapperley Hospital. "Mapperley Hospital 1880 -1980." Nottingham: Mapperley Hospital, 1980.
Nottingham No 3 Management Committee, "The Pioneer Years in Mental Health 1948-70," (Nottingham: Mapperley Hospital, 1970); courtesy of Duncan Macmillan Library, Nottinghamshire Healthcare NHS Trust.

University of Nottingham Library East Midlands Collection (UNLEMC) - information about local NHS services.

Media Archives

Nottingham Evening Post 1970 to date
Guardian Journal 1953-1973
Nottingham Recorder Nov 1981- Dec 1996
Newark Advertiser
Notts and Derby Drinker 1977-1982
Notts and District Drinker 1987-93
Notts and District Drinker 1984-87
Notts Drinker 1994-2002

FILMS/BROADCASTS

"St. Ann's" (1969, Thames Television) rebroadcast by Channel 4 on April 8th 1993.
"N Division: Under Pressure" (Central Television, 1982). The sixth in a series of six films looking at the Nottinghamshire police force. Shows stills of disturbances which occurred in Hyson Green on the night of July 10th 1981.
"N Division: Saturday's Match" (Central Television, 1982). The fifth in a series of six films, showing preparations being made for a match by police.

Both documentaries are available from the Media Archive for Central England *(MACE)*, University of Leicester.

"Cathy Come Home." (BBC: The Wednesday Play, 1966).
"Edna the Inebriate," (BBC: Play for Today, 1971).
"Cldnt give a XXX 4 lst ordrs" (BBC: Panorama, 2004)

Other Libraries and Sources

The Wellcome Trust: Wellcome Library, Special Collections GC/132/4; S.Sussman interview with Dr A. Minto. Psychiatry Interviews, 1988-1989. Tapes and transcripts of interviews conducted in 1988 by Sam Sussman with three Nottingham psychiatrists (A.D. Douglas, E.D. Oram and A. Minto).
Nottingham Central Library, Local Studies Library Oral History Collection project 'Making Ends Meet' recorded 1982-84 Notts Libraries. Tape A87 f
Alcohol Problems Advisory Service (APAS) – new archive developed as part of research process. Dates from 1976-2007. It includes Council on Alcoholism (former name of organisation) minutes of its Annual General Meetings, minutes of Executive Committee, 1976- 1997 and Board minutes 2005/2006. All documents viewed with permission of APAS.

REFERENCE SOURCES **205**

Philip McLean papers: Miscellaneous Papers 1962-2000 including correspondence, press cuttings and minutes on issues pertaining to alcohol.
Doug Cameron papers: Miscellaneous Papers 1989-95 including correspondence, press cuttings and minutes on issues pertaining to alcohol.
Framework Housing Association - annual reports 1990s to 2005.
Housing Aid - Nottingham city homelessness data 1981-19

REPORTS AND GUIDELINES

Official Reports

These are listed in chronological order to give an outline of the official policy over time.

Home Office. *Offences of Drunkenness*. London: HMSO, 1962.
Ministry of Health. *Hospital Treatment of Alcoholism:* Memorandum HM (62) 43 London, HMSO, 1962.
National Assistance Board. *Homeless Single Persons*. London: HMSO, 1966
Ministry of Health. *The Treatment of Alcoholism* Memorandum HM (68) 37. London: HMSO, 1968.
The Monopoly Commission. *A Report on the Supply of Beer. House of Commons, 1968-9*. London: HMSO, 1969.
DHSS Circular 16/71. *Development of Hospital Facilities for the Treatment of Alcoholism*. London: HMSO, 1971.
Home Office. *Report on the Habitual Drunken Offender*. London: HMSO, 1971.
Home Office. *Report of the Departmental Committee on Liquor Licensing* (The Erroll Report) Cmnd. 5154. London: HMSO, 1972.
DHSS Circular 21/73. *Community Services for Alcoholics*. London: HMSO, 1973.
Home Office. *Working Party on Vagrancy and Street Offences Working Paper.* London: HMSO, 1974.
DHSS. *Everybody's Business*. London: HMSO, 1976.
DHSS. *The Pattern and Range of Services for Problem Drinkers*. Report by the Advisory Committee on Alcoholism. London: HMSO, 1978.
The House of Commons Expenditure Committee. *Reduction of Pressure on the Prison System, England*. London: HMSO, 1978.
Parliamentary All Party Penal Affairs Group. *Too Many Prisoners*. London: Barry Rose, 1980.
Wilson, P. *Drinking in England and Wales*. London: OPCS, 1980.
The House of Commons. *Third Report from the Home Affairs Committee, Session 1979-80: Deaths in Police Custody*. London: HMSO, 1980.
DHSS. *Drinking Sensibly*. London: HMSO, 1981.

DHSS. *Care in Action.* London, HMSO, 1981.
DHSS. *NHS Management Inquiry Report* (Griffiths Report) London: HMSO, 1983.
Home Office Standing Conference on Crime Prevention. *Report of the Working Group on Young People and Alcohol.* London: HMSO, 1987.
Advisory Council on the Misuse of Drugs. *AIDS and Drug Misuse Part I.* London: HMSO, 1988.
Advisory Council on the Misuse of Drugs. *AIDS and Drug Misuse Part II.* London: HMSO, 1989.
Department of Health. *Caring for People: Community Care in the Next Decade and Beyond* (Cm. 849) London: HMSO, 1989.
Department of Health. *Working for Patients.* London: HMSO, 1989.
Department of Health. *General Practice in the National Health Service: A New Contract.* London: HMSO, 1989.
Department of Health. Circular: HN (89) 4: *Alcohol Misuse: Prevention and Local Co-ordination.* London: HMSO, 1989.
Department of Health. *Sensible Drinking: The Report of an Interdepartmental Working Group.* London: HMSO, 1995.
Department of Health. *Tackling Drugs Together: A Strategy for England 1995-8.* London: HMSO, 1995.
All-Party Group on Alcohol Misuse. *Alcohol and Crime: Breaking the Link.* London: HMSO, 1995.
Social Services Inspectorate. *Inspection of social services for people who misuse alcohol and drugs.* London: HMSO, 1995.
Health Advisory Service. *The substance of young needs: services for children and adolescents who misuse substances.* London: HMSO, 1996.
Department of Health. Task *Force to Review Services for Drug Misusers. Report of an Independent Review of Drug Treatment Services in England.* London: HMSO, 1996.
Department of Health. *The New NHS: Modern and Dependable.* London: HMSO, 1997.
Cabinet Office. *Tackling Drugs to Build a Better Britain: The Government's Ten-Year Strategy for Tackling Drugs Misuse.* London: HMSO, 1998.
Department of Health. *The NHS Plan.* London: HMSO, 2000.
Office of National Statistics. *Psychiatric morbidity among adults living in private households.* London: ONS, 2000.
Department of Culture Media and Sport. *Time for Reform: Proposals for the Modernization of Our Licensing Laws.* London: HMSO, 2001.
Cabinet Office. *Alcohol misuse: Interim Analytical Report.* London: HMSO, 2003.
Department of Health. *Choosing Health: Making Healthier Choices Easier.* London: HMSO, 2004.
Cabinet Office. *Alcohol Harm Reduction Strategy for England.* London: HMSO, 2004.

Department of Culture Media and Sport, Home Office, and Office of the Deputy Prime Minister. *Drinking Responsibly: The Government's Proposals* London: DCMS, ODPM, 2005.
Department of Health. *Models of Care for Alcohol Misusers.* London, HMSO, 2006.
Department of Health. *Safe. Sensible. Social: The Next Steps in the National Alcohol Strategy.* London: HMSO, 2007.
Department of Health. *Alcohol Units: A Brief Guide.* London: HMSO, 2008.
Department of Health. *Health Profile for England 2008.* London: HMSO, 2009.
Home Office. *Drugs: protecting families and communities.* London: HMSO, 2008.
National Treatment Agency. *Building recovery in communities: A consultation for developing recovery-orientated framework to replace Models of Care.* London: HMSO, 2011.
Home Office. *The drug strategy, 'Reducing demand, restricting supply, building recovery: supporting people to live a drug-free life.* London: HMSO, 2010.

Other Reports - in chronological order

Caloste Gulbenkian Foundation. *Community Work and Social Change: A Report on Training.* London: Longman, 1968.
Nottingham No. 3 Hospital Management Committee. *The Pioneer Years in Mental Health 1948-1970.* Nottingham: Mapperley Hospital, 1970.
Office of Health Economics. *Alcohol Abuse, Studies of Current Health Problems no. 34.* London: OHE, 1970.
Medical Council on Alcoholism. *Handbook on Alcohol and Alcoholism for Probation Officers.* London: MCA in collaboration with National Association of Probation Officers, 1975.
D.J. Armor, J.M. Polich and H.B Braiker. *RAND Report: Alcoholism and Treatment.* CA: Rand Corp, 1976.
P.W. Digby, *Hostels and Lodgings for Single People* (London: HMSO, 1976).
Joseph Rowntree Trust. *The Future of Voluntary Organisations.* London: Croom Helm, 1978.
Royal College of Psychiatrists. *Alcohol and Alcoholism:* A Report of a Special Committee of the Royal College of Psychiatrists. London: RCP, 1979.
Brewers' Society. *Statistical Handbook* . London: Brewers' Society, 1980.
Office of Health Economics. *Alcohol: Reducing the Harm, Studies of Current Health Problems No. 70.* London: OHE, 1981.
Benjamin W. and M. Vineall. *The UK Market for Beer, Wines and Spirits to 1990.* London: Stanisland Hall Associates, 1985.
Royal College of General Practitioners. *Alcohol: A Balanced View*: Reports from General Practice 24. London: RCGP, 1986.
Royal College of Psychiatrists. *Alcohol, our favourite drug.* London: Tavistock, 1986.

Royal College of Physicians. *A Great and Growing Evil: The Medical Consequences of Alcohol Abuse.* London: RCP, 1987.

Handy, C. *Report of the Charles Handy Working Party on Improving Effectiveness in Voluntary Organisations.* London: National Council for Voluntary Organisations, 1987.

Alcohol Concern. *Alcohol Services - the Future.* London: Alcohol Concern, 1987.

Bretman, A. *Lifestyle Survey.* Nottingham: Nottinghamshire Health Authority Health Policy Group, 1988.

E. Goddard and C. Ikin, *Drinking in England and Wales in 1987.* London: HMSO, 1988.

Unell, J. *Nottingham Safer Cities Project: Household Survey of Elderly People in the Meadows Area of Nottingham, to Investigate Lifestyle Patterns and Perceptions of Crime.* Nottingham: Nottingham Safer Cities Project, 1990.

Kendrick, D. *An evaluation of treatment for patients with alcohol problems. NHS Addiction services and the Nottingham Clinic.* Nottingham: Nottingham Health Authority, 1991.

Bean, P. and Pearson, Y. 'Crack and Cocaine Use in Nottingham in 1989/90 and in 1991/92' in Mott, J., ed, *Cocaine and crack in England and Wales, Research and Planning Unit Paper No. 70.* London: Home Office, 1992.

Roberts H. and R. Denglar. *Trent Lifestyle Survey: Interim Report to Trent Regional Health Authority.* Nottingham: Department of Public Health and Epidemiology, University of Nottingham, 1992.

Anderson, I. Kemp, P.A. and D. Quilgars. *Single Homeless People.* London: HMSO, 1993.

Bines, W. *The Health of Single Homeless People.* York: Centre for Housing Policy, University of York for the Joseph Rowntree Foundation, 1994.

F. Coffield and L. Gofton. *Drugs and Young People.* London: Institute for Public Policy Research, 1994.

Royal College of Physicians and British Paediatric Association. *Alcohol and the Young.* London: RCP, 1995.

Royal College of Physicians, Royal College of Psychiatrists and Royal College of General Practitioners. *Alcohol and the Heart in Perspective: Sensible Limits Reaffirmed.* London: RCP, 1995.

Sumner M. and H. Parker. *Low in Alcohol: A Review of International Research into Alcohol's Role in Crime Causation.* Manchester: University of Manchester, 1995.

Portman Group. *The Portman Group Code of Practice on the Naming, Packaging and Merchandising of Alcoholic Drinks.* London: Portman Group, 1996.

Parker, H. *Crack Cocaine and Drugs-Crime Careers*: Home Office Research and Statistics Directorate Research Findings No. 34. London: Home Office, 1996.

Brain K. and H. Parker. *Drinking with Design: Alcopops, Designer Drinks and Youth Culture.* London: Portman Group, 1997.

Alcohol Concern. *Measures for Measure, a Framework for Alcohol Policy.* London: Alcohol Concern, 1997.

Portman Group. *Keeping the Peace (updated): A Guide to the prevention of alcohol-related disorder.* London: Portman Group, 1998.

Standing Conference on Drug Abuse and the Children's Legal Centre. *Young people and drugs: policy guidance for drug interventions.* London: SCODA, 1999.

Alcohol Concern. Proposals for a National Strategy for England. London: Alcohol Concern, 1999.

Light R. and S. Heenan. *Controlling Supply: The Concept of 'Need' in Liquor Licensing.* Bristol: University of the West of England, 1999.

Wright, L. *Young People and Alcohol: What do 11-24 year olds know, think and do.* London: Health Education Authority, 1999.

Silburn, R., Lucas, D., Page R. and L. Hanna. *Neighbourhood Images in Nottingham.* York: Joseph Rowntree Foundation, 1999.

Society for the Study of Addiction. Tackling Alcohol Together. London: SSA and Free Association Books Ltd, 1999.

Standing Conference on Drug Abuse and the Children's Legal Centre. *Young People and Drugs: Policy Guidance for Drug Interventions.* London: SCODA, 1999.

Fitzpatrick, S. Kemp, P. and S. Klinker. *Single Homelessness - an Overview of Research in Britain.* York: Joseph Rowntree Foundation, 2000.

International Centre for Alcohol Policies. *The Geneva Partnership on Alcohol; Towards a Global Charter.* Geneva: ICAP, 2000.

International Center for Alcohol Policies. *The Limits of Binge Drinking.* Washington, DC: International Center for Alcohol Policies, 2000.

Levine, M. *Side and Closed Circuit Television (CCTV): Exploring Surveillance in Public Space.* Lancaster: University of Lancaster, 2000.

Royal College of Physicians. *Alcohol: Can the NHS afford it? Recommendations for a coherent alcohol strategy for hospitals.* London: RCP, 2001.

Royal College of Physicians and Royal College of Psychiatry, *Drugs: Dilemmas and Choices.* London: RCP 2000.

Pannell, J. *Older People and Homelessness in Nottingham: Final Report.* London; Nottingham: Framework Housing Association and Help the Aged, 2001.

British Beer and Pub Association. *Point of Sale Promotions: A Good Practice Guide for Licensees.* London: BBPA 2001.

N. Rehn, R. Room and G. Edwards. *Alcohol in the European Region – Consumption, Harm and Policies.* Geneva: WHO, 2001.

Young, S. *Poverty in Nottingham 2001: A Report Commissioned by Nottingham City Council.* Nottingham: The Observatory, 2001.

Deehan, A. Marshall, E. and E. Saville. *Drunks and Disorder: Processing Intoxicated Arrestees in Two City-Centre Custody Suites*: Police Research Series Paper 150. London: Policing and Reducing Crime Unit Research, 2002.

Engineer, R., Philips, A., Thompson, J. and J. Nicholls, *Drunk and Disorderly: A Qualitative Study of Binge Drinking among 18 to 24 Year Olds:* Home

Office Research Study 262. London: Home Office Research Development and Statistics Directorate, 2003.

Richardson A. and T. Budd. *Alcohol, Crime and Disorder: A Study of Young Adults:* Home Office Research Study No. 263. London: Home Office, 2003.

Crane, M. and A.M. Warnes. *Wet Day Centres in the United Kingdom: A Research Report and Manual.* Sheffield: Sheffield Institute for Studies on Ageing, 2003.

Portman Group. *Code of Practice on the Naming, Packaging and Promotion of Alcoholic Drinks.* London: Portman Group, 2003.

Richardson A. and T. Budd. *Alcohol, crime and disorder: a study of young adults.* London: Home Office Research, Development and Statistics Directorate, 2003.

Alcohol Concern. *The Role of Alcohol in the Night-Time Economy* (London: Alcohol Concern, 2004.

Association of Convenience Stores. *Responsible Retailing of Alcohol: Guidance for the Off-Trade.* British Retail Consortium and Wine and Spirit Association, 2004.

Hibell, B., Andersson, B., Bjarnason, T., Ahlström, S., Balakireva, O., Kokkevi, A. and M. Morgan. *The ESPAD Report: Alcohol and Other Drug Use among Students in 35 European Countries.* Stockholm: Swedish Council for Information on Alcohol and Other Drugs, Pompidou Group at the Council of Europe, 2004.

Smith, K. *Wet Day Centres for Street Drinkers.* Sheffield Institute for Studies on Ageing, Community Sciences Centre, 2004.

Academy of Medical Sciences. *Calling Time: the Nation's Drinking as a Major Health Issue.* London: Academy of Medical Sciences, 2004.

Turning Point. *Alcohol Consultation with Young People in England, 2004.* London: Turning Point 2004.

Audit Commission. *Inspection Report: Community Safety in Nottingham City.* Nottingham: Nottingham City Council and Police, 2005.

Alcohol Concern. *Health Select Committee on Public Health White Paper: A Response from Alcohol Concern.* London: Alcohol Concern, 2005.

Rochester, C. *Making Sense of Volunteering: A Literature Review.* London: Volunteering England, 2006.

Coleman, K., Hird C. and D. Povey, *Home Office Statistical Bulletin: Violent Crime Overview, Homicide and Gun Crime 2004/2005* Supplementary Volume to Crime in England and Wales 2004/2005. London: Home Office, 2006.

Raistrick, D., Heather N. and C. Godfrey. *Review of the Effectiveness of Treatment for Alcohol Problems.* London: National Treatment Agency, 2006.

National Probation Service. *Working with alcohol-misusing offenders – a strategy for delivery.* London, HMSO, 2006.

Office for National Statistics. *Over a third of adults exceed regular daily drinking limit.* Newport, UK: Office for National Statistics, 2007.

Berridge, V., Thom, B., and R. Herring. *The Normalisation of Binge Drinking? An Historical and Cross Cultural Investigation with Implications for Action.* London: Alcohol Education and Research Council, 2007.

National Centre for Social Research and the National Foundation for Educational Research. *Smoking, Drinking and Drug Use among Young People in England in 2006: Headline Figures*. Leeds: The Information Centre for Health and Social Care, 2007.

Thom, B. and M. Bayley, *Multi-Component Programmes: An Approach to Prevent and Reduce Alcohol-Related Harm.* York: Joseph Rowntree Foundation, 2007.

Valentine, G., Holloway, S.L., Jayne M. and C. Knell. *Drinking Places: Social Geographies of Consumption.* York: Joseph Rowntree Foundation, 2007.

General Lifestyle Survey (formerly the General Household Survey). *Smoking and Drinking 2009.* London: ONS, 2009.

Kneale, J. 'British Drinking from the Nineteenth Century to the Present,' in *Alcohol Health Committee: First Report of Session 2009-10* Vol. II, HC151-II, Ev 239-253.

Withington, P. and A. McShane. 'Fluctuations in English drinking habits: an historical overview' in *Report for the Parliamentary Select Committee on Health, April 2009* Vol. II, HC151-II Ev 231.

Nicholls, J. 'Drinking cultures and consumption in England: historical trends and policy implications', in *Alcohol Health Committee: First Report of Session 2009-10* Vol. II, HC151-II, Ev 239-53.

NHS Information Centre, *Statistics on Alcohol: England, 2011.* London: TheHealth and Social Care Information Centre, 2011.

British Beer and Pub Association. *Statistical Handbook 2011.* London: BBPA, 2011.

Hagger, M.S. Lonsdale, A.J. Baggott, R. Penny, G. and M. Bowen. *The Cost of Alcohol: The Advocacy for a Minimum Price per Unit in the UK.* London: AERC, 2011.

PRINTED SOURCES - in alphabetical order

Abel, E. L. "The gin epidemic: much ado about what?" *Alcohol and Alcoholism* 36, no. 5 (2001): pp. 401-405.

Abel-Smith, B. and P. Townsend. "The Poor and the Poorest." *Occasional Papers on Social Administration, no. 6.* London, George Bell, 1965.

Acker, C.J. and S.W. Tracy, *Altering American Consciousness: The History of Alcohol and Drug Use in the United States, 1800-2000.* Amherst, Mass: University of Massachusetts Press, 2004.

Addiction Counselling World. "12-Step Centres; Improve treatments and standards or fade way." *Addiction Counselling World* 4, no. 22 (1992).

Addison, P. and H. Jones, eds. *A companion to contemporary Britain, 1939-2000 Blackwell Companion to British History.* Oxford: Blackwell, 2005.

Adeney, M. *The Miner's Strike 1984-5: loss without limit.* London: Routledge, 1986.

Aggleton, P., G. Hart and P.M. Davies, eds. *AIDS: Individual, Cultural and Policy Dimensions*. Hamps: Falmer Press, 1990.

Agostinelli, G., J. M. Brown and W. R. Miller. "Effects of normative feedback on consumption among heavy drinking college students," *Journal of Drug Education* 25, no. 1 (1995): pp.31-40.

Agostinelli, G. and J. Grube. "Alcohol counter-advertising and the media: a review of recent research." *Alcohol Research & Health* 25, no 1 (2002): pp.15-21.

Ashfield, M. *Don't be late on Monday: Life in a Nottingham Lace Factory*. Derby: Derby Books Publishing Company Ltd, 2011.

Aitchison, C., N. MacLeod and S. Shaw. "Representing Landscapes." In *Leisure and Tourism Landscapes: Social and Cultural Geographies*. London: Routledge, 2000.

Akers, R.L. *Drugs, Alcohol and Society: Social structure, process and policy*. Belmont, CA: Wadsworth, 1992.

Alaszewski, A., L. Harrison and J Manthorpe, eds. *Risk, Health and Welfare*. Buckingham, Philadelphia: Open University Press, 1998.

Alcock, P., A. Erskine and M. May. *The student's companion to social policy* Oxford: Blackwell Publishing, 2003.

Alcohol Concern. "Alcopops Factsheet." London: Alcohol Concern, 2001.

Alcohol Concern. "Factsheet 1 Summary: Alcohol and the Night-time Economy." 2004.

Alexander, B.K. "The Roots of Addiction in Free Market Society." Vancouver: Canadian Centre for Policy Alternatives, 2001.

Allaman, A., Voller, F., Kubicka, L. and K. Bloomfield. "Drinking and the position of women in nine European countries." *Substance Abuse* 2, no 4 (2000): pp. 231-247.

Allsop, J. "Medical dominance in a changing world: the UK case." *Health Sociology Review* 15, no. 5 (October 2006): pp. 444-457.

Almeida-Filho, N., I. Lessa, L. Magalhães, M.J. Araújo, E. Aquino, I. Kawachi and S. A. James. "Alcohol drinking patterns by gender, ethnicity, and social class in Bahia, Brazil." *Rev Saúde Pública* 38, no. 1 (2004): pp. 45-54.

Altheide, D.L. "The impact of television news formats on social policy," *Journal of Broadcasting & Electronic Media* 35, no. 1 (1991): pp.3-21

Amin, A. and S. Graham. "The ordinary city." *Transactions of the Institute of British Geographers NS* 22, no.4 (1997): pp. 411-29.

Amos, D. M "Nineteenth-century social history, with particular reference to food, health and nutrition in the E. Midlands." PhD thesis: Nottingham, 2000.

Anderson, I. "Housing policy and street homelessness in Britain." *Housing Studies* 8, no. 1 (1993): pp.17-28.

Andreasson, R. and A. W. Jones. "Erik M.P. Widmark (1889-1945): Swedish pioneer in forensic alcohol toxicology." *Forensic Sci Int* 72, no. 1 (1995): pp.1-14.

Andreasson, R. and A. W. Jones. "Historical anecdote related to chemical tests for intoxication." *J Anal Toxicol* 20, no. 3 (1996): pp.207-208.

Andreasson, R. and A. W. Jones. "The life and work of Erik M. P. Widmark." *Am J Forensic Med Pathol* 17, no. 3 (1996): pp. 177-190.

Andrews, J. "Effectiveness of alcohol warning labels: a review and extension." *American Behavioural Scientist* 38, no. 4 (1995): pp. 622-632.

Archard, P. *Vagrancy, Alcoholism and Social Control*. London: Macmillan 1979.

Armstrong, D. *Political Anatomy of the Body*. Cambridge: Cambridge University Press, 1983.

Armstrong, D. "The rise of Surveillance Medicine." *Sociology of Health and Illness* 17, no.3 (1995): pp. 393-404.

Armstrong, E. and E. L. Abel. "Fetal Alcohol Syndrome: the Origins of a Moral Panic " *Alcohol and Alcoholism* 35, no. 3 (2000), pp. 276-282.

Armstrong, E. M. *Conceiving risk, bearing responsibility: fetal alcohol syndrome & the diagnosis of moral disorder*. Baltimore: The Johns Hopkins University Press, 2003.

Armstrong, G. *Football Hooligans: Knowing the Score*. Oxford: Berg, 1998.

Armstrong, G. and D. Hobbs. "Tackled from Behind." In *Football, Violence and Social Identity*, eds. R. Giulianotti, N. Bonney and M. Hepworth, pp. 196-228. London: Routledge, 1994.

Arnold, J.H. *History: A Very Short Introduction* Oxford: Oxford University Press, 2000

Atkinson, M.M. and W.D. Coleman. "Policy communities, policy networks and the problems of governance." *Governance* 5, no. 2 (1992): pp.154-180.

Atkinson, R. "Domestication by Cappuccino or a Revenge on Urban Space? Control and Empowerment in the Management of Public Spaces." *Urban Studies* 40, no. 9 (2003): pp. 1829-1843.

Austin, G A. and R. Room. *Alcohol in Western Society from Antiquity to 1800: A chronological history*. Santa Barbara, Oxford: ABC-Clio Information Services, 1985.

Babor, T.F."Partnership, profits and public health." *Addiction* 95, no. 2 (2000): pp. 193-5.

Babor, T.F. "Alcohol Police Research: A Quoi Bon?" *Addiction* 99, no. 9 (2004): pp. 1091 - 1092.

Babor, T. F., R. Caetano, S. Casswell, G. Edwards, N. Giesbrecht, K. Graham, J. Grube, P. Gruenewald, L. Hill, H. Holder, R. Homel, E. Osterberg, J. Rehm, R. Room and I. Rossow. *Alcohol: No Ordinary Commodity: Research and Public Policy*. Oxford: Oxford University Press, 2003.

Baer, J.S., Kivlahan, D.K., Blume, A. W., McKnight, P. and G. A. Marlatt. "Brief intervention for heavy drinking college students: Four-year follow-up and natural history." *American Journal of Public Health* 91, no. 8 (2001): pp.1310-1316.

Baer, J. S., Marlatt, G. A., Kivlahan, D. R., Fromme, K., Larimer, M. and E. Williams, "An experimental test of three methods of alcohol risk-reduction with young adults." *Journal of Consulting and Clinical Psychology* 60, no. 6 (1992): pp. 9784-979.

Baggott, R, "A Modern Approach to an Old Problem? Alcohol Policy and New Labour "*Policy and Politics* 38, no.1 (2010), pp. 135-152.

Baggott, R. *Alcohol strategy and the drinks industry: A partnership for prevention.* York: Joseph Rowntree Foundation, 2006.

Baggott, R. *Alcohol, Politics and Social Policy.* Aldershot: Avebury, 1990.

Baggott, R. *Health and Health Care in Britain.* London: Macmillan, 1994.

Baggott, R. "Licensing Law Reform and the Return of the Drink Question." *Parliamentary Affairs* 40, no 4 (1987): pp.501-516

Baggott, R. *Public Health: Policy and Politics.* Hampshire: Palgrave Macmillan, 2000.

Baggott, R. "Regulatory reform in Britain: the changing face of self regulation." *Public Administration* 67, no.4 (1989): pp.435-454.

Bailey, P. *Leisure and Class in Victorian England: Rational Recreation and the contest for control 1830-1885.* London: Routledge, Paul Kegan 1978.

Bakan, J. *The Corporation: The Pathological Pursuit of Profit and Power.* London: Constable and Robinson, 2004.

Balding, J. "Young People in 1996." Exeter: Schools Health Education Unit, University of Exeter, 1997.

Balding, J. and J. Regis. "More alcohol down fewer throats." *Education and Health* 13, no. 4 (1996): pp.61-64.

Bamford, T. *Commissioning and Purchasing.* London: Routledge, 2001.

Bandura, A. *Social Foundations of Thought and Action.* Englewood Cliffs, NJ: Prentice Hall, 1986.

Bannister, J., N. Fyfe and A. Kearns. "Closed circuit television and the city." In *Surveillance, Closed Circuit TV and Social Control*, eds. C. Norris, J. Moran and G. Armstrong. Aldershot: Ashgate, 1998.

Barnard, M. and A. Forsyth. "Alcopops and under-age drinking: changing trends in drink preference." *Health Education* 98, no. 6 (1998): pp.208-212.

Barr, A. *Drink: A social history.* London: Bantam Press, 1995.

Barrow, M. "Temperate feminists: The British Women's Temperance Association," Manchester, 1999.

Barrow, R. "Beer Can History." *Off License News*, December 12th 1985.

Barrows, S. and R. Room, eds. *Drinking: behaviour and belief in modern history.* Berkley University of California Press, 1991.

Barrows, S., R. Room and J. Verhey. *The social history of alcohol: drinking and culture in modern society: Conference: Papers.* Berkeley: Alcohol Research Group, Medical Research Institute of San Francisco, 1987.

Bartley, M. *Authorities and Partisans.* Edinburgh: Edinburgh University Press, 1993.

Baumgartner, F. and B. Jones. *Agendas and instability in American Politics*. Chicago: Chicago University Press, 1993.

Baumgartner, F.R. and B.D. Jones. "Agenda Dynamics and Policy Subsystems." *Journal of Politics* 53 (1991): pp.1044-74

BBC "Who are the Yardies?" *BBC News*, June 19th 1999. Available from http://news.bbc.co.uk/1/hi/uk/371604.stm [cited September 3rd 2011].

BBC "Short History of Immigration." *BBC News*: May 17th 2002. Available at http://news.bbc.co.uk/1/hi/in_depth/uk/2002/race/1994140.stm [Cited September 3rd 2011].

BBC. "Nottinghamshire brewing history." *BBC News*: February 2003 [Cited September 3rd 2011]. Available from http://www.bbc.co.uk/nottingham/features/2003/02/nottinghamshire_brewing_history.shtml. [Cited September 3rd 2011].

BBC. "Woman killed defending her shop". *BBC News*: September 30th 2003.

BBC. "The Victorian binge drinkers" *BBC News*, December 2nd 2005.

BBC. "Living in 'Gun City" *BBC News*, March 13th 2005.

BBC. "Cldnt give a XXXX 4 1st ordrs?" *BBC 1 Panorama:* broadcast June 6th 2004. Transcript of programme available from http://news.bbc.co.uk/nol/shared/spl/hi/programmes/panorama/transcripts/xxxx.txt [Cited September 3rd 2011].

BBC."Booze; what every teenager needs to know." *BBC1 Panorama:* broadcast November 19th 2006.

BBC. "Sorted for E's and Whizz." *BBC Radio 4*: broadcast October 4th 2007.

BBC. "Minimum alcohol price levels planned by coalition." *BBC News*, January 18th 2011.

BBC. "Why is alcohol consumption falling?" *BBC news magazine*, February 15th 2011.

BBC. "Rioters in Nottingham damage vehicles." *BBC News*, August 9th 2011.

Bean, P. T., C.K. Wilkinson, Whynes D.K. and J.A. Giggs. "Knowledge of drugs and consumption of alcohol among Nottingham 15-year-olds." *Health Education Journal* 47, no. 2/3 (1988): pp.79-81.

Beattie, J. "Transplacental alcohol intoxication." *Alcohol and Alcoholism* 21, no. 2 (1986): pp.163-166.

Beattie, J., D.C. Hull and F. Cockburn. "Children intoxicated by alcohol in Nottingham and Glasgow, 1973-84." *British Medical Journal* 292, no. 6519 (1986): pp.519-521.

Beauchamp, D. E. *Alcohol and Public Health Policy*. Philadelphia: Temple University Press, 1980.

Beck, U. *Risk Society: Towards a New Modernity*. Trans. M. Ritter, ed. M Featherstone, *Theory, Culture and Society*. New York: Sage, 1992.

Becker, H. *Outsiders: studies in the sociology of deviance*. New York: Free Press, 1966.

Becker, H. *Social problems: A modern approach*. New York: Wiley, 1966.

Beckett, B. "Rehabs Work: Research on Success " *Addiction Today* November 17th 2008.

Beckett, J. and K. Brand. *Nottingham*. Manchester: Manchester University Press, 1997.

Beckett, J. *A Centenary History of Nottingham.* Manchester: Manchester University Press, 1997.

Beckett, J. *Nottingham* Nottinghamshire: Thoroton Society, 2006 Available from http://www.thorotonsociety.org.uk/gateway/places/nottingham/nottingham4.htm. [Cited September 25th 2011].

Beckingham, D. "An historical geography of liberty: Lancashire and the Inebriates Acts," *Journal of Historical Geography* 36, no. 4 (2010) pp.388-401.

Beckingham, D. "Geographies of drink culture in Liverpool: Lessons from the drink capital of nineteenth-century England," *Drugs: Education, Prevention and Policy*, 15, no. 3 (2008.), pp. 305-313.

Begbie, H. *The General Life of William Booth: The Founder of the Salvation Army Vol 1*. New York: Macmillan, 1920.

Belina, B. and G. Helms. "Zero tolerance for the industrial past and other threats: policing and urban entrepreneurialism in Britain and Germany." *Urban Studies* 40, no.9 (2003): pp.1845-1867.

Bell, D. "Commensality, urbanity, hospitality." In *Critical hospitality studies*, eds. C. Lashley, P. Lynch and A. Morrison. London: Butterworth Heineman, 2005.

Bell, D. and J. Binnie. "What's eating Manchester? Gastro-culture and urban regeneration." In *Food and the city*, ed. K.A. Franck. Chichester: Wiley, 2005.

Bell, D. and G. Valentine. *Consuming geographies.* London: Routledge, 1997.

Bell, H. *Frontiers of Medicine in the Anglo-Egyptian Sudan, 1899-1940 Oxford Historical Monographs*. Oxford: Oxford University Press, 1999.

Bennet, J.M. *Ale, Beer and Brewsters in England: Women's Work in a Changing World, 1300-1600*. New York: Oxford University Press, 1996.

Bennett, J. R. "The experience of the campaign on the use and restriction of barbiturates." In *The Misuse of Psychotropic Drugs.*, eds. R. Murray, A. H. Ghodse, C. Harris, D. Williams and P. Williams. London: Gaskell. The Royal College of Psychiatrists, 1981.

Bennett, T. and R. Wright. "The impact of prescribing on the crimes of opioid users." *British Journal of Addiction*, 81, no. 2 (1986): pp.265-273.

Benson, J. *The Rise of Consumer Society in Britain 1880-1980*. London: Longmann, 1994.

Ben-Yehuda, N and E. Goode. *Moral panics: the social construction of deviance.* Oxford: Blackwell, 1994.

Benyon, J.T. and J. Solomos. *The Roots of Urban Unrest*. Oxford: Pergamon Press, 1987.

Berridge, V. *AIDS in the UK: The Making of Policy, 1981-1994*. Oxford: Oxford University Press, 1996.

Berridge, V. "Current and future alcohol policy: the relevance of history." *History and Policy* (2005). Available from http://www.historyandpolicy.org/papers/policy-paper-38.html [Cited September 25th 2011)

Berridge, V. "Disease, Risk, Harm and Safety: Trends in Post-war British Alcohol Policy." In *Images of Disease: Science, Public Policy and Health in Post-war Europe*, ed. I. Lowy and J. Krige, pp.41-52. Luxembourg: European Communities, 2001.

Berridge, V. "Drugs and social policy: the establishment of drug control in Britain 1900-1930." *British Journal of Addiction,* 79, no. 1 (1984): pp.17-29.

Berridge, V. *Health and Society in Britain since 1939, Economic History Society: New Studies in Economic and Social History* Cambridge: Cambridge University Press, 1999.

Berridge, V. "Historical Research." In *Studying the Organisation and Delivery of Health Services: research methods*, ed. N. Fulop, pp.140-153. London: Routledge, 2001.

Berridge, V. "Illicit drugs, infectious disease and public health: A historical perspective 2005." *Can J Infect Dis Med Microbiol* 16, no. 3 (2005): pp.193-196.

Berridge, V. *Making Health Policy; Networks in Research and Policy after 1945* Amsterdam, New York: Rodopi, 2005.

Berridge, V. *Medicine, the Market and the Mass Media: Producing Health in the Twentieth Century Studies in the Social History of Medicine*. London: Routledge, 2005.

Berridge, V. "New strategies for alcohol policy-lessons from history?" *Drugs: Education, Prevention, and Policy* 13, no. 2 (2006): pp. 105-108.

Berridge, V. *Opium and the People: Opiate use and Drug Control policy in Nineteenth and Early Twentieth Century England*. London: Free Association Books, 1999.

Berridge, V. "Post-war smoking policy in the UK and the redefinition of public health." *Twentieth Century British History* 14, no. 1 (2003): pp.61-82.

Berridge, V. "Public health activism: lessons from history?" *British Medical Journal* 335 (7633) (2007): pp.1310-1312.

Berridge, V. *Temperance: its history and impact on current and future alcohol policy, JRF Drug and alcohol research programme*. York: Joseph Rowntree Foundation, 2005.

Berridge, V. "What's Happening in History" *Addiction* 81, no. 6 (1986), pp. 721-723.

Berridge, V. and S.S. Blume. *Poor Health: Social Inequality Before and After the Black Report* London: Routledge, 2003.

Berridge, V. and S. Bourne. "Illicit drugs, infectious disease and public health: A historical perspective." *Can J Infect Dis Med Microbiol* 16, no. 3 (2005): pp.193-196.

Berridge, V. and K. Loughlin. "Smoking and the New Health Education in Britain 1950s-1970s." *Am J Public Health* 95, no. 6 (2005): pp. 956-64.

Berridge, V. and B. Thom. "Research and policy: What determines the relationship?" *Policy Studies* 17, no. 1 (1996): pp. 23 - 34

Berridge, V., C. Webster and G. Walt. "Mobilisation for total welfare 1948-74." In *Caring for Health; History and Diversity*, ed. C Webster. Oxford: Oxford University Press, 1993.

Besley, T. *Counseling youth: Foucault, power, and the ethics of subjectivity.* Rotterdam: Sense Publishers 2006.

Bessant, J., R. Watts, T. Dalton and P. Smyth. *Talking Policy: How Social Policy Is Made.* Crows Nest, NSW: Allen & Unwin, 2006

Best, D., M. Gossop, J. Harris, L-H. Man, V. Manning, J. Marshall and J. Strang. "Prior Alcoholics Anonymous (AA) Affiliation and the Acceptability of the Twelve Steps to Patients Entering UK Statutory Addiction Treatment." *Journal of Studies on Alcohol.* 64, no. 2 (2003): pp.257-61.

Best, J. *Threatened children: Rhetoric and Concern about Child-victims.* Chicago: University of Chicago Press, 1990.

Betts, G. *Local Government and Inequalities in Health.* Avebury, Hants: Ashgate Publishing, 1993.

Bevir, M. and F. Trentmann. "Civic Choices: Retrieving Perspectives on Rationality, Consumption, and Citizenship." In *Citizenship and Consumption*, eds. S. Soper and F. Trentmann, pp. 19-33. Basingstoke, Hamps: Palgrave Macmillan, 2007.

Bevir, M. and F. Trentmann. "Social Justice and Modern Capitalism: Historiographical Problems, Theoretical Perspectives." *European Legacy* 6, no.2 (2001): pp.141-158.

Bianchini, F. "Night Cultures, Night Economies" *Planning Practice and Research* 10, no. 2 (1995): pp. 121-126.

Biggs, S. and L.B. Helms. *The Practice of American Policymaking.* New York: M.E Sharpe, Inc, 2007.

Bindman, D. *Hogarth and his times: serious, exh.cat.* London: British Museum, 1997.

Black, N. "Evidence based policy: proceed with care." *BMJ* 323, no.7307 (2001): pp. 275-279.

Blackman, S.J. *Chilling out: the cultural politics of substance consumption, youth and drug.* Maidenhead: Open University Press, 2004.

Blocker, J. S. *Alcohol, Reform, and Society: The Liquor Issue in Social Context.* Westport, CT: Greenwood Press, 1979.

Blocker, J. S., D.M. Fahey and I. R. Tyrrell. *Alcohol and temperance in modern history: an international encyclopedia.* Santa Barbara, Calif.; Oxford: ABC-CLIO, 2003.

Bloom, S.L. *Creating sanctuary: toward the evolution of sane societies* London: Routledge, 1997.

Bloomfield, K. "A comparison of alcohol consumption between lesbians and heterosexual women in an urban population." *Drug and Alcohol Dependence* 33, no.3 (1993): pp.257-269.

Bloomfield, K., G. Gmel, N. Rehn and T. Stockwell. "International Comparisons of Alcohol Consumption." *Alcohol Research & Health* 27, no. 1 (2003): pp.95-109.

Bobak, M., M. McKee, R. Rose and M. Marmot. "Alcohol consumption in a national sample of the Russian population" *Addiction* 94, no. 6 (1999): pp.857-866

Body-Gendrot, S. *The social control of cities: a comparative perspective*. Oxford: Blackwell, 2000.

Bohlmann, R.E. "Drunken husbands, drunken state: The Woman's Christian Temperance Union's challenge to American families and public communities in Chicago, 1874-1920 (Illinois)." PhD thesis: University of Iowa, 2001.

Bojke, C., H. Gravelle and D. Wilkin. "Is bigger better for primary care groups and trusts?" *BMJ* 322, no. 7303 (2001) pp.599-602

Bornat, J., R. Perks, P. Thompson and J. Walmsley. *Oral History, Health and Welfare*. London: Routledge, 2000.

Borsay, P. "Binge drinking and moral panics: historical parallels?" *History and Policy*. Policy Paper 62 (2007).

Borsay, P. "Bingeing Britain." *BBC History*, July 2005, pp.44-48.

Borsay, P. *A History of Leisure: The British Experience since 1500*. Basingstoke, New York: Palgrave Macmillan, 2006.

Bosworth, E. C. "Public healthcare in Nottingham, 18th century to 1945." Nottingham 1998.

Bottoms, A.E. "Crime Prevention in the 1990s." *Policing and Society* 1, no.1 (1990): pp. 3-22.

Boyden, J. "Some Reflections on Scientific Conceptualisations of Childhood and Youth." In *Managing Reproductive Life*, ed. S. Tremayne, pp. 175-193. Oxford: Berghahn Books, 2001.

Brain, K., H. Parker and T. Carnwath. "Drinking with Design: young drinkers as psychoactive consumers " *Drugs: Education, Prevention & Policy* 7, no. 1 (2000): pp.5-20.

Brandon, D., K. Wells, C. Francis and E. Ramsay. *The survivors: a study of homeless young newcomers to London and the responses made to them*. London: Routledge, 1980.

Brandt, A.M. and P. Rozen. *Morality and Health: Interdisciplinary perspectives*. London; New York: Routledge, 1997.

Brandwood, G., A. Davison and M. Slaughter. *Licensed to Sell: The History and Heritage of the Public House*. Swindon: English Heritage, 2004.

Brass, D. J. and M. E. Burkhardt. "Changing patterns or patterns of change: the effects of a change in technology on social network structure and power." *Administrative Science Quarterly* 35, no. 1 (1990): pp.104-127.

Brenton, M. *The Voluntary Sector in British Social Services*. London: Longman, 1985.

Brint, S. *In an Age of Experts: The Changing Role of Professionals in Politics and Public Life*. Princeton, NJ: Princeton University Press, 1994.

Brown, A. *Fanatics! : Power, Identity and Fandom in Football*. London, New York: Routledge, 1998.

Brown, J. and S. Greenacre. "Manchester City Centre Safe: a demonstration project." In *Licensed premises: Law and Practice*, ed. P. Kolvin, pp.702-730. Haywards Heath: Tottel, 2005.

Brown, J.M. "The Effectiveness of Treatment." In *The Essential Handbook of Treatment and Prevention of Alcohol Problems*, eds. N. Heather and T. Stockwell, pp.9-20. New York: John Wiley & Sons, 2004.

Brownson, R. C., C. Royer, R. Ewing and T.D. McBride. "Researchers and Policy makers Travelers in Parallel Universes." *American Journal of Preventive Medicine* 30, no. 2 (2006): pp.164-72.

Bruun, K., M. Lumio, K. Mekela, L. Pan, P. Popham, R. Room, W. Schmidt, O. Skog, P. Sulkunnen and E. Osterberg. *Alcohol Control Policies in Public Health Perspective*. Helsinki: Finnish Foundation for Alcohol Studies; WHO Regional Office for Europe; Addiction Research Foundation of Ontario, 1975.

Budd, J., P. Gray and R. McCron. *The Tyne Tees alcohol education campaign: an evaluation*. London Health Education Council, 1983.

Budd, L., J. Charlesworth and R Paton, eds. *Making policy happen*. London: Routledge, 2006.

Burnett, J. *Liquid Pleasures*. London, New York: Routledge, 1999.

Burnham, J.C. *Bad habits*. New York: New York University Press, 1993.

Burns, E. *The Spirits of America: A Social History of Alcohol*. Philadelphia: Temple University Press 2004.

Burns, T. *Community mental health teams: a guide to current practices* Oxford: Oxford University Press, 2004.

Burns, T. "Psychiatry in the future: Changes in UK mental health care over the past 15 years" *Psychiatric Bulletin* 28, no.8 (2004): pp.275-276.

Buse, K. and G. Walt. *Making Health Policy*. Maidenhead: Open University Press, 2005.

Butler J.R. and M.S.B. Vaile. *Health and Health Services: An Introduction to Health Care in Britain*. London: Routledge, 1984.

Butler, T. and G. Robson. "Negotiating their way in: the middle classes, gentrification and the deployment of capital in a globalising metropolis." *Urban Studies* 40, no.9 (2003): pp.1791-809.

Button, M. *Private Policing*. Devon: Willan Publishing, 2002.

Bynum, W. F, R. Porter and M. Shepherd, *The anatomy of madness: essays in the history of psychiatry, Volume 3*. (London, Routledge, 2004).

Bynum, W. F., 'The rise of science in medicine, 1850–1913', in W F Bynum, A. Hardy, S. Jacyna, C. Lawrence and E. M .Tansey, *The western medical tradition 1800 to 2000*. Cambridge: Cambridge University Press, 2006, pp. 111–132.

Caddy, G.R and S.H Lovibond. "Self-regulation and discriminated aversive conditioning in the modification of alcoholics' drinking behaviour." *Behaviour Therapy* 7, no.2 (1976): pp.223-300.

Camberwell Council on Alcoholism. *Women and Alcohol*. London: Tavistock, 1980.
Cameron, D. "Community management of "Determined Drinkers." PhD thesis: University of Glasgow, 1991.
Cameron, D. "I see managerialism as a virus," *The Guardian*, April 5th 2002.
Cameron, D. *Liberating Solutions to Alcohol Problems*. London: Jason Aronson, 1995.
Cameron, D. "Why alcohol dependence - and why now?" In *The Misuse of alcohol: crucial issues in dependence, treatment & prevention*, ed. N. Heather, I. Robertson and P. Davies, pp. 59-71. London: Croom Helm, 1985.
Cameron, D. and M.T. Spence. "Lessons from an Out-patient Controlled Drinking Group." *Alcohol and Alcoholism* 11, no. 2 (1976): pp. 44-55
Cameron, D., M. Thomas, S. Madden, C. Thornton, A. Bergmark, H. Garretsen and M. Terzidou. "Intoxicated Across Europe: In Search of Meaning." *Addiction Research & Theory* 8, no. 3 (2000): pp.233-242.
Campbell, J.L. "Institutional Analysis and the Role of Ideas in Political Economy." *Theory and Society* 27, no.3 (1998), pp.377-409.
Campbell, N.D. *Discovering Addiction*. Michigan: University of Michigan Press, 2007.
Caplan, G. *An Approach to Community Mental Health*. London: Tavistock, 1961.
Carlson, P. and D. Vagero. "The social pattern of heavy drinking in Russia during transition; Evidence from Taganrog 1993."*European Journal of Public Health* 8, no. 4 (1998): pp.280-285.
Cartwright, A.K.J., S.J. Shaw and T.A. Spratley. "Designing a Comprehensive Community Response to Problems of Alcohol Abuse. Report to the Department of Health and Social Security." London: Maudsley Alcohol Pilot Project, 1975.
Castree, N "The epistemology of particulars: human geography, case studies and 'context." *Geoforum* 36, no.5 (2005): pp. 541-544.
Caudill, B. D., G. T. Wilson and D. B. Abrams. "Alcohol and self-disclosure: analyses of interpersonal behavior in male and female social drinkers." *J Stud Alcohol* 48, no. 5 (1987): pp.401-409.
Chamberlain, M. and P. Thompson. *Narrative and Genre*. London: Routledge, 2000.
Chamberlayne, P., J. Bornat and T. Wengraf,. *The Turn to Biographical Methods in Social Science; Comparative issues and examples* London: Routledge, 2000.
Chapman, S.D. "Industry and Trade, 1750-1900." In *A Centenary History of Nottingham*, ed. J.V. Beckett. Manchester: Manchester University Press, 1997.
Chatterton, P. "Will the real creative city please stand up?" *City* 4, no. 3 (2000): pp.390-397.
Chatterton, P. and R. Hollands. "Theorising urban playscapes: producing, regulating and consuming youthful nightlife city spaces." *Urban Studies* 39, no. 1 (2002): pp.95-116.
Chatterton, P. and R. Hollands. *Urban Nightscapes: Youth Cultures, Pleasure Spaces and Corporate Power*. London: Routledge, 2003

Chavigny, K. A. "Reforming Drunkards in Nineteenth Century American; Religion, therapy, medicine." In *Altering American Consciousness*, eds. S.W. Tracy and C.J. Acker, pp.108-23. Massachusetts: University of Massachusetts Press, 2004.

Chesher, G. and J. Greeley."Tolerance to the effects of alcohol" *Alcohol, Drugs and Driving* 8, no. 2 (1992): pp.93-106.

Chick, J., H. Howlett, M. Y. Morgan, B. Ritson and UKMAS Investigators. "United Kingdom Multicentre Acamprosate Study (UKMAS): a 6 Month Prospective Study of Acamprosate versus Placebo in Prevention Relapse after Withdrawal from Alcohol." *Alcohol and Alcoholism* 35, no. 2 (2000): pp.176-187.

Chikritzhs, T. and T. R. Stockwell. "The impact of later trading hours for Australian public houses (hotels) on levels of violence." *Journal of Studies on Alcohol* 63, no.5 (2002): pp. 591-599.

Chinn, C. *The Worked all their lives: Women of the urban poor in England 1880-1939*. Manchester: Manchester University Press, 1988.

Clark, P. ed. *The Cambridge Urban History of Britain*. Cambridge: Cambridge University Press 2000.

Clark, P. *The English Alehouse: A Social History 1200-1830* London: Longman, 1983.

Clarke, J. and C. Critcher. *The Devil Makes Work: Leisure in Capitalist Britain*. Basingstoke: Palgrave Macmillan, 1985.

Clarke, L. "The Opening of Doors in British mental hospitals in the 1950s." *History of Psychiatry* 4, no.16 (1993): pp.527-551.

Clarke, L *The Time of the Communities: People, Places and Events, Community psychiatry*. London: Jessica Kingsley, 2003.

Clayson, C. "The Role of Licensing law in Limiting the Misuse of Alcohol." In *Alcoholism: New Knowledge and New Responses*, eds. M. Grant and G. Edwards. London: Croom Helm, 1977.

Clements, S. "Feminism, citizenship and social activity: The role and importance of local women's organisations in Nottingham 1918-1969." PhD thesis: Nottingham, 2008.

Clifford Engs, R. *Clean Living Movements: American Cycles of Health reform*. Westport, Ct: Praeger, 2001.

Coates, K. and R. Silburn. *Poverty: The Forgotten Englishmen*. Harmondsworth, Middlesex: Penguin, 1970.

Coates, K. and R. Silburn. *St Ann's: Poverty, deprivation and morale in a Nottingham community*. Nottingham: Spokesman, 1967.

Cochrane, A.L. *Effectiveness and Efficiency: random reflections on health services*. London: Nuffield Provincial Hospitals Trust, 1972.

Cochrane, A.L. "1931-1971: a critical review with particular reference to the medical profession." In *Medicines for the year 2000*, pp.1-11. London: Office of Health Economics, 1979.

Cochrane, M., T. Spratley and H. Shelley. "Detoxification: a toxic metaphor?" *Journal of Substance Misuse for Nursing Health and Social Care* 3, no. 3 (1998): pp.178-180.

Coffield, F. and L. Gofton. *Drugs and Young People*. London: Institute for Public Policy Research, 1994.
Cohen, D. and M. O'Connor. *Comparison and History: Europe in Cross-National Perspective*. London, New York: Routledge, 2004
Cohen, S. *Folk Devils and Moral Panics: The Creation of the Mods and Rockers*. 3rd ed. MacGibbon and Kee: London, 2002.
Colebatch, H.K. *Policy, Concepts in the Social Sciences*. Maidenhead: Open University Press, 2002.
Coleman, J.C. *Youth policy in the 1990s: the way forward*. New York: Routledge, 1992.
Coleman, L. and S. Cater. "Changing the culture of young people's binge drinking: From motivations to practical solutions." *Drugs: Education, Prevention & Policy* 14, no.4 (2007): pp.305-317.
Coleman, L. and S. Cater. *Underage 'risky' Drinking*. York: Joseph Rowntree Foundation, 2005.
Coleman, W.D. and G. Skogstad. "Policy communities and policy networks; a structural approach." In *Policy communities and public policy in Canada*, eds. W.D. Coleman and G. Skogstad, pp. 14-33. Mississauga ON: Copp Clark Pitman, 1990.
Collingridge, D. and C. Reeve. *Science Speaks to Power: The Role of Experts in Policy Making*. New York: St. Martin's Press, 1986.
Collins, D.C. and R.A. Kearns. "Under curfew and under siege? Legal geographies of young people." *Geoforum* 32, no.3 (2001): pp.389-404.
Collins, J. J. and W. E. Schlenger. "Acute and chronic effects of alcohol use on violence." *J Stud Alcohol* 49, no. 6 (1988): pp.516-521.
Collins, T. and W. Vamplew. *Mud, sweat and beers: a cultural history of sport and alcohol, Global sport cultures*. Oxford: Berg, 2002.
Colson, E. and T. Scudder. *For Prayer and Profit: The Ritual, Economic and Social Importance of Beer in Gwembe District, Zambia*. Stanford: Stanford University Press, 1988.
Conrad, P., and J.W. Schneider. *Deviance and Medicalization: From Badness to Sickness*. Philadelphia: Temple University Press, 1992.
Convery, F.J. "Making a difference - how environmental economists can influence the policy process - a case study of David W Pearce " *Environmental and Resource Economics* 37, no. 1 (2007): pp.7-32.
Cook, C.C. *Alcohol, Addiction and Christian Ethics*. Cambridge: Cambridge University Press 2006.
Cook, C.C.H. "The Minnesota Model in the Management of Drug and Alcohol Dependency: miracle, method or myth? Part I." *British Journal of Addiction* 83, no.6 (1988): pp.625-634.
Cook, C.C.H. "The Minnesota Model in the Management of Drug and Alcohol Dependency: miracle, method or myth? Part II." *British Journal of Addiction* 83, no.7 (1988): pp.735-748.

Cook, T. W. *Governing with the News: The News Media as a Political Institution.* Chicago: University of Chicago 1998.

Cooper, D. *Psychiatry and Anti-Psychiatry*, London: Paladin, 1967.

Cooper, J. *Psychiatrists and primary care in Nottingham.* eds. A.W. Clare and M. Lader, *In Psychiatry and General Practice.* London: Academic Press, 1982.

Cordon, J.D. "Hostel for Offenders with Alcoholic Problems 28 Addison Street, Nottingham." *Alcohol and Alcoholism* 5, no. 4 (1970): pp.167-168

Coulson, P. "Licensing and the Law: An Overview." Paper presented at the 24 Hour City: Selected Papers from the First National Conference on the Night-time Economy, Manchester 1994.

Courtwright, D. *Dark paradise: A history of opiate addiction in America.* Cambridge: Harvard University Press, 2001.

Courtwright, D. *Forces of Habit; Drugs and the Making of the Modern World.* Cambs, Massachusetts and London: Harvard University Press, 2001.

Cousins, R. *Newark Inns and Public Houses.* Nottingham: Nottingham County Council, 1991.

Craig, G., N. Derricourt and M. Loney. *Community Work and the State. Towards a radical practice, Community Work 8.* London: Routledge and Kegan Paul, 1982.

Craig, G., K. Popple and M. Shaw. *Community Development in Theory and Practice: an International Reader.* Nottingham: Spokesman, 2008.

Crane, M. and A. Warnes. "Wet day centres in Britain." *Drug and Alcohol Findings,* no. 12 (2005): pp.24-9.

Crewe, L. and J. Beaverstock. "Fashioning the city: Cultures of consumption in contemporary urban spaces " *Geoforum* 29, no. 3 (1998): pp.287-308

Critcher, C. "Moral panics and newspaper coverage of binge drinking." In *Pulling Newspapers Apart,* pp.154-162, ed. Bob Franklin. London: Routledge, 2008.

Critchlow, B. "The powers of John Barleycorn. Beliefs about the effects of alcohol on social behavior." *Am Psychol* 41, no. 7 (1986): pp.751-64.

Cronin, A.M. *Advertising Myths: The Strange Half-lives of Images and Commodities, Business / Economics /Finance* London: Routledge, 2004.

Crook, R. and J. Ayee. "Urban Service Partnerships, 'Street-Level Bureaucrats' and Environmental Sanitation in Kumasi and Accra, Ghana: Coping with Organisational Change in the Public Bureaucracy." *Development Policy Review* 24, no. 1 (2006): pp.51-73.

Crossley, B. and J.C. Denmark. "Community care: a study of the psychiatric morbidity of a Salvation Army hostel." *British Journal of Sociology* 20, no.4 (1969): pp.443-449.

Crouch, C. and R. Dore, eds. *Corporatism and Accountability: Organized Interests in British Public Life* Oxford: Clarendon Press, 1990.

Crowley, J. W. *The white logic: alcoholism and gender in American modernist fiction.* Amherst: University of Massachusetts Press, 1994.

Curran, J. and J. Seaton. *Power without Responsibility: The Press, Broadcasting, and New Media in Britain.* 6th ed. London, New York: Routledge, 2003

Cutler, D. L. and C. Huffine. "Heroes in Community Psychiatry Professor Gerald Caplan." *Community Mental Health Journal* 40, no. 3 (2004): pp.193-197

Dance, A.R. *Narrow Marsh*. Nottingham: Arundel Books, 2008.

Daniels, S. and S. Rycroft. "Mapping the Modern City: Alan Sillitoe's Nottingham Novels " *Transactions of the Institute of British Geographers NS, New Series* 18, no. 4 (1993): pp.460-80.

Daunton, M.J., D.M. Pallister and P. Clark, eds. *The Cambridge Urban History of Britain. Vol.3, 1840-1950.*Cambridge: Cambridge University Press, 2000.

Davies, D.L. "Normal drinking in recovered alcohol addicts." *Q.J. Stud. Alcohol* 23 (1962): pp.94 -104.

Davies, J. *Youth and the Condition of Britain: Images of Adolescent Conflict*. London: Athlone, 1990.

Davies, J. and B. Stacey. *Teenagers and Alcohol. A Developmental Study in Glasgow*. London: HMSO, 1972.

Davies, J.B. *The Myth of Addiction*. London: Routledge 1997.

Davies, J.K. and M.P Kelly. *Healthy cities: research and practice*. London: Routledge, 1993.

Davies, K. and J. Barnard. "Working with other agencies." In *Care of drug users in general practice: a harm reduction approach*, ed. B Beaumont, pp.157-176. Abingdon, Oxon: Radcliffe Publishing, 2004.

Davies, P. and D. Walsh. *Alcohol problems and alcohol control in Europe*. London: Croom Helm, 1983.

Davies, S. and S. Payne. "Patients repeatedly admitted to psychiatric wards: a four-year follow-up." *Psychiatric Bulletin* 20, no.6 (1996): pp.342-344.

Davis Smith, J. and M. Oppenheimer. "The Labour Movement and Voluntary Action in the UK and Australia: a Comparative Perspective." *Labour History* 88 (2005).

Davis Smith, J., C. Rochester and R. Hedley. *An Introduction to the Voluntary Sector*. London: Routledge, 1994.

Davis, S. N., M. Crawford and J. Sebrechts. *Coming into her own: educational success in girls and women*. San Francisco, Calif.: Jossey-Bass, 1999.

Davison, J. *Gangsta: The Sinister Spread of Yardie Gun Culture*. London: Vision paperbacks, 1997.

Day, P. and D. Schuler. *Community Practice in the Network Society: Local Action, Global Interaction*. London: Routledge, 2004

Day, P., D.M. Fox, R. Maxwell and E. Scrivens. *The State, Politics and Health: essays for Rudolf Klein*. Oxford: Blackwells, 1996.

de Garine, I. and V.C. de Garine. *Drinking: anthropological approaches*. Oxford: Berghahn, 2001.

De Jong, F. and H. Jansen. *The Construction of an Urban Past: Narrative and System in Urban History*. Oxford: Berg, 2001

De Leon, G. *The Therapeutic Community*. 7th ed. New York: Springer Publishing, 2000.

Deehan, A., E. Marshall and E. Saville. *Police Research Series Paper 150: Drunks and Disorder: Processing intoxicated arrestees in two city-centre custody suites.* London: Policing and Reducing Crime Unit Research Home Office, Development and Statistics Directorate, 2002.

Dempsey, H.A. *Firewater: the impact of the whisky trade on the Blackfoot nation.* Calgary: Fifth House Publishers, 2002.

Dennis, R. *English Industrial Cities of the Nineteenth Century: A Social Geography.* Cambridge: Cambridge University Press 1984.

Dickenson, J. P. and P. T. H. Unwin. *Viticulture in colonial Latin America: essays on alcohol, the vine and wine in Spanish America and Brazil.* Liverpool: University of Liverpool, Institute of Latin American Studies, 1992.

DigGuarde, K. I. *Binge Drinking Research Progress.* New York: Nova Science, 2009.

Dimeo, P. *Drugs, alcohol and sport: Sport in the global society.* London: Routledge, 2006.

Dingle, A.E. *The Campaign for Prohibition in Victorian England: The United Kingdom Alliance 1872-1895.* London: Croom Helm, 1980.

Dingle, A.E. "Drink and Working Class Standards in Britain; 1870-1914." *Economic History Review* 25, no. 4 (1972): pp. 608-622

Dingwall, R. "Litigation and the threat to medicine." In *Challenging Medicine*, eds. J. Gabe and D. Kelleher, pp. 46-64. London: Routledge, 1994.

Doern, K. G. "Temperance and feminism in England, c.1790-1890: women's weapons - prayer, pen and platform." PhD thesis: Sussex, 2001.

Donovan, D. M., R. L. Umlauf and P. M. Salzberg. "Bad drivers: identification of a target group for alcohol-related prevention and early intervention." *J Stud Alcohol* 51, no. 2 (1990): pp.136-41.

Dorey, P. *Developments in British public policy.* London: Thousand Oaks: Sage, 2005.

Dorn, N. *Alcohol, Youth and the State: Drinking Practices, Controls and Health Education.* London: Croom Helm, 1983.

Douglas, M. *Constructive drinking.* Cambridge: Cambridge University Press, 1987.

Drummond, C. "An alcohol strategy for England: the good, the bad and the ugly." *Alcohol and Alcoholism* 39, no. 5 (2004): pp.377-379.

Duke, K. *Drugs, prison and Policy-making.* London: Palgrave Macmillan, 2003.

Duke, K. "Getting Beyond the Official Line: Reflections on Dilemmas of Access, Knowledge and Power in Researching Policy Networks." *Journal of Social Policy* 31, no. 1 (2002): pp. 39-59.

Duke, M.H. "Obituary: Dr. Brian Lake." *Church Times* January 25th 2008. Available at http://www.churchtimes.co.uk/content.asp?id=50389 [Cited 3rd April 2010]

Dupuis, R. "Acceptance - Birth of CTA in the 60s." In *British Pastoral Foundation.* Prenton, Birkenhead: British Pastoral Foundation, undated.

Earnshaw, S. *The Pub in Literature.* Manchester, New York: Manchester University Press, 2000.

Eberstadt, N. "Russia: Too Sick to Matter? Vodka and heart disease weaken the Russian bear " *Policy Review* No. 95 (1999): pp.3-26

Eddy, R. *Alcohol in History: an account of intemperance in all ages: together with a history of the various methods employed for its removal*. Mauston: Independent Order Good Templars, 1883.

Edensor, T. "Caudan: domesticating the global waterfront." In *Small cities: urban experience beyond the metropolis*, eds. D. Bell and M. Jayne; London: Routledge, 2006.

Edwards, G. *Alcohol: the ambiguous molecule*. London: Penguin, 2000.

Edwards, G. *Alcohol Policy and the Public Good*. Oxford: Oxford University Press, 1994.

Edwards, G. *Alcohol: the world's favourite drug*. New York: Penguin Books, 2000.

Edwards, G. *The Treatment of Drinking Problems*. 2nd ed. Oxford: Blackwell Scientific Publications, 1987.

Edwards, G. and M.M. Gross. "Alcohol dependence: Provisional description of a clinical syndrome." *British Medical Journal* 1, no. 6017 (1976): pp. 1058-1061.

Edwards, G., J. Orford, S. Egert, S. Guthrie, A. Hawker, C. Hensman, M. Mitcheson, E. Oppenheimer and C. Taylor. "Alcoholism: A Controlled Trial of "Treatment" and "Advice"." *Journal of Studies on Alcohol* 38, no. 5 (1977): pp. 1004-1031.

Edwards, G., R. West, T. Barbor, W. Hall and J. Marsden. "An invitation to the alcohol industry lobby to help decide public funding of alcohol research and professional training: a decision that should be reversed." *Addiction* 99, no. 10 (2004): pp.1235-1236.

Ellickson, P., R. Collins, K. Hambarsoonians and D. McCaffery. "Does advertising promote adolescent drinking?" *Addiction* 100, no. 2 (2005): pp. 235-246.

Erikson, R.S., G.C. Wright and J.P. McIver. *Statehouse democracy: Public opinion and policy in the American states*. Cambridge: Cambridge University Press, 1993.

Estabrook, C. *Urbane and Rustic England: Cultural Ties and Social Spheres in the Provinces, 1660-1780*. Manchester: Manchester University Press, 1998.

Ettore, B. "A study of alcoholism treatment units: Treatment activities and the institutional response." *Alcohol and Alcoholism* 19, no. 3 (1984): pp.243-255.

Ettore, E. *Women and alcohol: a private pleasure or public problem?* London: The Women's Press, 1997.

Exworthy, M., L. Berney and M. Powell. "How great expectations in Westminster may be dashed locally': the local implementation of national policy on health inequalities." *Policy and Politics* 30, no. 1 (2002): pp. 79-96

Exworthy, M. and M. Powell. "Big windows and little windows: implementation in the congested state." *Public Administration* 82 (2004): pp. 263-281.

Farooq, S. and F.A. Minhas. "Community psychiatry in developing countries — a misnomer?" *Psychiatric Bulletin* 25, no. 6 (2001): pp. 226-227.

Farquharson, K. "A Different Kind of Snowball: Identifying Key Policy makers "*International Journal of Social Research Methodology* 8, no. 4 (2005): pp. 345-353

Fass, P.S. "Cultural History/Social History: Some Reflections on a Continuing Dialogue." *Journal of Social History* 37, no. 1 (2003): pp. 39–46.

Featherstone, M. *Consumer culture and postmodernity.* London: Sage, 1991.

Federal Alcohol Administration. *Legislative History of the Federal Alcohol Administration Act.* Washington: United States of America Treasury, 1935.

Feek, W, *Working effectively.* London: Bedford Square Press, 1988.

Feinmann, J. "Addiction Centre Breaks New Ground." *General Practitioner,* (November 23rd 1990), p.45.

Fellstrom, C. *Hoods: The gangs of Nottingham* Lancs: Milo Books, 2008.

Fenwick, J. and M. Bailey. "Local government reorganisation in the UK: Decentralisation or corporatism?" *International Journal of Public Sector Management* 12, no. 3 (1999): pp. 249-261.

Ferrell, J. and N. Websdale. *Making trouble: cultural constructions of crime, deviance, and control.* New York: Aldine de Gruyter, 1999.

Fillingham, P. and C. Richards. *Nottingham in the 1980s.* Stroud: The History Press Ltd, 2002.

Fingarette, H. *Heavy Drinking - The Myth of Alcoholism as a Disease.* Berkeley: University of California Press, 1988.

Finlayson, G. *Citizen, state, and social welfare in Britain 1830-1990.* Oxford: Clarendon Press, 1994.

Fischer, W., W. Hamilton, C. McLaughlin and R. Zmud. "The Elusive Product Champion." *Research Management* 29, no. 3 (1986): pp.13-16.

Fischer-Tiné, H. "Britain's other civilising mission; Class prejudice, European 'loaferism' and the workhouse–system in colonial India." *Indian Economic & Social History Review* 42, no. 3 (2005): pp. 295-338.

Fisher, J. *Advertising, alcohol consumption and abuse: a worldwide survey.* Westport, CT Greenwood Press, 1993.

Fitzpatrick, K. and M. Lagory. *Unhealthy Places: The Ecology of Risk in the Urban Landscape.* London: Routledge, 2000

Fitzpatrick, S. and A. Jones. "Pursuing Social Justice or Social Cohesion? Coercion in Street Homelessness Policies in England." *Journal of Social Policy* 34, no. 3 (2005): pp. 389-406.

Fleming, A. *Alcohol: the delightful poison: a history* New York: Dell Publishing 1979.

Forbes, D., R. Hayes and J. Reason. "Voluntary but not amateur." London: London Voluntary Service Council, 1990.

Forsyth, J. and D.M. Fahey. *The collected writings of Jessie Forsyth, 1847-1937: the Good Templars and temperance reform on three continents, Interdisciplinary studies in alcohol use and abuse; Vol. 1.* Lewiston, N.Y.: E. Mellen Press, 1988.

Fossey, E, W. Loretto and M. Plant. "Alcohol and Youth." In *Alcohol Problems in the Community*, ed. L Harrison, pp. 52-75. London: Routledge, 1996.

Foster, J. H., R. Herring, H. S. Waller and B. Thom. "The Licensing Act 2003: A step in the right direction?" *Journal of Substance Use* 14, no. 2 (2009): pp.113-123

Foucault, M. *The Birth of the Clinic: An Archaeology of Medical Perception*. New York: Vintage, 1975.

Foucault, M. *Discipline and punishment: The birth of the prison*. New York: Pantheon, 1977.

Foucault, M. *Madness and civilization*. New York: Pantheon 1965.

Frank, L.D., H. Frumkin and R. Jackson. *Urban Sprawl and Public Health*. Washington, DC: Island Press 2004.

Frey Jr., D. A. "Bacchus and Civic Order: The Culture of Drink in Early Modern Germany." *Journal of Social History* 36, no. 4 (2003): pp. 1110-1112.

Frisby, D. *Cityscapes of modernity: Critical Explorations* Cambridge: Polity Press, 2001.

Frosdick, S. and P. Marsh. *Football Hooliganism*. Devon: Willan Publishing, 2005.

Frumkin, H., L. D. Frank and R. Jackson. *Urban Sprawl and Public Health: Designing, Planning, and Building for Healthy Communities*. Washington, DC: Island Press 2004.

Fukuyama, F. *The End of Order: SMF Centre for Post-Collectivist Studies Paper No. 3*. London: The Social Market Foundation, 1997.

Fumerton, P. "Not Home: Alehouses, Ballads and the Vagrant Husband in Early Modern England." *Journal of Medieval and Early Modern Studies* 32, no. 3 (2002): pp.493-518.

Fyfe, N.R. "Out of the shadows: exploring contemporary geographies of voluntarism " *Progress in Human Geography* 27, no. 4 (2003): pp.397-413.

Gaffney, D., A. M. Pollock, D. Price and J. Shaoul. "The private finance initiative: NHS capital expenditure and the private finance initiative expansion or contraction?" *British Medical Journal* 319, no.7201 (1999): pp. 48-51.

Gage, A. J. and C. Suzuki. "Risk factors for alcohol use among male adolescents and emerging adults in Haiti." *J Adolesc* 29, no. 2 (2006): pp.241-60.

Galanter, M. *Alcohol Problems in Adolescents and Young Adults: Epidemiology, Neurobiology, Prevention, Treatment* New York: Springer 2005.

Gamella, J. F. *Drugs and alcohol in the Pacific: new consumption trends and their consequences, The Pacific world. Lands, peoples and history of the Pacific, 1500-1900; v. 14*. Aldershot: Ashgate, 2002.

Garcia-Andrade, C., Wall, T. L. and C. L Ehlers. "Alcohol expectancies in a Native American population." *Alcohol Clin Exp Res* 20, no. 8 (1996): pp. 1438-42.

Garnham, N. "The Mass Media, Cultural Identity and the Public Sphere in the Modern World." *Public Culture* 5, no. 2 (1993): pp. 251-65.

Gately, I. *Drink: a cultural history of alcohol*. New York: Gotham Books, 2008.

Gefou-Madianou, D. *Alcohol, Gender, and Culture*. New York: Routledge, 1992.

Gelder, K. and S. Thornton. *The subcultures reader*. London: Routledge, 1997.
George, M. D. *London Life in the Eighteenth Century*. London: Routledge, 1997.
Gerstein, D.R. *Towards the Prevention of Alcohol Problems*. Washington, D.C: National Academy Press, 1984.
Ghodse, H., G. Edwards, J. Stapleton, T. Bewley and M. Al-Samarrai. "A Comparison of Drug-Related Problems in London Accident and Emergency Departments 1975-1982." *British Journal of Psychiatry* 148, no.6 (1986): pp. 658-662.
Giggs, J.A. "Drug Abuse and Urban Ecological Structure: The Nottingham Case." In *Spatial Epidemiology*, ed. R.W. Thomas, pp.218- 239. London: Pion, 1990.
Giggs, J.A. "Ethnic status and mental illness in urban areas." In *Health, Race & Ethnicity*, eds. T. Rathwell and D. Phillips, pp. 137-174. London: Routledge, 1986.
Giggs, J.A. "Housing, Population and Transport." In *A Centenary History of Nottingham*, ed. J.V. Beckett, pp.435-462. Manchester: Manchester University Press, 1997.
Giggs, J.A. "Mental disorder and ecological structure in Nottingham." *Social Science and Medicine* 23, no. 10 (1986): pp. 945-961.
Giggs, J.A, P. Bean, D. Whynes and C. Wilkinson. "Class A Drug Users: prevalence and characteristics in Greater Nottingham." *British Journal of Addiction*, 84, no. 12 (1989): pp.1473-1480.
Giggs, J.A. and D.K. Whynes. "Homeless people in Nottingham." *East Midlands Geographer* 11, no. 2 (1988): pp. 57-67.
Gilboa, E. "Effects of Global Television News on US Policy in International Conflict." In *Media and Conflict in the Twenty-First Century*, ed. P. Seib, pp 1-32. New York: Palgrave Macmillan, 2005.
Gill, J.S. "Reported levels of alcohol consumption and binge drinking within the UK undergraduate student population over the last 25 years." *Alcohol and Alcoholism* 37, no. 2 (2002): pp. 109-120.
Gillam, S., S. Abbott and J. Banks-Smith. "Primary care groups: Can primary care groups and trusts improve health?" *British Medical Journal* 323, no. 7304 (2001): pp. 89-92.
Gillies, P.A., J.C.G. Pearson and J.M. Elwood. *Regional Health Authority Survey of Smoking in 15-16 year olds*. Nottingham: Report to the Health Education Council. Trent Department of Community Medicine and Epidemiology, University of Nottingham, 1986.
Gillis, J.R. *Youth and History: Tradition and Change in European Age Relations, 1870-Present*. New York: Academic Press, 1981.
Girouard, M. *Victorian pubs*. London: Studio Vista, 1975.
Glatt, M. "Treatment Centre for Alcoholics in a Public Mental Hospital: Its Establishment and its Working." *British Journal of Addiction* 52, no.1-2 (1955): pp.55-133.

Gmel, G., H. Rehm and E. Kuntsche. "Binge Drinking in Europe: definitions, epidemiology and consequences." *Sucht* 49 (2003): pp. 105-116.

Gochfeld, M. "Chronologic History of Occupational Medicine." *Journal of Environmental Medicine* 47, no. 2 (2005): pp. 96-114.

Goddard, E. and C. Ikin. *Drinking in England and Wales in 1987*. London: HMSO, 1988.

Gofton, L. "On the town: Drink and the 'new lawlessness'." *Youth and Society* 29, no.2 (1990): pp.33-39.

Gofton, L. R. "Folk Devils and the Demon Drink: Drinking Rituals and Social Integration in North East England." *Drogalkohol, Alkohol and Drogen* 12 (1988): pp.181-196.

Golby, J. M. and A. W. Purdue. *The civilisation of the crowd*. London: Batsford, 1984.

Gold, M. S. and N.S. Miller. *Alcohol* Vol. 2 *Drugs of Abuse: A Comprehensive Series for Clinicians*. London, New York: Plenum Medical, 1991.

Gomberg, E. S. "Women and alcohol: use and abuse." *J Nerv Ment Dis* 181, no. 4 (1993): pp. 211-219.

Gomm, R., M. Hammersley and P. Foster. *Case Study Method: Key Issues, Key Texts*. London: Sage, 2000.

Goodwin, D. "Inpatient Treatment of Alcoholism - New Life for the Minneapolis Plan." *New England Journal of Medicine* 325 (1991): pp. 804-806.

Goodwin, D. W. *Alcoholism: The Facts*. Oxford, New York, Toronto: Oxford University Press, 1981.

Gorsky, M. "Local leadership in public health: the role of the medical officer of health in Britain, 1872–1974." *J Epidemiol Community Health* 61, no.6 (2007): pp. 468-472.

Gorsky, M. "Public health in interwar England and Wales: did it fail?" *Dynamis* 28 (2008): pp.175-198.

Gossop, M., L. Green and G. Phillips."What happens to opiate addicts immediately after treatment: A prospective follow up study." *British Medical Journal of Social Psychiatry* 194, no. 6584 (1987): pp. 1377-1388.

Gotham, H. J., K. J. Sher and P. K. Wood. "Predicting stability and change in frequency of intoxication from the college years to beyond: individual-difference and role transition variables." *J Abnorm Psychol* 106, no. 4 (1997): pp. 619-629.

Gough, B. and G. Edwards. "The beer talking: four lads, a carry out and the reproduction of masculinities." *Sociological Review* 46, no. 2 (1998): pp.409-435.

Gourvish, T.R. and R.G. Wilson. *The British Brewing Industry 1830-1980*. Cambridge: Cambridge University Press, 1994.

Graber, D.A. *Processing Politics: Learning from Television in the Internet Age*. Chicago: University of Chicago, 2001.

Grant, M. and J. Litvak. *Drinking patterns and their consequences.* London, Philadelphia: Taylor and Francis, 1998.

Grant, M. and J. O'Connor. *Corporate Responsibility and Alcohol: The Need and Potential for Partnership.* New York: Routledge, 2005.

Grant, M, M Plant and A. Williams. *Economics and Alcohol: Consumption and Controls.* London, Canberra: Croom Helm in Association with the Alcohol Education Centre, 1983.

Gray, D. *Nottingham through 500 years: A History of Town Government.* 2nd ed. Nottingham: Nottingham City, 1960.

Gray, D. *Nottingham: Settlement to city.* A companion volume to Nottingham through 500 years. 2nd ed. Leeds: The Amethyst Press, 1983.

Gray, G.E. *Concise guide to evidence-based psychiatry.* Arlington, V.A: American Psychiatric Publishing, 2004.

Grazian, D. *On the Make: The Hustle of Urban Nightlife.* Chicago: University of Chicago Press Ltd, 2008.

Great Britain Historical GIS Project. *A vision of Britain between 1801 and 2001: Nottingham Unitary Authority.* Portsmouth: Dept. of Geography, University of Portsmouth, 2004

Greenaway, J. "Agendas, Venues and Alliances: New Opportunities for the Alcohol Control Movement in England," *Drugs: education, prevention and policy,* 15, no. 5 (2008), pp. 487-501.

Greenaway, J. "Calling 'Time' on Last Orders: The Rise and Fall of the Public House Closing Hours in Britain." *Revue française de civilisation* 14, no. 2 (2007): pp. 181-96.

Greenaway, J. *Drink and British Politics since 1830.* Hamps: Palgrave Macmillan, 2003.

Greenaway, J. "The "improved" public house, 1870-1950: the key to civilized drinking or the primrose path to drunkenness?" *Addiction* 93, no. 2 (1998): pp. 173-181.

Greene, B. T. "An examination of the relationship between crime and substance use in a drug/alcohol treatment population." *Int J Addict* 16, no. 4 (1981): pp.627-645.

Greener, I. *Healthcare in the UK: Understanding Continuity and Change.* Bristol: The Policy Press, 2009.

Greve, J. *Homelessness in Britain.* York: Joseph Rowntree Foundation, 1991.

Griffin, C. *Representations of youth: the study of youth and adolescence in Britain and America. Feminist perspectives.* Cambridge: Polity Press, 1993.

Grube, J. "Alcohol portrayals and alcohol advertising on television: Content and effects on children and adolescents." *Alcohol Health and Research World* 17, no.1 (1995): pp.61-66.

Grube, J. and P. Nygaard. "Adolescent drinking and alcohol policy." *Contemporary Drug Problems* 28, no. 1 (2001): pp.87-131.

Gruenewald, P.J., R. Lipton and L. Remer. "Evaluating the Alcohol Environment: Community Geography and Alcohol Problems." *Alcohol Research & Health* 26, no. 1 (2002): pp. 42-48.

Gunthorpe, K. "Between dependency and adulthood: the treatment of youth in British politics, 1959-70.", Leeds 1995.

Gurr, T. *History of violent crime*. London: Sage, 1989.

Gusfield, J.R *Symbolic Crusade*. Chicago: University of Illinois Press, 1986.

Gutzke, D.W. *Alcohol in the British Isles from Roman times to 1996: an annotated bibliography, Bibliographies and indexes in world history; no. 44*. Westport, Conn.; London: Greenwood Press, 1996.

Gutzke, D.W. "The Cry of Children: the Edwardian medical campaign against maternal drinking." *British Journal of Addiction* 79, no.4 (1984): pp.71-84.

Gutzke, D.W. *Pubs and Progressives: Reinventing the Public House in England, 1896-1960*. : Northern Illinois University: Press De Kalb, Illinois, 2005.

Guy Peters, B. and J. Pierre, eds. *Handbook of Public Policy*. London: Sage Publications, 2006.

Habermas, J. *The structural transformation of the public sphere: inquiry into a category of bourgeois society*. Cambridge: Polity Press, 1974.

Hadfield, P., S. Lister and P. Traynor. "The Orientation and Integration of Local and National Alcohol Policy in England and Wales." London: AERC, 2009.

Hadfield, P., S. Lister and P. Traynor. "This town's a different town today': Policing and regulating the night-time Economy." *Criminology & Criminal Justice* 9, no. 4 (2010): pp.465-485.

Hadfield, P.M. *Bar wars: contesting the night in contemporary British cities*. Oxford: Oxford University Press, 2006.

Hagan, J. *Disreputable pleasures: Crime and Deviance in Canada*. New York, Toronto: McGraw-Hill Ryerson, 1984.

Haigh, R., P. Campling and J. Cox. *Therapeutic Communities; Past, Present and Future*. London: Jessica Kingsley Publishers, 1998.

Haley, J. *Strategies for Psychotherapy*. New York: Grune and Stratton, 1963.

Hall, C. *Cultures of empire: colonisers in Britain and the Empire in nineteenth and twentieth centuries: a reader*. Manchester: Manchester University Press, 2000.

Hall, P. "Policy Paradigms, Social Learning and the State." *Comparative Politics* 25, no. 3 (1993): pp. 275-296.

Hall, P. "Social Capital in Britain" *British Journal of Political Science* 29, no. 3 (1999): pp. 417-462.

Hall, S. "The Treatment of 'Football Hooligans' in the Press'." In *Football Hooliganism: The Wider Context*, eds. Ingham et al. London: Inter-Action Inprint 1978.

Hall, S., C. Critcher, T. Jefferson, J. Clarke and B. Roberts. *Policing the Crisis: Mugging, The State and Law and Order*. Basingstoke: Macmillan, 1978.

Hall, T. and P. Hubbard. *The entrepreneurial city: geographies of politics, regimes and representation*. London: Wiley, 1998.

Hall, W. and A. Carter. "Drug Addiction, Society and Ethics." In *Principles of Health Care Ethics*, eds. R.E. Ashcroft and J. McMillan. Chichester: John Wiley & Sons, 2007.

Hallett, M. *The Spectacle of Difference*. London, New Haven: Yale University Press, 1999.

Ham, C. *Health Policy in Britain*. Hamps., New York: Palgrave Macmillan, 2004.

Ham, C. *Management and Competition in the New NHS*. Oxford: Radcliffe Medical Press, 1994.

Ham, C. and C. Heginbotham. *Purchasing Together*. London: King's Fund, 1991.

Hammersley, R. and J. Ditton. "Binge or bout? Quantity and rate of drinking by young people in the evening in licensed premises." *Drugs: Education, Prevention & Policy* 12, no.6 (2005): pp. 493-500.

Hanlon, N., G. Halseth, R. Clasby and V. Pow. "The place embeddedness of social care: Restructuring work and welfare." *Health & Place* 13, no. 2 (2007): pp.466-481

Hannigan, J. *Fantasy city: pleasure and profit in the postmodern metropolis*. London: Routledge, 1998.

Hanson, D.J. *Preventing Alcohol Abuse: Alcohol, Culture and Control*. Westport, Conn. : Praeger/Greenwood, 1995.

Harbour, H. *Strong Reasons against Strong Drink; or, Alcohol, its history and nature*. London: Jarrold & Sons, 1891.

Hardill, I. *Discovering Cities: Nottingham*. eds. P.S Fox and C.M Law, *Discovering Cities* Sheffield: Geographical Society, 2002.

Hardill, I., D.T. Graham and E. Kofman. *Human Geography in the UK*. London: Routledge, 2001.

Harding, J. "Helping the Socially Isolated." *British Hospital Journal and Social Services Review*, October 16th (1971): pp. 2142-2143.

Harding, T. *AIDS in Prison*. Geneva: University Institute of Legal Medicine, 1987.

Hardy, C. and N. Arthur. *Nottingham since 1900: Eighty Years in Photographs*. Nottingham: Archive Publications, 1987.

Harnett, R., B. Thom, R. Herring and M. Kelly. "Alcohol in transition: towards a model of young men's drinking styles." *Journal of Youth Studies* 3, no.1 (2000): pp. 61-77.

Harris, J. *This Drinking Nation*. Oxford, New York: Maxwell Macmillan International, 1994.

Harrison, B. *Drink and the Victorians: The Temperance Question in England, 1815-1872*. London: Faber and Faber, 1971.

Harrison, G. "Residence of incident cohort of psychotic patients after 13 years of follow up" *British Medical Journal* 308, no.6932 (1994): pp. 813-816

Harrison, L. *Alcohol Problems in the Community*. London: Routledge, 1996.

Harrison, S. and W. I. U. Ahmad. "Medical Autonomy and the UK State 1975 to 2025." *Sociology* 34, no.1 (2000): pp. 129-146

Hart, L. "A review of treatment and rehabilitation legislation regarding alcohol abusers and alcoholics in the United States: 1920-1971." *Int J Addict* 12, no. 5 (1977): pp. 667-78.

Hastings, G., S. Anderson, E. Cooke and R. Gordon. "Alcohol marketing and young people's drinking: a review of the research." *Journal of Public Health Policy* 26, no.3 (2005): pp. 296-311.

Hatton, J., A. Burton, H. Nash, E. Munn, L. Burgoyne and N. Sheron. "Drinking Patterns, dependency and life time drinking history in alcohol-related liver disease." *Addiction* 104, no. 4 (2009): pp. 587-592.

Hawker, A. *Adolescents and Alcohol*. London: Edsal, 1978.

Hawkins, K.H. and C.L. Pass. *The Brewing Industry: A Study in Industrial Organisation and Public Policy*. Heineman Educational: London, 1979.

Haworth, A. and R. Simpson, eds. *Moonshine Markets: Issues in Unrecorded Alcohol Beverage Production and Consumption*. New York: Brunner-Routledge, 2003.

Heath, D. B. *International Handbook on Alcohol and Culture*. Westport, CT: Greenwood Press, 1995.

Heath, D. B. "Sociocultural Variants in Alcoholism." In *Encyclopedic Handbook of Alcoholism*, eds. E.M. Pattison and E. Kaufman, pp. 426-440. New York: Gardner Press, 1982.

Heather, N. "Relationships between delinquency and drunkenness among Scottish young offenders." *British Journal of Alcohol and Alcoholism* 16, no.2 (1981): pp.150-161.

Heather, N. "United Kingdom Alcohol Treatment Trial (UKATT); Hypothesis, Design and Methods." *Alcohol and Alcoholism* 36, no. 1 (2001): pp. 11-21.

Heather, N. and I. Robertson. *Controlled Drinking*. 2nd ed. New York: Methuen, 1981.

Heather, N. *Problem drinking: The New Approach*. Harmondsworth: Penguin Books, 1985.

Heather, N. and T. Stockwell. *The Essential Handbook of Treatment and Prevention of Alcohol Problems*. Hoboken, NJ: Wiley, 2004.

Heckathorn, D.D. "Respondent-Driven Sampling: A New Approach to the Study of Hidden Populations." *Social Problems* 44, no.2 (1997): pp.174-199.

Heifer, U., M. Neuhausen, F. Pluisch and C. Schyma. "Alcohol and safety in street traffic: investigations in epidemiology and the approximation of traffic laws in Europe." *Blutalkohol* 29, no. 1 (1992): pp.1-52.

Heron, C. *Booze: a distilled history* Toronto, Ont.: Between the Lines, 2003.

Herring, R., V. Berridge and B. Thom. "Binge Drinking: an exploration of a confused concept " *Journal of Epidemiology and Community Health* 62, no. 6 (2008): pp.476-479.

Herring, R. and B. Thom. "The right to take risks: Alcohol and older people." *Social Policy and Administration* 31, no. 3 (1997): pp.233-246.

Herring, R., B. Thom, J. Foster, C. Franey and C. Salazar. "Local responses to the Alcohol Licensing Act 2003: the case of Greater London." *Drugs: education, prevention and policy.* 15, no. 3 (2008): pp.251-265.

Hey, V. *Patriarchy and pub culture.* London: Tavistock, 1986.

Hibbert, A., A. Godwin and F. Dear. *Rapid psychiatry.* Oxford: Blackwell, 2003.

Hill, J. "Leisure." In *A Centenary History of Nottingham,* ed. J.V. Beckett. Manchester, Manchester University Press, 1997.

Hill, M. and P. Hupe. *Implementing Public Policy.* London: Sage, 2002.

Hilton, M. *Consumerism in Twentieth-Century Britain: The Search for a Historical Movement.* Cambridge: Cambridge University Press, 2003.

Hilton, M. "The duties of citizens, the rights of consumers." *Consumer Policy Review* 15, no. 1 (2005): pp.6-12.

Hjern, B. and D. O. Porter. "Implementation Structures: A New Unit of Administrative Analysis." *Organization Studies* 2, no. 3 (1981): pp. 211-227.

Hobbs, D. "The night-time economy." In *Alcohol Concern Research Forum Papers.* London: Alcohol Concern, 2003.

Hobbs, D., P. Hadfield, S. Lister and S. Winlow. *Bouncers: Violence and Governance in the Night-time Economy.* Oxford: Oxford University Press, 2003.

Hobbs, D., S. Lister, P. Hadfield, S. Winslow and S. Hall. "Receiving shadows: governance and liminality in the night-time economy." *British Journal of Sociology* 51, no.4 (2000): pp.701-717.

Hohenberg, P. and L. Lees. *The Making of Urban Europe, 1000-1994.* Cambridge, Massachusetts Harvard University Press, 1995.

Hollands, R. "Division in the dark: Youth cultures, transitions and segmented consumption spaces in the night-time economy." *Journal of Youth Studies* 5, no. 2 (2002): pp.1-20.

Holloway, C. and S. Otto. *Getting organised: a handbook for non-statutory organisations.* London: Bedford Square Press, 1985.

Holt, M.P. *Alcohol: A Social and Cultural History.* Oxford: Berg, 2006.

Holt, M.P. "Wine, Community and Reformation in Sixteenth-Century Burgundy" *Past and Present* 138, no.1 (1993): pp. 58-93.

Holt, R. *Sport and the British; a Modern History, Oxford Studies in Social History.* Oxford: Clarendon Press, 1992.

Hood, C. "A Public Management for All Seasons." *Public Administration* 69, no.1 (1991): pp. 3-19.

Hopkins, M. and M. Maguire. "Targeted Policing Initiative- Reducing Alcohol Related Violence in Nottinghamshire." Cardiff: Cardiff University, May 2002.

Hopkins, M. and P. Sparrow. "Sobering Up: Arrest Referral and Brief Intervention for Alcohol Users in the Custody Suite." *Criminology and Criminal Justice* 6, no.4 (2006): pp. 389-410.

Hore, B.D. "Alcohol and crime." *Alcohol and Alcoholism* 23, no. 6 (1988): pp. 435-439.

Hore, B.D. *Alcohol Dependence*. ed. W. Linford Rees, *Postgraduate Psychiatry Series*. London: Butterworths, 1976.
Hore, B.D. "The Manchester Detoxification Centre." *British Journal of Addiction* 75, no. 2 (1980): pp. 197-205.
Hore, B.D. "Society's response to alcohol consumption and problem development" *Alcohol and Alcoholism*, 23, no. 4 (1988): pp.253-257.
Hore, B.D. and E. Smith "Who goes to alcoholic units." *British Journal of Addiction*, 70, no.3 (1975): pp. 263-270.
Horowitz, D.L. *The Deadly Ethnic Riot*. Berkeley, Calif.; London: University of California Press, 2000.
Hough, M. and G. Hunter. "The 2003 Licensing Act's impact on crime and disorder." *Criminology and Criminal Justice* 8, no. 3 (2008): pp.239-260.
Howard, M. R. "Red jackets and red noses: alcohol and the British Napoleonic soldier." *J R Soc Med* 93, no. 1 (2000): pp. 38-41.
Howat, J. Nottingham and the Hospital Plan: a follow-up study of long-stay in-patients, *The British Journal of Psychiatry*, 135, no.1 (1979), pp. 42-51
Howell, M. C. and W. Prevenier. *From reliable sources: an introduction to historical methods* New York: Cornell University, 2001.
Hoynes, W. *Public television for sale: media, the market, and the public sphere*. Boulder, Colo Westview Press, 1994.
Hubbard, P. "Screen-shifting: consumption, 'riskless risks' and the changing geographies of cinema." *Environment and Planning* A 34, no.7 (2002): pp.1239-1258.
Hubbard, R. L., W. E. Schlenger, J. V. Rachal, R. M. Bray, S. G. Craddock, E. R. Cavanaugh and H. M. Ginzburg. "Patterns of alcohol and drug abuse in drug treatment clients from different ethnic backgrounds." *Ann N Y Acad Sci* 472, no.1 (1986): pp. 60-74.
Hudebine, H. "Applying cognitive policy analysis to the drug issue: Harm reduction and the reversal of the Deviantization of drug users in Britain 1985-1997." *Addiction Research & Theory* 13, no. 3 (2005): pp. 231-243.
Hudson, J. and S. Lowe. *Understanding the Policy Process*. 2nd ed. Bristol: The Policy Press, 2004.
Hughes, R., R. Lart and P. Higate. *Drugs: policy and politics*. Maidenhead: Open University Press, 2006.
Hunt, G. and S. Saterlee. "Darts, Drink and the Pub: The Culture of Female Drinking." *Sociological Review* 35, no.3 (1987): pp. 571-601.
Hunt, G.P., K. Mackenzie and K. Joe-Laider. "Alcohol and masculinity: the case of ethnic youth gangs." In *Drinking Cultures*, ed. T.M. Wilson, pp. 225-254. Oxford: Berg, 2005.
Hutson, S. and M. Liddiard. "Youth Homelessness: Marginalising the Marginalised?" In *Towards a Classless Society?* ed. H. Jones pp. 96-120. London: Routledge, 1997.

Hutt, C. *The Death of the English Pub*. London: Hutchinson, 1973.
Institute of Alcohol Studies. *Alcohol Consumption and Harm in UK and EU*. St. Ives: IAS, 2006.
Institute of Alcohol Studies. *Alcohol Consumption and Harm in the UK and EU*. St. Ives: IAS, 2010.
Institute of Alcohol Studies. *Alcohol: Tax, Price and Public Health*. St. Ives: IAS, 2006.
Institute of Alcohol Studies. *Binge Drinking: Nature, Prevalence and Causes*. St. Ives: IAS, 2005.
Institute of Alcohol Studies. "Book Review: Dealing with Drink." *Alcohol Alert*, no. 2 (1999): pp.11-13.
Institute of Alcohol Studies. *Drinking in Great Britain*. St. Ives: IAS 2006.
Institute of Alcohol Studies. "*Factsheet: Women and Alcohol*." St. Ives: IAS, 2008.
Institute of Alcohol Studies. "*What is Problem Drinking?*" St. Ives: IAS, 2002.
Jackson, C. and P. Tinkler. "'Ladettes' and 'Modern Girls': 'troublesome' young femininities." *Sociological Review* 55, no.2 (2007): pp. 251-272.
Jackson, L. "The Coffee Club Menace. Policing Youth, Leisure and Sexuality in Postwar Manchester " *Cultural and Social History* 5, no. 3 (2008): pp.289-308.
Jackson, M. *The English Pub*. London: Collins, 1976.
Järvinen, M. and R. Room. *Youth drinking cultures*. Aldershot: Ashgate, 2007.
Jarvis, G. and H. Parker. "Young Heroin Users and Crime." *British Journal of Criminology & Criminal Justice* 29, no. 2 (1989): pp.175-185.
Jayne, M., S.L. Holloway and G. Valentine. "Drunk and disorderly: alcohol, urban life and public space." *Progress in Human Geography* 30, no. 4 (2006): pp.451-468.
Jayne, M., S.L. Holloway and G. Valentine. "Geographies of alcohol, drinking and drunkenness: a review of progress." *Progress in Human Geography* 32, no.2 (2008): pp.247-263
Jayne, M., S.L. Holloway and G. Valentine. "The place of drink: Geographical contributions to alcohol studies "*Drugs: Education, Prevention, and Policy* 15, no. 3 (2008): pp. 219-232.
Jefferies, B.M.H., C. Power and O. Manor. "Adolescent drinking and adult binge drinking in a national birth cohort." *Addiction* 100, no.4 (2005): pp.543-549.
Jellinek, E.M. *The Disease Concept of Alcoholism*. New Jersey: Hillhouse Press, 1960.
Jellinek, E.M. "Immanuel Kant on drinking." *Quarterly Journal of Studies on Alcohol* 1 (1941): pp.777-778.
Jenkins, K. and A. Munslow. *The Nature of History Reader*. London: Routledge, 2004.
Jenkins-Smith, H. C. and P. A. Sabatier. "The dynamics of policy-oriented learning." In *Policy change and learning - an advocacy coalition approach*, ed. P. A. Sabatier and H.C. Jenkins-Smith, pp. 41-56. San Francisco: Westview Press., 1993.

Jennings, P. *The Local: A History of the English Pub*. Stroud: Tempus Publishing, 2007.
Jochelson, K. "Nanny or Steward? The role of government in public health." In *King's Fund Working Paper*. London: Kings Fund, 2003.
Johns, R. I. *Nottingham's Family First 1965-2005*. Nottingham: Family First Ltd, 2006.
Johns, R. I. *St Ann's Nottingham: inner-city voices*. Warwick: Plowright Press, 2002.
Johnston Conover, P. "The Influence of Group Identifications on Political Perception and Evaluation" *The Journal of Politics* 46, no. 3 (1984): pp. 760-785
Jones, H. and S. MacGregor. *Social issues and party politics*. London: Routledge, 1998.
Jones, K.L and D.W. Smith. "Outcome of offspring of Chronic Alcoholic Women." *The Lancet* 303 no.7866 (1974): pp. 1076-1078.
Jones, K.L and D.W. Smith. "Recognition of the Fetal Alcohol Syndrome in Early Infancy." *The Lancet* 302, no. 7836 (1973): pp.999-1001.
Jones, M. "Industrial rehabilitation of mental patients still in hospital." *The Lancet* 271, no. 6950 pp.985-986 (1956).
Jones, M. *Social psychiatry. A study of therapeutic communities* (London: Routledge and Kegan, 1952).
Jones, M. *The Therapeutic Community*. New York: Basic Books, 1953.
Jones, N. "Politics and the Press." In *Pulling Newspapers Apart*, ed. B. Franklin, pp. 172-180. London: Routledge, 2008.
Joseph Rowntree Trust. "Drinking in the UK: an exploration of trends." York: JRF, 2009.
Joseph Rowntree Trust. "The Future of Voluntary Organisations." London: Croom Helm, 1978.
Kantor, G. K. and M. A. Straus. "Substance abuse as a precipitant of wife abuse victimizations." *Am J Drug Alcohol Abuse* 15, no. 2 (1989): pp.173-189.
Katz, A. H. "Self-Help and Mutual Aid: An Emerging Social Movement?" *Annual Review of Sociology* 7, no.1 (1981): pp. 129-155.
Katz, M. B. *Improving Poor People: the welfare state, the 'underclass' and urban schools as history*. Princeton, N.J., Chichester: Princeton University Press, 1995.
Kearns, W., K. Murray-Sykes and P. Mullen. "District planning teams in England." *Public Health* 96, no. 2 (1982): pp. 86-95.
Keenan, T. and W. Hui Kyong Chun. *New Media, Old Media: A History and Theory Reader*. London: Routledge, 2005.
Kemp, P.A. "The characteristics of single homeless people." In *Homelessness and social policy*, ed. R. Burrows, N. Pleace and D. Quilgars, pp. 69-87. London: Routledge, 1997.
Kendall, J. *The Voluntary Sector*. London: Routledge, 2003.
Kendall, J. and M. Knapp. *The Voluntary Sector in the United Kingdom*. Manchester: Manchester University Press, 1996.

Kessel, N., B.D. Hore, J.D. Makenjuola, A.D. Redmond, C.J. Rossall, D.W. Rees, T.G. Chand, M. Gordon and P.C. Wallace. "The Manchester detoxification service. Description and evaluation." *The Lancet* 1, no. 8381 (1984): pp.839-842.

Kessel, N. and H.J. Walton. *Alcoholism*. London: Pelican Books, 1965.

Kift, D. *The Victorian Music Hall: culture, class and conflict*. Cambridge: Cambridge University Press, 1996.

Kingdon, D. "Implications of Social Policy." In *Homelessness and Mental Health*, ed. D. Bhugra, pp. 267-295. Cambridge: Cambridge University Press, 1996.

Kingdon, J.W. *Agendas, alternatives and public policies*. 2nd ed. New York: Longman, 2003.

Kingsley, C. *Sanitary and Social Lectures and Essays*. London: Macmillan, 1902.

Kitteringham, D. B. "Health and safety in the collieries of the East Midlands, 1850-1911.", PhD thesis: Nottingham, 2005.

Klee, H. and P. Reid. "Drugs and Youth Homelessness: Reducing the risk " *Drugs: education, prevention and policy* 5, no. 3 (1998): pp.269-280

Klein, N. *No logo: taking aim at the brand bullies*. London: Flamingo, 2000.

Klein, R. *The New Politics of the NHS: From Creation to Re-invention*. Oxon: Radcliffe Publishing, 2006.

Kneale, J. "The place of drink: temperance and the public 1856-1914." *Social and Cultural Geography* 2, no. 1 (2001): pp.43-59.

Kneale, J. and S. French. "Mapping alcohol: Health, policy and the geographies of problem drinking in Britain." *Drugs: Education, Prevention, and Policy* 15, no. 3 (2008): pp. 233-249

Knight, B. *Voluntary Action*. London: Centris, 1993.

Kolvin, P. *Licensed premises: law and practice*. Haywards Heath: Tottel Publishing, 2005.

Kruzich, D. J., H. D. Silsby, J. D. Gold and M.R. Hawkins. "An evaluation and education program for driving while intoxicated offenders." *J Subst Abuse Treat* 3, no. 4 (1986): pp.263-270.

Kumar, K *From post-industrial to post-modern society*. Oxford: Blackwell, 1995.

Ku min, B.A. and B. A Tlusty. *The world of the tavern: public houses in early modern Europe*. Aldershot, Hants: Ashgate, 2002.

Kunkel, D., D. Linz, M. Metzger and L. Zwarun. "Effects of Showing Risk in Beer Commercials to Young Drinkers." *Journal of Broadcasting & Electronic Media* 50, no. 1 (2006): pp.52-77.

Kuntsche, E., J. Rehm and G. Gmel. "Characteristics of binge drinkers in Europe." *Soc Sci Med* 59, no.1 (2004): pp. 113-127.

Kurtz, E. *Not-God: a history of Alcoholics Anonymous*. San Francisco: Harper and Row, 1979.

Kurzer, P. *Markets and Moral Regulation*. Cambridge: Cambridge University Press, 2001.

Kyvig, D.E. *Law, alcohol and order: perspectives on national prohibition, Contributions in American History.* Westport; London: Greenwood, 1985.

Kyvig, D.E. *Repealing National Prohibition.* Kent: Ohio Kent State University Press, 2002.

La Hausse, P. *Brewers, beerhalls and boycotts: a history of liquor in South Africa.* Johannesburg: Ravan Press, 1988.

Lampard, R. "An examination of the relationship between marital dissolution and employment." In *Social Change and the Experience of Unemployment*, eds. D. Gallie, C. Marsh and C. Vogler, pp. 264-298. Oxford: Oxford University Press, 1994.

Lange, J. E., R. B. Voas and M. B. Johnson. "South of the border: a legal haven for underage drinking." *Addiction* 97, no. 9 (2002): pp. 1195-1203.

Langhamer, C. "Adultery in Post-war England" *History Workshop Journal* 62, no. 1 (2006): pp. 86-115.

Lart, R. "Drugs and Health Policy." In *Drugs: Policy and Politics*, eds. R. Lart, P. Higate and R. Hughes. Maidenhead: Open University Press, 2006.

Lash, S. and J. Urry. *Economies of Signs and Space.* London: Sage, 1994.

Laumann, E.O. and D. Knoke. *The Organizational State.* Madison: University of Wisconsin Press, 1987.

Lavoie, F., T. Borkman and B. Gidron. *Self-help and mutual aid groups: international and multicultural perspectives.* Binghamton, NY: Haworth Press, 1994.

Lawler, J. and E. Harlow. "Postmodernization: A Phase We're Going Through? Management in Social Care." *British Journal of Social Work* 35, no. 7 (2005): pp.1163-1174.

Le Grand, J. *Motivation, Agency and Public Policy.* Paperback ed. Oxford: Oxford University Press, 2006.

Le Grand, J. 'Quasi Markets and Social Policy'." *Economic Journal* 101, September (1991): pp. 1256- 1267.

Leach, J, and J.K. Wing. "Social Policies and Social Surveys." In *Helping destitute men*, pp.25-43. London: Tavistock, 1980.

Learmonth, M. "Managerialism and public attitudes to U.K. managers." *Journal of Management in Medicine* 11, no.4 (1997): pp. 214-221.

Ledermann, S. *Alcool, Alcoolisme, Alcoolisation.* Paris: Presses Universitaires de France, 1956.

Lees, F.R. *The illustrated history of alcohol.* London: John Chapman, 1846.

Lees, L. "The relationships between gender and crime in the Midlands during the 17th century." PhD thesis: Nottingham Trent, 1999.

Lender, M. "Drunkenness as an offense in early New England. A study of "Puritan" attitudes." *Q J Stud Alcohol* 34, no. 2 (1973): pp. 353-66.

Leon, D.A. and J. McCambridge. "Liver cirrhosis mortality rates in Britain from 1950 to 2002: an analysis of routine data." *The Lancet* 367, no. 9504 (2006): pp. 52-56.

Leon, D.A., L. Saburova, S. Tomkins, E. Andreev, N. Kiryanov, M. McKee and V. M. Shkolnikov. "Hazardous alcohol drinking and premature mortality in Russia: a population based case-control study." *The Lancet* 369, no. 9578 (2007): pp.2001-2009.

L'Etang, J. *Public Relations in Britain: A History of Professional Practice in the Twentieth Century* London: Lawrence Erlbaum Associates, 2004

Lettieri, D. J, J. S. Brook and D.W. Brook. *Alcohol and Substance Abuse in Adolescence*. New York, London: Haworth Press 1985.

Levine, M. *SIDE and Closed Circuit Television (CCTV): Exploring Surveillance in Public Space*. Lancaster: University of Lancaster, 2000.

Lewis, C. "The future of British brewing: strategies for survival." *Strategic Change* 10, no. 3 (2001): pp. 151-161.

Lewis, J. "The Origins and development of public health in the UK." In *Oxford Textbook of Public Health,* eds. W. Holland, R. Detels and G. Knox. Oxford: Oxford University Press, 1991.

Lewis, J. *The politics of motherhood*. London: Croom Helm, 1980.

Lewis, J. "Reviewing the Relationship between the Voluntary Sector and the State in Britain in the 1990s." *Voluntas: International Journal of Voluntary or Nonprofit Organisations* 10, no. 3 (1999): pp. 255-270

Lewis, J. *What Price Community Medicine? The Philosophy, Practice and Politics of Public Health since 1919*. Brighton: Wheatsheaf, 1986.

Lewis, M. A. *A rum state: alcohol and state policy in Australia, 1788-1988*. Canberra: AGPS Press, 1992.

Light, R. and S. Heenan. "Controlling Supply: the concept of 'need' in liquor licensing." Bristol: University of the West of England, 1999.

Lindstrom, L. *Managing Alcoholism: Matching Clients to Treatment*. Oxford: Oxford University Press, 1992.

Lipsky, M. *Street-level Bureaucracy; Dilemmas of the Individual in Public Services*. New York: Russell Sage Foundation, 1980

Lister, S., D. Hobbs, S. Hall and S. Winslow. "Violence in the night-time economy; bouncers: the reporting, recording and prosecution of assaults." *Policing and Society* 10, no.4 (2000): pp.283-402.

Lister Sharp, D. "Underage Drinking in the United Kingdom since 1970: Public Policy, the Lane and Adolescent Drinking Behaviour." *Alcohol and alcoholism* 29, no. 5 (1994): pp. 555-563.

Litten, R.Z. and J.P. Allen. *Measuring Alcohol Consumption: Psychological and Biomedical Methods*. Totowa, NJ: Humana Press, 1992.

Lloyd, T.O. *Empire to welfare state; English history 1906-1967* London: Oxford University Press, 1970.

Lodge Patch, I.C. "Homeless men in London: Demographic findings in a lodging house sample." *British Journal of Psychiatry* 118, no. 544 (1971): pp. 313-317

Long C. G., Williams M. and C. R. Hollin. "Treating alcohol problems: a study of programme effectiveness and cost effectiveness according to length and delivery of treatment " *Addiction* 93, no. 4 (1998): pp. 561-571.

Longmate, N. *The Waterdrinkers: A History of Temperance*. London: Hamilton 1968.

Lovatt, A and J. O'Connor. "Cities and the Night-time Economy" *Planning Practice and Research* 10, no. 2 (1995): pp. 127-134

Lovell, H. "The role of individuals in policy change: the case of UK low-energy housing." *Environment and Planning C: Government and Policy* 27, no. 3 (2009): pp.491-511

Lowe, G., D. R. Foxcroft and D. Sibley. *Adolescent Drinking and Family Life*. London: Hardwood Academic Publishers, 1993.

Lowe, R. *The Welfare State in Britain since 1945*. 3rd ed. New York: Palgrave Macmillan, 2005.

Ludtke, A. *The History of Everyday Life: Reconstructing Historical Experiences and Ways of Life*. Princeton, N.J: Princeton University Press, 1995.

Ludwig, A. M and A. Wikler. "'Craving' and relapse to drink." *Q J Stud Alcohol* 35, no. 1 (1974): pp.108-130.

Lundahl, M. *Knut Wicksell on Poverty: No Place Is Too Exalted*. New York: Routledge, 2005.

Lyon, D. *Surveillance Society: Monitoring Everyday Life*. Buckingham: Open University Press, 2001.

MacAndrew, C. and R. Edgerton. *Drunken comportment: A social explanation*. Chicago: Aldine Publishing Company, 1969.

MacDonald, T.H. *Rethinking Health Promotion: A Global Approach*. London: Routledge, 1998.

MacGregor, S. *Drugs and British Society: Responses to a Social Problem in the 1980s*. London: Routledge, 1989.

MacGregor, S. *Drugs Services in England and the Impact of the Central Funding Initiative*, London: ISDD, 1990.

MacGregor, S. "Promoting new services: The Central Funding Initiative and other mechanisms" in: J Strang, M Gossop, ed. *Heroin Addiction and Drug Policy: The British System*. Oxford: Oxford University Press, 1994, pp. 259-269.

MacMillan, D. "Community treatment of mental illness." *The Lancet* 272, no. 7039 (1958): pp. 201-204.

MacMillan, D. "Mental Health Services of Nottingham." *Journal of Social Psychiatry* 4, no.1 (1958): pp. 5-9.

MacMillan, D. "Recent developments in community mental health." *The Lancet* 281, no.7281 (1963): pp.567-571.

Maguire, M. and M. Hopkins. "Data analysis for problem-solving: alcohol and city centre violence." In *Crime Reduction and Problem-Oriented Policing*, ed. K. Bullock and N Tilley, pp. 126-153. Devon: Willan, 2003.

Mahone, S. and M. Vaughan. *Psychiatry and Empire* Basingstoke, Hamps: Palgrave Macmillan, 2008.

Mahoney, J. "Path Dependence in Historical Sociology." *Theory and Society* 29, no. 4 (2000): pp. 507-548.

Mainelli, M. and I. Harris. "Quality Management in Charities." In *The Charities Finance Handbook 1993/94,* pp.98-107: Dalkeith, Midlothian: Charles Letts & Co, 1993.

Majone, G. *Evidence, argument and persuasion in the policy process.* New Haven, CT: Yale University Press, 1989.

Malcolmson, R. *Popular recreations in English society 1700-1850.* Cambridge: Cambridge University Press, 1973.

Malone, D. and T. Friedman. "Drunken patients in the general hospital: their care and management." *Postgrad Med J* 81, no. 953 (2005): pp.161-166.

Malyutina, S., M. Bobak, S. Kurilovitch, E. Ryizova, Y. Nikitin and M. Marmot. "Alcohol consumption and binge drinking in Novosibirsk, Russia, 1985-95." *Addiction* 96, no. 7 (2001): pp.987-995

Mansukhani, R. *The Pub Report: British Pubs in the 1980s.* London: Euromonitor Publications, 1985.

Mark, T.L., J.D. Dilonardo, M. Chalk and R. Coffey. "Trends in inpatient detoxification services, 1992–1997." *Journal of Substance Abuse Treatment* 23, no.4 (2002): pp.253- 260.

Markham, S.K. and L. Aiman-Smith. "Product Champions: Truths, Myths and Management " *Research-Technology Management* 44, no. 3 (2001): pp. 44-50.

Markowitz, S. and M G. Grossman. "Alcohol Regulation and Domestic Violence towards Children." *Contemporary Economic Policy* 16, no. 3 (1998): pp.309-320.

Marks, I. "Phobic Disorders Four Years after Treatment: A Prospective Follow-up " *The British Journal of Psychiatry* 118 (1971): pp. 683-688.

Marmot, M. "The Rising Tide of Alcohol." *Addiction* 99, no. 9 (2004): p. 1090.

Marsh, A., J. Dobbs and A. White. *Adolescent drinking.* London: HMSO, 1986.

Marsh, P., K Fox, G. Carnibella, J. McCann and J. Marsh. *Football Violence in Europe: A report to the Amsterdam Group.* Oxford: The social issues research centre, 1996.

Marsh, P. and K.F. Kibby, *Drinking and Public Disorder.* Oxford: Alden Press, 1992.

Martin, A. L. *Alcohol, sex and gender in late medieval and early modern Europe, Early modern history.* New York, Basingstoke: Palgrave, 2001.

Martin, A. L. "Drinking and alehouses in the diary of an English mercer's apprentice, 1663-1674." In *Alcohol: a social and cultural history,* ed. M.P Holt. Oxford: Berg, 2006.

Martin, A. L. "Fetal Alcohol Syndrome in Europe, 1300-1700: A Review of Data on Alcohol Consumption and a Hypothesis." *Food and Foodways* 11, no. 1 (2003): pp.1-26

Martin, S. "City grants, urban development grants and urban regeneration grants." In *Local Economic Policy,* ed. M. Campbel. London: Cassell, 1990.

Martinic, M. and F. Measham. "Extreme drinking." In *Swimming with Crocodiles: the Culture of Extreme Drinking.,* ed. M. Martinic and F. Measham, pp.1-12. London: Routledge, 2008.

Martinic, M. and F. Measham. *Swimming with crocodiles: the culture of extreme drinking*. Abingdon, Oxon: Routledge, 2008.

Mass-Observation. *The pub and the people: A Worktown Study*. London: The Cresset Library, 1987.

Mathews, P.S. "Treatment of alcoholism: The American experience, 1850-2000." PhD thesis: Florida State University, 2001.

May, C. "A burning issue? Adolescent alcohol use in Britain 1970-1991." *Alcohol and Alcoholism* 27, no. 2 (1992): pp. 109-115.

May, C. "Response: The Sins of the Few." *Alcohol and Alcoholism* 6 (1992): pp.710-711.

Mayhew, K., C. Deer and M. Dua. "The Move to Mass Higher Education in the UK: Many Questions and Some Answers." *Oxford Review of Education. Special Issue: Business, Education and Vocationalism* 30, no. 1 (2004): pp. 65-82.

McAlaney, J. and J. McMahon. "Establishing rates of binge drinking in the UK: Anomalies in the date." *Alcohol and Alcoholism* 41, no.4 (2006): pp. 355-357.

McCabe, S. and P. Wallington. *The police, public order, and civil liberties: legacies of the miners' strike*. London: Routledge, 1988.

McClellan, M.L "'Lady lushes': Women alcoholics and American society, 1880-1960 ", PhD thesis Stanford University, 2000

McCusker, C.G. and K. Brown. "Alcohol-predictive cues enhance tolerance to and precipitate "craving" for alcohol in social drinkers." *Journal of Studies on Alcohol* 51, no. 6 (1990): pp. 494-499.

McDowell, L. *Redundant Masculinities? Employment change and white working class youth* Oxford: Blackwell Publishing, 2003.

McGuire, A., J. Henderson and G. Mooney. *The Economics of Health Care*. London: Routledge, 1988.

McIntosh, M.C. and E. M Sellers. "Drug Use as a Lifestyle in the 1980s." *Can Fam Physician* 29, Oct (1983): pp.1876-1877.

McKibben, M. *Pop fiction? The truth about alcopops*. London: Alcohol Concern 1996.

McKibben, M. "Letter: More "alcopops" have come on market since study was done " *BMJ* 313, no. 7969 (1996): p.1397.

McLean, P.C. "Alcoholism." In *Mental Illness: Changes and Trends*, ed. P. T. Bean, pp. 297-328. London: Wiley and Sons, 1983.

MCM. "WTAG binge-drinking research. Report of research and consultation." MCM Research Ltd for Wine Intelligence, 2004.

McMahan, E.M. and K.L Rogers. *Interactive Oral History Interviewing, LEA's Communication Series*. Mahwah, New Jersey: Lawrence Erlbaum Associates, 1994.

McRobbie, A. *Feminism and youth culture*. London: Macmillan, 1991.

McShane, A. and J. Kneale. "Histories and geographies of intoxicants and intoxication – an introduction." *Social History of Alcohol and Drugs*, 25, nos 1-2 (2011): pp.6-14.

McVay, D. *Notts County Football Club*, 1988.

Measham, F. "The 'big bang' approach to sessional drinking: changing patterns of alcohol consumption amongst young people in North West England." *Addiction Research & Theory* 4, no. 3 (1996): pp. 283-299.

Measham, F "The decline of ecstasy, the rise of 'binge' drinking and the persistence of pleasure." *Probation Journal* 51, no. 4 (2004): pp. 309–326.

Measham, F "Play space: historical and socio-cultural reflections on drugs, licensed leisure locations, commercialisation and control." *International Journal of Drug Policy* 15, nos.5-6 (2004): pp. 337-345.

Measham, F. and K. Brain. "Binge drinking, British alcohol policy and the new culture of intoxication." *Crime Media Culture* 1, no. 3 (2005): pp. 262-283.

Medical News Today. "Campaign Welcome Parliamentary Report Exposing Serious Failings in Treatment for Alcohol Dependents across England." May 21st 2009.

Meinke, T. "The Role of Power Relations and Ideas in State Policy-Making." In *Annual meeting of the MPSA Annual National Conference*. Hilton, Chicago, 2008.

Meller, H.E. *Town, Plans and Society in Modern Britain*. Cambridge: Cambridge University Press 1997.

Merryfield, A. "The dialectics of dystopia: disorder and zero tolerance in the city." *International Journal of Urban and Regional Research* 24, no.2 (2000): pp. 473-489.

Midanik, L. "Biomedicalization and Alcohol Studies: Implications for Policy " *Journal of Public Health Policy* 25, no. 2 (2004): pp. 211-228.

Midanik, L. *Biomedicalization of Alcohol Studies: Ideological shifts and Institutional Challenges*. New Brunswick, New Jersey: Transaction, 2006.

Milbourne, P. *Rural Poverty: Marginalisation and Exclusion in Britain and the United States*. London: Routledge, 2004

Miles, M. and T. Hall. *Urban Futures: Critical Commentaries on Shaping Cities*. London: Routledge, 2003.

Miles, S. *Youth lifestyles in a changing world*. Buckingham: Open University Press, 2000.

Miles, S. and R. Paddison. "Urban consumption: an historical note." *Urban Studies* 35, nos. 5-6 (1998): pp. 815-832.

Miller, P.M and M. Plant. "Drinking, smoking and illicit drug use among 15 and 16 year olds in the United Kingdom." *British Medical Journal* 313, no. 7054 (1996): pp. 3943-3997.

Miller, W.B "Lower-class culture as a generating milieu of gang delinquency." *Journal of Social Issues* 14, no. 3 (1958): pp. 5-19.

Miller, W. R. and R. K. Hester. "The effectiveness of alcoholism treatment: What research reveals." In *Treating Addictive Behaviors: Processes of Change*, eds. Miller W. R. and N. Heather, pp.121-174. New York: Plenum Press 1986.

Miller, W. R. and C. A. Taylor. "Relative effectiveness of bibliotherapy, individual and group self-control training in the treatment of problem drinkers." *Addictive Behaviours* 5, no.1 (1980), pp. 13-24

Milligan, C. and N.R. Fyfe. "Putting the Voluntary Sector in its Place: Geographical Perspectives on Voluntary Activity and Social Welfare in Glasgow." *Journal of Social Policy* 33, no.1 (2004): pp. 73-93.

Minto, A. and F.J. Roberts. "Temposil; a New Drug in the Treatment of Alcoholism." *Journal of Mental Science* 106, no.2 (1960): pp. 288-295.

Mitchell, C. N. "The intoxicated offender; refuting the legal and medical myths." *Int J Law Psychiatry* 11, no. 1 (1988): pp. 77-103.

Mitchell, D. *The Right to the City.* New York: Guilford Press, 2003.

Mitchell, T. *Intoxicated identities: alcohol's power in Mexican history and culture.* London: Routledge, 2004.

Miyazawa, K. and S. Miyazawa. *Crime Prevention in the Urban Community.* Deventer: Kluwer Law and Taxation Publishers, 1995

Mold, A. *Heroin: the treatment of addiction in twentieth-century Britain.* DeKalb, Illinois: Northern Illinois University Press, 2008.

Mold, A. and V. Berridge. "Crisis and Opportunity in Drug Policy: Changing the Direction of British Drug Services in the 1980s." *Journal of Policy History* 19, no. 1 (2007): pp. 29-48.

Mold, A. and V. Berridge. *Voluntary Action and Illegal Drugs: Health and Society in Britain Since the 1960s.* Basingstoke, Hamps: Palgrave Macmillan, 2010.

Monkkonen, E.H. "A disorderly people? Urban order in the nineteenth and twentieth centuries." *The Journal of American History* 68, no.3 (1981): pp. 539-559.

Montgomery, J. "The Evening Economy of Cities." *Town and Country Planning* 63, no. 11 (1994): pp. 302-307.

Montgomery, J.R. "The story of Temple Bar: Creating Dublin's Cultural Quarter." *Planning Practice and Research* 10, no. 2 (1995): pp. 135-172.

Moore, L., C. Smith and J. Catford. "Binge drinking: prevalence, patterns and policy." *Health Education Research* 9, no. 4 (1994): pp. 497-505.

Moore, S. and D. Rosenthal. *Sexuality in adolescence.* London: Routledge, 1993.

Moore, S., J. Shepherd, N. Perham and B. Cusens. "The prevalence of alcohol intoxication in the night-time economy." *Alcohol and Alcoholism* 42, no. 6 (2007): pp. 629-634.

Morris, C. *The Journeys of Celia Fiennes.* London: Cresset Press, 1949.

Morris, D. "Charities in the contract culture: survival of the largest?" *Legal Studies* 20, no. 3 (2006): pp. 409-27.

Morris, D. *The Soccer Tribe.* London: Jonathon Cape, 1981.

Morrison, B. L. "Ordering disorderly women: female drunkenness in England, c.1870-1920." PhD thesis: Keele University, 2005.

Moss, M.C and E. Beresford Davies. *A Survey of Alcoholism in an English County.* Altrincham: St. Ann's Press, 1967.

Muller, R. and H. Klingemann. *From science to action? 100 years later - alcohol policies revisited.* Dordrecht; London: Kluwer Academic, 2004.

Muncie, J. *Youth and Crime: A Critical Introduction.* London: Sage, 2004.

Murdock, C.G. *Domesticating Drink: Women, Men, and Alcohol in America, 1870-1940* Baltimore: John Hopkins University Press, 1998.

Murgraff, V., A. Parrott and P. Bennett. "Risky single-occasion drinking amongst young people; definition, correlates, policy, and intervention: a broad overview of research findings." *Alcohol and Alcoholism* 34, no.1 (1999): pp. 3-14.

Nayak, A. "Last of the 'real Geordies'? White masculinities and the subcultural response to deindustrialisation." *Environment and Planning D: Society and Space* 21, no.1 (2003): pp.7-25.

Nelson, J. and D. Young. "Do Advertising Bans Work? An International Comparison." *International Journal of Advertising* 20, no.3 (2001): pp. 273-296.

Nencini, P. "The rules of drug taking: wine and poppy derivatives in the ancient world. I. General introduction." *Subst Use Misuse* 32, no. 1 (1997): pp. 89-96.

Nencini, P. "The rules of drug taking: wine and poppy derivatives in the ancient world. III. Wine as an instrument of aggressive behavior and of ritual madness." *Subst Use Misuse* 32, no. 3 (1997): pp. 361-367.

Nencini, P. "The rules of drug taking: wine and poppy derivatives in the ancient world. V. Sobriety or postponement of drunkenness?" *Subst Use Misuse* 32, no. 5 (1997): pp. 629-633.

Neufeld, V. and N. Johnson. *Forging Links for Health Research: Perspectives from the Council on Health Research for Development*. Ottawa, Canada: International Research Development Centre, 2001.

Neve, M. "A Commentary on the History of Social Psychiatry and Psychotherapy in Twentieth-Century Germany, Holland and Great Britain." *Medical History* 48, no.4 (2004): pp.407-412.

Newburn, T. and M. Shiner. *Teenage Kicks? Young People and Alcohol: A Review of the Literature*. York: Joseph Rowntree Foundation, 2001.

Newhouse, E. *Alcohol: Cradle to Grave*. ed. A. Lucas. Enumclaw, WA: Issues Press, 2006.

Newson, J. and E. Newson. *Patterns of Infant Care in an Urban Community*. London: George Allen and Unwin, 1963.

Nicholls, J. "England's Bane? Tradition and English Drinking Culture." In *Centre for History in Public Health: Alcohol Seminar Series*. London School of Hygiene and Tropical Medicine, 2008.

Nicholls, J. "Liberties and licenses: Alcohol in Liberal Thought." *International Journal of Cultural Studies* 9, no. 2 (2006): pp.131-151

Nicholls, J. *The Politics of Alcohol; a History of the Drink Question in England*. Manchester: Manchester University Press, 2009.

Nicholls, J. "Alcohol policy comment: determinants, influences and the media." *Alcohol Policy UK*, March 28th 2011. Available at http://www.alcoholpolicy.net/2011/03/alcohol-policy-comment-determinants-influences-and-the-media.html [Cited October 6th 2011].

Nielsen, J. "Alcohol prices, alcohol consumption, delirium tremens and mortality in chronic alcoholism from 1911 to 1961." *Ugeskr Laeger* 130, no. 23 (1968): pp. 987-992.

Nightingale, A. *Murder and Crime in Nottingham.* Stroud: History Press Ltd, 2007.

Nilssen, O. "The Tromsø study: Identification of and a controlled intervention on a population of early stage risk drinkers.» *Preventive Medicine* 20, no.4 (1991): pp. 518-528.

Nix, J. "Interpreting the warehouse landscape: Nottingham's lace market, 1850-1920." PhD: London, 1997.

Nixon, S. *Advertising cultures: gender, commerce, creativity.* London: Sage, 2003.

Norman, P., P. Bennett and H. Lewis. "Understanding binge drinking among young people: an application of the Theory of Planned Behaviour " *Health Education Research* 13, no. 2 (1998): pp.163-169.

Norstrom, T. "Effects on criminal violence of different beverage types and private and public drinking." *Addiction* 93, no.5 (1998): pp. 689-99.

Norton, A. " Alcohol-related crime: The good practice of the magistrates courts," *Alcohol and Alcoholism* 33, no. 1 (1998): pp. 78-82.

Nottinghamshire Heritage Gateway. *Nottingham.* Thoroton Society: Available from http://www.thorotonsociety.org.uk/gateway/places/nottingham/nottingham6.htm. [Cited September 26th 2011].

Nottinghamshire Police. "Crime continues to fall in Nottinghamshire." *Engaging: Stakeholder Bulletin,* no. 34. Nottingham: Nottinghamshire Police 2007.

O'Mally, P. and M. Valverde. "Pleasure, freedom and drugs: the use of 'pleasure' in liberal governance of drugs and alcohol consumption." *Sociology* 38, no.1 (2004): pp. 25-42.

O'Brien, J. *Women's' liberation in labour history.* Spokesman Pamphlet No.24. Nottingham: Bertrand Russell Peace Foundation, 1972.

Oc, T. and S. Tiesdell. *Safer city centres: reviving the public realm.* London: Paul Chapman, 1997.

O'Connor, J. *The Young Drinkers.* London: Tavistock, 1978.

Oldenburg, B. F., J. F. Sallis, Ffrench M. L. and N. Owen. "Health promotion research and the diffusion and institutionalization of interventions" *Health Education Research* 14, no. 1 (1999): pp. 121-130.

O'Neill, J. "Family Life in the Twentieth Century." In *A Centenary History of Nottingham,* ed. J.V. Beckett, pp. 513-532. Manchester: Manchester University Press, 1997.

Orange, J. *History and antiquities of Nottingham, 1799-1878.* London: Hamilton 1840

Oldfield, G. *The Illustrated History of Nottingham Suburbs Revised.* Derby: Breedon Publishing, 2009)

Orford, J. and G. Edwards. *Alcoholism. A comparison of treatment and advice.* Oxford: Oxford University Press, 1977.

Orford, J. and J. Harwin, *Alcohol and the Family.* London: Croom Helm in association with the Alcohol Education Centre, 1982.

Orrells, K. "Representations of gin in 18th-century London, c.1736-c.1760." PhD thesis: University of York 2005.

Orwell, G. *Down and out in Paris and London,* London: Victor Gollancz Ltd, 1933.
Osgerby, B. *Youth media.* London: Routledge, 2004.
Pacione, M. *Britain's Cities: Geographies of Division in Urban Britain.* London: Routledge, 1997.
Pacione, M. *Urban Geography: A Global Perspective.* London: Routledge, 2005.
Pain, R. "Gender, race, age and fear in the city." *Urban Studies* 38, nos. 5-6 (2001): pp. 899-913.
Palmer, G. "The New You: Class and Transformation in Lifestyle Television." In *Understanding reality television,* eds. S. Holmes and D. Jermyn, pp. 173-190. London: Routledge, 2004.
Pandina, R. J. and V. Johnson. "Familial drinking history as a predictor of alcohol and drug consumption among adolescent children." *J Stud Alcohol* 50, no. 3 (1989): pp. 245-253.
Park, C-Y. "Women and philanthropy in England, c.1880-1920: with particular reference to the Midlands. PhD thesis: University of Nottingham, 2004.
Park, C-Y. "The Normalization of 'Sensible' Recreational Drug Use" *Sociology* 36, no. 4 (2002): pp. 941-964.
Parker, H., F. Measham and J. Aldridge. *Illegal Leisure: The Normalization of Adolescent Drug Use.* London: Routledge, 1998.
Parker, H. and R. Newcombe. "Heroin use and acquisitive crime in an English community." *The British Journal of Sociology* 38, no. 3 (1987): pp. 331-350.
Parker, H., R. Newcombe and K. Bakx. *Living with Heroin: the impact of a drugs epidemic on an English community.* Milton Keynes: Open University Press, 1988.
Parker, H. and L. Williams. "Intoxicated weekends: young adults work hard-play hard lifestyles, public health and public disorder " *Drugs: Education, Prevention and Policy* 10, no. 4 (2003): pp. 345-367
Parkinson, M. *Cities and Regions: Institutions, Relationships and Economic Consequences.* Liverpool: European Institute for Urban Affairs, John Moores University on behalf of the Core Cities Working Group, 2004.
Parr, H. "Feeling, Reading and Making Bodies in Space." *The Geographical Review,* 91, nos. 1-2 (2001): pp. 158-167.
Parsons, T. *The Social System.* Illinois: Free Press, 1951.
Patchell, J. "Landscapes of Voluntarism: New Spaces of Health, Welfare and Governance " *Canadian Geographer / Le Géographe canadien* 51, no. 3 (2007): pp. 403-5.
Patkart A.A., P.C. Naik, C.A. Marsden, P.C. McLean, D.A. Kendall, and T. Al-Chalabi. "[3H]-Imipramine binding in Type 1 and Type 2 Alcoholism." *Human Psychopharmocology* 10, no. 3 (1995): pp. 15-320
Paul, H.W. *Bacchic Medicine: wine and alcohol therapies from Napoleon to the French.* New York: Rudolphi, 2001.
Paulson, R. *Hogarth: Art and politics, 1750-1764.* Cambridge: Lutterworth Press, 1993.

Paulson, R. *Hogarth's graphic works*. 3rd ed. London: The Print Room, 1989.
Pauly, P. J. "Is liquor intoxicating? Scientists, prohibition, and the normalization of drinking." *Am J Public Health* 84, no. 2 (1994): pp. 305-313.
Pearson, G. *Hooligan. A History of Respectable Fears*. London: Macmillan, 1983.
Pearson, G. "Victorian Boys. Here we are! [1983]." In *The Subcultures Reader*, eds. K. Gelder and S. Thornton, pp.281-301. London: Routledge, 1997.
Peele, S. *Diseasing of America*. Boston: Houghton Mifflin, 1989.
Peele, S. "Recovering from an all-or-nothing approach to alcohol." *Psychology Today*, no. Sept/Oct (1996): pp.35-43 & pp. 68-70.
Perks, R. and A. Thomson. *The Oral History Reader*. London: Routledge, 1998.
Peters, T.J. *Alcohol Misuse: A European Perspective*. Australia: Harwood Academic, 1996.
Petersen, A. and D. Lupton. *The New Public Health: Health and Self in the Age of Risk* London: Sage, 1996.
Peterson, J. B., Finn, P. R. and R.O Pihl. "Cognitive dysfunction and the inherited predisposition to alcoholism." *J Stud Alcohol* 53, no. 2 (1992): pp.154-160.
Phillips, S. "Jesse Boot and the rise of Boots the Chemists." *The Pharmaceutical Journal* 269, no. Dec 21/28 (2002): pp.925-928.
Piasecki, T. M., Sher, K. J., Slutske, W. S. and K. M Jackson. "Hangover frequency and risk for alcohol use disorders: evidence from a longitudinal high-risk study." *J Abnorm Psychol* 114, no. 2 (2005): pp. 223-234.
Pidgeon, J. "Unity in action." *Social Work Today*. Jan (1991): pp. 16-17.
Pihl, R. O., Smith, M. and B. Farrell. "Individual characteristics of aggressive beer and distilled beverage drinkers." *Int J Addict* 19, no. 6 (1984): pp. 689-696.
Pile, S. and N. Thrift. *Mapping the Subject*. London: Routledge, 1995.
Pillmann, F., Ullrich, S., Draba, S., Sannemuller, U. and A. Marneros. "Acute effects of alcohol and chronic alcoholism as causes of violent crime." *Nervenarzt* 71, no. 9 (2000): pp. 715-721.
Pincock, S. "Binge drinking on rise in UK and elsewhere. Government report shows increases in alcohol consumption, cirrhosis, and premature deaths." *The Lancet* 362, no. 9390 (2003): pp. 1126-1127.
Plant, M. and M. Plant. *Risk-takers: alcohol, drugs, sex, and youth*. New York; Tavistock: Routledge, 1992.
Plant, M. *Women and alcohol*. London: Free Association Books, 1997.
Plant, M. and L. Harrison. "Prevention and Harm Minimisation in the UK." In *Alcohol Concern Research Forum Paper*. London: Alcohol Concern, 2003.
Plant, M., D. F. Peck and E. Samuel. *Alcohol, Drugs and School-leavers*. London: Tavistock, 1985.
Plant, M., E. Single and T. Stockwell. *Alcohol: Minimising the Harm: What Works?* London: Free Association Books, 1997.
Plant, M. and M. Plant. "Alcohol education and harm minimisation." In *Alcohol: Minimising the Harm: What Works?* eds. M.A. Plant, E. Single and T. Stockwell, pp. 193-210. London: Free Association Books, 1997.

Plant, M. and M. Plant. *Binge Britain.* Oxford: Oxford University Press, 2006.
Pleace, N. and D. Quilgars. "Youth Homelessness." In *Young People, Housing and Social Policy*, ed. J. Rugg, pp. 93-108. London: Routledge, 1999.
Poikolainen, K.and J. Simpura. "One-year drinking history and mortality." *Prev Med* 12, no. 5 (1983): pp. 709-14.
Polich, J.M., D.J. Armor and H.B. Braiker. *The course of alcoholism: Four years after treatment.* New York: Wiley, 1981.
Pomfret, D.M. "Representations of Adolescence in the Modern City: Voluntary Provision and Work in Nottingham and Saint-Etienne, 1890-1914." *Journal of Family History* 26, no. 4 (2001): pp. 455-479.
Pomfret, D.M. *Young people and the European city: age relations in Nottingham and Saint-Etienne, 1890-1940*, eds. Jean-Luc Pinol and Richard Rodger, *Historical Urban Studies.* Aldershot: Ashgate, 2004.
Portans, I., White, J. M. and P. K Staiger. "Acute tolerance to alcohol: changes in subjective effects among social drinkers." *Psychopharmacology (Berl)* 97, no. 3 (1989): pp. 365-369.
Porter, D. *Health, Civilization and the State: a History of Public Health from Ancient to Modern Times.* London: Routledge, 1999.
Porter, D and R. Porter, *Doctors, Politics and Society: Historical Essays.* Amsterdam, Atlanta GA: Adolphi, 1993.
Porter, R. "The Drinking Man's Disease: the 'pre-history' of alcoholism in Georgian Britain." *British Journal of Addiction* 80, no.4 (1985): pp. 385-396.
Porter, R. "Two Cheers for Psychiatry! The Social History of Mental Disorder in Twentieth Century Britain, 1841-1991." In *150 Years of British Psychiatry Volume Two - The Aftermath*, eds. H. Freeman and Berrios G.E. London: Athlone, 1996.
Porter. D. and R. Porter. "What was social medicine? An historiographical essay." *J Hist Sociol* 1, no.1 (1988): pp. 90-106.
Pratt, A. and M. Lavalette. *Social Policy: A Conceptual and Theoretical Introduction.* 2nd ed. London: Sage, 2001.
Pratt, J. and M. Salter. "A Fresh Look at Football Hooliganism." *Leisure Studies* 3, no. 2 (1984): pp. 201-219.
Pratten, J.D. "The development of the modern UK public house: Part 1: The traditional British public house of the twentieth century." *International Journal of Contemporary Hospitality Management* 19 no. 4 (2007): pp.335 - 342.
Pratten, J.D. "The development of the UK public house: Part 2: signs of change to the UK public house 1959-1989 " *International Journal of Contemporary Hospitality Management* 19, no. 6 (2007): pp. 513-519
Pratten, J.D. "The development of the modern UK public house: Part 3: the emergence of the modern public house 1989-2005 " *International Journal of Contemporary Hospitality Management* 19, no. 7 (2007): pp.612-618.
Pressman, J.L. and A.Wildavsky. *Implementation: how great expectations in Washington are dashed in Oakland.* 3rd ed. Berkeley: University of California, 1984.

Prestwich, P.E. *Drink and the Politics of Social Reform: Antialcoholism in France since 1870*. Palo Alto, CA: Society for the Promotion of Science and Scholarship, 1988.
Price, R. *British Society, 1680-1880: Dynamism, Containment and Change*. Cambridge: Cambridge University Press, 1999.
Pridemore, W.A. "Heavy Drinking and Suicide in Russia." *Soc Forces* 85, no. 1 (2006): pp. 413-430.
Prochaska, J. and C. DiClemente."Toward a comprehensive model of change." In *Treating Addictive Behaviors: Processes of Change*, eds. W. R. Miller and N Heather, pp. 3-27. New York: Plenum, 1986.
Prochaska, J. and C. DiClemente."*The Transtheoretical Approach*. Illinois: Dow Jones-Irwin, 1984.
Prochaska, J. and C. DiClemente." "Stages and processes of self-change of smoking: Toward an integrative model of change." *Journal of Consulting and Clinical Psychology* 51, no.3 (1983): pp. 390-395.
Pugh, M. *State and Society: A Social and Political History of Britain, 1870-1997*. London: Arnold, 1999.
Purdy, M. and D. Banks. *The Sociology and Politics of Health: A Reader* London: Routledge, 2001
Raco, M. "Remaking place and securitising space: urban regeneration and the strategies, tactics and practices of policing in the UK." *Urban Studies* 40, no.9 (2003): pp.1869-1887.
Radstone, S. *Memory and methodology*. Oxford; New York: Berg, 2000.
Raleigh Yow, V. *Recording Oral History: A Guide for the Humanities and Social Sciences*. 2nd ed. Walnut Creek, CA: AltaMira Press, 2005.
Rao, R. "Alcohol misuse and ethnicity: Hidden populations need specific services." *BMJ* 332 no. 7543 (2006): p. 682.
Rao, R., K. Wolf and E. Marshall. "Alcohol use and misuse in Older People: a local prevalence study comparing English and Irish inner city residents living in the UK." *Journal of Substance Use* 13, no.1 (2008): pp.17-26.
Rapoport, R. and R. Rapoport. "Community as the Doctor." *Human Organization* 16, no. 4 (1957): pp.28-31
Rapoport, R. N. *Community as Doctor*. London: Tavistock, 1960.
Rathwell, T. *Strategic planning in the health sector* London: Routledge, 1987.
Ravetz, A. *Council Housing and Culture: The History of a Social Experiment*. London: Routledge, 2001.
Redfield, M. and J. Farrell Brodie. *High Anxieties: Cultural Studies in Addiction*. Berkeley CA: University of California Press, 2002.
Reed, T. L. *The transforming draught: Jekyll and Hyde, Robert Louis Stevenson and the Victorian alcohol debate*. Jefferson, London: McFarland & Co, 2006.
Rehm, J., M.J. Ashley, R. Room, E. Single, S. Bondy, R. Ferrence and N. Giesbrecht. "On the Emerging Paradigm of Drinking Patterns and Their Social and Health Consequences." *Addiction* 91, no.11 (1996): pp.1615-1621.

Reid, D. A. "Mass Leisure in Britain." In *Twentieth Century Mass Society in Britain and the Netherlands,* eds. R. Moore and H. Van Nierop, pp. 132-159. Oxford: Berg, 2006.

Reid, D. A. "Playing and Praying." In *Cambridge Urban History of Britain: 1840-1950,* ed. M.J. Daunton, pp. 745-810. Cambridge: Cambridge University Press, 2000.

Reiner, R. "Policing a Postmodern Society." In *Policing: Key Reading,* ed. T. Newburn, pp. 675-697. Devon: Willan Publishing, 2005.

Reiss, A.J. and J.A. Roth. *Understanding and Preventing Violence Vol. 3.* Washington DC: National Academy Press, 1994.

Rennie, Y., J. P. Conrad and S. Dinitz. *Search for the Criminal Man; a Conceptual History of the Dangerous Offender,* New York: Lexicon Books, 1978.

Reuter, P. and A. Stevens. *An Analysis of UK Drug Policy.* London: UK Drugs Policy Commission, 2007.

Riccucci, N.M. *How Management Matters: Street-level bureaucrats and welfare reform.* Washington, D.C: Georgetown University Press, 2005.

Rice, R. E. and C. K. Atkin. *Public communication campaigns.* London: Sage, 2000.

Richards, C. and P. Fillingham. *Nottingham in the 1980s (Archive Photographs) Images of England.* Stroud: Tempus Publishing, 2002.

Ritchie, D.A. *Doing Oral History: A Practical Guide.* Second ed. Oxford, New York: Oxford University Press, 2003.

Ritson, B. "Hostel for Offenders with Alcoholic Problems 28 Addison Street Nottingham." *Alcohol and Alcoholism* 5, no.4 (1970): p.167.

Ritson, B. and C. Hassal. *The Management of Alcoholism.* Edinburgh: E&S Livingstone, 1970.

Ritson, E. B. and C. P. Thompson. "Planning a Rural Alcoholism Program" *Addiction* 65, no. 3 (1970): pp. 199-202.

Roberts, G. J. "Medical Defence Union response to concern over Mental Health Act." *Bulletin of the Royal College of Psychiatrists* 10, Feb (1986): p.38.

Roberts, M. "From 'creative city' to 'no-go areas' – The expansion of the night-time economy in British town and city centres." *Cities* 23, no. 5 (2006): pp. 331-338.

Roberts, N.C. and P.J King. "Policy Entrepreneurs: Their Activity, Structure and Function in the Policy Process." *Public Administration, Research and Theory* 1, no. 2 (1991): pp.147-175.

Robertson, I. "Controlled drinking - an approach to management." *Drug and Alcohol Review* 4, no. 2 (1985): pp. 257-266.

Robinson, D. "The Erroll Report: Key Proposals and Public Reaction." *Addiction* 69, no. 2 (1974): pp. 99-104.

Robinson, D. *From Drinking to Alcoholism: A Sociological Commentary.* London: Wiley and Sons, 1976.

Robson, P. and M. Poustie. *Homelessness and the Law in Britain.* London: Butterworths/Planning Exchange, 1996.

Rochester, C. and M. Harris. *The Voluntary Organisations and Social Policy; In Britain*. Basingstoke: Palgrave, 2001.

Rodger, R. "Taking Stock: Perspectives on British Urban History." *Urban History Review (Revue d'histoire urbaine)* 32, no. 1 (2003): pp. 54-63.

Rogers, E. *Diffusion of innovations*. New York: Free Press of Glencoe, Macmillan Company, 1962.

Roizen, J. "Epidemiological issues in alcohol-related violence, Vol. 13." In *Recent Developments in Alcoholism*, ed. M. Galanter, pp. 7-40. New York: Plenum Press, 1997.

Roizen, R. "The great controlled-drinking controversy." In *Recent developments in alcoholism*, ed. M. Galanter, pp. 245-279. New York: Plenum, 1987.

Rojek, C. *Decentering leisure. Rethinking leisure theory*. London: Sage, 1995.

Room, R. "Alcohol Control and Public Health." *Ann. Rev. Public Health* 5, pp. 293-317 (1984).

Room, R. "Alcohol, The Individual and Society: What History Teaches Us." *Addiction* 92 no.3s1 (1997): pp. 7-12.

Room, R. "Disabling the public interest: alcohol strategies and policies for England." *Addiction* 99, no.9 (2004): pp. 1083-1089.

Room, R. "A Farewell to Alcoholism? A Commentary on the WHO Expert Advisory Committee Report." *British Journal of Addiction,* 76 no. 2 (1981): pp. 115-123..

Room, R. "Social science research and alcohol policy making." In *Alcohol: the development of sociological perspectives on Use and Abuse*, ed. P. Roman, pp.311-335. New Brunswick: Rutgers Centre of Alcohol Studies, 1991.

Room, R. and M. Järvinen. *Youth drinking cultures: European experiences, Volume 13*. Aldershot, Hamps: Ashgate, 2007.

Rorabaugh, W.J. *The Alcoholic Republic*. New York: Oxford University Press, 1979.

Rose, K. D. *American women and the repeal of prohibition* New York: New York University Press, 1997.

Rose, N. *Governing the Soul: The Shaping of the Private Self*. Second ed. London: Free Association Books, 1999.

Rose, N. and P. Miller. *Governing the Present: Administering Economic, Social and Personal Life*. Cambridge: Polity Press, 2008.

Rose, N. and P. Miller. "Political Power Beyond the State: Problematics of Government " *British Journal of Sociology* 43, no. 2 (1992): pp. 172-205.

Rosen, G. *A History of Public Health*. Vol. 1, *MD monographs on medical history*. New York: MD Publications, 1958.

Rosenberg, H., J. Melville, D. Levell and J. E. Hodge. "A 10-year follow-up survey of the acceptability of controlled drinking in Britain." *Journal of Studies on Alcohol* 53, no. 5 (1992): pp. 441-446.

Rosenstone, R. A. and A. Munslow. *Experiments in Rethinking History*. London: Routledge, 2004

Rossi, E. *The Collected Papers of Milton H. Erickson's on Hypnosis*. New York: Irvington, 1974.

Roth, M. "Carnival, Creativity and the Sublimation of Drunkenness." *Mosaic: A Journal for the Interdisciplinary Study of Literature* 30, no. 2 (1997): pp. 1-18.

Roth, M. "The Golden Age of Drinking and the Fall into Addiction." *Janus Head* 7 no. 1 (2004): pp. 11-33.

Rotskoff, L. *Love on the rocks: men, women, and alcohol in post-World War II America.* Chapel Hill, N.C.; London: University of North Carolina Press, 2002.

Rowley, J.J. "Drink and the Public House in Nottingham 1830-60." *Thoroton Society Transactions (Transactions of the Thoroton Society of Nottinghamshire)* 79 (1975): pp. 72-81.

Roy, L. "The psychiatric careers of male shelter users in Nottingham." *Psychiatric Bulletin* 16, no.11 (1992): pp. 685-687.

Royce, J.E. *Alcohol Problems and Alcoholism.* London: Collier Macmillan 1981.

Royuela, V. and J. Surinach. "Constituents of Quality of Life and Urban Size " *Social Indicators Research* 74, no. 3 (2005): pp. 549-572

Ruddick, S. "Modernism and Resistance: How ' Homeless' Youth Subcultures make a Difference." In *Cool Places: Geographies of Youth Cultures*, eds. G. Valentine and T. Skelton, pp. 344-362. London: Routledge, 1998

Rumball, D. and T. Waller. *Treating Problem Drinkers and Drug Misusers in the Community.* Oxford: Blackwell Science 2004.

Rumbarger, J.J. *Profits, Power and Prohibition: American Reform and the Industrialising of America.* Albany State: University of New York Press, 1989.

Rutherford, D. "The drinks cabinet: UK alcohol policy." *Contemporary British History, 1743-7997,* 5, no. 3 (1991): pp. 450-467.

Ryana, T., L. Webb and P.S. Meierc. "A systems approach to care pathways into in-patient alcohol detoxification: Outcomes from a retrospective study " *Drug and Alcohol Dependence* 85, no. 1 (2006): pp.28-34

Rykwert, J. *The Seduction of Place: The History and Future of the City.* Oxford: Oxford University Press 2004.

Sabatier, P.A. *Theories of the Policy Process.* 2nd ed. Colorado: Westview Press, 2007.

Sabatier, P.A. "Toward better theories of the policy process." *Political Science and Politics* 24, no. 2 (1991): pp. 147-56.

Sabatier, P.A. and H.C. Jenkins-Smith. *Policy change and Learning: an Advocacy Coalition Approach.* Boulder, CO: Westview Press, 1993.

Sackett, D.L., W. Rosenberg, J. Gray, R.B. Haynes and W.S Richardson, "Evidence based medicine: what it is and what it isn't " *British Medical Journal* 312, no. 7023 (1996): pp. 71-72.

Saffer, H. "Alcohol Advertising and Youth." *Journal of Studies on Alcohol*, Suppl. 14 (2002): pp. 173-181.

Saint-Martin, D. *Building the New Managerialist State: Consultants and the Politics of Public Sector Reform in Comparative Perspective Oxford*: Oxford University Press, 2000.

Saito, K. "Labour in the Nottingham lace industry, 1918-39.". PhD thesis: University of Leicester, 1996.
Salaman, L. and S. Anheier. *The Emerging Nonprofit Sector*. Baltimore/London: John Hopkins Press, 1995.
Salamon, L.M. "The Voluntary Sector and the Future of the Welfare State" *Nonprofit and Voluntary Sector Quarterly* 18, no. 1 (1989): pp. 11-24
Sandland, R. and P. Bartlett. *Mental Health Law*. Oxford: Oxford University Press, 2007.
Saunders, P. "The Good Practice of Police: An Alternative Approach in Dealing with Offenders who abuse/misuse Alcohol." *Alcohol and Alcoholism* 33, no. 1 (1998): pp.73-77.
Savage, J. *Teenage: The Creation of Youth Culture 1875-1945* London: Vintage, 2008.
Savage, M. and A. Warde. *Sociology, capitalism and modernity*. New York: Continuum, 1993.
Scally, G., and J. Womack. "The importance of the past in public health." *J. Epidemiol. Community Health* 58, no.9 (2004): pp. 751-755.
Scannell, P. "Public Service Broadcasting and Modern Public Life." *Media, Culture & Society* 11, no. 2 (1989): pp. 135-166.
Schnabel, J. "Neuroscience: Rethinking rehab." *Nature* 458 (2009): pp. 25-27.
Schon, D. "Champions for new radical inventions." *Harvard Business Review* March /April (1967): pp. 77-86.
Schuckit, M. *Drug and Alcohol Abuse, Critical issues in Psychiatry*. New York: Plenum 1979.
Scodel, J. *Excess and the Mean in Early Modern English Literature*. Princeton, N.J: Princeton University Press, 2002.
Scott, A.J. *The cultural economy of cities: essays on the geographies of image producing industries*. London: Sage, 2000.
Searle, G. R. *Morality and the Market in Victorian Britain*. Oxford: Clarendon Press, 1998.
Seddon, T. "Coerced drug treatment in the criminal justice system." *Criminology and Criminal Justice* 7, no. 3 (2007): pp. 269-286.
Shapiro, R. and B. Page. *The Rational Public: Fifty Years of Trends in Americans' Policy Preferences* Chicago: University Of Chicago Press, 1992.
Sheard, S. and H. Power, eds. *Body and City: Histories of Urban Public Health*. Aldershot: Ashgate, 2000.
Shepherd, J. P., Robinson, L. and B. G. Levers. "Roots of urban violence." *Injury* 21, no. 3 (1990): pp. 39-41.
Shivy, V.A. and L.M Koehly, "Social Network Analysis: A New Methodology for Counseling Research." *Journal of Counseling Psychology* 45, no. 1 (1998): pp. 3-17.
Shorter, E. *A History of Psychiatry: From the Era of the Asylum to the Age of Prozac*, New York: Wiley, 1997.

Shorthose, J. "Nottingham's de facto Cultural Quarter; The Lace Market, Independents and a Convivial Ecology." In *City of quarters: urban villages in the contemporary city*, eds. M. Jayne and D. Bell, pp. 149-62. Aldershot: Ashgate Publishing.

Silburn, R., D. Lucas, R. Page and L. Hanna. "Neighbourhood Images in Nottingham." In *JRF Regeneration research programme*, York: Joseph Rowntree Foundation, 1999.

Sillitoe, A. *Saturday Night and Sunday Morning*. London: Flamingo, 1994.

Silverman, E.B. and J.-A. Della-Giustina. "Urban policing and fear of crime." *Urban Studies* 38, nos. 5-6 (2001): pp. 941-957.

Simpson, A. "Stacking the Decks: A Study in Racial Inequality in Council Housing in Nottingham." pp.289-90. Nottingham: Nottingham and District Community Relations Council, 1981.

Sipila, J. "Community Structure and Deviant Behavior among Adolescents." *Youth and Society* 16, no. 4 (1985): pp. 471-497

Smart, C. "Social policy and drug addiction: a critical study of policy development." *British Journal of Addiction* 79, no.1 (1984): pp. 31-39.

Smith, J. *An Introduction to the Voluntary Sector*. London: Routledge, 1995.

Smith, K. *Wet Day Centres for Street Drinkers*. Sheffield: Sheffield Institute for Studies on Ageing, Community Sciences Centre, 2004.

Smith, M.A. *Sex, Gender and Power: The enigma of the Public House*. Hebden Bridge: Lambert Print & Design, 2003.

Smith, M.A. "Social usage of the public drinking house: changing aspects of class and leisure." *British Journal of Sociology* 34, no.3 (1983): pp. 367-385.

Smith, M.J. *Pressure, Power and Policy: State Autonomy and Policy Networks in Britain and the United States,* Pittsburgh: University of Pittsburgh Press, 1993.

Smith, N. *The new urban frontier: gentrification and the revanchist city*. London: Routledge, 1996.

Smith Wilson, D. "A New Look at the Affluent Worker: The Good Working Mother in Post-War Britain," *Twentieth Century British History* 17, no.2 (2006): pp. 210-222.

Smyth, J. D. "Competition as a means of procuring public services: Lessons for the UK from the US experience." *International Journal of Public Sector Management* 10, no. 1-2 (1997): pp.21-46

Snape, S and P. Taylor. *Partnerships between Health and Local Government, Medical Policy*. London: Routledge, 2004.

Snow, G.E. "Socialism, alcoholism and the Russian working classes before 1917." In *Drinking: Behavior and Belief in Modern History*, eds. S. Barrows and R. Room. Berkeley: University of California Press, 1991.

Sobell, M.B. and L.C. Sobell. "Alcoholics treated by individualized behaviour therapy: One year treatment outcome." *Behav Res Ther* 11, no.4 (1973): pp. 599-618.

Sobell, M.B. and L.C. Sobell. "Second year treatment outcome of alcoholics treated by individualized behavior therapy: Results." *Behav Res Ther* 14, no.3 (1976): pp.195-215.

Söderqvist, T. *The Historiography of Contemporary Science and Technology, Studies in the History of Science, Technology and Medicine* London: Routledge, 1997.

Solomon, J. and J. Benyon. "The Simmering Cities: Urban Unrest during the Thatcher Years." *Parliamentary Affairs* 41, no. 3 (1988): pp. 402-422.

Sommer, B.W. and M.K. Quinlan. *The Oral History Manual*. Walnut Creek, CA Rowman AltaMira, 2002.

Spear, H.B. "The Early Years of Britain's Drug Situation in practice, up to the 1960s." In *Heroin Addiction and the British System: Volume One*, eds. J. Strang and M. Gossop. London: Routledge, 2005.

Spear, H.B. *Heroin Addiction Care and Control 1916-1984*. London: Drugscope, 2002.

Spence, N. *British Cities: An Analysis of Urban Change*. Vol. 26, *Urban and Regional Planning*. Oxford: Pergamon Press, 1982.

Spiller, B. *Victorian Public Houses*. Newton Abbot: David & Charles, 1972.

Spinner, R. J., Poliakoff, M. B. and R. L. Tiel. "The origin of "Saturday night palsy?" *Neurosurgery* 51, no. 3 (2002): pp.737-741

Squires, P. *ASBO Nation*. Bristol: Policy Press, 2008.

Stacey, B. and J. Davies. "Drinking behaviour in childhood and adolescence: An Evaluative Review." *British Journal of Addiction* 65, no.3 (1970): pp 203-12.

Stainback, R. D. *Alcohol and Sport*. Champaign, IL: Human Kinetics, 1997.

Stapleton, B. and J. Thomas. *Gales: A Study in Brewing, Business and Family History*. Aldershot: Ashgate, 2000.

Startt, J.D and W.D. Sloan. *Historical Methods in Mass Communication* London: Lawrence Erlbaum Associates, 1989.

Stein, H. F. "Recent developments in alcoholism: substance and symbol." *Recent Dev Alcohol* Review 11 (1993): pp. 153-164.

Stevenson, W.C. *Making and Managing a Pub*. Newton Abbot: David and Charles, 1981.

Stewarts, J. *The Battle for Health: A Political History of the Socialist Medical Association, 1930-51*. Aldershot: Ashgate 1999.

Stimson, G.V. "AIDS and injecting drug use in the United Kingdom, 1987–1993: The policy response and the prevention of the epidemic " *Social Science & Medicine* 41, no. 5 (1995): pp.699-716.

Stimson, G.V. "British Drug Policies in the 1980s: a preliminary analysis and suggestions for research." *Addiction* 82, no. 5 (1987): pp. 477- 488.

Stimson, G.V. "Reviewing policy and practice: New ideas about the drugs problem." In *AIDS and Drug Misuse*, eds. J. Strang and G.V. Stimson. London: Routledge, 1990.

Stimson, G.V. and R. Lart. "HIV, Drugs, and Public Health in England: New Words, Old Tunes." *Substance Use & Misuse* 26, no. 12 (1991): pp. 1263 - 1277.

Stimson, G.V. "Drinking in Context: A Collective Responsibility " In *ICAP Reviews 2*, pp. 1-12: International Centre for Alcohol Policies, 2006.

Stimson, G.V., M. Grant, M. Choquet and P. Garrison *Drinking in Context: Patterns, Interventions, and Partnerships*. London: Routledge, 2006.

Stimson, G.V. and R. Lart. "The relationship between the state and local practice in the development of national policy between 1920 and 1990." In *Heroin Addiction and the British System*, eds. J. Strang and M. Gossop, p.179. London: Routledge, 2005.

Stimson, G.V. and R. Lart. "The relationship between the state and local practice in the development of national policy on drugs between 1920 and 1990." In *Heroin addiction and drug policy - the British system*, eds. J. Strang and M. Gossop, pp. 331-41. Oxford: Oxford University Press, 1994.

Stimson, G.V. and B. Thom. "Reducing drug and alcohol related harm." *Drugs: Education, Prevention and Policy* 4, no. 1 (1997): pp. 3-6.

Stöhr, W.B. *Global challenge and local response: initiatives for economic regeneration* London: Mansell Publishing Ltd, 1990.

Stone, D A. "Causal Stories and the Formation of Policy Agendas." *Political Science Quarterly* 104, no. 2 (1989): pp. 281-300

Stone, D A. *Policy Paradox: The Art of Political Decision Making*. 3rd ed. New York: W. W. Norton & Company, 2001.

Stout, R.L., A. Rubin, W. Zwick, W. Zywiak, and L. Bellino. "Optimizing the cost-effectiveness of alcohol treatment. A rationale for extended case monitoring" *Addictive Behaviors* 24, no. 1 (1999): pp.17-35

Strang, J. and M. Gossop. *Heroin Addiction and the British System Volume I: Origins and Evolution*. London: Routledge, 2004.

Strong, P.M. "Doctors and dirty work - the case of alcoholism." *Sociology of Health and Illness* 2, no.1 (1980): pp. 24-47.

Strug, D. and S. Pryadarsini. *Alcohol Interventions: Historical and Sociocultural Approaches* New York: Haworth Press, 1985.

Sturdy, S. *Medicine, Health and the Public Sphere in Britain, 1600-2000*. London: Routledge, 2002

Sullivan, H. and C. Skelcher. *Working Across Boundaries: Collaboration in Public Services*. Basingstoke: Palgrave Macmillan, 2002.

Tabakoff, B. and P.L. Hoffman. "Tolerance and the etiology of alcoholism: Hypothesis and mechanism" *Alcoholism: Clinical and Experimental Research* 12, no. 1 (1988): pp.184-186.

Talbot, D. *Regulating the Night: Race, Culture and Exclusion in the Making of the Night-time Economy*. Aldershot: Ashgate, 2007.

Tarschys, D. "The Success of a Failure: Gorbachev's Alcohol Policy, 1985-88 " *Europe-Asia Studies* 45, no. 1 (1993): pp. 7-25.

The Civic Trust. "Nightvision: Town centres for all." London: The Civic Trust, 2006.

The Daily Express. "Alcohol abuse: middle class women are new bingers." October 4th 2011.

The Daily Mail. "Girls Behaving Sadly; Femail Special Investigation." October 7th 2004

The Daily Mail. "Just a Quiet Night on Our Streets, Was It?" November 25th 2005.

The Daily Mail. "Why middle class women are dying for a drink," June 3rd 2010.

The Daily Mail. "Hiding under her hood: The smirking 11-year-old girl in 'large scale riot rampage' refuses to apologise," August 11th 2011.

The Guardian. "Under the influence: Part one." November 20th 2004.

The Guardian. "Under the influence: Part Two." November 20th 2004.

The Guardian. "Reading the Riots study to examine causes and effects of August unrest," September 5th 2011.

The Independent. "A new drop in health centre for young people in Nottingham." June 15th 1993.

The Independent. "Boozers lose out to designer bar culture." November 1st 2001.

The Independent. "Blunkett confirms five-year jail term for gun possession." January 6th 2003.

The Independent. "When in Rome, do as young Romans do: binge like a Brit." August 11th 2005.

The Independent. "Jowell: we got it wrong on 24hr drinking", August 28th 2005.

The Observer. "Britain: a nation in grip of drink crisis." November 21st 2004.

The Observer. "On the Streets of Binge Britain." September 5th 2004.

The Observer. "A tale of two cities." Review. May 22nd 2005

The Observer. "Binge drink panic mirrors Hogarth's 'gin craze'." September 9th 2007.

The Sunday Mirror. "Not One Pub in Britain is Now Open 24 Hours." November 19th 2006.

The Sunday Times, "Labour concealed its doubts over 24-hour drinking initiative," June 6th 2004.

The Telegraph. "City of guns, drugs and murder hires a reputation manager." October 13th 2005.

The Thoroton Society. "The Old Inns of Brewhouse Yard." In *Nottingham's Stuart and Georgian Inns. Trans. of the Thoroton Society 13*, pp. 57-69. Nottingham: Thoroton Society, 1910.

The Times, "Nottingham grabs a piazza of the action." April 3rd 2007.

Thom, B. *Dealing with drink; alcohol and social policy.* London: Free Association Books, 1999.

Thom, B. "From Alcoholism Treatment to the Alcohol Harm Reduction Strategy for England: An Overview of Alcohol Policy since 1950 " *Am J Addict.* 14, no. 5 (2005): pp. 416-425.

Thom, B. "Who makes alcohol policy? Science and policy networks 1950-2000." Clio Medica/The Wellcome Series in the History of Medicine, Networks in Research and Policy after 1945. ed. V. Berridge. *Clio Med* 75 (2005): pp. 75-99

Thom, B. "Women and Alcohol: The Emergence of a Risk Group." In *Gender, drink, and drugs*, ed. M. McDonald, pp. 33-54. Oxford: Berg, 1994.

Thom, B and M. Bayley. "Multi-component programmes: An approach to prevent and reduce alcohol-related harm." In *Drug and alcohol research programme series*. York: Joseph Rowntree Foundation, 2007.

Thom, B. and V. Berridge. "Special Units for Common Problems: The Birth of Alcohol Treatment Units in England." *Social History of Medicine* 8, no.1 (1995): pp.75-93.

Thom, B., R. Herring and V. Berridge. "Workshop Report. Part of: The normalisation of binge drinking? An historical and cross cultural investigation with implications for action." In *Binge drinking: Challenges and Opportunities*. London: Alcohol Education and Research Council, 2007.

Thomas, C.J. and R.D.F. Bromley. "City-centre Revitalisation: Problems of Fragmentation and Fear in the Evening and Night-time City." *Urban Studies* 37, no. 8 (2000): pp.1403-1429.

Thompson, E.P. *The Making of the Working Class*. New York: Random House, 1966.

Thompson, F. M. L. *The Cambridge Social History of Britain, 1750-1950*. Cambridge: Cambridge University Press, 1990.

Thompson, K. *Moral Panics*. London: Routledge, 1998.

Thompson, P. "The Voice from the Past." In *The Nature of History Reader*, eds. K. Jenkins and A. Munslow, pp.107-109. London: Routledge, 2004.

Thompson, P. *The Voice of the Past: Oral History*. Oxford: Oxford University Press, 2000.

Thornicroft, G. "The NHS and Community Care Act, 1990: Recent government policy and legislation." *Psychiatric Bulletin* 18, no.1 (1994): pp. 13-17.

Thornton, S. *Club Cultures: Music, Media and Subcultural Capital* Cambridge: Polity, 1995.

Thoroton, R. *The Antiquities of Nottinghamshire*. Nottingham: G. Burbage, 1790.

Tiesdell, S. "Tensions between revitalization and conservation: Nottingham's Lace Market " *Cities* 12, no. 4 (1995): pp.231-241

Tilley, H. and R.J Gordon, eds. *Ordering Africa: Anthropology, European Imperialism and the Politics of Knowledge*. Manchester: Manchester University Press, 2007.

Tilley, N. *Crime Prevention Unit Series Paper No.42. Understanding Car parks, Crime and CCTV: Evaluation lessons from Safer Cities*. London: Police Research Group Home Office Police Department, 1993.

Time Magazine, "A Cry from the Streets." September 8th 1958.

Tolley, B.H. "Education." In *A Centenary History of Nottingham*, ed. J.V. Beckett, pp. 549-565. Manchester: Manchester University Press, 1997.

Tonkiss, F. *Space, the City and Social Theory*. Cambridge: Polity, 2005.
Townsend, P. "Measuring Poverty." *British Journal of Sociology* 5, no. 2 (1954): pp. 130-137.
Tracy, S. *Bands, booze and broads*. Edinburgh: Mainstream Publishing, 1995.
Transchel, K. *Under the influence: working-class drinking, temperance, and Cultural Revolution in Russia, 1895-1932*. Pittsburgh; University of Pittsburgh Press, 2006.
Treml, V.G. *Alcohol in the USSR: A Statistical Study, Duke Press Policy Studies*. Durham N.C: Duke University Press, 1982.
Trentmann, F. and V. Taylor. "From users to consumers: Water politics in Nineteenth-Century London." In *The Making of the Consumer: Knowledge, Power and Identity in the Modern World*, ed. F. Trentmann, pp. 53-79. Oxford: Berg, 2006.
Trinder, L. and S. Reynolds. *Evidence-based practice: a critical appraisal*. Oxford: Blackwell Science, 2000.
Trinkle, D.A. *Writing, Teaching, and Researching History in the Electronic Age: Historians and Computers*. London: M. E. Sharpe, 1998
Trotter, T. *An essay, medical, philosophical, and chemical on drunkenness and its effects on the human body with an introduction by Roy Porter.* ed. R. Porter. London: Routledge, 1988.
Valentine, G. *Social Geography: space and society*. Harlow: Pearson Education Ltd, 2001.
Valentine, G. and T. Skelton. *Cool Places: Geographies of Youth*. London: Routledge, 1998.
Vallee, B. L. "Alcohol in the western world." *Sci Am* 278, no. 6 (1998): pp.80-85.
Valverde, M. *Diseases of the will: alcohol and the dilemmas of freedom, Cambridge studies in law and society*. Cambridge: Cambridge University press, 1998.
Van Wersch, A. and W. Walker. "Binge-drinking in Britain as a Social and Cultural Phenomenon: The Development of a Grounded Theoretical Model " *Journal of Health Psychology* 14, no. 1 (2009): pp. 124-134.
Vansina, J. *Oral Tradition: A Study in Historical Methodology*. New Brunswick, N.J: Aldine Transaction, 2006.
Vizzard, W. J. *In the cross fire: a political history of the Bureau of Alcohol, Tobacco, and Firearms, Explorations in public policy*. Boulder, Colo.; London: Lynne Rienner, 1997.
Wagner, P. *A sociology of modernity: liberty and discipline*. London; New York: Routledge, 1994
Waller, P.J. *The Urban English Landscape*. Oxford: Oxford University Press, 2000.
Wallerstein, R. S. *Hospital Treatment of Alcoholism* New York: Basic Books 1957.
Walt, G. *Health policy: an introduction to process and power.* London: Zed Books, 1994.
Walt, G. and L. Gilson. "Reforming the health sector in developing countries: the central role of policy analysis." *Health Policy Plan* 9, no. 4 (1994): pp. 353-370.

Walton, J.K. "Towns and Consumerism." In *The Cambridge Urban History of Britain Vol. III 1840-1950*, eds. P. Clark, D. M. Palliser and M.J. Daunton, pp.715-744. Cambridge: Cambridge University Press, 2000.

Ward, B.W. and J. Gryczynski. "Social Learning Theory and effects of living arrangements on heavy alcohol use: Results from a national study of college students." *Journal of Studies on Alcohol and Drugs* 70, no. 3 (2009): pp. 364-372.

Wardhaugh, J. *Sub City: Young People, Homelessness and Crime*. Aldershot: Ashgate, 2000.

Warner, J. "Can Legislation Prevent Debauchery? Mother Gin and Public Health in 18th-Century England." *American Journal of Public Health* 91, no. 3 (2001): pp.375-384.

Warner, J. *Craze: gin and debauchery in an age of reason*. New York: Random House, 2002.

Warner, J. "Gin and Gender in Early Eighteenth-century London." *Eighteenth-Century Life* 24, no.2 (2000): pp. 85-105.

Warner, J. "Historical perspectives on the shifting boundaries around youth and alcohol. The example of pre-industrial England, 1350-1750 " *Addiction* 93, no. 5 (1998): pp. 641-657.

Warner, J. "Resolv'd to drink no more": addiction as a preindustrial construct." *J Stud Alcohol* 55, no. 6 (1994): pp.685-691.

Warner, J. "Shifting categories of the social harms associated with alcohol: examples from late medieval and early modern England." *Am J Public Health* 87, no. 11 (1997): pp.1788-1797.

Warner Osborn, M. "Diseased Imaginations: Constructing Delirium Tremens in Philadelphia, 1813-1832 " *Social History of Medicine* 19, no. 2 (2006): pp. 191-208.

Waterson, J. "Gender Divisions and Drinking Problems." In *Alcohol problems in the community* ed. L. Harrison, pp. 170-99. London: Routledge, 1996.

Waterson, J. *Women and alcohol in social context*. Hamps: Palgrave, 2000.

Webster, C. *Caring for Health, History and Diversity*. ed. C. Webster. *Health and Disease Series: book 6*. Buckingham: Open University Press, 1995.

Webster, C. "Psychiatry and the early National Health Service: the role of the Mental Health Standing Committee." In *150 Years of Psychiatry, 1841-1991*, eds. Berrios G.E and H. Freeman. London: Royal College of Psychiatrists, 1991.

Webster, C. *Understanding Race and Crime*. Berkshire: Open University Press: McGraw-Hill International, 2007.

Wells, F. A. "'Present Day Economic Structure'." In *Nottingham and its Region*, ed. K.C. Edwards. Nottingham: British Association, 1966.

Welshman, J. "The Medical Officer of Health in England and Wales, 1900-1974: watchdog or lapdog?" *Journal of Public Health* 19, no. 4 (1997): pp. 443-450.

White, S. *Russia goes dry: alcohol, state and society*. Cambridge: Cambridge University Press, 1996.

White, S. *Russia's New Politics: The Management of Post Communist Society*. Cambridge: Cambridge University Press, 2000.

Whynes, D.K, P. Bean, Giggs J.A. and C. Wilkinson. "Managing Drug Use." *Addiction* 84, no. 5 (1989): pp. 533-540.

Whynes, D.K."Mobility and the Single Homeless " *Area* 23, no. 2 (1991): pp. 111-118

Whynes, D.K. and J.A. Giggs. "The health of the Nottingham homeless." *Public Health* 106, no. 4 (1992): pp. 307-314.

Wiener, C. *The politics of alcoholism: building an arena around a social problem*. New Brunswick, New Jersey: Transactions Books, 1981.

Wild, T. C., K. Graham and J. Rehm. "Blame and punishment for intoxicated aggression: when is the perpetrator culpable?" *Addiction* 93, no. 5 (1998): pp. 677-687.

Willems, P. J. A., F. J. J. Letemendia and F. Arroyave. "A Two-Year Follow-up Study Comparing Short with Long Stay In-patient Treatment of Alcoholics" *The British Journal of Psychiatry* 122, no.6 (1973): pp. 637-648.

Williams, R.J. *The Anxious City: British Urbanism in the Late Twentieth Century*. London: Routledge, 2004.

Willie, C.V. *Race, ethnicity, and socioeconomic status: a theoretical analysis of their Interrelationship*. New York: General Hall Inc., 1983.

Wills, A. "Youth culture and crime: what can we learn from history?" *BBC History Magazine*. Available from http://www.bbchistorymagazine.com/feature/youth-culture-and-crime-what-can-we-learn-history [Cited September 30th 2011]

Wilson FW (1978). 'Spiritual therapy in the therapeutic community' in Vamos P, Brown D, ed. Proceedings of the 2nd World Conference of Therapeutic Communities: *The Addiction Therapist, Special Edition* 4: pp. 204-205.

Wilson, T.M. *Drinking cultures: Alcohol and Identity*. New York: Berg, 2005.

Winlow, S. and S. Hall. *Violent Night; Urban Leisure and Contemporary Culture*. Oxford: Berg, 2006.

Winskill, P.T. *The temperance movement and its workers: a record of social, moral, religious and political progress* London: Blackie, 1892.

Winterton, R. and J. Winterton. *Coal, crisis, and conflict: the 1984-85 miners' strike in Yorkshire*. Manchester: Manchester University Press, 1989.

Witz, A. *Professions and Patriarchy*. London: Routledge, 1992.

Wojtczak, H. *English Social History: Women of Nineteenth-Century Hastings and St.Leonards*. Hastings: Hastings Press, 2002.

Worpole, K. *Towns for People: Transforming Urban Life*. Bucks: Open University Press, 1992

Wright, G. and B. Curtis, J. *The Inns and pubs of Nottinghamshire. The stories behind the names*. Nottingham: Nottingham County Council, 1995.

Wright, N. "A day at the cricket: The breath alcohol consequences of a type of very English binge drinking." *Addiction Research and Theory* 14, no. 2 (2006): pp. 133 -137

Wright, N. and D. Cameron. "The Influence of Habitual Alcohol Intake on Breath-alcohol Concentrations following Prolonged Drinking." *Alcohol & Alcoholism* 33, no. 5 (1998): pp. 495-501.

Wright, N. and C. Thompson. "Withdrawal from Alcohol using Monitored Alcohol Consumption: A Case Report." *Alcohol and Alcoholism* 37, no. 4 (2002): pp. 344-346.

Wyn, J. and R. White. *Rethinking Youth*. St Leonards, NSW: Allen & Unwin 1997.

Wyness, M. "Parental responsibilities, social policy and the maintenance of boundaries." *Sociological Review* 45, no.2 (1997): pp. 305-324.

Wynne, D. and J. O'Connor. "Consumption and the postmodern city." *Urban Studies* 35, nos 5-6 (1998): pp. 841-864.

Wynne-Harley, D. "Community Care in the United Kingdom." In *Futurecare: new directions in planning health and care environments*, eds. M.S. Valins and D. Salter, pp. 35-54. Oxford: Blackwell Science, 1996.

Yarwood, R. "Crime and Policing in the British Countryside: Some Agendas for Contemporary Geographical Research " *Sociologia Ruralis* 41, no. 2 (2001): pp. 201-219.

Yates, G. L., R. MacKenzie, Pennbridge. J. and E. Cohen. "A risk profile comparison of runaway and non-runaway youth." *American Journal of Public Health* 78, no. 7 (1988): pp.820-821.

Yates, R. *Out of the shadows*. London: NACRO, 1981

Yates, R. 'A brief moment of glory: the impact of the therapeutic community movement on the drug treatment systems in the UK', *International Journal of Social Welfare* 12, no.3, pp. 239-243.

Yin, R. K. *Case study research: Design and methods*. 3rd ed. Newbury Park, CA: Sage, 2002.

Young, J. *A Short History of Ale*: Newton Abbot: David & Charles, 1979.

Youngs, F.A. Jr. *Guide to the Local Administrative Units of England, Vol II: Northern England*. London: Offices of the Royal Historical Society, 1991.

Yow, V. "Do I Like Them Too Much?" Effects of the Oral History Interview on the Interviewer and Vice-Versa." *Oral History Review* 24, no. 1 (1997): pp. 55-79.

Zimmerman, J. *Distilling democracy: alcohol education in America's public schools, 1880-1925*. Lawrence: University Press of Kansas, 1999.

Zohar, A. "Emergent Order and Self-Organization: A Case Study of Alcoholics Anonymous " *Nonprofit and Voluntary Sector Quarterly*, 26, no. 4 (1997): pp. 527-552.

Zolkiewski, J. "Marketization and the delivery of UK health services" *Journal of Business Research* 57, no. 9 (2004): pp. 1012-1020

Zukin, S. "Urban lifestyles: diversity and standardisation in spaces of consumption." *Urban Studies* 35, nos 5-6 (1998): pp. 825-839.

INDEX

24-hour city 144, 179. *See also* night-time economy
1971 12, 47, 48

A

abstinence 9, 13, 21, 22, 50, 51, 124, 126, 132, 184, 197
   v. controlled drinking 85, 121
addiction 9, 16, 42, 44, 63, 65, 78, 80, 81, 97, 98, 100, 117, 125, 136–139, 161, 177
aftercare 34, 59, 89, 132
AIDS/HIV. *See* HIV/AIDS
alcohol
   unit of. *See* daily limit
Alcohol Concern 160, 162, 175, 188, 194
alcohol dependence syndrome 58
Alcohol Harm Reduction Strategy for England (2004) 176, 181, 195, 202
Alcoholics Anonymous 10, 11, 19, 21, 22, 29, 135
alcohol industry 142
alcohol misuse 181
alcohol problem 6, 77, 101, 105, 132
Alcohol Problem Advisory Service (APAS) 43, 66, 88, 89, 99, 100, 125, 137. *See also* Nottinghamshire Council on Alcoholism
Alcohol Treatment Units (ATUs) 21, 56
amphetamine. *See* Speed
Antabuse 32
asylum 192

B

binge drinking 16, 42, 159, 160, 165, 178, 180, 181. *See also* bout drinking
bout drinking 51. *See also* binge drinking
British drink culture 176
British Government 104, 123
Bruun, Kettil 49, 63

C

Camberwell Council on Alcoholism 34, 56
CCTV 142, 169, 170, 173, 179, 192. *See also* surveillance
charitable sector 61. *See also* voluntary sector
churches 61, 92
circuit drinking 13, 105, 196

Clarke, Kenneth 75, 80, 127, 138, 143, 158, 172, 180
cocaine 142, 148, 150
Community Alcohol Teams (CATs) 85
community based care. *See* shared care
community psychiatric nurses 88, 89
consumption 3, 11, 67, 68, 104, 106, 116, 144, 184, 197–199
  and public health 49
  and success ethic 189
  at home 102
  control of 23, 132, 184
  decline in 188
  excessive 59
  increase in 20, 77, 101, 142, 176, 189
  measurement of 84
  patterns 190
  per capita 55, 103, 176
  women's 70
contract culture 85, 126, 194
controlled drinking 85, 97, 98, 121, 126, 132–136, 139
Councils on Alcoholism 61, 126
counselling 89, 93, 132
Crime and Disorder Act (1998) 136, 166

D

daily limit 149, 176
Davies, DL 97
day care 35, 125, 131, 132, 134
Department of Health and Social Security (DHSS) 48
Department of Health (DH) 126–128, 166, 188
detoxification 12, 48, 49, 54, 55, 57, 58, 61, 86, 88, 91–93, 124–126, 132, 134, 135
doctors 30, 86, 98. *See also* general practioners; psychiatrists
drink driving 69, 78, 118
Drug and Alcohol Action Team (DAAT) 151, 194
drugs
  addiction 21, 54, 65
  illicit use 83, 103, 106
  treatment 84, 87, 89, 123, 136, 166, 197
drunkenness 5, 6, 9, 19, 21, 24, 25, 105, 113, 116
  decriminalising 54
  legislation 3
  public 40, 48, 49, 115
  rates of arrest 21, 23, 69, 108
  rise in 77

E

ecstasy 142, 148
Edwards, Griffith 9, 34, 56, 58, 63, 87
epidemiology 60
evidence based medicine (EBM) 131, 138
extra contractual referral (ECR) 126, 137

F

Family First, Nottingham 38, 45, 79, 89
feminism 68
Framework 94–96, 134, 198. *See also* Nottingham Help the Homeless HA; Macedon Housing HA

G

general practitioners 97
Glatt, Max 33, 44
Gosling, Ray 23, 26, 27, 38, 39, 42, 70
Green, Steven 14, 165, 167, 168, 172, 173, 177

H

Habitual Drunkards Act (1879) 48
habitual drunken offenders 40, 48, 91
Habitual Drunken Offenders report (1971) 191
Handel Street wet centre 13, 83, 93–96, 100, 114, 144, 158, 198
harm reduction 122
health and social services 90
Helping Hand 60, 66. *See also* Turning Point
HIV/AIDS 12, 83, 84
home detoxification 125, 132
homelessness 13, 37, 40, 47, 57, 68, 86, 90, 101, 103, 106, 115, 190, 191, 198. *See also* street drinkers; vagrants
  and alcoholism 61, 86
Home Office 12, 41, 46, 63, 64, 91, 99, 114, 117, 120, 136, 150, 153, 155, 166, 170, 171, 175, 178–180, 191, 201, 202
hostels 35, 48, 55, 66, 90–92, 95, 134
Hostels Liaison Group (HLG) 89, 90, 92, 93, 96, 99

I

inebriates 48
inpatient units 21, 124, 125, 133
  v. outpatient care 51, 125, 131, 133
intoxication 59, 121, 134, 180, 200. *See also* drunkeness; inebriates

J

Jellinek, EM 9, 21, 51, 63
Jones, Maxwell 32

L

Ledermann, Sully 49
Leeds detoxification centre 61
Licensing Act 72
   1961 6, 20, 67, 72, 196
   1964 6, 20, 67, 72, 113, 147, 189, 196
   1988 13, 101, 102, 112, 113, 116, 142, 148, 189
   2003 176, 195

M

Macedon Housing HA 92, 95
Manchester Detoxification Centre 100
Mapperley Hospital 11, 12, 19, 30, 30–33, 44, 45, 47, 50, 51, 54, 86, 93, 94, 193, 201
McLean, Philip 56–59, 61, 62, 65, 66, 86–89, 92, 98–100, 125, 132, 133, 137, 139
Medical Officers of Health 64
medical profession 7, 58. *See also* doctors; general practitioners
Mental Health Act (1959) 44
middle class alcoholics 5, 56, 119, 156, 189, 201
Ministry of Health 11, 19, 33, 40, 41, 44, 193
Minnesota Model 124, 132, 136, 137
Minto, Alfred 32, 34, 35, 38, 39, 43–45, 50, 51, 193, 201
moderation 85, 103, 121

N

National Council on Alcoholism 12, 60, 62, 194
national drugs strategy 151, 166, 167. *See also* Tackling Drugs to Build a Better Britain (1998)
National Health Service (NHS) 9, 13, 17, 19, 21, 32, 41, 43, 44, 54, 58, 59, 61, 83, 87, 93, 121, 122, 124, 125, 127–131, 133, 134, 136, 137, 139, 171, 193, 194, 200, 201
   and Community Care Act (1990) 122, 136
national strategy 143, 194
New Directions in Alcoholism Group 121
night-time economy 14, 116, 141, 148, 150, 152, 156, 157, 165, 168, 169, 172–174, 177, 194, 196. *See also* 24-hour city
non-statutory sector. *See* voluntary sector
Nottingham Alcohol and Drug Team (NADT) 86, 100, 125, 131–135, 171

Nottingham Help the Homeless Association 39, 62, 92, 93, 95, 96, 100. *See also* Framework
Nottingham Help the Homeless HA 39, 62, 92, 93, 95, 96, 100
Nottinghamshire Council on Alcoholism 12, 59, 60, 193. *See also* Alcohol Problem Advisory Service

O

outpatient. *See* community based care
outpatient care 51, 52, 58, 88, 125, 131, 132. *See also* inpatient units

P

policy entrepreneurs 177, 195
population approach 12, 62
Portman Group 157, 158, 160, 175
primary care 84, 85, 166. *See also* community based care; general practitioners
probation service 51, 54, 59, 93, 166
product champions 195. *See also* policy entrepeneurs
psychiatric hospitals 21, 30, 52, 53
psychiatrists 36, 39, 41, 47, 50, 52, 54, 56, 63, 65, 97
public health view. *See* population approach

R

recovery movement 197
regeneration 146, 152, 155
rehabilitation 21, 33, 34, 44, 48, 54, 56, 57, 59, 62, 91, 123, 124, 197
Ritson, Bruce 50, 51, 53, 54, 56, 63, 64
Royal College of General Practitioners 97
Royal College of Physicians 97, 137, 196
Royal College of Psychiatrists 41, 50, 63, 65, 97

S

Safer Cities 114
self-help 39, 43, 53
shared care 125
Sillitoe, Alan 2, 15, 22, 28, 41, 42
social workers 11, 19, 33, 36, 37, 51, 52, 53, 89
speed 150, 161, 170, 192
street drinkers 13, 94, 96, 134, 170. *See also* vagrants
surveillance 70, 90, 169, 170, 192, 197, 199, 201. *See also* CCTV

T

Tackling Drugs to Build a Better Britain (1998) 136, 143, 151, 178

The Pattern and Range of Services for Problem Drinkers (1978) 50, 63, 99
therapeutic community 51, 54, 55, 123, 136
Time for Reform (2001) 165, 177
Turning Point 66
Twelve Steps treatment programmes 22. *See also* self-help

U

unemployment 4, 25, 28, 32, 86, 90, 101, 103, 106, 189, 191

V

vagrants 21, 24, 55, 92
voluntary sector 13, 87, 88, 93, 106, 125, 166, 193. *See also* charitable sector

W

wet centre. *See* Handel Street wet centre
withdrawal symptoms 31, 50, 132, 135
World Health Organisation (WHO) 9, 21, 49, 63, 137
Wright, Neil 133, 134

www.ingramcontent.com/pod-product-compliance
Lightning Source LLC
Chambersburg PA
CBHW071405300426
44114CB00016B/2184